PRIVACY 2000

1st ed., 1997

by Mark Nestmann

Privacy 2000

Asset Protection International
5468 Dundas St. W. #931
Toronto, ON M9B 6E3
Canada

Phone/fax: 416-352-5086

Internet: http://www.nestmann.com

E-mail: assetpro@nestmann.com

Produced in association with Scope International, Ltd.
Forestside House
Rowlands Castle
Hants PO9 6EE England, U.K.
Phone: 44-1705-631751
Fax: 44-1705-631322

Copyright © 1997 by Mark Nestmann

ISBN 0-9657151-3-2

All rights reserved. Copying any portion of this publication or placing it on any electronic medium without publisher's written permission is prohibited by law. Violators risk criminal penalties and U.S. $50,000 damages.

This publication is sold with the understanding that it does not render legal or other professional services or advice. If legal advice or other expert assistance is required, the services of a competent professional should be sought. Readers who have general questions about this publication or its contents, or suggestions for future editions, may contact the author at the above address or via e-mail. The author is also available for speaking engagements.

Additional copies of this title are available.

Table of Contents

Chapter 1: HORROR STORIES FROM THE SURVEILLANCE STATE — 1

Absolute Power Corrupts Absolutely — 2
Cash Police
Privacy Criminalized
Informants
Corruption
Criminal Abuse and Fraud
Entrapment
Illegal Access to Databases
Conclusion

Chapter 2: THE U.S. SURVEILLANCE INFRASTRUCTURE — 18

U.S. Constitution (1789) — 19
Fourth Amendment
Right to Privacy?

Private Express Statutes (1872) — 20
Mail Covers
Intelligence Agency "Mailtaps"
Warrantless Opening of Mail
Mail Drops

IRS (1913) — 22
Octopus
Dossiers
Powers
Code
Criminal Prosecution
Tax Equity and Fiscal Responsibility Act (1982)
Strategic Plan (1984)
    Independent Contractors
    Tax Gap
    Electronic Filing
Tax Reform Act (1986)
Market Segment Specialization Program (1993)
Compliance 2000 (1994)

Emergency Powers — 30
Trading With the Enemy Act (1917)
National Emergencies Act (1976)
International Emergency Economic Powers Act (1977)

i

Social Security Act (1935) 33

Department of Defense (1947) 35
    National Security Agency (1952)
    Foreign Intelligence Surveillance Act (1978)

Safe Streets Act (1968) 38
    Electronic Monitoring
    Computer Monitoring
    Dialing Records
    Nationwide Caller ID (1995)

Fair Credit Reporting Act (1970) 42
    Public Records
    Cluster Modeling
    Medical Records

Racketeering and Corrupt Organizations Act (1970) 48
    Criminal Forfeiture
    Extraterritorial Application

Bank Secrecy Act (1970) 55
    Abuses and Challenges
    Right to Financial Privacy Act (1978)
    Structuring (1986)
    BSA Reporting Requirements: Financial Institutions
    BSA Reporting Requirements: Trades and Businesses
    BSA Reporting Requirements: International Investments
    BSA Reporting Requirements: International Funds Transfers
    BSA Reporting Requirements: Suspicious Transactions

Privacy Act (1974) 68
    Project Match (1977)
    Computer Matching and Privacy Protection Act (1988)

Comprehensive Forfeiture Act (1984) 70
    Forfeiture in English Common Law
    Civil Forfeiture

Money Laundering Control Act (1986) 73
    MLCA-RICO Compared
    MLCA Section 1957
    MLCA-Internal Revenue Code Interaction

Anti-Drug Abuse Act (1988) 79
    Kerry Agreements
    Financial Crimes Enforcement Network
    Global Surveillance?

Annunzio-Wylie Anti-Money Laundering Act (1992) — 83

Money Laundering Suppression Act (1994) — 84

Chapter 3: THE GLOBAL SURVEILLANCE INFRASTRUCTURE — 85

Restatement (Third) of Foreign Relations Law (1988) — 86

Bilateral Information Exchange and Forfeiture Agreements — 88
Tax Treaties
Tax Information Exchange Agreements
Mutual Legal Assistance Treaties
Memoranda of Understanding

International Tax and Forfeiture Agreements — 90
Council of Europe/OECD Convention on Mutual Administrative Assistance in Tax Matters (1988)
United Nations Convention Against Illicit Traffic in Narcotic Drugs and Psychotropic Substances (1988)
Financial Action Task Force (1988)
Council of Europe Laundering Convention (1990)

Surveillance in Offshore Financial Centers — 94
Crown Offshore Financial Centers
    The Crown
    Enforcement and Executive Powers
    Statute of Elizabeth (1571)
    No Solid Economies
    Regulation
    Intelligence
    Homogenization
Switzerland
Austria

Chapter 4: COUNTER-SURVEILLANCE? — 102

Expectations of Privacy — 103
English Common Law
U.S. Common Law
Curtilage
Attorney-Client Privilege
Investments

Contracts With the Government — 112
Corporation Acts
    Limited Partnership Acts
        Charging Orders

    Hybrid Limited Partnership-Foreign Trust Structures
   Tenancy by the Entireties

Privacy   120
  Schindler's List
  Cash
  Funding
  Non-Reportable Foreign Investments
    Real Estate
    Safekeeping
    Foreign Insurance Contracts
    Securities
  Asset Protection Trusts
  Civil Law
  Liechtenstein
  Secure Communications
  Alternative Travel Documents and Citizenship

REFERENCES   132

Appendix A: A GUIDE TO CITATIONS USED IN THIS BOOK   137

Appendix B: U.S. GOVERNMENT REPORTING FORMS   138
 Form 720 (Quarterly Federal Excise Tax Return)
 Form 926 (Return by a U.S. Transferor of Property to a Foreign Corporation, Foreign Estate or Trust, or Foreign Partnership
 Form 1041 (U.S. Income Tax Return for Estates and Trusts)
 Form 3520 (Creation of or Transfers to Certain Foreign Trusts)
 Form 3520-A (Annual Return of Foreign Trust With U.S. Beneficiaries)
 Form 4789 (Currency Transaction Report)
 Form 4790 (Report of International Transportation of Currency or Monetary Instruments)
 Form 5471 (Annual Information Return of U.S. Persons With Respect to Certain Foreign Corporations)
 Form 8300 (Receipt of Cash Payments Over $10,000 Received in a Trade or Business)
 Publication 1544 (Reporting Cash Payments of Over $10,000)
 Form 8362 (Currency Transaction Report by Casinos)
 Form 8621 (Return of a Shareholder of a Passive Foreign Investment Company or Qualified Electing Fund)
 Form TD F 90-22.1 (Annual Report of Foreign Bank and Financial Accounts)
 Form TD F 90-22.47 (Suspicious Activity Report)

INDEX   247

Chapter 1:

HORROR STORIES FROM THE SURVEILLANCE STATE

Absolute Power Corrupts Absolutely

There is no financial privacy in the United States. Governments, credit bureaus and insurance companies maintain dossiers on wealthy Americans. Investigators can identify and locate assets at the touch of a button. Deep pockets are at high risk to lawsuits and government surveillance.

Supreme Court Justice William O. Douglas wrote:

We are rapidly entering the age of no privacy, where everyone is open to surveillance at all times. Secret observation booths in government offices and closed circuit television circuits in industry, extending even to restrooms, are common. Personality tests seek to ferret out a man's innermost thoughts. Federal agents are often 'wired' so that their conversations are either recorded on their persons or transmitted to tape recorders some blocks away.

The dossiers on all citizens mount in number and increase in size. Now they are being put on computers so that by pressing one button all the miserable, the sick, the suspect, the unpopular, the offbeat people of the nation can be instantly identified. Taken individually, each step may be of little consequence. But when viewed as a whole, there begins to emerge a society quite unlike any we have seen—a society in which government may intrude into the secret regions of a man's life at will.

In recent decades, surveillance has grown far more pervasive and efficient. To accumulate wealth privately, persons must avoid the **global surveillance infrastructure**. This infrastructure is discussed in Chapter 3.

This infrastructure invites absolute power and absolute corruption. Consider the tragic case of 62-year-old Donald Scott. On the morning of October 2, 1992, Ventura County, California resident Scott awoke to hear the door to his home being battered down and a cry for help from his wife. He rushed downstairs with a handgun. An armed man ordered him to lower his gun. Scott did so, only to be shot twice in the chest by the man. He died instantly.

Scott's killers were members of a heavily-armed task force consisting of 31 officers and agents from the Los Angeles County sheriff's department, Drug Enforcement Agency, California Bureau of Narcotics, the California National Guard—and the National Park Service. The task force claimed that the search resulted from a tip they had received that Scott was growing marijuana on his 200-acre estate. But no drugs of any kind were found.

Scott's killing aroused a national uproar. An investigation by Ventura County District Attorney Bradbury revealed,

> The statement of Probable Cause upon which the warrant was based includes a number of statements which could be considered false ... In addition, there are a number of facts that could be considered material omissions.

Preparation for the raid included analyzing the values of surrounding parcels of land and reviewing the personal and financial records of the Scotts, including a report from an anonymous informant that Scott's wife "was spending $100 bills." **Based on the profile created by the computer, the Scotts were deemed "promising" targets for property seizure.**

According to a report on the incident issued by the Ventura County District Attorney:

> We find no reason why law enforcement officers who were investigating suspected narcotics violations would have any interest in the value of [Scott's ranch] or the value of property sold in the same area other than if they had a motive to forfeit that property.

Boosting Government Revenues

Millions of Americans meet the same financial profile as the Scotts: upper-middle-class to wealthy, owning primarily or exclusively **visible** assets, and making at least occasional transactions to protect their privacy.

If such "evidence" is insufficient to obtain probable cause for a search warrant, you have the word of a prosecuting attorney that allegedly **false statements** and **material omissions** may be used to obtain probable cause if sufficient assets are at stake.

You also have the word of the Supreme Court, two U.S. Attorney Generals and the former director of the Treasury Department's Office of Financial Enforcement that a legitimate purpose in U.S. asset forfeiture policy is to enhance government revenues.

• In *Caplin & Drysdale, Chartered v. United States,* 491 U.S. 615 (1989), the Supreme Court declared that the federal government has a **legitimate financial interest** in maximizing forfeiture to raise revenues.

• In 1989, acting U.S. Attorney General S.G. Dennis, Jr. sent a memo warning U.S. Attorneys nationwide that the Department of Justice was far short of its "goal" for the year in forfeiture revenues:

> If inadequate forfeiture resources are available to achieve [this] goal, you will be expected to divert personnel from other activities or to seek assistance from other U.S. Attorneys' offices, the Criminal Division, and the Executive Office for U.S. Attorneys.

• In 1990, Attorney General Richard Thornburgh sent out a similar memo urging U.S. attorneys to "increase production" to achieve the Department's goal of $470 million in forfeiture deposits:

We must significantly increase production to reach our budget target. Failure to achieve the $470 million projection would expose the Department's forfeiture program to criticism and undermine confidence in our budget projections. Every effort must be made to increase forfeiture income during the remaining three months.

• In 1991, Amy Rudnick, director of the Office of Financial Enforcement at the Treasury Department described the philosophy of the government's asset forfeiture program in *Bank Management* magazine:

The more assets you can identify and seize, the more money you've got, either going into the general treasury or into asset forfeiture funds. That money can be used to help law enforcement in criminal prosecutions. I see this as a moneymaking enterprise for the government, and anything that's going to make money is not going to die too quickly.

Outside the federal government, federal forfeiture laws offer substantial incentives to state, local, and county governments: "Adopt" local property under federal forfeiture laws, pay a commission to the federal agency administering the law and keep the remainder. With budget cutbacks and shrinking tax bases, forfeited assets are a valuable supplement to law enforcement budgets. Since the law enforcement authority making the seizure keeps up to 80 percent of the proceeds if forfeiture occurs, huge incentives to maximize property seizures exist.

To train prosecutors in forfeiture basics, the Bureau of Justice Assistance, funded by the Department of Justice, has published 14 volumes on the subject. Titles include *Disclosing Hidden Assets: Plea Bargains and the Use of the Polygraph* and *Tracing Money Flows Through Financial Institutions*. Such technical assistance, combined with the computer matching of data in state and federal databases, represents a major initiative toward making the U.S. surveillance infrastructure self-funding by giving local governments a stake in its success.

This surveillance infrastructure now has global connections. This book describes treaties, connections between intelligence agencies and the global application of law. All tend to globalize the U.S. surveillance infrastructure, creating **global surveillance**. Surveillance is **particularly** pervasive in some "tax haven" jurisdictions, as discussed in Chapter 3.

No Presumption of Innocence for Property

In a U.S. **civil forfeiture** proceeding, there is no presumption of innocence for property. The burden of proof is reversed from that of a criminal proceeding; the owner or lienholder must prove that his property was not associated with a crime, or that he is an "innocent owner."

Proving innocence means a great deal more than demonstrating lack of guilt. In 1991, reporters from *The Pittsburgh Press* reviewed records of 25,000 seizures by the Drug Enforcement Administration. In **80 percent** of them, owners or lienholders of seized properties were **never charged with any crime**.

Forfeiture abuse is not limited to DEA or Customs seizures:

- **Stay current on mortgage payments, lose your home.** In 1986, Anthony Ferrer told Great Western Bank on a mortgage application that he made $2,500/month working for a garage door company. The bank didn't verify the income because Ferrer was putting down 25 percent and thus entitled to an "easy qualifier" loan. Six years later, when the U.S. Attorney's office asked for confirmation of this employment, the company's owner denied it. **Ferrer was current in his loan payments, but in 1992, a judge ordered the civil forfeiture of his home.** *United States v. 403 1/2 Skyline Drive, La Habra Heights, Calif.*, 797 F.Supp. 796 (C.D.Calif. 1992)

The Financial Institutions Reform, Recovery, and Enhancement Act (18 U.S.C. 1014) makes it illegal to make a false statement on a loan application from any institution insured by the Federal Deposit Insurance Commission and authorizes the civil forfeiture of any property obtained in this manner. In Ferrer's case, the alleged misrepresentation occurred three years **before** the Act's adoption in 1989, but the U.S. District Court agreed to the law's retroactive application. Its reasoning: the action was brought in a **civil** proceeding against the **property**, not against Ferrer. Therefore, the constitutional prohibition against *ex post facto* laws in **criminal** cases didn't apply.

Using the powers granted it in 1988, the federal government has begun a systematic effort to cross-match mortgage applications with tax returns to discover properties that are candidates for forfeiture. (See "The Pinocchio Papers," *Los Angeles Times*, July 21, 1993.)

- **Defend a client too vigorously, have your law firm's assets frozen.** In 1992, the Office of Thrift Supervision obtained an "asset preservation order" against millions of dollars of assets owned by a prominent law firm, Kaye, Scholare, Fierman, Hays & Handler. (An asset preservation order is similar to an asset freeze, except that the assets can be used under the supervision of the agency issuing the order.) The agency demanded a $275 million fine for the firm's alleged interference with the agency's investigation of the firm's client, allegedly involved in the 1989 collapse of a savings and loan institution.

Under the Federal Deposit Insurance Act (12 U.S.C. 1818), as amended, federal regulators can preserve the assets of an "insured depository institution" or an "institution-affiliated party" (such as an attorney representing the institution) by issuing a judicially-enforceable administrative order, **without going to court**. With all its assets "preserved," Kaye, Scholare agreed to pay a $44 million fine, without the opportunity to argue its case in court. The firm's malpractice coverage paid for much of the fine, but the firm's partner's were forced to dig into their own pockets to pay the multi-million dollar balance.

- **Kill an "endangered rat," lose the right to farm your property.** In 1993, Taung Ming-Lin, a Taiwanese immigrant who doesn't speak English, fulfilled a lifelong dream of purchasing property in the United States. Before buying a 720-acre farm in the California desert, he asked his attorney to check with county officials to verify that the land was zoned for agriculture. Go ahead and farm it, they told him. Lin then prepared the land to grow vegetables used in oriental cuisine, catering to Southern California's booming Asian population.

A year later, officials from the U.S. Fish & Wildlife Service showed Lin a dead rat, told him it and several other dead rodents had been found on his land, and indicted him for violating the Endangered Species Act (ESA). The agents then confiscated Lin's $50,000 tractor, which they claimed Lin used to deliberately kill an endangered species—a criminal offense in which the "instruments of the crime" may be forfeited. The forfeiture was later dismissed, but in the meantime, Lin was **forbidden to cultivate his own land.**

The endangered species specified in the indictment—the Tipton kangaroo rat—can only be distinguished from the non-endangered Herman's kangaroo rat by the size of the rear feet. The Tipton variety's rear feet are **1/100 of an inch longer.**

- **Admit a patient to a hospital "unnecessarily," forfeit your medical practice.** Federal prosecutors can seize the assets of physicians defrauding Medicare and Medicaid. "Fraud" is defined broadly. Any **"unnecessary" admission** is a forfeitable offense for the physician ordering it if the government can demonstrate that the physician directly or indirectly benefited from it. Physician peer-review panels have found that as many as 25 percent of hospital admissions are unnecessary.

Civil forfeiture of monies earned fraudulently, and criminal prosecution, is permitted if the government can demonstrate conversion of funds involving fraudulent or false billing for a medical product, service, or test; inflated cost of a service or procedure performed by a health care provider; or a kickback to a health-care provider on a sale of any medical product, including durable medical equipment, or any medical service.

Civil forfeitures ordered by U.S. courts can now be enforced **internationally,** even in jurisdictions that do not recognize this practice. For instance, in 1994, a court in the United Kingdom authorized a civil forfeiture ordered by a U.S. court to proceed against assets located in the United Kingdom. Again, we have the globalization of surveillance.

Cash Police

"This is the goose that laid the golden egg"

—Cary Copeland, Director of Asset Forfeiture Division, Department of Justice

Congress has passed laws requiring that many large cash transactions be reported to the IRS. Other laws permit the **confiscation** of cash. Government initiatives exist to make cash **more traceable**, and ultimately, to **eliminate** cash.

The Controlled Substances Act (21 U.S.C. 881(a)(6)) permits the civil forfeiture of proceeds of narcotics transactions, or property facilitating or purchased with such proceeds. Most street-level narcotics transactions involve an exchange of cash for narcotics, so the seizure of cash has become a common tactic in the "War on Drugs." But the government has gone far beyond street-level narcotics sales in its efforts to seize cash.

Virtually all law enforcement agencies, and many courts, have concluded that the presence of narcotics residues on cash provides probable cause that the currency was generated in narcotics transactions. **But according to statements from 21 federal agencies that seize cash, drug-contaminated currency is not destroyed. It's deposited in banks and re-enters circulation. Are we to conclude that such recirculated currency represents "the probable proceeds of narcotics transactions?"**

Moreover, for a decade, the Drug Enforcement Administration—under whose authority many such seizures take place—has known that much of the currency circulating in the United States is contaminated with drug residues. In 1985, a DEA laboratory issued a classified report concluding that; "The Federal Reserve may be contaminating the currency through normal procedures."

Researchers found that belts from the Fed's high-speed sorting machines are contaminated with cocaine, tainting vast amounts of currency. **How did cocaine get into the Federal Reserve's sorting machines to begin with?** The study doesn't speculate, only recommending that the DEA **discontinue** seizing currency contaminated with drug residues, and concluding, "Forensic usefulness of trace analysis is at best limited." This report was only made public in 1992.

In Valusia County, Florida, sheriff's deputies seized more than $8 million in cash from motorists on Interstate 95 between 1989 and 1992. Typically, the deputies stopped vehicles that met a secret "drug courier" profile. If any cash were found in the car, the sheriff would bring a drug-sniffing dog to inspect it. Deputies claimed that the dog "alerting" (barking or wagging his tail) after sniffing the cash constituted probable cause to seize it as the "probable proceeds of a narcotics transaction."

To recover their cash, victims had to prove in court that they earned it legitimately. Except for the largest seizures, the cost of a court fight exceeded the value of the currency. Most cases were settled out of court, with fines and attorney's fees deducted from the amount returned.

In 1991, plant nursery owner Willie Jones paid for an airline ticket in currency at the Nashville airport. The ticket agent informed the airport Drug Interdiction Unit of the purchase. While Jones was waiting in line to board his flight, two representatives from this unit asked him to step aside. Jones did so and consented to a search, in which the officers found $9,000 in additional currency. After a drug-sniffing dog alerted to the presence of narcotics residues on the currency, officers confiscated the money.

The publicity surrounding the DEA report, introduced in Willie Jones' successful appeal, led to some courts imposing stricter probable cause requirements for cash seizures. *Jones v. Drug Enforcement Administration*, 698 F. Supp. (M.D. Tenn. 1993). These **minimal** additional requirements may include receiving a tip from a confidential informant that the cash was generated in a narcotics transaction; not receiving a reasonable explanation for the origin of the cash; and/or that the person carrying it used a pseudonym.

To make cash transactions less private, in 1989, Massachusetts Senator John Kerry introduced an act that called for **machine-readable bar codes** on all U.S. currency. Kerry recommended that optical scanning devices track serial numbers on these bills. **Persons would disclose their identity in every cash transaction.**

That same year, Treasury Secretary Donald Regan suggested that all $50s and $100s be recalled and replaced with a new currency. The changeover would occur in ten days, and the "old money" would no longer be legal tender after that time. Regan recommended that anyone turning in more than $1,000 be required to prove that the cash was legally earned, tax-paid income. Otherwise, the funds would be impounded and their former owner could face criminal charges. Federal legislation mandating a new more traceable currency was introduced in 1991, 1992, 1994 and 1995, but not yet enacted.

Eliminating cash and substituting electronic debits provides even more efficient surveillance. In 1993, Maryland became the first state to complete a statewide network to issue welfare benefits electronically. Food stamps have been replaced with plastic cards, in an effort to reduce fraud. Some recipients used food stamps to purchase drugs or other items on the black market. A welfare agency sets up an account in the recipient's name and credits it every month with food stamps and other benefits. The recipient uses a debit card to draw against the benefits.

This initiative is an example of how privacy-reducing technology arrives through the back door to help build a **surveillance infrastructure**. The technology is first introduced to groups that have no effective way to refuse it (other than turn down benefits). Based on its "success" in these groups, the technology is introduced elsewhere. Will Social Security and Medicaid recipients be next?

Privacy Criminalized

A person trying to establish privacy in financial transactions is all the proof I need that he is engaged in criminal activity.

—Testimony from an IRS Criminal Investigation Division agent

The government has built a surveillance infrastructure that **identifies** visible assets, ties the **owner** of those assets to potentially suspect activities or cash transactions and brings the most promising targets to the attention of officials who have a financial stake in seizing these assets. Yet any efforts to protect one's privacy from this surveillance infrastructure, according to the government, **in itself** demonstrates criminal activity. The mere purchase of this book could undoubtedly be used to demonstrate a person's interest in privacy and therefore a criminal mindset.

Consider the case of Daniel Aversa, who conspired with a friend to hide income from Aversa's wife. The scheme triggered reports of suspicious transactions in their respective bank accounts. Aversa was charged with a federal crime: trying to avoid filing a government reporting form. When the U.S. Attorney announced Aversa's indictment, he implied that his office had broken up a **major money-laundering ring.** Yet Aversa's only "crime" was trying to protect his privacy.

Aversa Judge Loughlin wrote:

Defendants should never have been prosecuted for structuring currency transactions ... where evidence showed that defendants were not attempting to avoid paying tax on money or disguise where it came from ... The evidence shows that [Aversa] did not believe that [he] was breaking any law ... This is a case that was never contemplated by the drafters of the statute and that never should have been brought by the U.S. Attorney. **There is only one explanation for the bringing of these charges—it was easy** [emphasis added]. *United States v. Aversa*, 762 F.Supp. 441 (D.N.H. 1991).

Yet Loughlin had no choice but to sentence Aversa to the mandatory prison term. The Federal Appeals Court overturned Aversa's conviction, because he had not "willfully" violated the structuring law. However, 1994 amendments **eliminate** the willfulness requirement. **Anyone** can be imprisoned for trying to disguise cash transactions involving their own lawfully earned, after-tax earnings.

Employees of banks and other financial institutions that are not sufficiently vigilant to transactions such as Aversa's may be criminally liable. In one case, bankers were convicted of money laundering and bank fraud **without** the government even demonstrating they "ought to have known" about their customers' illegal activities.

Defendants Antonio Giraldi and Maria Lourdes Reategui were "relationship bankers" with Bankers Trust Co. and American Express International Bank. They were introduced to a "Mr. Villagomez," an investor they believed was a wealthy Mexican businessman with millions of dollars to invest in the United States. Villagomez was actually a money launderer for a narcotics trafficking ring.

Prosecutors didn't contest the defendants' good-faith belief that Villagomez was a legitimate businessman. Instead, the government brought money laundering and bank fraud charges against them based on evidence showing that:

1) the banks had "know your customer" rules requiring employees to understand a customer's business and be alert to unusual transactions (Chapter 2); and
2) bank forms completed by the defendants relating to Villagomez contained factual inaccuracies.

Prosecutors argued the only possible reason for these inaccuracies was to mislead the bank, and that such evidence demonstrated consciousness of guilt. **The government made no claim that the bankers knew or even "should have known" about Villagomez' relationship to narcotics trafficking.** On this basis, Giraldi was convicted of money laundering, conspiracy to commit money laundering, and bank fraud. Reategui was convicted of conspiracy and bank fraud. *United States v. Giraldi and Reategui*, CR-B9-3-028-S1 (S.D.Tex. 1994).

In an earlier case, Harlan Vander Zee, a bank official in Texas, was accused of complicity in money laundering. He described his harrowing experience with the government's surveillance infrastructure in congressional hearings in 1992. In 1987, a Mexican national approached Vander Zee with $300,000 in currency to deposit. To determine the proper reporting procedure, Vander Zee contacted **five separate federal agencies**. Each agency assured him—once on a recorded phone line—that the bank merely needed to complete a "Currency Transaction Report" for each transaction.

Vander Zee did so, and filed additional Currency Transaction Reports when the man returned with more currency to deposit. But three years later, he was indicted on three counts of money laundering, based on testimony from a paid informant. A jury acquitted him, but he was re-indicted on an additional conspiracy charge. The U.S. District Court granted a defense motion for dismissal once the second trial began.

Prosecutors seized the depositor's money, and refused to release it until Vander Zee's bank agreed to **not** pay for his defense and **not** to allow him to return to work. The decree also indemnified the government from any claim by the bank for false or malicious prosecution. Loss of the funds would have reduced the bank's capital below regulatory minimums, forcing it to close. To remain open, the bank signed the decree. Vander Zee lost not only his life savings, but his career.

Informants

Dozens of agencies pay **informant commissions** to persons who provide information that leads to asset forfeiture. The U.S. government pays out nearly $100 million each year in informant commissions as high as 25 percent of the value of the seized property. At airports, railroad stations, bus stations, and hotels, ticket agents, security personnel, and desk clerks supplement their income by tipping off local police to anyone acting suspiciously or carrying large quantities of currency.

There is no requirement that an informant gather evidence against a person **legally** to be eligible for a commission. The *IRS Manual* states:

> In receiving unsolicited information for the first time from an informant, the Service may accept the information and, in accordance with its value, may pay for such information even if it may have been obtained illegally by the informant.

This policy also applies to information provided by other agencies. For instance, the courts have ruled that evidence seized illegally by the FBI, even though currently inadmissible in a criminal proceeding, may be used by the IRS in a collection action.

Informant commissions **need not** be reported to the IRS on Form 1099. The 1996 *Instructions to Filers of Forms 1099, 1098, 5498, and W-2G* reads:

Fees Paid to Informants. A payment to an informant as an award, fee, or reward for information about criminal activity is not required to be reported if the payment is made by a federal, state, or local government agency, or by a non-profit organization under Section 501(c)(3) that makes the payment to further the charitable purpose of lessening the burdens of government.

Some cities have set up spy networks to maximize forfeiture revenues. According to documents obtained from the government in the Willie Jones case, in Nashville, agents from the DEA visit managers of local hotels to encourage them to spy on their guests. They are asked to tip off the local DEA office when guests engage in "large" currency transactions, make more than the "ordinary" number of phone calls, or host "excessive" numbers of visitors. **Managers who inform on their guests under these guidelines are eligible for rewards if their tips lead to forfeitures**. The same "guidelines" are in effect in many other cities as well.

False and/or malicious information from informants may lead to seizures that are hard to reverse. In 1989, Matthew Farrell, the owner of a 60-acre farm in Missouri, had his farm seized based on the testimony of a convicted drug dealer turned paid informant. The informant claimed that Farrell had sold him marijuana and described Farrell as creating a multi-million dollar drug cultivation operation that included tractors outfitted with special lights to harvest his crop at night.

Based on the informant's allegations, the county sheriff searched Farrell's home and farm. He found **no sign of drugs** or any other criminal activity. Despite this lack of evidence, the sheriff obtained a warrant to seize the farm. Farrell eventually recovered his property, but only after spending thousands of dollars in attorneys' fees and agreeing not to sue. **The county took no legal action against the informant.**

Sentencing laws that provide "mandatory minimums" for many crimes create powerful incentives for criminals to cooperate with prosecutors and become informants. The truth may be the largest casualty of such arrangements. According to Judge Stephen Trott of the U.S. Ninth Circuit Court of Appeals,

> Criminals will do anything to stay out of prison, including lying, committing perjury, manufacturing evidence, soliciting others to corroborate their lies with more lies and double-crossing anyone with whom they come into contact, including—and especially—the prosecutor.

Corruption

Forfeiture laws **increase** the street-level supply of narcotics and otherwise provide incentives to encourage criminal activity. Seizing agencies keep up to 100 percent of the currency or proceeds from property they seize. But seizures of narcotics, gambling equipment, illegal weapons, child pornography, etc. are destroyed and generate no revenues. **Strong incentives exist for police to maximize property seizures by delaying arrests of persons engaged in sales of illegal commodities until they have sold all or most of their supply.**

A 1994 research paper from Miller & Selva describes how this process operates. One researcher worked as an undercover informant for several months, conducting street-level drug busts in several Tennessee cities. He found that narcotics agents were instructed to maximize cash seizures, even at the expense of getting drugs off the street.

Time and again, when the researcher brought to his supervisors' attention the presence of large quantities of narcotics that could be seized, he was ordered to concentrate on currency and property seizures. In one case, a supervisor instructed the researcher to observe a drug dealer's cocaine transactions so that officers could postpone making the bust until after the shipment was converted to cash.

Have drug dealers and police evolved a symbiotic relationship that maximizes both the distribution of drugs and the production of cash?

As forfeiture programs come under increased scrutiny, investigators have found massive corruption:

- **Los Angeles.** In 1994, three former sheriff's deputies were convicted of stealing confiscated drug money, laundering it through a gun store, and failing to declare it on their tax returns. They joined 23 other Los Angeles County deputies convicted in the 1989 Operation Big Spender federal investigation, which found that anti-drug teams beat suspects and stole money and property after it was confiscated. According to U.S. Attorney Barbara Scheper, the deputies split about $750,000 taken in three sting operations.

- **Fort Lauderdale.** In 1993, reporters from a local newspaper discovered that during the tenure of Broward County Sheriff Nick Navarro, millions of dollars of seized assets went into secret office accounts, was left in uncashed checks, or was misspent.

About $2.6 million in cash seized as evidence in criminal cases was deposited in four bank accounts. The accounts had not been audited or reconciled in more than three years, and financial documents given to the county commission did not disclose them. Seized monies were also used to set up a **cocaine manufacturing laboratory** that manufactured "crack" for use in "reverse sting" operations; i.e., undercover agents selling the drugs to prospective buyers and then arresting them, confiscating their currency.

- **Miami.** In 1993, one FBI and three Customs agents were snared in a sting aimed at uncovering lawmen that allegedly ripped off drug dealers and laundered the money. The agents were charged with stealing and laundering $200,000.

- **New York.** In 1993, former police officer Michael Dowd pled guilty to drug trafficking and taking bribes from drug gangs. He told the court he stole guns, cash and drugs seized from criminal suspects by police and sold them back to drug traffickers. Dowd said he averaged $8,000 a week in bribes, split six ways with co-conspirators.

Criminal Abuse and Fraud

Power placed in irresponsible hands leads to **criminal abuse and fraud**. The surveillance and seizure powers granted by Congress to the Internal Revenue Service are an open invitation for criminal misconduct:

- **IRS agents kidnap children.** IRS agents detained seven children at a Detroit-area day care center, changed the locks on the doors, then called the children's parents. The children were released only after their parents paid fees due the school that the IRS applied to a tax levy.

- **IRS agents attack vehicle to seize it.** An Alaska couple, disputing a tax assessment, had it tripled. To enforce the assessment, IRS agents seized the couple's car while they were in it. Smashing the windows, the agents dragged the couple from the vehicle, leaving them bleeding on the pavement as a tow truck hauled their vehicle away.

- **IRS agents, U.S. marshals, beat pregnant woman.** A woman objected to the confiscation of vehicles on her property by IRS agents accompanied by armed U.S. marshals. Seven-months pregnant with twins, she was beaten to the ground with the butt of an automatic weapon. One twin was born dead, the other brain-damaged.

In 1976, Idaho Senator Frank Church convened hearings of the Select Committee to Study Governmental Operations with Respect to Intelligence Activities on the domestic intelligence activities of the IRS. Testimony revealed that the IRS maintained a "hit list" developed to audit, harass and intimidate 8,000 individuals and 3,000 organizations, "although clearly from the nature of these organizations, they [were] not suspected of owing taxes."

The hearings also revealed that the IRS engaged in undercover **political** surveillance of persons with controversial or unpopular views, including copying down license plate numbers of persons attending political gatherings, then auditing them. IRS Commissioner Donald Alexander described how the White House, the CIA, and FBI regularly requested and could receive the tax returns of any person or organization. After listening to Alexander's testimony, Senator Church concluded:

> [W]hat your testimony shows is [that] every taxpayer in this country is on notice that when his tax return is filed ... any agency ... that can claim an official interest can get into that tax return for its own purposes ... [W]hat better form is there to intimidate people, harass people, force them to comply with whatever it is some other agency may have in mind, than to have his tax return and information that it may contain?

However, **criminal abuse and fraud** continues two decades later. In 1992, the former branch chief of an IRS compliance center was indicted for filing false income tax returns using the names and Social Security Numbers of individuals he knew would not file. The returns showed large refunds due, which he pocketed. If this scam hadn't been uncovered, the individuals named on the returns would have been responsible for paying back the government nearly $500,000, plus penalties and interest. In another incident, a retired chief of the IRS Criminal Investigation Division was indicted for selling confidential government records to a California private investigator while still employed by the IRS.

According to testimony from William Duncan, a former agent with the IRS Criminal Investigation Division, agency attorneys are encouraged to **lie** to cover up agency misdeeds:

> To my knowledge, not one of the IRS attorneys has been punished, additional IRS executives have provided false, misleading, or incomplete testimony to investigators, and the conspiracy to cover up the illegal acts continues.

Entrapment

Undercover operations where the government **encourages** persons to violate the law are used in narcotics, money laundering and many other investigations.

After rejecting repeated offers from an undercover IRS agent to launder money through a pawnshop controlled by the government, Royal Lamar Hardy was approached by a second undercover agent from the Drug Enforcement Administration. That agent asked Hardy if he knew anyone who had extra cash available to launder through the agent's check-cashing business (another undercover operation). Hardy mentioned that he knew of a pawnshop (the IRS operation) that had repeatedly asked him to exchange cash for travelers' checks. **For providing this "lead," Hardy was indicted for money laundering.**

The government created the crime, supplied the means to commit it, laundered more than $300,000 in currency and repeatedly tried to involve Hardy in the illegal activity. The government's informants admitted they had no evidence that Hardy was predisposed to launder money, and that they had created the entire operation to entice him into committing criminal acts.

In the majority opinion of *Jacobson v. United States*, 112 S.Ct. 1535 (1992), Supreme Court Justice White wrote:

> Government agents may not originate a criminal design, implant in an innocent person's mind the disposition to commit a criminal act, and then induce commission of the crime so that the government may prosecute.

This is **exactly** what the government did in Hardy's case, violating the clear standards set by the Supreme Court. Hardy was acquitted, but only after spending thousands of dollars in legal fees.

Illegal Access to Databases

The surveillance infrastructure is easily misused for prurient interest or personal gain. Consider the following account from *The Gary Allen Report*, made possible by legislation and regulations issued to encourage the federal government to swap information with the states to eliminate welfare fraud:

George was attracted to her the moment he saw her while he was driving to work. She was in her mid-thirties, elegantly dressed, with long blonde hair that fluttered in the breeze as she drove her red Porsche convertible in the adjacent lane of the crowded California freeway. Letting her get a little ahead of him, George was able to read her vanity license plate: MINE.

When he arrived at his office in the local government building that housed the Department of Health and Human Services, where he worked in the social welfare division, George quickly brought up his file of codes on his computer terminal; tracking down that beauty would be a snap, he mused to himself. After all, he had access to numerous government records and private data banks. Checking people out was part of his job to distinguish valid welfare applicants from chiselers and illegal aliens. It was all part of the administration's drive to reduce waste, fraud and abuse in federal welfare programs.

At the computer prompt, George entered his authorization code on the keyboard, hit the 'execute' button and accessed the Department of Motor Vehicles database. He typed in the license plate letters 'MINE' and ordered a search of the DMV files. After less than a minute's wait, the monitor screen displayed the information he wanted: License tag: MINE. Vehicle: 1983 Porsche 944. Owner: Julie Jameson, 1509 Appleton Drive, Laguna Heights, CA. Driver's license: U0834725. Date of Birth: 5/14/52. Sex: Female. Height: 5'6". Weight: 105 lbs. Social Security Number (SSN): 552-58-2436.

Entering another data bank, George used the SSN as the key data element to search wage records that employers are required to file with state unemployment compensation and tax offices. Julie's record came up with more information: SSN #552-58-2436. JULIE JAMESON. Employer: Toltech Manufacturing, Inc., 921 Wilshire Blvd., Los Angeles, CA. Employed from 1/10/77—current. Position: National Director of Sales and Marketing. Gross pay for 1993: $93,124. Earnings for First Quarter, 1994: $25,542.

"Not bad," thought George. Next, he typed Julie's address into the computer and told it to search the records of the Laguna Heights deed registration office. Soon the screen filled with a new data record: 1509 Appleton Drive. Block 351, Lot 3. Land Assessment: $35,685. Total Assessment: $114,006. Built: 1978. Use: Residential. Deed of trust recorded: October 11, 1978. Loan Instrument: 23997. Amount: $75,000, between Joseph James and Julie Jameson Nelson and First National Savings & Loan. Other personal assets listed as collateral: 25-foot sailboat, assessed at $16,000.

Julie Jameson had once been Julie Nelson. George decided to check county divorce records to see what was on file. He found the record: Divorce awarded 7/18/85. *Julie Jameson Nelson v. Joseph James Nelson.* Married: 6/12/76. Children: Anthony Michael, born 4/3/78; Carolyn Marie, born 12/24/80. Grounds for divorce: Infidelity. Divorce sought by: wife. Race: husband, Caucasian; wife, Caucasian. Number of previous marriages: husband, none; wife, one. Date first marriage was terminated: 9/24/74 in Reno, Nevada.

Being a curious fellow, George then decided to check local school enrollment records. He found that 'Tony' went to Ben Franklin High School. Carolyn Marie was enrolled at Montgomery Special Education Institute, a school for children with learning disabilities.

Next, George decided to look into IRS files. But such records are confidential, so George's office computer terminal could not access the IRS data in Washington by an on-line connection. Instead, he put Julie's name and SSN on a request list that was mailed by his welfare office to the IRS the next day. In less than a week, George received a magnetic storage tape from the IRS that contained tax information on Julie Jameson's other sources of income.

Data from Form 1090 (Unearned Income) revealed that her interest income included $2,100 from a $23,000 Certificate of Deposit from First National Bank, $4,200 from a $48,000 CD at the same bank and another $1,600 from a $28,000 passbook savings account. Dividend income was also listed—including $9,754 from 4,000 shares of Toltech Manufacturing stock. Capital gains income of $5,600 came in from the sale of IBM stock. Even $3,235 in winnings from betting on the horses at Los Alamitos Race Track was listed.

Chuckling to himself, George mentally reviewed what he had learned about his mark. Julie Jameson was recently divorced after a nine-year marriage; it had been her second marriage and she had ended it with a divorce by charging her husband with adultery—and had apparently wound up with a hefty settlement as well as custody of the kids; she lived in an expensive home in a nice neighborhood (George had driven by to check it out); she worked at a secure high-paying job; she had additional income from interest and dividends; she enjoyed sailing and betting on the ponies; her six-year-old daughter had a learning disability; and she owned a status-symbol car. He decided he had enough information to make a phone call and strike up an acquaintance!

The Taxpayer Browsing Protection Act of 1997 prohibits such browsing, **but only by IRS employees**. Other records are similarly vulnerable. In 1991, the investigative arm of the U.S. Department of Health and Human Services began an investigation of unauthorized access into the Social Security Administration's payroll records. What appeared at first to be the activities of a single law-breaking employee turned out to be a nationwide network for stolen data, including data from criminal records maintained in the FBI's National Crime Information Center database.

The wholesale price of Social Security payroll records is as low as $20, according to indictments returned in the investigation, and sell for as much as $350. Criminal records from the FBI cost about $10 each. According to a regional inspector general for the Social Security Administration, drug dealers use the service to determine if their customers can pay for the narcotics they had ordered—and to make certain they didn't work for a law enforcement agency.

One reason more such investigations don't occur is that the government has little interest in shutting down this market. Bureaucrats don't want the public to understand how vulnerable individual records are, and prosecutors don't wish to reveal their own illicit information sources.

Rothfedder in *Privacy for Sale* relates the following example: In 1988 a black market data broker tried to bribe an IRS clerk to obtain a target's tax records. The clerk took the money, but informed his superiors of the payoff. The broker was arrested for attempted bribery and conspiracy to traffic in illegal information. Meeting with prosecutors, the broker disclosed his client list, which included high-level operatives in the CIA and other intelligence agencies. He threatened to enter this list into the public record if he was indicted, thereby exposing the illegal information gathering requests of his intelligence clients.

The strategy succeeded. No charges were brought against him. He merely agreed not to violate the law and to inform the IRS and the FBI of any unauthorized disclosure of, and/or access to, taxpayer information or investigative files of those or other federal agencies of which he was aware. **Far from shutting down his business, the government allowed the black market broker to put his competitors out of business by informing on them.**

Conclusion

The creation of a surveillance infrastructure making possible **absolute power** and **absolute corruption** requires stealth and the **appearance** of randomness. However, as the remainder of this book documents, this infrastructure's threads are too closely woven and its inter-relationships too compelling to not have been created from a blueprint.

First the government sets up a surveillance infrastructure, and then it passes laws permitting the confiscation of assets that infrastructure identifies. For instance, in the United States, the Bank Secrecy Act (Chapter 2) sets up a surveillance infrastructure for cash transactions. Amendments to the Act permit unreported cash transactions to be forfeited. **Is the expanding pattern of surveillance and seizure really accidental?**

Chapter 2:

THE U.S. SURVEILLANCE INFRASTRUCTURE

U.S. Constitution (1789)

While the U.S. Constitution contains several **implied** privacy rights, U.S. **Common Law** (i.e., **decisional** or judge-made law) supports no theory of a **constitutional** right to **financial** privacy, and only a limited constitutional right to **personal** privacy. U.S. statutory and decisional law essentially **eliminates** financial privacy.

Fourth Amendment

The Fourth Amendment to the U.S. Constitution provides:

The right of the people to be secure in their persons, houses, papers, and effects, against unreasonable searches and seizures, shall not be violated, and no warrants shall issue, but upon probable cause, supported by oath or affirmation, and particularly describing the place to be searched, and the persons and things to be seized.

With narrow exceptions, you may demand that police demonstrate **probable cause** to search your person, papers, luggage, vehicle or home. **Probable cause**, according to *Black's Law Dictionary*, is "reasonable cause; having more evidence for than against ... more than mere suspicion but less than the quantum of evidence required for conviction."

You may be asked to voluntarily give up this right; don't. Voluntary consent is valid even if you didn't know you had a right to refuse and may be given by another occupant of your home or passenger in your vehicle. *Scheckloth v. Bustamonte*, 412 U.S. 218 (1973).

Probable cause for **arrest** usually provides probable cause for **search**. Even incident to arrest, a warrant is required to search a car's locked trunk, or, in the home, any area out of the "plain view" of the arresting officer. *Chimel v. California*, 395 U.S. 752 (1969). You may refuse consent for a warrantless search of your **home** unless probable cause (not mere suspicion) exists that evidence of a crime is being destroyed. *Vale v. Louisiana*, 399 U.S. 30 (1970).

The Customs Service need not demonstrate probable cause to conduct a search. The Supreme Court has upheld "stop and frisk" searches **without** probable cause, without consent, and **without** arrest if the government reasonably suspects possession of weapons or narcotics. *Terry v. Ohio*, 392 U.S. 1 (1968). It also has ruled that persons have less expectation of privacy in a vehicle than in a home and therefore upheld the use of "random" drunk driver checkpoints where drivers are stopped, questioned, and often asked to submit to "voluntary" searches. *United States v. Chadwick*, 433 U.S. 1 (1976).

Police can stop and **question** you anytime, without probable cause. In a vehicle, you may be **briefly** detained while the government confirms your identity and that there are no outstanding warrants for your arrest. Your driver's license may not be withheld as a condition for a voluntary search.

Other than for the preceding exceptions, if the government conducts a search without your permission and without probable cause, you may bring a tort claim against the arresting officer and/or jurisdiction. The claim will be adjudicated by the court to determine if probable cause existed. If probable cause did not exist, any property seized in the search in theory must be returned, but often is not.

Right to Privacy?

The Supreme Court in 1965 recognized a constitutional right to privacy in *Griswold v. Connecticut*, 381 U.S. 479 (1965). A decade later, the Court limited this right to "matters relating to marriage, procreation, contraception, family relationships, and child rearing and education." *Paul v. Davis*, 424 U.S. 693 (1976).

The right to privacy does not extend to personal records that may tend to self-incriminate held by a regulated third party. *California Bankers Association v. Shultz*, 416 U.S. 21 (1974); *United States v. Miller*, 425 U.S. 435 (1976). The government may even force a person to deliver personal records to it, and subsequently use those records against that person in a civil or **criminal** proceeding. *United States v. Doe*, 104 S.Ct. 1237 (1984). (See "Bank Secrecy Act.") This is despite the wording of the Fifth Amendment, which states in part: "No person shall ... be compelled in any criminal case to be a witness against himself."

The Privacy Act (1974) and Right to Financial Privacy Act (1978) define a federal **statutory** right to privacy with respect to the government, but exceptions and amendments, and court decisions interpreting these statutes, tend to **eliminate** such rights. (See "Privacy Act" and "Right to Financial Privacy Act.")

This legal framework has permitted the development of a pervasive surveillance infrastructure in the United States, with **global** connections.

Private Express Statutes (1872)

In 1872, Congress imposed a government **monopoly** over first class mail delivery. This monopoly facilitates surveillance by requiring the delivery of most correspondence by a single carrier.

The monitoring and warrantless opening of mail by police, intelligence agencies and the Postal Service is legal or condoned under various circumstances. For instance, all packages sent from "source areas for the distribution of narcotics and/or controlled substances" might be inspected by drug-sniffing dogs. Court testimony from federal agents indicates that **every major city in the United States is considered such a "source area."**

The Postal Service also sells change-of-address information to direct marketing companies (and provides it to government agencies) and has established an **intelligence unit** to target for surveillance persons engaged in "suspicious mailing patterns."

Mail surveillance programs carried out by or with the cooperation of the Postal Service include mail covers, intelligence agency "mailtaps," and warrantless opening of mail.

Mail Covers

The monitoring of mail by a government agency is a "mail cover." The mail is only monitored, not opened; no warrant is required. The agency conducting the investigation records the address, sender, return address, meter number, place and date of postmark and class of mail for all mail delivered to the target address. Mail covers can be extended indefinitely.

International correspondence is a frequent target of mail covers. In the 1960s, the IRS photocopied all correspondence between Switzerland and the United States. It matched the postal codes on the envelopes with the names and addresses of Swiss banks and audited persons who had received correspondence from these banks. Many account-holders were prosecuted for income tax evasion.

Intelligence Agency "Mailtaps"

The courts have ruled that opening mail requires probable cause of criminal wrongdoing. But according to testimony before Congress from Professor Mel Crain of San Diego State University, while employed by the CIA,

> I found myself extensively involved in mail-tapping of American citizens ... The letters were opened, reproduced, and sent on their way without interrupting mail flow or their opening in any way being detected.

Targets were chosen, according to the National Center for Security Studies, "on [the agents'] own interpretation of current events." This operation was curtailed in the 1970s in the wake of the Watergate scandal, although **unofficial** reports of illegal mail opening by U.S. intelligence agencies continue. In the meantime, the CIA built a database of 1.5 million persons whose names were listed in the illegally opened correspondence. Portions of this list may have been merged with the CIA's DESIST anti-terrorist database.

The FBI also illegally opened mail during this period from a list of about 600 "subversives," mostly opponents of the War in Vietnam. However, only about 25 percent of the mail that was opened came from persons on this list. As with the CIA, individual FBI agents used their "judgment" to determine what other mail to open.

Warrantless Opening of Mail

The Postal Service may allow mail to be detained while a law enforcement agency decides if it has probable cause to examine the contents. However, the definition of probable cause is remarkably broad, as the following example, taken from documents filed in federal court, demonstrates:

> The Chicago Division of the U.S. Postal Inspection Service has implemented an Express Mail Profile program at the Air Mail Facility at Chicago O'Hare International Airport. This program consists of a physical profile of Express Mail parcels which have been mailed to or from locations within the Northern District of Illinois. Targets were cities and/or areas of the United States which have been identified by law enforcement personnel as being source areas for the distribution of narcotics and/or controlled substances.
>
> After the packages are identified, they are placed in front of Drug Enforcement Agency dogs trained to sniff for the smell of drugs. If the dogs 'alert' to the presence of drugs, the packages are then opened for inspection. Should drugs be found, the package is delivered to the address, and the recipient arrested.
>
> The positive reaction of the dogs, according to the affidavit, provides probable cause for the packages to be opened. Many packages opened contain no drugs, only cash, **which in some cases may be seized if it contains narcotics residues**. Packages may then be resealed and delivered to the addressee with no indication a search has occurred.

Mail Drops

Mail drops or mail receiving services are available in many countries. A mail drop may facilitate privacy when receiving or sending sensitive correspondence, but may be compromised. International investors can use mail drops outside their domestic jurisdiction to defeat mail covers of their international correspondence.

Law enforcement agencies associate mail drops with criminal activity. Some advertisements for mail drops in privacy-oriented publications are a ploy to get your name and address, which is cross-referenced with lists of missing or wanted persons. This is known as "reverse skip tracing." Persons contemplating the use of mail drops should make certain a mail drop actually exists before using it.

IRS (1913)

The 16th Amendment to the U.S. Constitution states:

The Congress shall have the power to lay and collect taxes on incomes, from whatever source derived, without apportionment among the several States, and without regard to census or enumeration.

Some persons, including Benson in *The Law That Never Was,* argue persuasively that the 16th Amendment was not properly ratified, and that Secretary of State Knox **falsely certified** to Congress that three-fourths of the states had ratified the amendment. However valid these arguments, they have been rejected by U.S. courts.

United States v. Thomas, 788 F.2d 1250 (7th Cir. 1986); *United States v. Foster*, 789 F.2d 457 (7th Cir. 1986); *United States v. Ferguson*, 793 F.2d 828 (7th Cir. 1986)

Today, U.S. citizens and permanent residents are taxed on and required to report their worldwide income. **Gift and estate taxes** apply to a U.S. citizen or permanent resident's worldwide **assets** taxed at their "highest and best use."

Octopus

U.S. **citizenship** subjects income and assets to U.S. jurisdiction and subjects citizens to U.S. income tax liability on their **worldwide** income. Seven other factors may produce such liability: residence, domicile, marital status, source of income, location of assets, timing, and status of beneficiaries.

Eliminating U.S. taxation requires eliminating each of these criteria. For most U.S. citizens, this requires giving up citizenship.

Dossiers

The first federal income tax was only 6 percent, paid only by those earning $500,000 per year or more. Tax rates gradually increased. Efforts by U.S. persons to minimize tax liability increased as well.

Laws passed by Congress and regulations adopted pursuant to them have constructed a massive surveillance infrastructure and database to collect income tax and to prevent defections from the system. Enforcement of these laws outside U.S. jurisdiction (**extraterritorial** enforcement) broadens this infrastructure. (See "Bilateral Information Exchange and Forfeiture Agreements.")

Submission of a tax return provides data that with the aid of computers compiles dossiers. IRS computers analyze individual returns compared to other returns of people with similar income and occupations. This "Discriminate Function System" (DIF), identifies returns that have a **potential** for adjustment. If the computer detects differences that exceed predetermined variances, the return becomes subject to review by a human agent.

Every tax return filed with the IRS undergoes such analysis. The **effective** audit rate for U.S. tax returns is therefore 100 percent.

Powers

Congress has provided the IRS with collection powers greater than any other federal agency. Historically, these powers have often been misused. Chapter 1 contains numerous examples.

The IRS need not demonstrate its assessments are accurate before imposing taxes. To collect assessments, the IRS may, without a trial or judgment:

- sell a person's principle residence at auction and use the proceeds to pay off taxes that it claims that person owes;

- seize bank accounts, securities accounts, and property in safety deposit box;

- issue an "administrative subpoena" (rather than a warrant) to compel third parties to turn over records that may be used in a civil or **criminal** proceeding;

- seize wages and salaries and force a person to support their family on no more than the standard deduction for that person and dependents; and

- confiscate Social Security or pension checks, even if that revenue is a person's sole source of income.

An uncollected tax assessment automatically imposes a lien against **all** property and property rights of the taxpayer. It also attaches to all property acquired after imposition of the lien. Property owned, or deemed owned, by the taxpayer, is subject to seizure by "**any means**." Property exempt from seizure under state laws, such as homestead statutes, is not exempt from lien.

The lien follows property wherever transferred. Transfers to a third party are voided unless that party can demonstrate that it did not know of the lien and paid fair market value for the property. Third-party holders of property (banks, etc.) are subject to the lien and relieved of liability **only** if they surrender the property. Failure to surrender renders the third party personally liable up to the value of the property not surrendered. The third party has no standing to challenge the assessment.

Code

The text of the Internal Revenue Code (Title 26 of the U.S. Code) fills several thousand pages and has sections numbered to 9,722. Much of the Code and regulations issued pursuant to it consists of **reporting requirements**, data from which helps create IRS dossiers. These regulations occupy several thousand more pages, and the *IRS Manual*, which sets out IRS procedures, fills an entire bookshelf. But the biggest problem of the Code is not its length or complexity, but its **inconsistency, unpredictability** and **retroactive application.**

A good example of inconsistency and unpredictability are the "commodity reporting" requirements added to the Code in 1982. In these amendments, Congress required "brokers" in "certain commodities" to report sales of these commodities by "unincorporated individuals" to the IRS on Form 1099.

When the IRS issued preliminary regulations, guidelines were vague. "Broker" was left undefined. Nor did the regulations stipulate a reporting threshold. Compliance and enforcement were wildly inconsistent. Some "brokers" ignored the regulations and were not penalized. Others were fined for not reporting to the IRS the purchase of a single silver dime. In one case a broker who completed hundreds of reporting forms by hand was fined $50,000 for not submitting them on **magnetic tape.** Finally, in 1992—10 years later—the IRS issued final regulations.

Inconsistency and unpredictability are inevitable for industries affected by any of the 50 "major rulemaking" assignments the IRS has yet to complete, some dating back to the early 1980s, along with nearly 600 major sets of regulations. Under these circumstances, it falls to individual IRS agents to interpret the "preliminary rules" or whatever other rules apply as best they can.

The Supreme Court has also ruled that the Code may be amended retroactively, despite the U.S. Constitution's prohibition of *ex post facto* laws. For instance, in *United States v. Carlton,* 114 S.Ct. 2081 (1994) the Court reconfirmed the constitutionality of a retroactive change in estate tax laws.

Criminal Prosecution

Each year, the several thousand taxpayers are indicted for criminal tax offenses: tax evasion, tax fraud, failure to file or increasingly, money laundering. More than 90 percent of IRS criminal prosecutions end in conviction or plea agreement.

Tax evasion and failure to file charges increasingly are replaced or augmented by perjury and fraud charges. Misdemeanor perjury sanctions are imposed by 26 U.S.C. 7207, which prohibits submission or delivery to the IRS of any document or statement known by the taxpayer to be false. Knowledge need not be proven directly, but may be inferred by the surrounding circumstances. Violations are punishable by a fine up to $10,000 ($50,000 for corporations) and up to one year in prison.

The felony perjury statute, 26 U.S.C. 7206(1), covers more serious violations. The penalty is a fine up to $10,000 ($50,000 for corporations) or up to three years imprisonment, **plus** the costs of prosecuting the case. 18 U.S.C. 1001 makes it a crime to willfully make any false statement on any matter within the jurisdiction of any department or agency of the U.S. government and carries a fine up to $10,000, up to five years imprisonment, or both. This statute covers **any** false statement or document given to **any** representative of the federal government in **any** inquiry.

Submission of a fraudulent asset listing in an IRS collection proceeding may trigger a felony perjury prosecution. Another common cause of action for such prosecution involves submission of an allegedly false Form W-9 to an employer. For instance, a taxpayer may claim 10 deductions when he may only legitimately claim two or three. Even submission of a false return **where there is no tax liability** can result in prosecution.

The increased use of tax fraud and perjury charges also helps the government enforce tax laws **globally.** In recent years, the government has negotiated treaties with other countries in which signatories are obliged to set aside confidentiality laws to exchange documents, if tax fraud is alleged. "Simple" tax evasion, which many of these treaties exempt, under the IRS definition exists only in the rare case when the agency does not allege the taxpayer submitted false documents or declarations. (See "Bilateral Information Exchange and Forfeiture Agreements.")

Tax Equity and Fiscal Responsibility Act (1982)

In 1982, Congress adopted legislation greatly expanding the powers of the IRS to gather information for criminal investigations. The Act **eliminates** the constitutional requirement that gathering evidence in a criminal investigation be supported by a warrant backed by probable cause.

The courts dismissed all constitutional challenges, culminating in *In Matter of Newton*, 718 F.2d 1015 (1983), in which a federal appeals court held that absent an explicit congressional grant of professional privilege, the IRS authority to gather information from third parties (in this case, an accountant) could not be obstructed.

Once the IRS has prepared a summons, it goes to federal court in an *ex parte* (without notice to the defendant) proceeding to obtain a subpoena. The IRS need only demonstrate that the investigation will be conducted pursuant to a legitimate purpose; the inquiry will be relevant to that purpose; the information sought is not in the possession of the IRS; and the administrative steps required by the Code have been followed.

The Act as amended also:

• greatly expands the types of income reported to the IRS. It requires banks and brokers to report all income, trades and redemptions, including interest, dividends, and the gross proceeds from sales, redemptions, exchanges and account closings. Banks and brokers must deduct 31 percent of the earnings of anyone who does not disclose their "Taxpayer Identification Number;" for almost everyone, their Social Security Number.

• requires that companies doing business as "brokers" maintain a list of the names and addresses of all customers, available for warrantless IRS inspection.

• requires that anyone who pays an "unincorporated entity" more than $600 in a year to submit a Form 1099 to the IRS. (One of the few exemptions is for **government informants**.)

• bans new issues of publicly-traded bearer stocks and bonds. (Bearer securities are instruments that can be owned anonymously. They are the property of the person "bearing" them and are not registered.)

• requires that anyone turning in a bearer instrument for redemption identify himself with a Taxpayer Identification Number. Otherwise, the holder forfeits 31 percent of interest and principal.

Strategic Plan (1984)

> *It is with considerable pride that I approve the Strategic Plan to carry out the mission of the Service. The Plan consists of the Statement of Strategic Direction and the 55 initiatives to translate them into action. It provides a strong foundation for directing tax administration efforts well into the 1990s and lays the groundwork for the Service's entry into the 21st century. Within the next five to 10 years, paper returns will be a thing of the past. And tax-processing procedures that now take weeks and months will be reduced dramatically. Early indications are that the automated system enables us not only to collect more efficiently but to collect more dollars in less time.*

— Roscoe Eggar, Jr., IRS Commissioner, "Internal Revenue Service Strategic Plan," document #6941, May 9, 1984

The IRS Strategic Plan is the centerpiece of the agency's effort to remake itself to more efficiently collect taxes. While not meeting Eggar's target of eliminating paper returns by 1994, the Plan has intensified collection efforts against the self-employed and underground entrepreneurs and helped move the IRS toward automated processing of tax data. It has also led to a vastly expanded U.S. and global surveillance infrastructure.

Independent Contractors. Key targets of the Strategic Plan are the self-employed; persons who work as independent contractors. Self-employed persons often fall through the surveillance infrastructure of information reporting and tax withholding. The Strategic Plan cannot be effective if large numbers of persons work as independent contractors.

In 1988, the IRS began intensive audits of companies using independent contractors, seeking to narrow the definition of work qualifying for that status. Typically, it seeks both back taxes and a 100 percent penalty for improper classification. The agency boasts of "eliminating" more than 400,000 self-employed persons since 1985.

In many cases, the IRS disallows independent contractor claims it approved in previous audits, despite a 1978 law that established a "safe haven" for employers who in past IRS examinations had incurred no liability for independent contractors holding substantially similar positions.

One firm that appeared to be ideal for independent contractor arrangements—a maid service that treated individual maids working for it as independent contractors—was declared by the IRS to be employing them. The IRS also tried to penalize several Pennsylvania corporations for paying dentists as independent contractors, even though under state law it would be illegal to hire the dentists as employees.

Tax Gap. Another goal of the Strategic Plan is to reduce or eliminate accounts receivable and the so-called "tax gap;" i.e., untaxed transactions in the underground economy. According to IRS calculations, U.S. taxpayers owe it $111 billion. These accounts receivable represent taxes assessed or otherwise calculated, but not paid. In addition, the IRS postulates the existence of an annual tax gap exceeding

$120 billion; the difference between what it believes Americans owe and what they actually admit to owing.

These numbers are inflated hugely by the IRS. A 1993 report from the General Accounting Office slashed the IRS' estimate of uncollected accounts receivable **83 percent**. The GAO says the real balance should be $19 billion, not the $111 billion estimated by the IRS.

The calculation of an annual $120 billion tax gap is similarly suspect. It postulates the existence of an underground economy with revenues exceeding $500 billion—well over 10 percent of the U.S. Gross National Product. But the calculations ignore the expenses of underground entrepreneurs. Assuming the IRS estimate of total underground revenues is correct, and further assuming a profit margin of 20 percent, the net revenues of the underground economy come to $100 billion. If 30 percent of this income represents uncollected tax, it implies an annual tax gap of only $30 billion—75 percent less than the IRS estimate.

Electronic Filing. Another provision of the Strategic Plan is a transition from paper filing to electronic filing. The objective, according to the Plan, is to "audit every taxpayer, every year," and eventually, institute a "return-free system."

In 1994, 20 million Americans filed their taxes electronically. To encourage more electronic filing, the IRS has introduced legislation that would require all tax preparers to file client returns electronically.

Electronic filing makes audits easier and more productive, because processing tax data by computer is more efficient than organizing the same quantity of data manually. A 1979 study concluded that it cost the IRS $400 to process 100,000 documents submitted on magnetic media, compared to $20,000 to process the same number of documents on paper. This gives computer processing a 50:1 cost advantage over manual processing; the advantage is surely much greater today, given the huge advances in computer technology since 1979.

A "return-free system" would be even more efficient. For more than 40 years, the IRS has proposed a tax infrastructure that would "eliminate the need for filing tax returns by wage earners when tax is withheld by employers." The legal and surveillance infrastructure for a return-free system was not available then, but could be much more easily constructed today. The IRS would send taxpayers a bill for the tax it has calculated they owe. Unpaid bills would be satisfied by levies against bank accounts or other property.

The 1993 North American Free Trade Agreement (NAFTA) provides a major step toward a return-free system. This Act authorizes the overhauling of the federal tax deposit program that collects more than $700 billion annually from U.S. employees through employer withholding. Employer accounts are debited directly through a central clearing agency. This system also makes it easier for the IRS to levy employee wages, as the agency simply increases the amount electronically deducted each paycheck from the employer's account. All employer tax payments must be made electronically by the year 2000.

Tax Reform Act (1986)

This Act retroactively disqualified deductions and extended depreciation schedules used by hundreds of thousands of taxpayers and investors. It led to a collapse of real estate values, as the favorable tax policy afforded real estate was a large part of its economic value. In turn, the collapse of real estate values led directly to the collapse of hundreds of banks and savings & loan institutions and a $500 billion federal bailout.

The Act also significantly expands the IRS surveillance infrastructure. It requires parents to insert the Social Security Numbers of their children on tax returns to obtain a deduction for them. **This provision assures a cradle-to-grave identification card for every U.S. citizen.**

The Act further requires that all interest earned from municipal bonds be reported to the IRS, even though such interest is tax-exempt. In 1992, the Long Term Family Security Act proposed a 2.5 percent tax on income from municipal bonds. This amendment did not pass. Was the Tax Reform Act's municipal bond income reporting provision intended to pave the way for this initiative?

Recall from "Octopus" that U.S. citizens are taxed on their **worldwide** income. However, tax on some types of income is **deferrable.** Until 1986, U.S. investors could invest and reinvest income in numerous offshore mutual funds while deferring current income tax, and convert ordinary income into capital gain upon the sale of the shares. If they held the shares until death, their heirs could obtain a tax-free "step-up" in their value, effectively eliminating tax across generations.

The "Passive Foreign Investment Company" provisions of the Tax Reform Act ended this treatment. A U.S. investor purchasing shares, no matter how few, in a PFIC must pay tax on any gain resulting from the "disposition" (sale or exchange) of PFIC stock, or on the receipt of an "excess distribution" (payment of a larger-than-normal dividend). The regulations assume the gains or distribution were earned pro rata over the period the shares were held. The income is taxed at the highest income tax rate applicable to the year in which it is allocated, **without** taking into account the taxpayer's actual marginal rate. In addition, **interest** is added to the tax for each year of deferral.

Market Segment Specialization Program (1993)

This 1993 initiative changes IRS business auditing tactics. Instead of auditing taxpayers in a particular **income segment**, IRS auditors specializing in particular **market categories** audit all businesses in these categories. An outgrowth of the Strategic Plan, this program enlists individual businesses in each market category to submit income and expense information to formulate audit guides. The IRS can then investigate any business in the category with net income below a certain range.

The first phase of the program involved preparing audit guides for targeted professions and industries. The IRS requested that targeted industries submit data to help it prepare the audit guides. **Essentially, it asked companies to provide data to help audit their competitors.** The guides led to development of program guidelines that purport to show businesses in each profession or industry what expenses and income are usual and customary. More than 20 such guides have now been published.

Targeted industries and professions include: attorneys, taxis, the music industry, construction, real estate, gasoline retailers, laundromats, air charter companies, automobile dealerships, commercial fishing, the ministry, restaurants, trucking, mortuaries, bed and breakfasts, reforestation, and travel agencies.

Compliance 2000 (1994)

This latest initiative to improve taxpayer compliance, now postponed, was to create a new database that could instantly analyze any financial transaction for which a computer record existed. Federal financial databases were to be enhanced with state, local, and commercial sources.

While the IRS withdrew this proposal after protest from civil liberties groups, it **already exists** in another form: the Treasury Department's Financial Crimes Enforcement Network. (See "Financial Crimes Enforcement Network.") The IRS uses data from FinCEN to match taxpayer income to "lifestyle" to identify prosperous nonfilers and for related purposes. The announcement in the December 20, 1994 *Federal Register* of how Compliance 2000 was to be used in effect describes how the IRS **already uses** lifestyle analysis to monitor the transactions of **"any individual who has business and/or financial activities:"**

> These [activities] may be grouped by industry, occupation, or financial transactions, included in commercial databases, or in information provided by state and local licensing agencies ... Examples of other information would include data from commercial databases, any state's Department of Motor Vehicles, credit bureaus, state and local real estate records, commercial publications, newspapers, airplane and pilot information, U.S. Coast Guard vessel registration information, any state's Department of Natural Resources information, as well as other state and local records. In addition, federal government databases may also be accessed, such as federal employment files, federal licensing data, etc.
>
> **... This system is exempt from the access and contest provisions of the Privacy Act** ... Closer cooperation between the IRS, the states, and commercial databases could significantly impact the levels of compliance [emphasis added].

Emergency Powers

Without seeking congressional or court approval, the U.S. President may seize property, organize and control the means of production, seize commodities, assign military forces abroad, institute martial law, seize and control all transportation and communication, nullify contracts, and regulate travel.

These powers may seem remote, but have worldwide impact. For instance, the President's emergency powers have been used on many occasions to freeze foreign-owned assets in the United States. Such powers have expanded in tandem with the U.S. and global surveillance infrastructure. Has this infrastructure been developed to seize and/or forfeit assets identified through global surveillance?

Executive Orders providing emergency powers to the President include:

- E.O. 11002 authorizes the Postal Service to register the location and identity of every U.S. citizen in preparation for other emergency procedures.

- E.O. 11921 calls for the control of all "devices capable of emitting electro-magnetic radiation." Does this mean **confiscation**, of radios, televisions and computers? It also authorizes the "utilization of excess and surplus real and personal property." Could this mean that property owned by persons who have "surplus" wealth may be confiscated and sold?

- E.O. 10995 authorizes the federal takeover of all other "communications media."

- E.O. 11004 authorizes relocation of individuals from their homes to new areas designated by the government.

- E.O. 11000 authorizes the enlistment of civilians into work brigades under the command of the military.

- E.O. 10999 authorizes the federal takeover of all modes of transportation, highways, etc. President Bush invoked this Executive Order in 1990 in preparation for war with Iraq.

- E.O. 11005 and E.O. 11003 authorize the federal takeover of all other modes of transportation including airports, railroads inland waterways, and public storage facilities.

- E.O. 10998 authorizes the federal takeover of the nation's food supply, and to divert it to whatever purposes directed by the President.

Trading With the Enemy Act (1917)

This Act provides an efficient collection mechanism for assets identified by the global surveillance infrastructure. The Act, amendments to it, and legislation drawing upon it have been used to shut down the U.S. banking system; force U.S. persons to sell precious metals to the government; and confiscate foreign-owned U.S. property.

When enacted in 1917, persons subject to the Act's jurisdiction were "other than citizens of the United States." However, Section 2 of the Emergency Banking

Act of March 9, 1933, amended it to also apply to **all U.S. persons**. Section 5(b) of the revised Act now reads:

> During time of war or **during any other period of national emergency declared by the President**, the President may, through any agency that he may designate, or otherwise, investigate, regulate, or prohibit, under such rules and regulations as he may prescribe, by means of licenses or otherwise, any transactions in foreign exchange, transfers of credit between or payments by banking institutions as defined by the president, and export, hoarding, melting, or earmarking of gold and silver coin or bullion or currency, by **any person within the United States or anyplace subject to the jurisdiction thereof** [emphasis added].

Drawing upon the authority in Sec. 5(b), the Emergency Banking Act (1933) imposed a National Banking Holiday, prohibiting depositors access to their accounts. More than 4,000 banks never reopened. On April 5, 1933, President Franklin Roosevelt again used Sec. 5(b) to issue an Executive Order requiring all U.S. persons to deliver all gold coin, bullion and gold certificates to the Federal Reserve. Anyone failing to comply could be fined up to $10,000, jailed up to 10 years, or both.

Persons turning in gold were reimbursed with Federal Reserve Notes at the official value of gold; $20.67/ounce. Roosevelt then devalued the dollar to $35/ounce. **In effect, the government paid gold owners only about 65 percent of the market value of their holdings, confiscating the remainder of its value.** The prohibition on private gold ownership was later extended to silver, and was not repealed until 1975.

President Nixon in 1969 combined many of the powers granted him under previous Executive Orders and the Act into E.O. 11490. This Executive Order stated that all power might be transferred to the President under "any national emergency **type** situation that might conceivably confront the nation." It authorizes the President to "utilize non-industrial facilities in the event of an emergency in order to reduce requirements for new construction and to provide facilities in a minimum period of time." Do these words authorize the confiscation of commercial and residential property in peacetime?

E.O. 11490 also calls for the president to "develop plans and procedures for the provision of logistical support to members of foreign forces, their employees and dependents as may be present in the United States." Does this mean the military can force private citizens to accommodate foreign soldiers on their property—a violation of the Third Amendment? E.O. 11490 also permits the president to seize all public power sources and freeze wages, prices and bank accounts. In 1971, President Nixon invoked this Executive Order to impose wage and price controls and suspends gold payments to foreign central banks.

National Emergencies Act (1976)

The Act was enacted after 1973 hearings before the Senate Special Committee on National Emergencies and Delegated Emergency Powers examined the U.S. Code and all statutory emergency powers. It identified 470 such grants of power. It also identified four proclamations of national emergency (1933, 1950, 1970 and 1971) that were only revoked upon passage of the Act. **However, none of the President's emergency powers were revoked.**

International Emergency Economic Powers Act (1977)

In the event of an "unusual or extraordinary threat" to the U.S. economy if that threat exists "in whole or in substantial part outside the United States," this Act authorizes the president to:

> require licenses for any activity; require anyone to keep and furnish any records; and investigate, regulate, prohibit, direct, compel, nullify, void, prevent, or prohibit any transaction, acquisition, holding, use, transfer, withdrawal, transportation, importation or exportation, dealing, or exercising any right, power, or privilege with respect to **any property** [emphasis added].

Persons violating these rules are subject to civil fines of $10,000 per violation. Criminal penalties for willful violations provide for up to a $50,000 fine and 10-year prison sentence. The money laundering statutes provide for the forfeiture of any assets obtained or involved in or connected to the violation.

When President Franklin Roosevelt ordered the forced sale of privately owned gold in 1933, many persons didn't comply. Except for persons holding bullion in exchange warehouses or other centralized locations, the Trading with the Enemy Act was essentially unenforceable.

With today's modern surveillance infrastructure, and the widespread use of computerized records, more recent Executive Orders issued under the authority of the IEEPA have been enforced much more efficiently. For instance, when President Clinton ordered the U.S. assets of certain Islamic fundamentalist groups frozen in 1995, the funds were restrained in a few **hours.**

Social Security Act (1935)

The Social Security Number is one of the most important elements of the U.S. surveillance infrastructure. Even though until the 1970s, Social Security cards were issued with the warning, "not for identification," they are now *de facto* national identification cards from birth until death.

In many states, a person's driver's license number is their SSN. Credit records are indexed by SSN. Some banks and credit unions even use SSNs as account number. Universities use SSNs for both student and faculty ID numbers. Health plans use SSNs to identify their policyholders.

At Social Security's inception, only workers in commercial and industrial occupations were covered. The military, the self-employed, and agricultural and domestic workers were exempt. Over time, Congress brought all these work categories into the system.

The Social Security Administration created the SSN so that it could distinguish between recipients with similar or the same names, and to establish eligibility for benefits. However, other government agencies found the number convenient to uniquely identify individuals. In the 1950s and 1960s, the IRS and state motor vehicle agencies began indexing persons by SSN.

Federal legislation first permitted, then required states to collect SSNs to administer various federal mandates. The Tax Reform Act (1976) allows any public agency that administers taxes, general public assistance, driver's licenses or motor vehicle registrations to require SSN disclosure. In 1988, Congress enacted the Family Support Act, which mandates that states require parents to submit SSNs to obtain birth certificates for their children. Even if the parents do not apply for a SSN for the baby, the government will know their SSNs, and be alerted to the new arrival.

But the banner year for federal mandates requiring SSN disclosure was 1996. That year's immigration reform act requires states to issue driver's licenses with the SSN displayed or electronically encoded, or alternatively to collect SSNs and turn the data over to the Social Security Administration for validation. The immigration reform act requires states to require SSNs before issuing professional, occupational or marriage licenses, or permitting persons to participate in a divorce action, child-support decision, or paternity determination. And in the name of "administrative simplification," federal law now requires that any person seeking health care in the United States, **even if self-paid**, submit a "unique identifying number."

The use of SSNs as a **universal identifier** also presents many opportunities for **impersonation** and **fraud**. There are no restrictions on the private use of SSNs, or on government retrieval of data held by private companies that use the number as an identifier. Confidential data may be retrieved over the phone from banks, credit card companies and insurance companies by anyone who provides a name and matching SSN. Knowledge of a person's SSN is often equated with proof of his identity.

Impersonation scams may result in civil and **criminal** liability against **victims:**

• A thief used the SSN of a Delta Airlines flight attendant to apply for credit cards under the attendant's name, then used the cards to charge thousands of dollars of merchandise. The flight attendant learned of the impersonation only when detained by a Customs officer during a routine border crossing. She was jailed, her passport confiscated, and her employment suspended.

• A Philadelphia resident received a letter from the IRS saying that she owed $6,000 in taxes, interest and penalties for an inheritance. The money had actually gone to an illegal alien who had used the resident's SSN to obtain employment.

• A Chicago resident was twice arrested and jailed for desertion from the Navy—even though he never enlisted. An impersonator had used his SSN to enlist, then deserted.

The damage to SSN impersonation victims is compounded when bogus information is transferred between credit bureaus or other companies. Even if the original mistake is corrected, it can be difficult or impossible to persuade companies or law enforcement to remove the incorrect information or drop a criminal investigation. Indeed, erroneous data can lead to decisions to deny a person the most basic privileges. Private data banks indexed by SSN track worker's compensation claims or "problem" tenants. A "hit" based on an erroneous report can make it difficult or impossible to obtain employment or housing.

This danger would be less serious if it were difficult to obtain SSNs; it isn't. Many persons list SSNs on checks. Doctors and other professionals often list the number on their stationary or on prescription forms. Driver's license and motor vehicles records are open to the public in most states; many contain SSNs. Given a name and address, private investigators or credit-reporting agencies can usually obtain a person's SSN. Some investigators claim a success ratio exceeding 80 percent.

These threats to individuals from **private misuse** of SSNs and data tied to SSNs pale in comparison to the threat of misuse of such data by **governments.** The reality is that governments **already** use SSNs as a national identifier to **target** persons for **surveillance, IRS audits,** even **property seizures.**

Department of Defense (1947)

Congress in 1947 combined the Departments of the Army, Navy and War into a single agency: the Department of Defense.

Before 1947, the United States had never maintained a sizeable standing army. The Department of War was active only in wartime. 1947 marked the beginning of the "military-industrial complex" that became so pervasive that when former General Eisenhower departed the presidency in 1961, he addressed the nation on its dangers.

The danger of the military-industrial complex is its ability to sustain a continuous threat of **crisis.** In wars, government powers, and the infrastructure created to enforce them, become more pervasive. The legacy of the military-industrial complex is not just weapons or war, but a greatly enhanced surveillance infrastructure.

National Security Agency (1952)

This agency, established by President Truman in 1952 by Executive Order, is the largest intelligence arm of the Department of Defense. Its mandate is the **global** monitoring of voice and other communications through a global network of monitoring stations and satellites. The agency has more than 100,000 employees and a "black" (off the books) budget exceeding $15 billion annually.

The NSA has interpreted its responsibilities as including the collection of **domestic intelligence**; assisting U.S. law enforcement agencies to conduct operations they are prohibited by statute from otherwise engaging in; and engaging in politically motivated eavesdropping. Legislation passed in 1978 seeks to restrict the NSA's domestic intelligence gathering authority, but the wording of **regulations written by the NSA itself** to invoke this law effectively bypasses this intent. (See "Foreign Intelligence Surveillance Act.")

Through a network of more than 2,000 monitoring stations around the world, including 150 in the United States, the NSA can monitor any information transmitted over wire and (especially) through the air. Voice, data, Teletype, facsimile transmissions, and telephone beeper signals are all vulnerable to NSA monitoring. So are mobile radio systems, local area network communications, radio PBXs and cordless and cellular telephones. To analyze this data, the agency has built the world's largest computer complex at its headquarters at Fort Meade, Maryland.

Information from non-U.S. monitoring stations is shared with the NSA pursuant to agreement. For instance, the "U.K.-U.S.A" Agreement (1947) between the United States, United Kingdom, Canada, Australia and New Zealand insures that all five nations share intelligence data captured throughout the world. **This agreement in itself sets up a global surveillance infrastructure**.

The capabilities of the NSA's 50 or so **surveillance satellites** are classified Top Secret, but details of their capabilities occasionally come to light. In 1988, Janes, a defense publishing company, printed a photograph of a Soviet warship photographed in amazing detail by a NSA satellite. Details only a few inches high—the equivalent of a license plate number or street sign—could clearly be identified.

Non-military satellites can also be used to gauge the likely capabilities of NSA satellites. For instance, a research satellite launched in 1994 is equipped with radar that can reportedly penetrate dry sand up to 13 feet thick as well as ice, dust, ash and vegetation. The official purpose of this radar is to "shed light on the climatic effects of volcanic ash" and "find traces of river tributaries buried by the Sahara desert." Is there any doubt that NSA satellites have even more sophisticated radars?

The domestic intelligence activities of the NSA were highlighted in 1976 hearings before the Senate Intelligence Committee. Witnesses described initiatives such as Project Minaret, in which the NSA monitored dissidents on "watch lists" provided by the FBI, CIA, Secret Service and the Defense Intelligence Agency; and Project Shamrock, in which from 1945 to 1975 the NSA inspected **daily** all overseas cables. According to the Committee's final report, Shamrock was the "largest governmental interception program affecting Americans, dwarfing the CIA's mail opening program by comparison." (See "Private Express Statutes.")

The NSA also admitted that it routinely monitored all international telephone communications. According to a report from the House Government Operations Committee that was never published:

> The NSA captures data as it is transmitted through the air and under the ground. Such messages are then processed through computers that are programmed to isolate encrypted messages, as well as messages containing "trig-

ger" words, word combinations, entities, names, addresses and combinations of addresses. The intercepted messages that are in code or cipher are, whenever possible, solved. These messages and messages selected by "target procedures" are then inspected by human analysts. Messages which the NSA electronically scans and judges to be of no interest to the NSA or its consumers [i.e., other federal agencies]—annually accounting for tens of millions of communications of U.S. citizens—**are not considered by the NSA to have been intercepted or acquired** [emphasis added].

Other NSA operations are smaller in scope, but no less invasive. For instance, when the Drug Enforcement Agency decided it couldn't tap all the phones in Grand Central Station without violating federal wiretapping statutes, it turned to the NSA to do so remotely. The agency worked in concert with the DEA to develop trigger words with which to screen these calls.

Political appointees and even relatives of presidents may also become NSA targets. The agency eavesdropped on former United Nations' representative Andrew Young when he met with a representative of the Palestinian Liberation Organization. When Billy Carter, the brother of former President Jimmy Carter, offered his services to the Libyan government, the NSA monitored the conversation—and turned the transcript over to the President.

Foreign Intelligence Surveillance Act (1978)

Until 1978, the NSA claimed it had "inherent presidential authority" to eavesdrop on anyone it viewed as a legitimate foreign intelligence target. In response to the abuses uncovered in its 1975 and 1976 hearings, Congress passed the Foreign Intelligence Surveillance Act (50 U.S.C. 1801). However, the mechanisms this Act sets forth for NSA domestic operations operate in **total secrecy** and may be bypassed through Executive Order. The result is no effective limitation on NSA domestic intelligence gathering.

The Act also establishes a **secret court,** the "Foreign Intelligence Surveillance Court," to review applications for **domestic** wiretaps and other surveillance for **foreign** intelligence purposes. This court consists of seven judges appointed by the Chief Justice of the U.S. Supreme Court. The Court deliberates behind closed doors and its decisions are never published. Since 1979, hundreds of wiretaps have been authorized by this Court each year. **The applications need not be based on probable cause. No application has ever been turned down.**

Until 1981, the Court also reviewed Department of Justice applications for the FBI to conduct surreptitious entries domestically into "non-residential premises under the direction and control of a foreign power." President Reagan in 1981 issued an Executive Order stipulating that court approval of such jobs was unnecessary since the president had the inherent authority to order them. The Court concurred.

The Act stipulates that "electronic surveillance" means "the acquisition by an electronic, mechanical or other surveillance device" of the approved targets. But it does not define "acquisition." This task was left to the NSA, which defined the term as "the interception **by the NSA** through electronic means of a communication to which it is not an intended party" [emphasis added].

By inserting "by the NSA" in this definition, the agency **excluded** from the Act and the Foreign Intelligence Surveillance Court **all interceptions received from any non-NSA source**. For instance, if the NSA acquires intelligence from MI-5 (British Intelligence) through the U.K.-U.S.A. intelligence-sharing agreement, the data would be excluded from these provisions.

Safe Streets Act (1968)

The evil incident to invasion of the privacy of the telephone is far greater than that involved in tampering with the mails. Whenever a telephone line is tapped, the privacy of the persons at both ends of the line is invaded, and all conversations between them upon any subject, and although proper, confidential, and privileged, may be overheard. Moreover, the tapping of one man's telephone line involves the tapping of the telephone of every other person whom he may call, or who may call him. As a means of espionage, writs of assistance and general warrants are but puny instruments of tyranny and oppression when compared with wiretapping.

Justice Brandeis, *Olmstead et al. v. United States*, 277 U.S. 438 (1928)

The "Omnibus Crime Control Act," 18 U.S.C. 2515, set up a procedure under which law enforcement officials could obtain court orders for electronic surveillance; i.e., remotely monitor conversations, data transmissions, and/or movements. The Act also prohibits electronic surveillance without a warrant supported by probable cause and bans the sale of fully assembled electronic surveillance devices.

The Act covers two groups of surveillance devices: wiretaps and "bugs." A **wiretap** is the act, process, or equipment used to monitor and/or record the content of messages transmitted over wires or through the air without degrading the quality of transmission or interfering with it in any way, without detection. The product of a wiretap is the content of messages so transmitted. A **bug** is a device or system used to monitor all target area audio. The product of a bug is target area audio.

Exemptions to the Act apply to telephone companies and other "electronic communication services," which have unlimited authority to listen in on conversations or data transmissions to prevent fraud:

> ...[A]n officer, employee, or agent of wire or electronic communication service [may] ... intercept, disclose, or use that communication in the normal course of his employment while engaged in any activity which is a necessary incident to the rendition of his service or to the protection of the rights or property of the provider of that service.

Nor is a warrant required for the Federal Communications Commission to monitor transmissions or if at least one party to a conversation (including law enforcement) is aware of the monitoring.

A practical, if not legal, exemption to the Act exists in that the proliferation of beepers and cellular and cordless telephones has made it unenforceable. Amendments to the Act prohibit monitoring cellular and cordless telephone **radio signals**, but the ease of monitoring makes the prohibition unenforceable. **The problem is so acute that bar associations in several states have warned attorneys that using such phones to discuss sensitive client matters may violate attorney-client privilege.**

A 1988 program produced by Home Box Office, "No Place to Hide," presented evidence that radio hobbyists listened in to former President Reagan's unprotected cellular conversations as he traveled in limousines around Washington, D.C. More recently, excerpts from the cellular phone conversations of Vice-President Gore were published. Politicians in Canada and Australia and England's Prince Charles have been embarrassed when details of their cellular conversations were made public.

Nor is the Act's ban on fully-assembled electronic surveillance devices of practical value, as "surveillance shops" offer such equipment fully-assembled if the purchaser signs an affidavit that it will be exported. Moreover, it takes only a few minutes to construct an electronic monitoring device with components purchased over-the-counter at an electronic hobby store.

Electronic Monitoring

Most counter-surveillance professionals claim that while most "sweeps" find no electronic surveillance devices, those that are found are almost always planted illegally. Court-authorized wiretaps, for instance, are almost always installed at a central switch, making on-site discovery impossible.

Illegal electronic monitoring is most common in divorce cases and corporate espionage. But there is little doubt that the **government** also conducts illegal electronic monitoring. The Nixon administration's illegal monitoring of journalists, war protestors, civil rights activists, etc. is thoroughly documented. More recently, the author has spoken to electronic counter-surveillance specialists who have discovered monitoring devices employing technologies only available to the government, but installed a manner suggesting they were not legally authorized.

Illegal monitoring of cellular and cordless conversations is even simpler. In one unit available only to law enforcement, Harris Corporation's "Triggerfish," all that is necessary is to dial the target number. Once entered into this device, all calls within range of the unit may be monitored. This makes it easy to circumvent the requirement that a warrant be obtained before monitoring cellular conversations.

Illegally installed wiretaps are typically established in the same building as the target telephone, frequently in an unlocked telephone closet. They take power from the line itself or use a battery to broadcast radio signals. Neither kind causes "pops" or "clicks" on the line or otherwise degrades sound quality.

Line-powered wiretaps are virtually impossible to detect electronically. (Therefore, those who offer "tap detectors" are frauds.) However, the added wire pair may be found in a careful visual inspection. Wiretaps that broadcast can transmit room audio a mile or more. The stronger the signal, and the longer the broadcasts, the more likely the wiretap can be detected electronically.

Only a small number of **authorized** electronic surveillances occur each year. For instance, in 1993, federal courts authorized about 1,500 wiretaps. In large-scale criminal investigations, the government will obtain a warrant for a **"roving wiretap."** Several or even dozens of phones that might be used by the surveillance target are monitored. Thousands of conversations not involving the subject may be recorded.

The most sophisticated roving wiretaps identify a "voiceprint" out of the thousands of telephone conversations taking place simultaneously in a telephone exchange. U.S. research to develop voiceprint-tapping systems is classified. Officially, the technology doesn't exist. However, the Canadian government acknowledges awarding in 1993 a $1.1 million grant to develop a "speaker identification system" which can isolate and identify voices from the millions of daily telephone conversations in Canada.

Other telephone monitoring techniques don't require wiretaps. One ingenious method is an ordinary extension telephone. An eavesdropper asks the telephone company to install an "extension phone" to an existing line. When the target picks up the phone, the tape begins rolling. Executives who install "private lines" that bypass a central PBX are particularly susceptible to this attack.

Electronic pagers have a similar vulnerability. In one case, a police chief obtained a court order to obtain the same pager number as a suspected drug dealer. Every time the suspect's pager went off, the police chief's device did as well. A person dialing the pager number had his number displayed not only on the drug dealer's pager, but the one carried by the police chief.

One of the most ingenious and commonly encountered **bugs** is a modified telephone. It operates normally but conducts room audio over spare wires in the telephone cable. Many telephones are room bugs as built. They may be remotely activated by telephone to transmit all room. Two examples are the Northern Telecom 2018 and the Comdial Executech II.

Wireless intercoms are also used as bugs. They transmit room audio as modulated low frequency signals over power lines; this is called "carrier current" or "line carrier." All an eavesdropper must do to construct an "intercom bug" is attach an amplifier across the wires (about $12 at Radio Shack) and connect the amplifier to speakers or a voice-activated tape recorder. Any office with an intercom speaker can be bugged in minutes.

Battery-powered bugs are the most portable, because they don't need to be hard-wired into an electrical grid. They may be installed on the underside of ashtrays, in wastebaskets, underneath desks, etc. Some, disguised as pens or some other common office item, can be installed in the presence of the target. Hard-wired bugs may be installed inside telephones, in light fixtures, electrical outlets, electric appliances, etc. Bugs may be designed with microphones designed to fit into unusual locations. A flexible "tube mike" may be placed in electrical outlets, keyholes, air ducts, etc. A "spike mike" is more rigid and can penetrate relatively hard surfaces such as walls. A "contact mike" can be attached to any interior surface.

A person can be "wired" to record and/or transmit conversation. This is common in undercover investigations, and is increasingly common in corporate espionage. A stereo tape recorder might be implanted in a shoulder holster, with microphones taped to the person's skin or installed in cufflinks or a tiepin. A pen or wristwatch can easily be transformed into a radio transmitter.

Computer Monitoring

A computer emits an "electronic signature" that can be monitored and decoded with the appropriate equipment. This is termed the Van Eck phenomenon, after the Dutch scientist who first publicized it. The U.S. government has moved aggressively to prevent detection of electronic signatures from computers and other equipment. Military computers are often enclosed in lead sheathing and are equipped with other so-called "Tempest" features to trap these emissions.

Exploitation of the Van Eck phenomenon appears to be responsible, in part, for the 1994 arrest for espionage of CIA employee Aldrich Ames. During its investigation of Ames, the FBI installed surveillance devices in his home. According to the Affidavit in Support of the Warrant for Ames' arrest, the FBI used "electronic surveillance of Ames' personal computer and software within his residence." The FBI could have planted a Van Eck device in Ames' computer to capture signals from the screen, keyboard strokes or both. It also could have focused an external antenna to monitor his computer remotely.

Dialing Records

A person's telephone dialing records do not convey the **content** of conversations, but provide a comprehensive record of who he has called and the length of conversations. Information conveyed from such records is analogous to that obtained in a mail cover of a person's correspondence. No expectation of privacy extends to these records (Chapter 4).

In 1992, Bell Atlantic, the parent company of C&P Telephone, revealed that it had received 22,000 requests from government agencies for dialing records in 1991 alone. Amendments in 1986 to the Safe Streets Act require that the subject of such an investigation be notified. However, the government may request a 30-day delay of such notification, which may be extended **indefinitely**.

Nationwide Caller ID (1995)

Caller ID displays the originating number of calls within a local area code, and beginning in 1995, nationwide. Some units also show the name of the caller along with the originating number. In an area equipped with caller ID service, all originating calls in which the service is not blocked send a caller ID signal. In areas with "enhanced 911" emergency service, calls to emergency services are accompanied by transmission of certain **medical records.**

A technology distinct from caller ID, but with similar capabilities, is **automatic number identification**. It permits an originating number to be displayed on calls to 800 (WATS) and 900 exchanges. Caller ID blocking does not block ANI.

Area codes and phone numbers collected through caller ID or ANI may be linked with customer records and other databases. Even the smallest businesses and agencies can equip themselves with such equipment. For instance, the "Octus Personal Telecommunications Assistant" may be installed on most personal computers.

The heart of the system is an electronic address book combined with caller ID. When a call comes in, the computer automatically consults a national white-pages database on CD-ROM, and displays the resulting name and address. Optional databases add a demographic profile of the caller's neighborhood. (See "Cluster Modeling.") This data is displayed in seconds.

Some companies place enticing advertisements and wait for calls to come in on their WATS lines. They don't answer the phone, but record the caller's number, match it to an address with a reverse directory on CD-ROM, and sell the information to direct marketing companies. Government agencies also place such ads to gather names of persons who may later be targeted for investigations. Could some advertisements for "alternative identity information" and related topics be such fronts?

Fair Credit Reporting Act (1970)

This Act (15 U.S.C. 1681 et. seq.) and regulations interpreting it permit "consumer reporting agencies" (e.g., credit bureaus) to furnish "consumer credit reports" to third parties:

- in response to a court order or administrative subpoena;

- in accordance with the written instructions of the consumer;

- in connection with a credit transaction involving the consumer, or a review or collection action regarding such transactions;

- in an application for employment or insurance coverage; or

- to determine the consumer's eligibility for a license or other benefit granted by a government agency required by law to consider an applicant's financial responsibility or status.

While it once was necessary for a government agency to obtain a court order to examine credit records, all that is required today is an **administrative subpoena**; a demand by a government agency that credit records are relevant to an ongoing investigation. (See "Tax Equity and Fiscal Responsibility Act.")

Consumers give **written instructions** permitting distribution of credit data more often than they might believe. Credit card agreements generally authorize issuers to "make credit, employment, and investigative inquiries as we deem appropriate for the extension of credit or collection of amounts owing on the account." Signing such an agreement authorizes the issuer not only to obtain credit records but also to review bank account balances to determine if the cardholder has sufficient funds to pay their bill.

Credit bureaus may distribute **partial** credit records without permission from the person on whom data is compiled. Such "headers," which may contain **Social Security Numbers** and other sensitive data, have been deemed by the Federal Trade Commission not to be "credit reports" and thus not subject to the Act's authority. Several credit bureaus market "credit risk evaluation services;" mathematical models that calculate the probability of a credit applicant falling behind on payments or declaring bankruptcy. Employers, banks, landlords and government agencies use such services to evaluate prospective employees, customers, tenants and investigative targets.

Information maintained by credit bureaus is much more extensive than often believed. Credit grantors continuously update the files. Each file contains the subject's name and address, age, and Social Security Number; employer, salary, and length of employment; the name and ages of spouse and children; and payment history on reported extensions of credit (credit cards, installment loans, mortgages, etc.).

Credit bureaus also contract with private companies to add records of judgments, state and federal tax liens, repossessions, bankruptcies, and lawsuits to credit files. This data is keyed to the subject's name and/or Social Security Number and is available at the touch of a button.

Public Records

Federal, state, and local governments maintain many records available to the public, including real estate ownership; voter's registration; motor vehicles; driver's licenses; professional licenses; and court records. Private companies also maintain records available to the public, including utility records and telephone listings. Dozens of companies now compile such data and make it available via computer. Trade in these records is not regulated by the Fair Credit Reporting Act, as public records and data assembled from them are not legally "credit reports." When used in conjunction with data in credit files, this data can create detailed personal and financial dossiers. A flyer offering such services shows how little they cost; discounted rates for multiple searches are also available:

Data sought: Home address. **Requires**: Last known phone number. **Cost**: $25

Data sought: Home address. **Requires**: License plate number. **Cost**: $30

Data sought: Home address. **Requires**: P.O. box number. **Cost**: $75

Data sought: Phone number. **Requires**: Last known address. **Cost**: $25

Data sought: Social Security Number. **Requires**: Full name and last known address. **Cost**: $35

Data sought: Phone number, past addresses, list of neighbors. **Requires:** Full name and last known address. **Cost:** $45

Data sought: Arrests, marriages, divorces, and business licenses. **Requires**: Full name and last known address. **Cost**: $30

Data sought: Real estate ownership. **Requires**: Full name and state. **Cost:** $85

Data sought: Consumer credit report. **Requires**: Full name and Social Security Number. **Cost**: $30

Data sought: Business credit report. **Requires**: Name and state of business. **Cost**: $75

Data sought: Assets in bank. **Requires**: Full name and Social Security Number. **Cost**: $150

Data sought : Vehicles owned. Requires: Name and address. Cost: $35

Criminal records are increasingly available via computer as the FBI's National Crime Information Center database expands and the agency implements its "NCIC 2000" program. This service is open to federal agencies, law enforcement, federally insured banks, private employers with defense or other federal or state government contracts, and many state agencies. However, illegal access is common.

Cluster Modeling

Any information voluntarily disclosed by a consumer may be analyzed. Data for such analysis comes from **public records** combined with records **of mail order purchases** and **credit card transactions**, overlain with **demographic profiles** of a where a person lives, his occupation, etc.

"Target marketing" or "cluster modeling" defines how an individual fits into an organization or group, predicting behavior based on characteristics of that group. Direct marketers employ target marketing to pinpoint consumer tastes. The government uses cluster modeling to update and analyze thousands of databases containing billions of records on virtually every U.S. citizen or resident.

In 1992, the FBI sought lists assembled from public records from three of the largest mailing list brokers in the country. These firms refused to rent the lists to the agency, although other companies provided the requested data. Could the FBI use the resulting data to predict what persons might be predisposed to commit crimes, or identify targets for investigation?

Records of goods or services purchased with a credit card or through the mail are the largest source of raw data for cluster marketing. Credit card agreements typically have language similar to the following:

We can furnish information concerning your account or credit file to consumer reporting agencies, our affiliates, and **others who may properly receive that information** [emphasis added].

Citicorp and American Express have for more than a decade analyzed the purchasing patterns of millions of credit card customers. Statements are analyzed to determine how often cardholders shop, how much they spend, and which stores, restaurants and hotels they prefer. Categories for analysis include dining, hotel, car rental, airline tickets, medical, automotive, retail shopping, specialty stores and cash advances. There are hundreds of sub-categories.

Any organization can create consumer profiles for its list. In 1992, the World Jewish Congress wanted to learn more about the 100,000 people on its donor list. It hired a consultant to match its names against a list of wealthy people culled from public records and information assembled by firms offering target marketing services. It found 250 "multi-millionaires" and another 2,500 "millionaires." The WJC then concentrated its marketing efforts on the most affluent portion of its list.

The IRS also analyzes public records and mailing lists to create consumer profiles. These profiles are then matched against declared income to determine whether anomalies exist. For instance, a person with a declared income of $15,000/year who lives in a $150,000 home might be deemed worthy for further investigation. The creation of a Treasury Department intelligence division makes such analysis routine. (See "Financial Crimes Enforcement Network.")

Medical Records

While the English Common Law inherited by the United States recognizes the confidential relationship between doctor and patient, this privilege has virtually ceased to exist in reference to the government and third-party payers of medical claims.

The structure of the U.S. medical system **forces** information disclosure. Insurance companies and the government demand waivers of confidentiality to confirm that claims are reimbursable. Doctors who accept payment from Medicare patients risk being disbarred from the program if they don't file the appropriate forms. Physicians who fail to disclose certain patient information, particularly when this data, if disclosed, may have led to lower reimbursement, are subject to stringent remedies, including fines, forfeitures, even **imprisonment**.

As the U.S. Attorney prosecuting a physician in Ohio remarked:

> The seizure of assets is a common tactic in the war on drugs. It will now become one of our major weapons in the war on health care fraud.

A variety of laws and legal doctrines also pierce medical confidentiality. In most states, physicians must notify law enforcement if they believe a patient poses a danger to others. Secrecy may be waived:

- in rape cases, if a defendant claims that medical or psychological records contain information that could help him argue his case;

- in assault cases, when patients have disclosed plans to harm someone physically;

- in child abuse cases; and

- in custody cases, when the information revealed may help a court decide the best interests of the child.

Nor does decisional law support the concept of medical confidentiality. In *Whalen v. Roe*, 429 U.S. 589 (1977), the Supreme Court ruled that there was no constitutional violation when the State of New York created a centralized computer listing of the names and addresses of all persons who had obtained prescriptions for certain drugs. It merely held that there had to be "adequate standards and procedures" for protecting this data from unauthorized disclosure. Even this extremely limited protection applies only to government agencies, not to the massive databases maintained by insurance companies and health maintenance organizations.

A few **states** have adopted constitutional amendments designed to protect privacy interests, including limitations on access to medical data. However, state courts have no jurisdiction over medical records crossing state lines. Reimbursement by insurance carriers operating nationally requires interstate transportation of medical records.

Patients who sign forms authorizing release of their medical records for insurance reimbursement lose control of these records, which may be conveyed to organizations that specialize in collecting these records.

The largest such company is the Medical Information Bureau. Its database contains summaries of health conditions on millions of Americans and Canadians. Insurance companies feed it data about persons who apply for insurance. Doctors and hospitals also supply data to the Bureau. When a person applies for life or health insurance coverage, the underwriter calls up Bureau records to determine if data exists that could help determine whether the policy will be issued, and at what price.

The Bureau is not a "credit reporting agency" and is therefore not subject to the Fair Credit Reporting Act's requirement that data shown to be erroneous be deleted from its database. When its files contain out-of-date or erroneous information, the data is not deleted. **When updated or corrected information is submitted, the Bureau simply adds the new information to what's already there.** If a physician erroneously informs the Bureau that a patient suffers from AIDS—and then attempts to correct the entry—the original entry is not deleted. A second entry saying that the patient doesn't have AIDS is superimposed on the first record.

Since physicians and hospitals in most states do not have a legal obligation to protect patient confidentiality, a burgeoning trade in medical records has developed. For instance, the Physician Computer Network, Inc. will lease a doctor's office or clinic a complete computer system at a below-market rate in exchange for access to patient records. The data is sold to drug companies eager to learn how their products are selling—and how physicians are prescribing them.

While physicians and drug companies claim this practice doesn't compromise privacy, the information may include a patient's age, sex, and an identification number; in most cases the patient's Social Security Number. Many smaller medical practices and independent pharmacies don't participate in these marketing schemes; most larger clinics, hospitals, and pharmacy chains do.

Mail-order drug companies are among the most aggressive marketers of these records. The largest such U.S. firm, Medco Containment Services, Inc., recently created a subsidiary that sells patient records, along with prescription data it buys from the American Association of Retired Persons.

Direct marketing companies also sell medical records. Metromail's "Patient Select" database, frequently rented by drug companies, contains 15 million names and includes the following categories:

- 2.7 million hypertensives [high blood pressure];

- 2.2 million hypercholesterolemics [high cholesterol];

- 1 million diabetics;

- 3.5 million arthritics [arthritis sufferers];

- 6 million allergy sufferers;

- 1 million heavy antacid users;

- 1 million ulcer sufferers;

- 281,000 estrogen replacement therapy users;

- 459,000 gastritis sufferers; and

- 150,000 osteoporosis victims.

Also available from Metromail are the names of Alzheimer's patients, individuals with bladder control problems, Parkinson's Disease sufferers and bald people.

Racketeering in Corrupt Organizations Act (1970)

This Act, codified at 18 U.S.C. 1961-1968 and popularly known as "RICO," was the culmination of longstanding efforts to enact legislation to dismantle **corrupt organizations**. Until RICO, no U.S. statute made it illegal to operate a "corrupt organization." Prosecutors might obtain convictions for crimes committed by **individual members** of such organizations, but could not attack the organization directly.

RICO's **criminal** provisions provide prosecutors with the power to seize all or essentially all of a defendant's assets prior to trial, and the Supreme Court has ruled that the government has a legitimate financial interest in maximizing forfeiture to raise revenue. *Caplin & Drysdale, Chartered v. United States*, 491 U.S. 617 (1989). Its **civil** provisions provide for **triple damages** and payment of attorney's fees.

The term **racketeering** is undefined in the RICO statute. 18 U.S.C. 1952, the Interstate and Foreign Travel or Transportation in Aid of Racketeering Enterprises, or "Travel Act," defines racketeering as

> the intent to distribute the proceeds of any unlawful activity; or commit any crime of violence to further any unlawful activity; or otherwise promote, manage, establish, carry on, or facilitate the promotion, management, establishment, or carrying on, of any unlawful activity.

Most readers undoubtedly believe that they are not racketeers. However, hundreds of thousands, if not millions, of U.S. businesses are **corrupt organizations** under RICO's broad definition. While the lower courts have often sought to restrict RICO's application, federal appellate courts and the Supreme Court have repeatedly noted the intent of Congress for RICO to be "broadly construed." So broadly construed it has been.

RICO makes it unlawful for any person (an individual, corporation, etc.) to use a **pattern of predicate offenses** or the **proceeds** of such offenses to invest in, acquire control over, or conduct the affairs of, any formal or informal interstate enterprise. A corrupt organization is any organization engaging in such a pattern.

The following federal and state offenses constitute RICO predicate crimes; those bolded are the ones that are most likely to apply to readers for reasons that will soon be apparent:

- bribery (18 U.S.C. 201)

- sports bribery (18 U.S.C. 224)

- counterfeiting (18 U.S.C. 471-473)

- felonious theft from interstate shipment (18 U.S.C. 659)
- embezzlement from pension and welfare funds (18 U.S.C. 664)
- extortionate credit transactions (18 U.S.C. 891-894)
- transmission of gambling information (18 U.S.C. 1084)
- **mail fraud (18 U.S.C. 1341)**
- **wire fraud (18 U.S.C. 1343)**
- dealing in obscene matter (18 U.S.C. 1461-1465)
- **obstruction of justice (18 U.S.C. 1503)**
- obstruction of criminal investigations (18 U.S.C. 1510)
- obstruction of state or local law enforcement efforts (18 U.S.C. 1511)
- interference with commerce, robbery or extortion (18 U.S.C. 1951)
- **racketeering (18 U.S.C. 1952)**
- interstate transportation of wagering paraphernalia (18 U.S.C. 1953)
- unlawful welfare fund payments (18 U.S.C. 1954)
- illegal gambling businesses (18 U.S.C. 1955)
- interstate transportation of stolen motor vehicles (18 U.S.C. 2112-2313)
- interstate transportation of stolen property (18 U.S.C. 2314-2315)
- trafficking in certain motor vehicles or motor vehicle parts (18 U.S.C 2320)
- trafficking in contraband cigarettes (18 U.S.C. 2341-2346)
- white slave traffic (18 U.S.C. 2421-2424)
- restricting payments and loans to labor organizations (29 U.S.C. 186)
- embezzlement from union funds (18 U.S.C. 501(c))

- **any offense involving fraud connected with a case under Title 11 (bankruptcy), securities fraud**, or the felonious manufacture, importation, receipt, fraudulent concealment, buying, selling, or otherwise dealing in narcotic or other dangerous drugs, punishable under any U.S. law;

- **any act indictable under the Bank Secrecy Act (18 U.S.C. 1829(b) and 31 U.S.C. 5311-5326);** and

- any act or threat of murder, kidnapping, gambling, arson, robbery, bribery, extortion, dealing in obscene matter, or dealing in narcotic or other dangerous drugs chargeable under **state law** and punishable by imprisonment for more than one year

RICO Section 1961(5) defines a **pattern of racketeering activity** (i.e., a pattern of predicate offenses) as:

[requiring] at least two acts of racketeering activity [predicate offenses] ... the last of which occurred within ten years (excluding any period of imprisonment) after the commission of a prior act of racketeering activity.

There is no requirement that a defendant be convicted of the predicate offense. The defendant need not be indicted; it is sufficient that he "could have been indicted."

Both criminal and civil RICO require that a person employ a pattern of predicate offenses or the proceeds thereof in a manner as to affect interstate commerce in one of four ways:

- investing the income derived from a pattern of predicate offenses in the enterprise;

- acquiring or maintaining an interest in an enterprise through a pattern of predicate offenses;

- conducting the affairs of an enterprise through a pattern of predicate offenses; or

- conspiring to conduct such activities.

The many predicate offenses under which RICO actions can be brought pose a **minefield** for businesses. Mail fraud and wire fraud are the most common RICO predicates. Other than civil RICO, there is no private cause of action for these offenses. In many cases, civil RICO is the **only** remedy for private persons victimized by corrupt organizations.

At first glance, the elements of mail fraud or wire fraud appear substantial. A plaintiff must establish:

- a **scheme or artifice** to defraud and obtain money or property by means of false pretenses, representations or promises;

- the use of **the mails or interstate wires** (i.e., the telephone or Internet) for the purpose of executing the scheme; and

- a **specific intent** to defraud, either by devising, participating or abetting the scheme.

The courts have interpreted this language broadly. **Scheme to defraud** includes any **trickery, deceit, half-truth, concealment of material facts, affirmative misrepresentation, or breach of fiduciary duties.** "Intent to defraud" may be inferred by a pattern of conduct, including **recklessness**, or from the nature of the scheme itself. *United States v. Beecroft*, 608 F.2d 753 (9th Cir. 1979).

Recklessness is conscious disregard of a substantial and identifiable risk; a gross indifference to the consequences of one's acts. It is not a defense to state "I didn't know" or "I didn't intend to" when a pattern of conduct clearly indicates otherwise. Is your medical practice, consulting business, professional organization or other enterprise operated in a reckless manner, potentially making it a corrupt organization subject to RICO? Consider the facts leading to a RICO civil suit in *RAGS Couture, Inc. v. Hyatt*, 774 F.2d 1350 (5th Cir. 1985):

Two sisters own a small tailoring business. When their sewing machines break down, they call a repairman, who fixes the machines and mails a bill. The bill is larger than the sisters anticipate and lists repairs they believe were never performed. Their lawyer agrees that the invoice lists some questionable items. He considers suits for breach of contract, misrepresentation and deceptive consumer practices, but there is not enough money at stake to justify the litigation expense. But when a second bill is sent, the lawyer can now allege two incidents of **mail fraud** in a 10-year period. A RICO case is born.

The U.S. District Court throws out the case, but the plaintiffs successfully appeal. An allegation of fraud under state law is transformed into a federal racketeering charge. Even if a conscious intent to defraud could not be proven, it could be inferred from the repairman's allegedly reckless conduct.

Civil remedies for RICO violations are provided for in Section 1964. Section 1964(a) gives a federal district court the power to order any person to divest himself of any interest, direct or indirect, in any enterprise; or dissolve the enterprise. Section 1964(b) provides for civil government actions, and empowers the court to issue restraining orders and take other actions to end prohibited activities.

Section 1964(c) provides that a private person suffering injury to his business or property is entitled to receive costs, attorney fees and **triple actual damages.** It is the latter provision that provides the incentive for the bulk of private RICO actions.

Criminal sanctions under RICO are set forth in Section 1963(a):

Whoever violates any provision of Section 1962 of this chapter shall be fined not more than $25,000 or imprisoned not more than 20 years, or both, and shall forfeit to the United States, **irrespective of any provision of state law**: (1) any interest the person has acquired or maintained in violation of Section 1962 (2) any (A) interest in; (B) security of; (C) claim against; or (D) **property or contractual right of any kind affording a source of influence over,** any enterprise which the person has established, operated, controlled, conducted or participated in the conduct of, in violation of Section 1962; and (3) any property constituting, or derived from, any proceeds which the person obtained, directly or indirectly, from racketeering activity or unlawful debt collection in violation of Section 1962 [emphasis added].

RICO's definition of corrupt organization potentially reaches many, if not most U.S. businesses. Its focus on patterns of specific criminal acts has permitted prosecutors and litigants to apply it to a wide variety of persons and situations.

In the 1980s, some lower courts reacted to the proliferation of private RICO actions by imposing stringent requirements on persons bringing such litigation. However, the Supreme Court removed all such limitations in 1985 on the grounds that it was not the role of the courts to impose such requirements beyond the statute's language. Congress alone had this responsibility. *Sedima, SPRL v. Imrex Co., Inc.*, 473 U.S. 479 (1985).

Every financial transaction should therefore be reviewed in terms of its potential application as a RICO predicate offense. Every business should be evaluated as a potential corrupt organization. While judges may employ various informal devices to discourage civil RICO complaints they believe are frivolous, there is no assurance that a particular judge will be sympathetic to such arguments. Under the statute as interpreted by the Supreme Court, all that is necessary to federalize a business or domestic dispute is finding two suitable predicate acts that allegedly form a pattern, affect interstate commerce, and relate to one another. *H.J., Inc. v. Northwestern Bell Co.*, 492 U.S. 229 (1989).

Plaintiffs have thus sought to apply civil RICO in contract disputes; zoning disputes; religious conflicts; divorces; invasion of privacy claims; and landlord-tenant disputes. For instance, in *Religious Technology Center v. Wollersheim*, 796 F.2d 1076 (9th Cir. 1986), *cert. denied*, 476 U.S. 1103 (1987), the Church of Scientology brought a RICO suit against a splinter church, alleging spiritual harm from alleged theft and distribution of religious manuscripts. In *Evans v. Dale*, 896 F.2d 975 (5th Cir. 1990), a wife made a claim under RICO in a divorce case that her husband and officers of a corporation had conspired to misrepresent the value of stocks subject to community property laws.

Nor have the courts limited the government's application of criminal RICO. According to an in-depth study by Professor Lynch of the Columbia University School of Law of RICO cases brought for prosecution:

> [I]t is very difficult to distinguish these cases from the typical run of fraud cases that are prosecuted ... without the assistance of RICO... The only apparent motivating factor for the use of RICO in these cases would appear to be prosecutorial interest in either the aggravated sentencing possible under RICO or the specific forfeiture remedy.

The RICO prosecution of Princeton/Newport, a private hedge fund in Princeton, New Jersey, is an apt illustration. To increase returns to investors, Princeton/Newport engaged in sophisticated tax avoidance strategies involving complex financial instruments. **Legal advisors retained by the firm approved these strategies.**

In 1987, U.S. Attorney Rudolph Giuliani (now mayor of New York City) dispatched 50 federal marshals outfitted with automatic weapons and bulletproof vests to raid Princeton/Newport. Giuliani indicted the company and its officers as a racketeering criminal enterprise based on alleged tax fraud. Prosecutors obtained pre-trial asset restraint of millions of dollars.

In his charge to the jury, Assistant Prosecutor Mark Hansen emphasized that a RICO conviction did not require conviction on the underlying predicate offenses:

You don't need a fancy tax-law expert because common sense tells you it's fraudulent, it's phony. **If it sounds sleazy, it's because it is sleazy.**

The jurors agreed and convicted the defendants, who were sentenced to jail. While the Federal Appeals Court ultimately reversed the convictions, this prosecution illustrates the risks to U.S. persons and companies who rely only on professional advisors, and not also on their sense of propriety, to address tax, compliance, and ethical issues in their businesses. It is the **client**, not the **lawyer**, who risks fines, forfeiture and/or imprisonment if a prosecutor can convince a jury that, "If the deal sounds sleazy, it's because it is sleazy." *United States v. Regan,* 858 F.2d 115 (2d Cir. 1988).

While the Department of Justice has formalized guidelines for U.S. Attorneys considering RICO criminal actions, such guidelines are **not** legally binding. The Supreme Court in *United States v. Caceres,* 440 U.S. 741 (1979) held that no court has a duty to enforce a regulation voluntarily promulgated by an agency. Moreover, the guidelines state that if RICO's forfeiture provisions will result in substantial revenues to the government, this is a "substantial purpose" permitting prosecution.

Criminal Forfeiture

Forfeiture after a RICO criminal conviction is **mandatory.** The determination in a **criminal forfeiture** is whether the defendant-owner is guilty of the charged offense and if his interest in property is sufficiently linked to the offense. If after conviction, the assets deemed to be so linked are not available for forfeiture, the court may order the forfeiture of **substitute untainted assets.**

Amendments to RICO in 1984 codify the **relation-back doctrine** with respect to criminal forfeiture. Under this legal fiction of English Common Law, as inherited in U.S. Common Law, all title to forfeitable assets transfers to the government **when the offense is committed.** The relation-back doctrine alerts business associates that they deal with the defendant at their peril. The defendant may therefore not be able to perform contractual obligations and become subject to suit for breach of contract.

Any property transferred by the defendant after the commission of the alleged predicate acts may be deemed tainted and thus subject to forfeiture. The recipient must establish that he is a "bona fide purchaser for value of such property who at the time of purchase was reasonably without cause to believe that the property was subject to forfeiture. Family members and business associates may have frozen assets acquired from the defendant even before the indictment was issued, dating back to the time the assets were allegedly tainted.

Another innovation in the 1984 amendments is **pre-trial asset restraint**. The U.S. District Court, upon application of the government, may approve restraining orders or take any other action to preserve the availability of property for forfeiture. No notice or hearing need be provided the defendant, if the government demonstrates probable cause that such notice would jeopardize the availability of the property for forfeiture.

Pre-trial restraining orders can deny a defendant the use of his assets to pay living expenses or even the costs of hiring defense counsel. In 1989, the Supreme Court ruled in *Caplin & Drysdale, Chartered v. United States,* 491 U.S. 617, that pre-trial restraint of assets that could have been used to pay an attorney did not violate the defendant's Sixth Amendment right to an attorney.

The Department of Justice interprets this decision as giving it authority to freeze **substitute assets** before trial. Even funds contributed by friends, family or business associates to a RICO defendant to mount a defense may be frozen. Prosecutors have used *Caplin & Drysdale* to seize assets that could be used to mount a criminal defense **without a hearing** and **without showing the assets are tainted** by any illegal activity. *United States v. Noriega,* 746 F.Supp. 1541 (S.D.Fla. 1990).

RICO's criminal forfeiture provisions have been liberally construed by the courts. In *United States v. Porcelli,* 865 F.2d 1352 (2d Cir. 1989), a RICO defendant was convicted of failing to pay New York sales taxes from several gas station franchises. He was ordered to forfeit not only an amount equal to the delinquent tax obligation, but also more than a dozen separate corporations through which he owned and operated a chain of gas stations.

The Eighth Amendment, which prohibits "excessive fines" from being imposed in criminal cases, requires that RICO forfeitures be roughly proportional to the crime. However, **"rough proportionality" leaves enormous discretion to the court.**

In *Alexander v. United States,* 113 S.Ct. 2766 (1993), the Supreme Court recognized the applicability of the Eighth Amendment in the context of criminal forfeiture. The defendant was sentenced to a five-year prison term and forfeited his $9 million business after being found guilty of selling four magazines and three videos found to be obscene. But the Court **declined** to call the sentence a violation of the Eighth Amendment, leaving the lower court to make that determination.

The awesome powers enjoyed by prosecutors in a criminal RICO case, combined with the surveillance infrastructure that may be applied against "hidden" wealth, are extraordinarily effective in separating a defendant from his assets. Only the money laundering statutes rival RICO in this regard.

Extraterritorial Application

RICO has extraterritorial reach; RICO predicate offenses committed anywhere in the world may trigger the statute if they affect U.S. interstate or foreign commerce. For instance, RICO may apply in jurisdictions that have signed Mutual Legal Assistance Treaties (MLATs) with the United States. While there is a widespread belief that MLATs cover only specific, "mutually-recognized crimes," this is **not** true; even if a MLAT signatory lacks a "racketeering" statute, RICO may still apply.

For instance, while the U.S.-Swiss MLAT generally requires dual criminality, Switzerland has no racketeering statute. Yet many RICO predicate offenses are stipulated as grounds for invoking the treaty. (See "Mutual Legal Assistance Treaties.")

International investors may ask what investments and structures will stand against RICO. Attorneys in the United States who form such structures emphasize that they are designed to protect assets against civil judgments. **A criminal RICO investigation or conviction can likely attach assets in any regulated offshore structure.**

Regulated persons—bankers, attorneys, trustees, etc.—might invoke the structure's anti-duress or flight provisions, but in a criminal or quasi-criminal investigation could risk fines, license revocation, or even incarceration for doing so.

Bank Secrecy Act (1970)

The "Financial Recordkeeping, Currency and Foreign Transactions Reporting Act" (codified as amended at 12 U.S.C. 1829(b) and 31 U.S.C. 5311-5326) represents a comprehensive federal effort to track currency and foreign financial transactions. As such, the Act represents not only an extension of the U.S. surveillance infrastructure, but its global expansion.

As amended, the Act requires U.S. financial and/or citizens to report:

• any transporting of more than $10,000 in currency, negotiable securities, or certain monetary instruments across a U.S. border. The applicable reporting form is Customs Form 4790.

• any transaction or series of transactions in currency with a financial institution or transactions in currency and/or other "monetary instruments" (cashier's checks, money orders, and travelers' checks) in "designated reporting transactions" with trades or businesses exceeding $10,000. The applicable Currency Transaction Reporting forms are IRS Forms 4789 and 8300.

• the existence of foreign bank, securities or "other financial accounts" with a cumulative balance exceeding $10,000. Such accounts must be disclosed each year on Schedule B of IRS Form 1040 (an individual's U.S. tax return) and on Treasury Form TD F 90-22.1.

Financial institutions are broadly defined:

- all banks, credit unions, and savings and loan institutions;

- all securities brokers and dealers;

- all investment companies and currency exchange houses;

- all "issuers, redeemers or cashiers" of travelers' checks, money orders, or similar instruments;

- all operators of credit card systems;

- all insurance companies, dealers in precious metals, stones, or jewels, pawn brokers, loan or finance companies, travel agencies, money transmitters, casinos, and telegraph companies;

- all automobile, aircraft, and boat dealers, real estate brokers and settlement agents;

- **all accountants and attorneys;**

- the U.S. Postal Service;

- any business or agency which engages in any activity which the Treasury Secretary determines by regulation to be similar to, related to, or a substitute for any business otherwise defined as a financial institution; and

- **all other businesses for which such reports would provide "a high degree of usefulness in criminal, tax, or regulatory matters"**

Persons violating the Act may be fined up to $500,000, imprisoned up to 10 years and forfeit all property "involved in" or "facilitating" such violations. Officers, directors and employees of financial institutions are **personally liable** for violations in which they knowingly participate. Two or more violations may bring about a RICO indictment, with correspondingly heavier penalties. **Informants** providing information leading to a criminal fine, civil penalty or forfeiture may receive commissions up to 25 percent of that sum, with a maximum reward of $150,000.

The Bank Secrecy Act was passed because Congress concluded that records of cash transactions have a "high degree of usefulness in criminal, tax, and regulatory investigations." However, there is no requirement that illegal or untaxed earnings be involved. Unreported transactions or accounts involving lawfully earned, after-tax earnings can result in civil and/or criminal liability. A person may violate the Act even if he is unaware of its requirements. Many efforts to avoid these requirements are likewise a crime, as are conspiracies to avoid or violate them.

The agency overseeing enforcement of the Act is the Treasury's intelligence division, the Financial Crimes Enforcement Network (FinCEN). FinCEN analyzes suspicious movements of money by analyzing the millions of forms filed pursuant to the Act, combining that data with information drawn from government, private, and foreign databases. The system creates a dossier of individuals who engage in large transactions in currency or currency equivalents, then matches these profiles against the typical patterns of tax evaders, money launderers, etc. (See "Financial Crimes Enforcement Network.")

The Customs Department oversees enforcement of the Act's border reporting requirements. A Customs official may stop and search, without a warrant, any vehicle, vessel, aircraft or other conveyance, envelope or other container, or person entering or departing the United States that the officer believes may contain currency or other monetary instruments transported in violation of the Act's reporting requirements. The Department's Treasury Enforcement Communications System (TECS-II) computer network is tied into FinCEN and the FBI's National Crime Information Center database. The system will report if a person crossing the border is has been arrested, convicted, or is under investigation for tax evasion, smuggling, narcotics offenses, or is wanted by any law enforcement agency for any crime.

TECS-II also constructs computerized profiles of individuals suspected of money laundering, drug smuggling, etc. By answering a few questions at a computer terminal, a Customs agent can determine whether to detain someone who appears to fit a criminal profile. The profile is secret, but some of the signs the Customs Department looks for, according to court testimony, include: paying for airline tickets in cash; not having a telephone listing that matches the name on the ticket; having a "known illicit drug center" or "money laundering center" as the point of departure or destination; appearing nervous; not checking any luggage; or making a very short visit outside the United States.

These profiles, which are now used by the DEA and other law enforcement agencies in narcotics investigations, have been uniformly accepted by U.S. courts, yet widely criticized as overbroad. For instance, in his dissenting opinion in *United States v. Hooper*, 935 F.2d 484, 499 (2d Cir. 1991), Federal Appellate Judge Pratt compared the DEA's drug courier profile to Humpty Dumpty's worldview in *Through the Looking Glass*:

> In our "Looking-Glass" world of drug enforcement, the DEA apparently seeks "to be master" by having "drug courier profile" mean, like a word means to Humpty Dumpty, "just what I choose it to mean -- neither more nor less."

Abuses and Challenges

Shortly after the Act's passage, the Nixon administration began using it to investigate political enemies; in particular, opponents of the Vietnam War. Typically, a federal agent would walk into a bank, flash a badge and request account records. Most of the time, access was granted "informally;" no subpoena or summons was necessary. No disclosure of the search was made to the subject of the investigation.

Legal challenges to the Act were dismissed. The first major challenge, *California Bankers Association v. Shultz,* 416 U.S. 21, came before the Supreme Court in 1974. The Association claimed that the Act's mandatory reporting provisions forced bank customers to submit evidence that could be used against those customers, thus violating constitutional privileges against compulsory self-incrimination (Fifth Amendment) and unreasonable search (Fourth Amendment).

The Court did not address the Association's position. Instead it held that the Association had no right to challenge the Act's constitutionality. The bank could not invoke a depositor's Fourth or Fifth Amendment rights.

In 1976, the Supreme Court ruled in *Fisher v. United States,* 425 U.S. 391 that, "A subpoena to a third party to obtain the records of the party does not violate the rights of a defendant, even in the midst of a criminal prosecution."

Fisher set the stage for the Court's decision that year in *United States v. Miller,* 425 U.S. 435. Miller's bank was served with secret subpoenas requiring it to turn over his account records to the government. The bank complied without notifying Miller or contesting the subpoenas. Miller's attorney argued that the subpoenas violated the Fourth Amendment. The Court ruled that "the depositor takes the risk, in revealing his affairs to another, that the information will be conveyed by the person to the government."

While in *California Banker's Association*, the Court ruled that a bank could not invoke the rights of a depositor to challenge such disclosure, it now concluded that the depositor had no such right. Information conveyed to a third-party recordkeeper loses all constitutional protection. Barring a statute restricting such disclosure, the government can demand any personal data maintained by any third-party recordkeeper.

In 1980, the Supreme Court ruled in *United States v. Payner,* 447 U.S. 727, that this principle applies even to **illegal** seizures against third-party recordkeepers. Payner had an account with a Bahamian bank being investigated by the IRS. In 1977, when a representative from the bank visited the United States, the IRS conducted an elaborate undercover operation to obtain the banking records he had brought with him. After luring the banker away from his hotel room, IRS agents broke in and photocopied papers in his briefcase, including records of Payner's account. Payner was convicted of tax evasion based on this evidence. The Court upheld this conviction.

The issue in *Payner* was the "supervisory power" doctrine of the courts; i.e., under what circumstances U.S. courts may invalidate indictments or convictions made possible only through government misconduct. In general, U.S. courts have ruled that this doctrine may be invoked only when the government's activity is "shocking to the conscience of the court." *United States v. Noriega,* 746 F.Supp. 1497 (S.D.Fla. 1990). In *Payner,* the Court concluded that the doctrine could not be used to suppress evidence obtained in violation of the constitutional rights of a **third party**; i.e., the banker whose briefcase was stolen.

Finally, in 1984, the Supreme Court decided in *United States v. Doe,* 104 S.Ct. 1237, that **individuals** have no constitutional right to avoid turning over incriminating documents to the federal government. The *Doe* decision stated in part: "The Fifth Amendment provides absolutely no protection for the contents of private papers of any kind." An individual may only refrain from offering self-incriminating **personal testimony.** He has no right to withhold pre-existing self-incriminating **documents,** even if the documents were prepared under compulsion of law.

Right to Financial Privacy Act (1978)

In this Act (12 U.S.C. 3401, et. seq.), Congress sought to reinstate some of the constitutional protections lost in *Miller*. However, the Act, weak to begin with, has since been amended to the point where it effectively **eliminates** any right to financial privacy.

The Act applies only to individuals. It totally exempts corporations, trusts, or limited partnerships by defining a "customer" as an individual or partnership of not more than five partners. Nor does it restrict state or local government investigations of account records. A state agency can obtain financial records and share them with its federal counterparts without violating the Act. Indeed, such cooperation was mandated in the Deficit Reduction Act (1984).

Even when a violation occurs, the Act imposes only a $100 fine, "without regard to the volume of records involved." Contrast this penalty to fines of up to $500,000 and prison sentences up to ten years that may be imposed on persons who fail to comply with the Bank Secrecy Act's reporting provisions.

The Right to Financial Privacy Act's premise is that account records maintained by financial institutions should remain confidential, and to give citizens the right to challenge disclosures of such records to the government. But it sets forth six separate procedures by which the government can obtain such records:

1) with the customer's written consent;

2) pursuant to a search warrant;

3) pursuant to an administrative subpoena;

4) pursuant to a formal written request;

5) pursuant to a judicial subpoena; and

6) pursuant to a grand jury subpoena.

Amendments to the Act mandate that financial institutions not reveal to their customers that their records are being reviewed in connection with a variety of crimes and procedures, or in preparation for confiscation. Other exemptions make the notification and challenge requirements essentially nonexistent. They include:

- **all disclosures to the IRS**. Section 3413(c) of the Act stipulates that "nothing in this chapter prohibits the disclosure of financial records in accordance with procedures authorized by Title 26;" i.e., the Internal Revenue Code. In 1979, a Federal Appeals Court ruled in *United States v. MacKay,* 608 F.2d 830 (10th Cir.) that the Act did not override the power of an IRS summons as defined in the Code. Subsequent decisions cited *MacKay* as upholding the IRS practice of issuing **unwritten** (i.e., verbal) summonses to banks. *Raikos v. Bloomfield State Bank,* 703 F.Supp. 1364 (S.D.Ind. 1989).

- **all disclosures to bank supervisory agencies**. Any agency involved in supervisory, regulatory, or monetary functions with a financial institution is exempt from the Act. This provision gives agencies such as the Federal Deposit Insurance Commission and the Federal Reserve free access to all bank records.

- **all disclosures in accordance with existing federal statutes or regulations**. If another federal law or regulation issued by an agency requires disclosure, the Act is null and void with respect to that law.

- **all disclosures in litigation involving the government**. If a government agency or prosecutor wants bank records in the course of a civil or criminal proceeding, its request overrides the Act.

Structuring (1986)

Amendments to the Bank Secrecy Act (31 U.S.C. 5324) define a new crime: **structuring.**

This is any act an individual takes in order to evade (or avoid) completing any Currency Transaction Report.

The anti-structuring statute reads in part:

a. **Domestic coin and currency transactions**. No person shall for the purpose of evading the reporting requirements of Section 5313(a) or Section 5325 or regulations prescribed under such Section 5325 with respect to such transaction—(1) cause or attempt to cause a domestic financial institution to fail to file a report required under Section 5313(a) or Section 5325 or regulations prescribed under Section 5325; (2) cause or attempt to cause a domestic financial institution to file a report required under Section 5313(a) or Section 5325 or regulations prescribed under Section 5325 that contains a material omission or misstatement of fact; or (3) structure or assist in structuring, or attempt to structure or assist in structuring, any transaction with one or more domestic financial institutions.

(Note: Title 31, Section 5313(a) is the section of the Bank Secrecy Act requiring financial institutions to report certain transactions in cash or monetary instruments that exceed $10,000. Section 5325 requires U.S. financial institutions that issue or sell bank checks, cashier's checks, traveler's checks, or money orders to any person in exchange for cash in amounts or denominations of $3,000 to $10,000 to comply with identification and recordkeeping requirements as stipulated by the Secretary of the Treasury.)

b. **International monetary instrument transactions**. No person shall, for the purpose of evading the reporting requirements of Section 5316—(1) fail to file report required by Section 5316, or cause or attempt to cause a person to fail to file such a report; (2) file or cause or attempt to cause a person to file a report required under Section 5316 that contains a material omission or misstatement of fact; (3) structure or assist in structuring, any importation or exportation of monetary instruments.

(Note: Section 5316 requires persons crossing a U.S. border with more than $10,000 in cash or certain cash equivalents to report that fact to U.S. Customs.)

Persons convicted of structuring may receive up to a five-year prison sentence, a $250,000 fine, and forfeit all property involved in or facilitating the transaction. Penalties are doubled for willful violations that occur in connection with another crime.

The act of structuring is **undefined** in law. The statute potentially makes any attempt made to protect financial privacy by engaging in transactions in cash or other reportable monetary instruments that ultimately exceed Bank Secrecy Act reporting thresholds illegal. Regulations issued to interpret Section 5324 stipulate that a person who deposits $9,000 in currency into an account on two consecutive days is structuring. But 12 consecutive $900 deposits may be structuring as well. The regulations don't address this possibility, or any of an infinite number of other possibilities.

Nor is "international" structuring defined. In theory, anyone transferring across a U.S. border **more** than $10,000 in cash or certain cash equivalents in a series of related installments **less** than $10,000 without completing Customs Form 4790 acts illegally. (See Chapter 4.)

A good example of the draconian effect of the structuring statute on persons who realize that a reporting requirement exists, but do not realize avoiding it is illegal, is illustrated in the following hypothetical situation, as postulated by Kacareb, in "An In-Depth Analysis of the New Money Laundering Statutes." (The author is an agent with the IRS Criminal Investigation Division.)

> An elderly widow with substantial assets in a bank account wishes to give cash gifts to her three grandchildren of $8,000 each. When she approaches the bank teller and asks to withdraw $24,000 in cash, she is told this requires the completion of a Currency Transaction Report.
>
> Since the widow doesn't want to file a form that may "red-flag" her account, she breaks up the $24,000 cash withdrawal into three transactions of $8,000 each. She goes to the bank three days in a row, each day to a different branch, and withdraws $8,000 each day. She then goes to each of her grandchildren's banks and deposits the cash in an account in each of their names.

Based on the widow's conduct, the bank informs the IRS of the suspected structured transaction on a Criminal Referral Form. The monies deposited into her grandchildren's account are subject to civil forfeiture and she faces potential criminal indictment for violation of Section 5324.

Nor has the government made any effort to alert persons to the structuring statute, although the Treasury Department proposed a publicity campaign after the Act's enactment. The March 11, 1988 *Federal Register* included the following suggestions:

1. Require that a short notice of the provisions of Section 5324 be posted at every location where customers may conduct cash transactions; e.g., bank teller's windows, casino gaming tables and cages.

2. Require that a short Treasury form notice of the provisions of Section 5324 be handed to any person conducting currency transactions over a certain amount; e.g., $1,000 or $3,000. Currency transactions would include deposits to accounts and purchases of monetary instruments such as cashier's checks, official bank checks, money orders or travelers' checks.

3. Require that all deposit tickets be imprinted with a short Treasury form notice of the provisions of Section 5324 that a person making a currency deposit over a certain amount; i.e., $1,000 or $3,000, sign the back of the deposit slip as an acknowledgement of reading such notice.

4. Require that a short Treasury form notice of the provisions of Section 5324 be sent to all customers by a certain date and to all new customers upon the opening of an account.

5. Require that a short Treasury form notice of the provisions of Section 5324 be included periodically, e.g., quarterly, in all customers' monthly statements of accounts, and upon opening a new account. In the event that financial institutions receive inquiries from customers as the result of any of the above proposals, Treasury could make available a form to give to customers giving a more detailed explanation of the provisions of Section 5324 and a toll-free number for the customer to call for further information.

None of these suggestions were implemented. The government made no effort to inform customers that any attempt to avoid reporting deposits or withdrawals of currency or other monetary instruments is illegal.

BSA Reporting Requirements: Financial Institutions

U.S. financial institutions are subject to Bank Secrecy Act reporting requirements.

The General Instructions for IRS Currency Transaction Report Form 4789 state:

Each financial institution ... must file a Form 4789 for each deposit, withdrawal, exchange of currency, or other payment or transfer, by, through, or to the financial institution which involves a transaction in currency of more than $10,000. Multiple transactions must be treated as a single transaction if the financial institution has knowledge that 1) they are by or on behalf of any person, and 2) result in either cash into or cash out of the financial institution totaling more than $10,000 during any one business day ... This form may also be filed for any suspicious transaction, even if it does not exceed $10,000.

Form 4789 defines "currency" as "the coins and currency of the United States or other country ... but does not include bank checks or other negotiable instruments not customarily accepted as money." A "transaction in currency" is one

involving the physical transfer of currency from one person to another. A transaction in currency does not include a transfer of funds by means of bank check, bank draft, wire transfer, or other written order that does not include the physical transfer of currency.

Information submitted to the IRS includes name, address, Social Security Number and identification data such as a driver's license number. Non-resident aliens must identify themselves with a passport, alien ID card, or other official document showing nationality and residence.

BSA Reporting Requirements: Trades and Businesses

U.S. trades and businesses are also subject to the reporting provisions of the Bank Secrecy Act.

Publication 1544, which contains instructions for Currency Transaction Form 8300 (used by trades and businesses for this purpose) defines "cash" as:

1) the coins and currency of the United States (and any other country), and 2) cashier's checks, bank drafts, travelers' checks, and money orders you receive, if they have a face value of **$10,000 or less** and you receive them in: a) a designated reporting transaction (defined later), or b) any transaction in which you know the payer is trying to avoid the reporting of the transaction on Form 8300.

A "designated reporting transaction" is

the retail sale of...: 1) a consumer durable, such as an automobile or boat ... property, other than land or buildings, that: a) is suitable for personal use, b) can reasonably be expected to last at least one year under ordinary use, c) has a sales price of more than $10,000, and d) can be seen or touched (tangible property). For example, a $20,000 car is a consumer durable, but a $20,000 dump truck or factory machine is not... 2) a collectible (a work of art, rug, antique, metal, gem, stamp, or coin); 3) travel or entertainment, if the total sales price of all items sold for the same trip or entertainment event in one transaction (or related transactions) is more than $10,000.

"Willful ignorance" of the transactions being related is a crime. Persons who know **or have reason to know** that a transaction represents an effort to avoid the reporting requirements, must report that transaction **regardless of its size**.

Attorneys are among the trades and businesses targeted for enforcement of these requirements. In *United States v. Goldberger & Dubin, P.C.*, 935 F.2d 501 (2d Cir. 1991) and *United States v. Leventhal*, 961 F.2d 936 (11th Cir. 1992), Federal Appeals Courts upheld the right of the IRS to demand client-identification information on Form 8300. The IRS may impose a civil penalty of $100,000 for failure to comply. **To challenge assessment of the penalty, the attorney must first pay it in full.**

Sting operations involving undercover agents from the IRS Criminal Investigation target cash businesses—car dealerships, precious metals dealers, jewelry dealers, etc. Typically, agents approach a merchant and try to convince him to accept more than $10,000 in currency or other monetary instruments without completing Form 8300. After the arrest, the IRS often issues a press release announcing the bust to "encourage" other merchants to comply.

Most "targeted industries" now realize that they are required to file Form 8300 for receipt of currency or monetary instruments above $10,000. As a result, the IRS now instigates technical reporting violations. For instance, an undercover agent may pay currency for a car, then casually mention that the purchase is for another person. This information must be noted on Form 8300 and the identity of the real purchaser disclosed. If the information is not included, the individual causing the form to be completed inaccurately may be subject to civil and/or criminal penalties and all property involved in or facilitating the transaction forfeited.

BSA Reporting Requirements: International Investments

The Bank Secrecy Act requires U.S. citizens and residents holding a cumulative total of $10,000 or more in certain "foreign financial accounts" to report their presence on Schedule B, line 11(a) of their federal income tax return and file a separate information return to Treasury. Schedule B must be completed for this purpose even if interest and dividend income is less than the reporting threshold. Penalties for "willful" non-compliance may result in prosecution under the BSA as well as tax fraud and perjury charges.

Treasury Form TD F 90-22.1, the "Foreign Bank Account Reporting Form," is submitted to a Treasury Department intelligence center in Detroit and its data then conveyed to the Financial Crimes Enforcement Network.

The reporting requirements for U.S. persons investing internationally are discussed further in Chapter 4.

BSA Reporting Requirements: International Funds Transfers

The Bank Secrecy Act requires any person transporting, causing to transport, or mailing more than $10,000 in cash or certain cash equivalents, or an equivalent amount of foreign currency, across a U.S. border to declare that fact on Customs Form 4790.

The requirements of the Bank Secrecy Act for U.S. persons moving money internationally are discussed in Chapter 4.

BSA Reporting Requirements: Suspicious Transactions

Amendments in 1988 to the Bank Secrecy Act require financial institutions to notify the government of any "suspicious transactions" engaged in by their customers. The institution must immediately inform the Financial Crimes Enforcement Network (FinCEN) and complete a "Criminal Referral Report." Failure to notify FinCEN of a transaction later deemed "suspicious," but that was not reported, may lead to civil and criminal liability for the institution **and** the employee permitting it to occur.

Financial institutions must now be alert to any of dozens of "suspicious activities" in which customers may engage—none of which are illegal, but taken as a pattern, may indicate criminal activity. **If the government determines after-the-fact that an institution failed to heed these indicia of wrongdoing, it may seize the account or the institution's collateral.** The government may take these indicia as **proven facts** to support its action. Since financial institutions do not know in advance which customers, if any, are engaged in illegal activity, **all customers** are subjected to pervasive, systematic, and continuous surveillance.

Indeed, the courts have concluded that the government isn't required to trace the proceeds of a specific transaction to a specific offense if available evidence gives rise to an **inference** that the funds are derived from illegal activity. *United States v. Blackmun,* 897 F.2d 309 (8th Cir. 1990). Similarly, courts have interpreted the "knowing" requirement as "ought to have known." The government is not required to prove any direct knowledge of wrongdoing; to obtain a criminal conviction, it merely must show that a defendant institution or employee **avoided** knowledge of certain facts.

To identify transactions that should be reported under the suspicious activity guidelines, banks are required to ask customers the origin of funds being deposited or transmitted. The *Code of Federal Regulations* (31 CFR Part 103 Appendix) outlines five hypothetical examples:

1. Linda Scott has had an account with the bank for 15 years and tries to deposit $15,000 in cash. The bank knows that she is an artist who exhibits and sells her artwork, and her art is currently on exhibit at the local gallery. The bank also knows that her paintings are worth $15,000. The bank can accept the money as long as she fills out a Currency Transaction Report. There is no need to inquire further about the source of the funds.

2. Dick Wallace recently opened a personal account and wants to transfer $18,000 in currency to a foreign bank. His identity was verified when he opened it, but not since. The bank cannot accept the money without inquiring

about the source of the money, recording it on a Currency Transaction Report, and reporting it to the IRS.

3. Dorothy Green, a partner at a law firm, wants to make a $50,000 cash deposit into the firm's trust account. The money came from three clients. The bank must know the names of the clients and their Social Security Numbers, and that information must be sent to the IRS.

4. Carlos Gomez enters a currency dealer's office and asks to buy $12,000 in travelers' checks with cash. The dealer must know the source of the money and whether he is acting on the behalf of another party, and that information must be sent to the IRS.

5. Gail Julian, a trusted employee of a large retail chain, makes three large cash deposits during one day totaling $48,000. The bank knows that Julian normally makes the store's deposit, but the store's exemption limit is only $45,000. The bank must have strong "know your customer" policies, but doesn't have to ask and record further information than the normal Currency Transaction Report requirement.

From a financial institution's perspective, a policy to detect and report suspicious transactions isn't enough. The policy must work **every time**. A single mistake can result in a criminal prosecution against the person making the mistake and sanctions against the bank.

One way to avert problems is to avoid the suspicious transactions to which financial institutions have been alerted. According to Michael Zeldin, former director of the U.S. Department of Justice's Asset Forfeiture Office, financial institutions should be aware of the following "non-industry-specific red flags" that may indicate criminal activity:

- loans to offshore companies that have no apparent connection to the customer's business;

- large cash transactions from businesses that are not typically cash-intensive;

- cash transactions with correspondent banks by other than armored carrier services;

- large wire transfers with offshore banks or businesses, especially if no connection to the customer's business is obvious;

- loans secured by obligations to offshore banks;

- established financial relationships with bank secrecy or tax haven countries;

- frequent or large wire transfers for persons with no account relationship with the financial institution;

- brokered deposit transactions where the broker's fees are paid for from the proceeds of related loans;

- loan production/sales used as a basis for officer bonuses;

- solicitation by persons who reportedly have access to millions of dollars from a confidential source, readily available for loans and/or deposits in U.S. financial institutions. (Rates and terms quoted are usually more favorable than funds available through normal sources.);

- financial statements showing concentrations of closely held companies or businesses that lack audited financial statements to support their stated value;

- loan proceeds used for purposes other than those stated;

- attempts to use cash to complete a transaction when such transactions are typically handled by checks or other monetary instruments;

- attempts to use monetary instruments endorsed to a third party to make purchases or investments;

- customers who are more concerned with cancellation privileges than with return on investment;

- reluctance to provide adequate identification information when opening an account or making a purchase;

- purchases (especially by cash/bank check/money order) that appear to be beyond the purchaser's means;

- customers whose business or residence is not near the financial institution or business at which they make a transaction, especially when branches are located closer to customer;

- businesses whose financial statements are inconsistent with similar businesses and (especially for large businesses) whose financial statements are not prepared by an accountant; or

- customers with backgrounds inconsistent with proposed business activities or purchases

Additional suggestions for evaluating suspicious transactions come from a booklet distributed by the Treasury Department to all U.S. banks entitled *Money Laundering: A Banker's Guide to Avoiding Problems*:

- opening accounts in several different names, none larger than $10,000;

- paying down a delinquent loan all at once;

- objecting to completing Currency Transaction Reports;

- changing currency from small to large denominations;

- buying cashier's checks, money orders or travelers' checks for less than the reporting limit;

- coming to the bank with another customer, and each making a currency transaction under the $10,000 ceiling;

- making deposits in currency, then having the money wired somewhere else;

- ordering internal transfers between accounts, followed by large outlays;

- appearing to use an account as a temporary repository for funds transferred overseas;

- making a transaction that involves a large number of $50 and $100 bills; or

- making a transaction without counting the currency first

According to the January 1991 *ABA Banking Journal,* the following situation is also a suspicious and should be reported:

> You are the personal banker for a successful local businessman in your small town. Three months ago, he opened a checking account for his 12-year-old son. You have noticed that about one month ago, the businessman began depositing a significant amount of business receipts into his son's account. The account balance has grown from $150 to $36,000. You have just received a call from the businessman. He has asked you to wire transfer $35,000 from the account to a major New York bank to the account of Spring Trust. You have never heard of Spring Trust.
>
> Is this a suspicious transaction? Yes, definitely, according to Charles Morley, head of the consulting firm The Morley Group and a former IRS agent and Senate investigator. **"We're not just talking drugs and drug cash,"** said Morley. "The businessman may be trying to evade taxes. **Or he may wish to hide money from his spouse"** [emphasis added].

Privacy Act (1974)

The Privacy Act (1974) (codified at 5 U.S.C. 552) was enacted to restrict the exchange of personal data between government agencies. However, like most other privacy legislation, the Act's primary effect is to legislate privacy reduction.

The Act stipulates that no agency may disclose any record contained in a "system of records" to any other person or agency except by written request **and** with the prior written consent of the individual to whom the records pertain **and** only "for a purpose that is compatible with the purposes for which it was collected." It requires agencies to maintain a list of such disclosures and stipulates (in conjunction with the Freedom of Information Act) and that citizens be given authority to examine their files and challenge information they believe to be inaccurate.

However, there are gaping loopholes in these requirements. No notification or consent is required if information or transfers of information is a "routine use;" if information is to be provided to another agency for civil or criminal law enforcement; if "national security" is at stake; or for data exchange with state and local authorities. New exemptions constantly are applied for, and approved. For instance, when the Financial Crimes Enforcement Network was created by Executive Order in 1990, the agency was quickly exempted from the Privacy Act's requirements that it:

- disclose the contents of its databases;

- permit public access to its databases;

- allow individuals to determine whether the agency maintained records containing information about them;

- permit individuals the right to amend incorrect information about themselves in a FinCEN database;

- not collect information beyond that "relevant and necessary to accomplish a FinCen purpose;" and

- maintain records to a discernible standard of accuracy.

Such loopholes have resulted in the Act having little practical effect in government efforts to gather and cross-reference information on citizens. For instance, many agencies co-mingle ordinary records with those having law enforcement or national security applications, thus exempting all such records from reporting requirements.

Project Match (1977)

In 1977, Joseph Califano, President Carter's Secretary of Health, Education and Welfare, initiated "Project Match," a program to compare names of federal employees with those of welfare recipients. The matches were keyed to employee and welfare recipient Social Security numbers. Agency lawyers advised Califano that Project Match violated the requirements of the Privacy Act in at least three ways:

1) records were not to be disclosed to another agency without the permission of the individual on whom the record was being kept;

2) records were not to be used for purposes inconsistent with the purpose for which they were originally collected; and

3) information could not be disclosed without an indication that a specific violation had occurred or might occur.

However, the matches proceeded in spite of these apparent violations.

In 1979, the White House's Office of Management and Budget issued computer matching "guidelines" permitting matches pending OMB approval. OMB **never** turned down such a request. In 1984, Congress came full-circle in passing the Deficit Reduction Act (42 U.S.C. 1320b-7(a) and (c)). This legislation avoided violating the Privacy Act by requiring the **states**—which were not subject to the Act's authority—to conduct computer matches to eliminate fraud and duplication in **federal** entitlement programs.

Computer Matching and Privacy Protection Act (1988)

Congress passed this Act to protect persons from having entitlement benefits eliminated due to an erroneous computer match. However, in mandating this protection, Congress also authorized the first full-scale effort to link data in federal, state and private databases. Any match may occur pursuant to a written agreement between agencies.

The full range of private and public databases now can be used for computer matching: court records, credit bureau records, Drug Enforcement Administration, Educational Testing Service, Immigration and Naturalization Service, IRS, Medicare, Medicaid, Medical Information Bureau, motor vehicle records, National Driver Registry, National Parent Locator, National Crime Information Center, Passport Office, Social Security Administration, etc.

Joint federal-state enforcement efforts made possible by the Act include initiatives:

• by the Department of Transportation to create a nationwide database of driver's license holders designed to prevent persons who have had their license suspended in one state from obtaining a license in another state;

• by the IRS to create an "Individual Master File" on every taxpayer and withhold tax refunds to persons who owe the federal government money; and

• by the Customs Service to supply data on customs declarations to state tax authorities, so that states can impose sales taxes on imported goods.

Comprehensive Forfeiture Act (1984)

Forfeiture in English Common Law

In the English Common Law, three types of forfeiture existed:

1) Under the principle of **deodand**, any object causing the death of a person was forfeited to the Crown. The forfeiture occurred even if the object's owner was not responsible for the death.

2) **Outlawry** was an even more ancient concept that holds that a criminal is "outside the law." All the criminal's property could be seized by anyone with the strength to hunt down the criminal and kill him. Outlawry evolved into a sanction by which all real property was forfeited to the Crown upon conviction of high treason. For all other felonies, it **escheated** (reverted to) the lord of the convicted felon. The forfeiture was said to be *in personam* ("against the person").

3) **Statutory forfeitures** authorized confiscation of property used illegally. For instance, vessels carrying contraband, involved in piracy and (later) in the slave trade could be forfeited. Again, it was not necessary to demonstrate that the owner was responsible for the illegal use of his property. The forfeiture was thus said to be *in rem* ("against the thing").

Only statutory forfeitures were directly inherited into U.S. law. But the RICO statute re-introduced to U.S. law *in personam* forfeiture. It also re-introduced the principle of outlawry that property far beyond the mere "fruits of crime" may be forfeited. This **ink drop theory** of forfeiture has spread to civil forfeiture through statute and decisional law.

Moreover, the principle of deodand—that property can be held accountable for crime regardless of the owner's personal liability—was inherited into U.S. civil forfeiture law. The doctrine that property involved in a crime becomes tainted and thus subject to forfeiture has existed in U.S. law since 1789. The **taint doctrine** derives from the deodand principle. An object tainted by association with crime cannot lose its taint, even if transferred or sold to another person. The Supreme Court upheld this doctrine as early as 1827, declaring that in a forfeiture *in rem*, "The thing is primarily considered the offender." *The Palmyra*, 25 U.S. (12 Wheat) 1.

The author's *Asset Protection 2000* discusses the confluence and merger of the deodand and outlawry principles in Anglo-American law—**deodand outlawry**—in greater detail.

Civil Forfeiture

Statutory forfeitures authorized under **civil forfeiture** laws exempt innocent owners only if a specific exemption exists. Property is assigned a "personality" and held accountable for its violation of law. The **property** is the defendant, not its owner. Hence the odd names in civil forfeiture cases; *United States v. $8,850*; *United States v. a Parcel of Land*, etc.

Until 1984, civil forfeiture in the United States was rare and existed primarily for violations of certain Customs statutes. The Comprehensive Forfeiture Act changed this status. It provided for:

- the civil forfeiture of property derived from, connected to, or facilitating drug-related offenses;

- the payment of informant commissions to individuals who provided information leading to forfeitures under this statute; and

- the creation of an "Asset Forfeiture Fund" at the Department of Justice to "share" forfeited revenues with other agencies.

Subsequent legislation expanded the list of offenses for which civil forfeiture was permitted to virtually **any crime** involving money. (See "Money Laundering Control Act.")

Civil forfeiture laws provide the government with unique advantages. A seizure or asset freeze is authorized in an *ex parte* hearing before a judge, magistrate or administrator. The Supreme Court has ruled that except when real property is involved, the property owner need not be informed of this hearing, and thus may not attend it, much less contest the seizure. *United States v. James Daniel Good Real Property*, 114 S.Ct. 492 (1993).

The government need only establish **probable cause** that there is a substantial connection between the seized property and illegal activity. Probable cause may be established by **hearsay evidence**. Indeed, according to a Department of Justice manual, "admissible hearsay" includes "tips from confidential informants." The testimony often consists of a government agent who testifies that a confidential informant said property was acquired with or facilitated illegal activity. On this evidence alone, the court may authorize property seizure.

Where an effort is made to claim restrained or seized property, the burden of proof shifts to the owner to demonstrate by a preponderance of the evidence that the seizure was in error. The owner must post a bond (ordinarily 10 percent of the property's value) to defray the government's expenses in defending its claim. If the owner cannot raise this bond, forfeiture occurs and title to the property transfers to the government. The bond may be waived if the owner requests an administrative hearing before the seizing agency, but the agency's decision may not be judicially appealed.

Some civil forfeiture statutes provide exemptions for innocent owners and lienholders. Demonstrating innocent ownership is difficult. The owner must prove a great deal more than that he is not a criminal. Unless the owner can demonstrate lack of knowledge of the illegal use of the property and (in some states) lack of consent of such use, the effort may be unsuccessful. *United States v. Lot 111 B*, 902 F.2d 1443 (9th Cir. 1990). The owner may also be required to prove that he or she is the "actual" owner of the property, not a nominee or "straw" owner in name only. *United States v. Accounts No. 3034504504 and 144-07143*, 971 F.2d 974 (3d Cir. 1992).

If a civil forfeiture statute lacks an innocent owner provision, the owner has no claim. In 1996, the Supreme Court upheld such a statute and the civil forfeiture of a joint ownership interest from a person both prosecution and defense agreed was innocent of any wrongdoing. *Bennis v. Michigan*, 116 S.Ct. 994.

At the state and local level, forfeiture may occur for violation of ordinances prohibiting prostitution (or soliciting prostitutes), zoning violations; illegal fishing or hunting; and other offenses. In some states, property connected to any indictable offense may be forfeited.

New Jersey is such a state. One New Jersey medical school graduate set up a counseling office in his parents' home in Monmouth County, New Jersey. Before doing so, he was assured by the local Mental Health Director that this was legal. A few weeks later, police arrested him for "practicing psychiatry without a license," and seized the contents of the home. New Jersey officials also seized a home because its owner allegedly stole a package from a neighbor and an **entire business** because it submitted a defective bid for a state purchasing contract.

Money Laundering Control Act (1986)

Until 1986, no federal statute criminalized financial transactions tied to illegal activity. The Money Laundering Control Act, part of the Anti-Drug Abuse Act (1986), corrected this "omission," and in so doing further expanded the U.S. surveillance infrastructure.

Borrowing criminal sanctions from the Racketeering and Corrupt Organizations Act (1970), the Money Laundering Control Act goes beyond RICO by requiring only one act (not a related pattern) to establish culpability. The Act's **civil forfeiture** provisions borrow from the Comprehensive Forfeiture Act (1984), and expand the universe of offenses for which civil forfeiture is a "remedy" to **thousands** of different crimes.

Unlike the Bank Secrecy Act, cash need not be involved in a money laundering offense. Any financial transaction tied to a "specified unlawful activity" qualifies, and there is no minimum threshold. The Act also makes it a crime to do business with persons who are "known criminals," even if the specific illegal act committed by such a person is unknown.

No uniform definition of the term "money laundering" exists. In a definition that seems deliberately incomplete (note the word "involves" rather than the term "consists of"), the U.S. Treasury states: "Money laundering involves disguising assets so they can be used without detection of the illegal activity that produced them."

Other governmental bodies have a much broader vision of money laundering. The President's Commission on Organized Crime in 1984 defined money laundering as the "process by which one conceals the existence, illegal source, or illegal application of income, and then disguises that income to make it appear legitimate." Under this interpretation, simply concealing the **existence** of income, no matter how legitimate its origin, is money laundering.

Section 1956 of the Act provides:

Whoever, knowing that the property involved in a financial transaction represents the proceeds of some form of unlawful activity, conducts or attempts to conduct such a financial transaction which in fact involves the proceeds of specified unlawful activity—(A)(i) with the intent to promote the carrying on of specified unlawful activity, or (ii) with intent to engage in conduct constituting a violation of section 7201 [tax fraud] or 7206 [tax perjury] of the Internal Revenue Code of 1986 (B) knowing that the transaction is designed in whole or in part—(i) to conceal or disguise the nature, the location, the source, the ownership, or the control of the proceeds of specified unlawful activity; or (ii) to avoid a transaction reporting requirement under state or federal law, shall be sentenced to a fine of not more than $500,000 or twice the value of the property involved in the transaction, whichever is greater, or imprisonment for not more than 20 years, or both.

(2) Whoever transports, transmits, or transfers, or attempts to transport, transmit, or transfer a monetary instrument or funds from a place in the United States to or through a place outside the United States or to a place in the United States from or through a place outside the United States—(A) with the intent to promote the carrying on of specified unlawful activity, or (B) knowing that the monetary instrument or funds involved in the transportation represent the proceeds of some form of unlawful activity and knowing that such transportation is designed in whole or in part—(i) to conceal or disguise the nature, the location, the source, the ownership, or the control of the proceeds of specified unlawful activity; or (ii) to avoid a transaction reporting requirement under state or federal law, shall be sentenced to a fine of not more than $500,000 or twice the value of the property involved in the transaction, whichever is greater, or imprisonment for not more than 20 years, or both.

Section 1956(c)(7) defines "specified unlawful activity" as encompassing:

(A) any act or activity constituting an offense listed in Section 1961(1) of this title [RICO offenses] except an act which is indictable [under the Bank Secrecy Act]; (B) with respect to a financial transaction occurring in whole or in part in the United States, an offense against a foreign nation involving the manufacture, importation, sale, or distribution of a controlled substance (as such term is defined for the purposes of the Controlled Substances Act); (C) any acts or acts constituting a continuing criminal enterprise, as that term is defined in Section 408 of the Controlled Substances Act

Section 1956(c)(7)(D) lists the following offenses as constituting specified unlawful activity; those bolded are the ones that are most likely to apply to readers:

- **18 U.S.C. 152 (concealment of assets; false oaths and claims**; bribery)

- 18 U.S.C. 215 (commissions or gifts for procuring loans)

- 18 U.S.C. 500-503 (certain counterfeiting offenses)

- 18 U.S.C. 513 (offenses involving securities of states and private entities)

- 18 U.S.C. 513 (offenses involving securities of states and private entities)

- 18 U.S.C. 542 (entry of goods by means of false statements)

- 18 U.S.C. 545 (smuggling goods into the United States)

- 18 U.S.C. 641 (offenses involving public money, property, or records)

- 18 U.S.C 656 (theft, embezzlement, or misapplication by bank officer or employee)

- **18 U.S.C. 657 (offenses involving lending, credit, and insurance institutions)**

- 18 U.S.C. 658 (fraud involving property mortgaged or pledged to farm credit agencies)

- **18 U.S.C. 666 (theft or bribery in programs receiving federal funds)**

- 18 U.S.C. 793, 794, or 798 (espionage)

- **18 U.S.C. 875 (offenses involving interstate communications)**

- 18 U.S.C. 1201 (kidnapping)

- 18 U.S.C. 1203 (hostage taking)

- **18 U.S.C. 1344 (bank fraud)**

- 18 U.S.C. 2113, 2114 (bank and postal robbery and theft)

- 18 U.S.C. 2319 (copyright infringement)

- 21 U.S.C. 830, Section 310 (offenses involving precursor and essential chemicals for narcotics production)

- 19 U.S.C 1590, Section 590 (aviation smuggling)

- 21 U.S.C. 857, Section 1822 (violations of the Mail Order Drug Paraphernalia Control Act)

- 22 U.S.C.S. 2778(c), Section 38(c) (violations of the Arms Export Control Act)

- 50 U.S.C.S. Appx. 2410, Section 11 (violations of the Export Administration Act of 1979)

- 50 U.S.C.S. 1705, Section 206 (violations of the International Emergency Economic Powers Act)

- 50 U.S.C. Appx. 16, Section 16 (violations of the Trading with the Enemy Act)

The courts have interpreted the "knowing" requirement of Sec. 1956 liberally. Prosecutors need not demonstrate that a defendant has **specific knowledge** of a particular illegal activity to obtain a conviction. The defendant need only know (through actual knowledge, facts and circumstances or "willful blindness") that the laundered property represents or was generated through some form of illegal activity. *United States v. Montague*, 29 F.3d 317 (7th Cir. 1994).

Amendments to the Act make **attempts** to conduct laundering transactions subject to the same sanctions, thus making possible **undercover sting operations** against suspected launderers.

MLCA-RICO Compared

Prescribed punishment under the Act borrows from RICO, as the government can obtain sanctions far exceeding the penalties for the underlying criminal conduct.

As in RICO, pre-trial restraint or seizure of any property involved in or traceable to illegal transactions is permitted. But while a RICO defendant must commit two specific and connected RICO predicate offenses within a 10-year period to be convicted or subject to a judgment, a single financial transaction connected to specified unlawful activity can result in a laundering conviction and/or forfeiture.

Criminal forfeiture provisions of the Act borrow from RICO, potentially reaching **all assets**, not just those criminally derived.

Unlike RICO, civil forfeiture is also permitted. 18 U.S.C. 981(a)(1)(A) stipulates that, "any property, real or personal," is subject to civil forfeiture if it is purchased with proceeds of, facilitates, or is "involved in" specified unlawful activity. The Act, in effect, expands the scope of civil forfeiture from Customs and narcotics violations to any criminal offense that involves money.

The MLCA also brings the merger of the ancient common law doctrines of deodand and outlawry to full fruition. If proceeds from criminally derived property are mingled with other, legitimate funds, the entire commingled sum may be forfeitable. Depositing $10 of "criminally derived proceeds" into a $100,000 bank account may make the **entire account** forfeitable. *United States v. All Monies ($477,048.62)*, 754 F.Supp. 1467 (D. Hawaii 1991).

"Clean" inventory in a business may be forfeited as property involved in an offense where it served to conceal or disguise the use of other inventory to launder criminal proceeds through the business. *United States v. All the Inventories of the Businesses Known as Khalife Bros. Jewelry*, 806 F.Supp. 648 (E.D. Mich. 1992). Merely spending in a manner calculated to conceal or disguise the true nature of criminal proceeds can render the property purchased subject to forfeiture. *United States v. Real Property in Mecklenberg County*, 814 F.Supp. 468 (W.D.N.C. 1993).

The powers enjoyed by prosecutors in a criminal RICO case thus apply to laundering prosecutions as well, with the added bonus of civil forfeiture remedies and a much wider variety of underlying offenses from which to choose. Furthermore, the money laundering statutes have extraterritorial reach, as does RICO, with comparable effects against assets outside U.S. territorial jurisdiction.

MLCA Section 1957

The corner grocer in a community is aware of the reputation of the local drug trafficker. That person comes to the store and buys five pounds of hamburger. The grocer has to know what he is coming in to buy groceries with is indeed the money derived from a particular designated crime. I don't have any problem whatsoever in holding the grocer accountable for money laundering.

—Florida Congressman Bill McCollum, *Congressional Record*, October 18, 1986

Section 1957 of the Money Laundering Control Act provides:

(a) Whoever ... knowingly engages or attempts to engage in a monetary transaction in criminally derived property that is of a value greater than $10,000 and is derived from specified unlawful activity, shall be punished as proved in subsection (b); (b)(1) Except as provided in paragraph (2), the punishment for an offense under this section is a fine under title 18, United States Code, or imprisonment for not more than ten years or both. (2) The court may impose an alternate fine to that imposable under paragraph (1) of not more than twice the amount of the criminally derived property involved in the transaction. (c) **In a prosecution for an offense under this section, the Government is not required to prove the defendant knew that the offense from which the criminally derived property was derived was a specified unlawful activity...** [emphasis added]

(f) As used in this section—(1) the term "monetary transaction" means the deposit, withdrawal, transfer, or exchange, in or affecting interstate or foreign commerce, of funds or a monetary instrument ... by, through, or to a financial institution ... but such term does not include any transaction necessary to preserve a person's right to representation as guaranteed by the Sixth Amendment of the Constitution; (2) the term "criminally derived property" means any property constituting, or derived from, proceeds obtained from a criminal offense."

Section 1957 makes it a crime to do business with persons with **reputations** as criminals, even if the person prosecuted is ignorant of the suspected criminal's specific illegal conduct. Unlike Section 1956, Section 1957 exempts transactions under $10,000. However, regulations issued to interpret Section 1957 stipulate that any pattern of "related transactions" totaling $10,000 or more in any 12-month period counts toward this amount. So if over a period of several months, a person who is a known criminal does $10,000 or more business with a merchant, the merchant could be held criminally accountable.

A monetary transaction under Section 1957 can either involve funds coming from or going to a known criminal. For instance, a bank or other financial institution may be convicted under Section 1957 if it advances more than $10,000 to a company that it knows **or has reason to believe** violated any law. Furthermore, banks ordinarily require borrowers to warrant that they will comply with all laws and regulations. A bank lending money to a company that it knows or has reason to believe is violating any law therefore becomes part of that company's criminal conspiracy, and is thus liable under Section 1956 as well.

Nowhere is this threat more compelling than with environmental laws. A bank lending funds to a manufacturer to install a pollution control system, realizing the existing system is not in full compliance with environmental laws, may violate both Sections 1956 and 1957. All receipts (payments on the loan) coming from such a facility violating environmental laws, property acquired from such receipts, and perhaps even the company controlling the facility, may be "proceeds." Bank officers may also face fines and imprisonment.

MLCA-Internal Revenue Code Interaction

The interaction of the anti-laundering statutes with the Internal Revenue Code is complex. Tax evasion is **not** a specified unlawful activity. However, felony violations of IRC Sections 7201 and 7206—tax fraud and tax perjury—can be. Willfully submitting false documents or testimony to the IRS in reference to the proceeds of specified unlawful activity may constitute a laundering violation.

For instance, failing to file a tax return that would have included illegally earned, unreported income, is **not** money laundering. Filing such a return that excludes or understates such income or contains material misrepresentations relating to it may constitute tax fraud and/or perjury and thus violate Section 1956 of the Money Laundering Control Act.

Even routine tax inquiries can lead to money laundering investigations. When a taxpayer's income and expenses are verified, IRS employees are now trained to check the agency's computerized data banks. These contain information from the agency's currency and banking reporting system, its information return master files, and also from the Financial Crimes Enforcement Network. All these sources may be used to pursue new avenues of inquiry.

A tax related money-laundering violation may occur for conduct as simple as mailing the IRS information later proven to be false. According to Comisky *et al.*, *Tax Fraud and Evasion*,

> This issue is of more than theoretical importance. Prior to the 1988 amendments adding the tax-intent crime [to the list of laundering predicate offenses], prosecutors used the mailing of federal tax returns to charge mail fraud as a

predicate under RICO. Mail fraud and wire fraud have long been RICO predicates. [Most] courts have permitted the mailing of [tax returns] to be charged as mail fraud. See, e.g. *United States v. Kellogg*, 955 F2d 1244 (9th Cir. 1992). Sec. 11.02[2][b].

Anti-Drug Abuse Act (1988)

Perhaps more than any other U.S. legislation, this Act globalizes the U.S. surveillance infrastructure. In addition to broadening the reporting requirements of the Bank Secrecy Act, stiffening the structuring statute, and implementing "know your customer" rules for banks to enforce "suspicious transaction" reporting requirements, this Act authorized a global surveillance network.

One element of this network is machine-readable passports authorized by the Act. In 1993, the State Department began issuing such passports, which provide an electronic record of U.S. passport holders' travel records. Could such passports, together with the Act's requirement of Social Security Number disclosure on passport applications, pave the way for U.S. border controls?

Another element requires the Treasury Secretary to negotiate with finance ministers of foreign countries to establish an "international currency control agency," adopt uniform Currency Transaction Report forms and anti-laundering statutes and obtain data regarding currency transactions larger than $10,000 (so-called Kerry Agreements).

Kerry Agreements

Massachusetts Senator John Kerry was responsible for inserting in the Act provisions requiring the Treasury Secretary to negotiate international agreements requiring other nations to implement their own currency reporting laws, and share the resulting data with the United States. This requirement, together with amendments to the Money Laundering Control Act stipulating that a financial transaction involving a **foreign felony** or **fraud against a foreign bank** are specified unlawful activities, may force U.S. financial institutions, in effect, to enforce the tax and currency laws of other nations. It also may force non-U.S. financial institutions in signatory nations to enforce U.S. tax and currency laws. As such, Kerry Agreements **globalize** such laws.

Kerry Agreements signed with Colombia, Ecuador, Panama, Peru and Venezuela make available to those governments the U.S. banking records of their citizens if evidence of money laundering is presented to U.S. authorities. While the agreements imply that only drug money laundering is covered, their language does not restrict data exchange for other laundering offenses. Any U.S. financial institution accepting or facilitating a transaction involving funds known or reasonably suspected to have been derived or transferred in violation of exchange control or tax laws in a signatory nation might be subject to criminal indictment.

Enforcement of such "fiscal" offenses has traditionally not extended internationally. Kerry Agreements, enforced to their logical potential, will **eliminate** the United States as a destination for flight capital for foreign persons seeking protection from corrupt governments and inflated currencies.

Financial Crimes Enforcement Network (1990)

We're a lot like Big Brother.

—FinCEN's former Director

The most significant global surveillance initiative in the Anti-Drug Abuse Act (1988), however, was the creation of a financial intelligence division in the Treasury Department, the Financial Crimes Enforcement Network (FinCEN).

Established in 1990 by executive order, FinCEN is a computerized operation that collects and analyzes data globally to unearth financial transactions of criminals and suspected criminals and identify their assets for confiscation. In building this surveillance infrastructure, FinCEN has exempted itself from most provisions of the Privacy Act, the Right to Financial Privacy Act and the Freedom of Information Act.

Initially, FinCEN's mission was to help detect narcotics traffickers as they laundered money. However, its efforts quickly expanded to initiatives involving not just drug money laundering, but all criminal activity; in particular, white-collar crimes and tax evasion. FinCEN has placed no limit on what data it might eventually collect or what activities, illicit or otherwise, might in the future be targeted.

FinCEN may be the world's most comprehensive source of financial intelligence. Using software designed by former **nuclear weapons designers**, the FinCEN Artificial Intelligence System (FAIS) seeks out unexplained, atypical money flows. It creates a dossier of individuals who engage in large transactions in currency or currency equivalents, then matches these profiles against the typical patterns of tax evaders, money launderers, etc. programmed into the system.

The FAIS uses a set of several hundred "rules" to mimic the thinking skills of human experts in identifying suspicious transactions. Transactions flagged by the FAIS are then examined by human operators and compared with personal and financial information drawn from the many databases to which FinCEN has access. For instance, FinCEN receives records from the Federal Reserve of **all** non-cash U.S. dollar transactions, **worldwide.** Transactions in U.S. dollars constitute about 60 percent of the world's financial activity, so the FinCEN-Fed data exchange means that the majority of the world's commercial activity may already be analyzed by FinCEN.

The FAIS analysis begins with the massive Currency and Banking Database, derived from filings of various forms pursuant to the Bank Secrecy Act:

• IRS Form 4789 (domestic transactions in currency or monetary instruments that exceed $10,000 by financial institutions)

- IRS Form 8300 (transactions over $10,000 in currency or certain monetary instruments with a U.S. "trade or business")

- Customs Form 4790 (transportation of $10,000 or more in currency or certain monetary instruments across a U.S. border)

- IRS Form 8362 (transactions over $10,000 in currency with casinos)

- Treasury Form TD F 90.22-1 (a U.S. person's report of foreign bank, securities, or "other financial accounts" that in aggregate exceed $10,000)

- Treasury Form TD F 90.22-47 (suspicious transactions)

FinCEN does not yet have **official** access to personal income tax returns, although the IRS has access to some of FinCEN's databases.

Coupled with a planned massively parallel computer system and data exchange with similar "Financial Intelligence Units" throughout the world, the FAIS appears to be the first step in giving governments the ability to monitor financial transactions as they occur, anywhere in the world.

FinCEN calls the U.S. model for this system the **Deposit Tracking System** (DTS). The proposed DTS will instantaneously track transactions in each of the hundreds of millions of U.S. bank and credit card accounts. It will create a continuously updated dossier on every person with a U.S. bank account or credit card. It is justified as needed to assess funding requirements for federal bank deposit insurance, to locate assets to enforce fines and forfeitures and to track financial transactions of suspected terrorists.

Once on-line, the DTS operations will impact every person investing or doing business in the United States or any other country with which FinCEN maintains intelligence links. Could the links that **already exist** with such intelligence agencies mean that financial records from Offshore Financial Centers are already accessible to FinCEN?

The DTS is also an open invitation for prosecutorial misconduct and bureaucratic abuse. According to the American Bankers Association:

> We doubt whether there are privacy safeguards that would be adequate to effectively protect this [DTS] database from use by government agencies and eventually, private parties. It is inconceivable to the ABA that such a database would be used only ... in deposit insurance coverage functions. Such a database ... would provide a wealth of information for investigations being conducted by the FBI, the Drug Enforcement Administration and the IRS, just to name a few. Like the baseball diamond in *Field of Dreams*, build this database and they will come. Eventually, whether legally or illegally, they will gain access to this database.

Political blackmail is only one of many potential uses for DTS information. For instance, the CIA routinely trades its silence regarding embarrassing personal or financial information it uncovers for information it wants. Will an independent Congressman determined to root out corruption in U.S. intelligence agencies survive a Deposit Tracking System counterattack when his credit card and telephone records are leaked to the press? Will persons identified as members of opposition political groups be electronically targeted for investigations, forfeitures, or electronic records altered to destroy their credit and thus their reputation? The DTS would make such operations possible at the touch of a button.

The list of prospective blackmailers could be expanded to every law enforcement agency in the world, pursuant to another FinCEN initiative: **Operation Gateway.** Gateway gives state and local law enforcement direct access to FinCEN's Financial Database. All queries are recorded and constantly compared against other requests. FinCEN automatically creates a dossier of persons suspected of crimes by any law-enforcement agency. The system is now on-line in all 50 states. The Gateway model is now being expanded globally with the worldwide development of Financial Intelligence Units (see Chapter 4).

In another respect, FinCEN's reach is already international. Within a few hours of the U.S.-led invasion of Kuwait on January 17, 1991, the U.S. Treasury Department's Office of Foreign Assets Control had with FinCEN's assistance identified and frozen 11 bank accounts, assets in California, Georgia and New York, and a $3.5 million real estate parcel. The properties belonged to persons and companies suspected of being fronts for Saddam Hussein or who were suspected of having traded with Iraq in violation of an Executive Order issued by President Bush pursuant to the International Emergency Economic Powers Act.

Global Surveillance?

The Anti-Drug Abuse Act (1988) calls for the Treasury Secretary to negotiate treaties to adopt uniform currency reporting transaction forms and anti-laundering statutes; i.e., to set up a global cash-monitoring system. Non-compliant countries are subject to sanctions. Also in 1988, the United States signed the Council of Europe/Organization for Economic Cooperation and Development's Convention on Mutual Administrative Assistance in Tax Matters that contained a blueprint for the global collection of taxes. (See "International Tax and Forfeiture Agreements.")

FinCEN is the agency tracking compliance with domestic currency reporting statutes and is preparing to monitor all bank and credit card transactions as they occur. FinCEN also has been instrumental in identifying assets to be frozen in international anti-laundering operations. The IRS already uses FinCEN in its tax investigations. Are these connections purely coincidental, or is FinCEN also the prototype of a global tax collection agency?

If so, current IRS initiatives to identify unreported income and non-filers may begin a worldwide trend. According to *Forbes* magazine,

In 1991 an IRS criminal investigator was sitting at his computer in Flint, Mich., searching a database of suspicious bank deposits of cash. The name of John E. Long appeared on his screen. At the next desk, an agent sorting paper criminal referral forms from banks saw the same name ... Building on those leads, the IRS got Long, his son-in-law and their wives to pay more than $12 million in back taxes, interest, penalties and forfeitures. It even collected a down payment by seizing a 50-foot yacht and $1.4 million of currency. The two men are now serving 21-month terms in prison camp, after which their wives will do shorter terms.

What happened? The family, which is largest promoter of country folk art shows in the nation, didn't book the cash it collected for admissions. Instead it deposited into its corporate accounts only the checks it received from renting booths, publishing a magazine and the like. Result: The Longs reported that their business was losing money, when in fact it was quite profitable.

But the computer knew better. An agent pulled from it reports of 63 suspicious cash deposits of under $10,000 made by Long and his son-in-law at eight banks. He then subpoenaed the banks' records—the Longs didn't even know this was happening—and entered into his personal computer the data on 2,000 deposits the family had made into 37 accounts. Computer sorting established which accounts contained skimmed money and which assets were purchased with unreported cash and thus subject to forfeiture.

Annunzio-Wylie Anti-Money Laundering Act (1992)

Continuing the globalization of the U.S. surveillance infrastructure, this Act authorizes the government to seize U.S. assets of foreign banks allegedly involved in illegal activity and permits any Federal District Court to file an order for a forfeiture in another country.

The Act also:

• authorizes regulators to shut down banks "knowingly" engaged in or facilitating money laundering and provides for the mandatory removal of officers and directors of financial institutions accused of any laundering offense. The "appropriate federal banking agency" may remove such persons and/or prohibit them from working for any other financial institution, **even if acquitted of all charges**.

• permits the Treasury Secretary to issue regulations that require financial institutions to report suspicious transactions that could involve a violation of **any law or regulation**, not just anti-laundering laws. Such regulations have now been issued. It also amends the Right to Financial Privacy Act to prohibit institutions from disclosing such reports to affected depositors. Depositors may not sue for damages, even if the resulting investigation uncovers no wrongdoing. Financial institutions that fail to report suspicious transactions that were not, but should have been, identified as suspicious face the penalties outlined in "BSA Reporting Requirements: Suspicious Transactions."

- requires financial institutions or merchants that sell or redeem monetary instruments (currency, cashier's checks, money orders, or travelers' checks) or transmit funds by wire to maintain records of international transactions, and make them available for warrantless inspection.

The Act's extraterritorial civil forfeiture provisions are particularly notable. In 1994, a U.S. District Court ordered that bank accounts in the United Kingdom belonging to an accused money launderer be forfeited to the federal government. *United States v. Meza*, 856 F.Supp. 759 (E.D.N.Y.). This case subjected **non-U.S.** accounts in **non-U.S.** banks to civil forfeiture, in a jurisdiction (the United Kingdom) in which civil forfeitures are otherwise not enforced.

U.K. law permits courts there to issue restraining orders to aid foreign civil proceedings in narcotics investigations. The English High Court of Justice concluded that there was no requirement that the foreign civil proceeding correspond to a proceeding permissible under English law. *In re Drug Trafficking Offenses Act 1986* (Designated Countries and Territories), Order 1990, DTA 76/90 (unreported).

That U.S. courts will exercise their authority to order forfeitures in the United Kingdom in cases not relating to drug trafficking appears guaranteed. The U.S.-U.K. **Mutual Legal Assistance Treaty** covers all non-misdemeanor U.S. criminal investigations, even if the conduct in question does not violate U.K. law. It also provides for cooperation in civil proceedings (such as civil forfeiture) brought in connection with a criminal investigation. Further, the U.K. Crown can extend this treaty to its dependent territories: Bermuda, the Cayman Islands, Gibraltar, Montserrat, the Turks & Caicos Islands, etc.) **Investors in these offshore financial centers should presume that U.S. civil forfeiture laws might be applied against their holdings.**

Money Laundering Suppression Act (1994)

In this Act, Congress restricted relations between the United States and countries that have not involved themselves fully in the global surveillance infrastructure.

The Act expands the definition of "monetary instrument" to include **bank drafts** transferred across a U.S. border. (See "BSA Reporting Requirements: International Funds Transfers.") The Conference Report accompanying the bill expresses concern that the new definition could delay inter-bank collection and reconciliation. To avoid unnecessary delays, the report suggests that Treasury exempt from reporting bank drafts originating in countries that have fully implemented the anti-laundering recommendations set forth by the Financial Action Task Force. (See "Financial Action Task Force.")

Treasury is to distinguish between countries that are implementing U.S.-type anti-laundering laws and those that are not. Offshore Financial Centers that do not have such laws will be placed at a competitive disadvantage, in that U.S. reconciliation and clearing operations will be delayed. "Problem" jurisdictions are to be identified in regulations. **Surveillance is globalized.**

Chapter 3

THE GLOBAL SURVEILLANCE INFRASTRUCTURE

Restatement (Third) of Foreign Relations Law (1988)

A court order ordinarily will have no effect outside the geographical area over which the court has authority; its **jurisdiction**. Where a court respects and defers to laws outside its jurisdiction, there is **comity**. A court seeking to enforce its jurisdiction beyond its territorial boundaries (**extraterritorial** jurisdiction) may interfere with comity.

Court orders issued in U.S. tax, racketeering, money laundering, anti-trust, insider trading, tax, and narcotics investigations often have extraterritorial effects. These laws impact all persons investing or doing business in **offshore financial centers**, criminals or not.

A principal reason offshore financial centers exist and prosper is because their laws offer businesses and investors advantages in comparison with other countries. These advantages may include low or non-existent taxes; a simplified regulatory structure; a predictable legal climate; and/or restrictions on the enforcement of foreign judgments.

Some countries, such as the United States, apply criminal penalties to activities that in offshore financial centers are legal or at worst subject to civil sanctions. Where conduct that constitutes a criminal offense in **both** countries (**dual criminality**) is alleged, the respective authorities are likely to cooperate in an investigation and/or legal proceeding, with or without a treaty mandating such cooperation.

Where laws between two countries are inconsistent, there is **conflict of law**. Conflict of law may or may not protect a person living, residing, or doing business in a country when that country seeks documents or assets located outside its territorial boundaries. For instance, a person provided official notice of a lawsuit against him (**service of process**) within the United States is obligated to produce documents located **outside** the United States if he is deemed in possession or control of these documents.

A person cannot produce documents or assets that do not exist, that are not in his possession or control, or are otherwise unobtainable. Absent an allegation of dual criminality or a treaty agreement, a **foreign third party** not coming within U.S. jurisdiction cannot be forced to produce such documents or assets.

For documents or assets under the control of a U.S. person or foreign third party deemed subject to U.S. jurisdiction, prosecutors may seek a "compelled waiver" order requiring the person or foreign third party to order a foreign financial institution or other foreign person to release records.

Consent is compelled, because if refused, the individual or foreign third party may be held in contempt. *Doe v. United States*, 487 U.S. 201 (1988). Whether such compelled consent will be honored depends on if the investment or other **contract** contains language prohibiting compelled consent that is enforceable under the foreign jurisdiction's law (see Chapter 4). This is a critical consideration for U.S. persons investing or doing business in offshore financial centers.

In the United States, the widely cited American Bar Association's Restatement (Third) of Foreign Relations Law provides for the extraterritorial enforcement of domestic court orders for the disclosure of information in the following manner:

Requests for Disclosure and Foreign Government Compulsion: Law of the United States. (1)(a) Where authorized by statute or rule of court, a court in the United States may order a person subject to its jurisdiction to produce documents, objects, or other information directly relevant, necessary, and material to an action or investigation, even if the information or the person in possession of the information is outside the United States.

(b) Failure to comply with an order to produce information may subject the person to whom the order is directed to sanctions, including finding of contempt, dismissal of a claim or defense or default judgment, or may lead to a determination by the court that the facts to which the order was addressed are as asserted by the opposing party.

(c) In issuing an order directing production of information located abroad, a court of the United States should take into account the importance to the investigation or litigation of the documents or other information requested; the degree of specificity of the request; whether the information originated in the United States; the extent to which compliance with the request would undermine important interests of the state where the information is located; and the possibility of alternative means of securing the information.

(2) If disclosure of information located outside the United States is prohibited by a law, regulation, or court order of the state in which the information or prospective witness is located, or by the state of nationality of the prospective witness,

(a) the person to whom the order is directed may be required by the court to make a good faith effort to secure permission from the foreign authorities to make the information available;

(b) the court should not ordinarily impose the sanctions of contempt, dismissal or default on the party that has failed to comply with the order for production except in cases of deliberate concealment or removal of information or of failure to make a good faith effort in accordance with paragraph (a)

(c) the court may, in appropriate cases, make findings of fact adverse to a party that has failed to comply with the order for production, even if the party has made a good faith effort to secure permission from the foreign authorities to make the information available and that effort has been unsuccessful.

Bilateral Information Exchange and Forfeiture Agreements

To expedite information exchanges and forfeitures, governments enter into agreements that obligate signatories to exchange documents and restrain and/or forfeit assets under mutually agreed conditions. These agreements have the effect of expanding the surveillance infrastructure globally, and making the laws of one jurisdiction apply in other jurisdictions, thereby reducing conflict of law.

The U.S. government has entered into several types of such bilateral agreements, including Tax Treaties, Tax Information Exchange Agreements, Memoranda of Understanding and Mutual Legal Assistance Treaties.

Lacking a bilateral agreement or one comprehensive enough to obtain the information sought, authorities may approach another country to obtain the data they seek. For instance, in 1992, the German government sought certain information concerning a tax file held by the Dutch tax authorities. Under the German-Dutch tax treaty, they were not entitled to that information. So the Germans asked the Canadians to ask the Dutch for this file—and obtained it through Canada.

Tax Treaties

These treaties require information exchange for civil and administrative enforcement of revenue laws. Recent Tax Treaties entered into by the U.S. government authorize the exchange of documentary information on dividends, interest, rents and royalties. They also call for the mutual collection of tax obligations.

As of mid-1996, the United States had tax treaties in effect with Aruba, Austria, Australia, Barbados, Belgium, Bermuda, Canada, China, Cyprus, Czech Republic, Denmark, Finland, France, French Guiana, Greece, Guadeloupe, Hungary, Iceland, India, Indonesia, Ireland, Israel, Italy, Jamaica, Japan, Korea, Luxembourg, Martinique, Malta, Mexico, Morocco, the Netherlands, Netherland Antilles (Curacao, Bonaire, St. Maarten & Saba), New Zealand, Norway, Pakistan, the Philippines, Poland, Romania, Slovak Republic, Spain, Sweden, Switzerland, Trinidad, Tobago, Tunisia, United Kingdom and the former Soviet Republics of Armenia, Azerbaijan, Belarus, Georgia, Kazakhstan, Kyrgyzstan, Moldova, Russia, Tajikistan, Turkmenistan, Ukraine and Uzbekistan.

Tax Information Exchange Agreements

Signatories to these treaties exchange data similar to that released in tax treaties, plus information relating to beneficial ownership of trusts and corporations. TIEAs may also call for bank-deposit information to be exchanged between tax authorities. In conjunction with Kerry Agreements, could TIEAs be used by signatories to eliminate capital flight into (or out of) the United States?

One incentive for countries to enter into TIEAs with the United States is eligibility for tax concessions under the Caribbean Basin Initiative. This program established favorable tariff arrangements for the exports of countries that signed such agreements with the United States.

As of mid-1996, the United States had TIEAs in effect with Barbados, Bermuda, Costa Rica, Dominica, Dominican Republic, Grenada, Guyana, Honduras, Jamaica, Marshall Islands, Mexico, Peru, St. Lucia and Tobago.

Mutual Legal Assistance Treaties

Mutual Legal Assistance Treaties (MLATs) provide for the exchange of financial and other records in the investigation of **suspected** criminal activities. Most MLATs negotiated by the United States do not require a judicial or administrative finding of probable cause to be invoked. **Reasonable suspicion** is sufficient. MLATs may also provide for extradition of criminal suspects and for "equitable sharing" of forfeited property.

The MLAT between the United States and the Crown of the Cayman Islands is a model for MLATs with many other offshore financial centers. The agreement covers all crimes recognized by both countries punishable by more than one year in prison. In addition, it covers offenses that are illegal in the United States, but not in the Cayman Islands, including insider trading and bribery of foreign officials. Pure tax offenses are excluded, but not if committed in conjunction with other crimes.

MLATs also override local confidentiality laws. For instance, the MLAT between the United States and the Crown of the Turks and Caicos Islands states:

A person who divulges any confidential information or gives any testimony in conformity with the [MLAT] request shall be deemed not to commit any offense under the Confidential Relationships Ordinance 1979 ... sub-section (6) of section 16 of the Banking Ordinance 1979 ... [or] section 202 of the Companies Ordinance 1981.

Persons doing business in jurisdictions that have signed MLATs with the United States should presume that U.S. criminal law is enforced there, whether or not that jurisdiction has enacted corresponding laws. Dual criminality is **not** required.

MLATs may also be used to enforce certain government **civil** judgments, including civil forfeitures. For instance, in 1993, the United States and Switzerland concluded negotiations expanding the U.S.-Swiss MLAT to include civil proceedings under the U.S. securities fraud statutes.

As of mid-1996, the United States had MLATs in effect with Anguilla, Argentina, the Bahamas, Belgium, British Virgin Islands, Canada, Cayman Islands, Italy, Jamaica, Mexico, Montserrat, Morocco, the Netherlands, Panama, Spain, Switzerland, Thailand, Turkey, the Turks & Caicos Islands, and the United Kingdom. MLATs with Austria, Colombia, Hungary, Korea, Nigeria and Uruguay are signed but not yet in effect.

Memoranda of Understanding

These administrative agreements, which under U.S. law do not have to be ratified by the Senate, cover a variety of subjects. For instance, MOUs assented to in 1994 by the Crown of the Cayman Islands and other Crown dependent territories, give the FBI limited investigative authority in Anguilla, the British Virgin Islands, the Cayman Islands, Montserrat, and the Turks and Caicos Islands. The FBI, working with local police, now may investigate white-collar crime in these jurisdictions. Any assets forfeited are split between the U.S. government and the dependent territory.

In the context of document exchanges, the United States has concluded MOUs with several nations concerning securities and anti-trust matters. The most sweeping such agreements are similar to MLATs in not requiring dual criminality to be invoked. for abandoning the requirement of dual criminality. As of mid-1996, the Securities and Exchange Commission had concluded MOUs with 27 countries, including Argentina, Brazil, Canada, China, Costa Rica, European Community, Egypt, France, Hong Kong, Israel, Italy, Indonesia, Japan, Luxembourg, Mexico, the Netherlands, Norway, Russia, Spain, Switzerland and the United Kingdom. Anti-trust MOUs are in effect with Canada, Australia and Germany, among other countries.

International Tax and Forfeiture Agreements

International agreements for mutual cooperation in collecting taxes and forfeiting the proceeds of crime follow the U.S. lead in seeking to eliminate the conflict of laws that is the essence of privacy and asset protection. They also establish global surveillance authorities and export the U.S. civil forfeiture laws that permit hearsay evidence to establish reasonable suspicion, shifting of the burden of proof to the defendant or property owner, confiscation of substitute untainted assets, informant commissions and sting operations. The agreements also require financial institutions to begin "know your customer" programs to identify suspicious transactions.

Council of Europe/OECD Convention on Mutual Administrative Assistance in Tax Matters (1988)

It is an established principal of international law that governments will not permit enforcement of foreign tax claims in their courts. The theory, known as the "revenue rule," was succinctly summarized in the Jersey (Channel Islands) case of *In re Tucker,* 1987-88 Jersey Law Reports 473: "Just as one State cannot send its police force into another State, so also it cannot send its tax-gatherers."

This Convention is an important step in restricting, even ending, the revenue rule. The objective of the treaty is:

> to place it beyond all doubt that a taxpayer may not resist recovery in the requested State by disputing in that country the validity of the instrument issued

by the applicant State or by alleging that the amount of the tax claim is erroneous because of payments he has already made.

The Convention covers all taxes—income tax, capital gains tax, value-added tax, etc., even if "the request concerns a tax which does not exist in the requested State." It also proposes an international tax collection agency to set up globally standardized tax forms and laws and global investigation and enforcement of tax assessments. This agency could seize property and assets for tax delinquencies anywhere in the world. Signatories would be required to seize property within their jurisdiction "to recover tax claims of the first-mentioned State as if they were its own tax claims."

The Convention went into effect in 1995 after being ratified by the United States, Sweden, Norway, Denmark and Finland.

United Nations Convention Against Illicit Traffic in Narcotic Drugs and Psychotropic Substances (1988)

In 1984, the United Nations' General Assembly requested that the U.N. Commission on Narcotic Drugs prepare a draft convention against illicit drug trafficking. This agreement was approved by more than 80 countries at a 1988 conference in Vienna, Austria and became known as the "U.N. Vienna Narcotics Convention." The Convention went into effect in 1990 and has now been signed by more than 100 nations.

The Convention's 14 articles address methods to combat narcotics cultivation, production and transportation; provide for "adequate" sanctions for drug offenses; strengthen extradition procedures; and develop techniques to trace the proceeds of narcotics trafficking. In addition, the Convention requires the criminalization of money laundering in narcotics cases, the setting aside of secrecy laws in laundering investigations, and the forfeiture of laundered proceeds. **Signatories therefore cannot claim a lack of dual criminality in international laundering investigations.** Further, the Convention permits signatories to shift the burden of proof from prosecutors to owners or lienholders of alleged laundered proceeds and encourages confiscation of substitute assets.

The first use of the Convention by U.S. prosecutors came in 1991. A criminal defendant with substantial overseas assets negotiated a plea bargain arrangement guaranteeing immunity from prosecution in exchange for disclosing the location of the foreign holdings. The United States then contacted governments that were Convention signatories with jurisdiction over those assets and requested their forfeiture. While the defendant objected to this use of the information he had provided, prosecutors only guaranteed immunity in criminal proceedings, not from forfeiture.

Countries that have signed, accepted, ratified, or declared the U.N. Vienna Narcotics Convention in effect include Afghanistan, Algeria, Antigua and Barbuda, Argentina, Armenia, Australia, Austria, Azerbaijan, the Bahamas, Bahrain, Bangladesh, Barbados, Belarus, Belgium, Bhutan, Bolivia, Bosnia, Brazil, Brunei, Bulgaria, Burundi, Burkina Faso, Cameroon, Canada, Chile, China, Colombia, Costa Rica, Croatia, Cuba, Cypress, Czech Republic, Denmark, Dominica, Dominican Republic,

Ecuador, El Salvador, Egypt, European Community, Finland, Fiji, France, Gabon, Germany, Ghana, Greece, Grenada, Guatemala, Guinea, Guyana, Holy See, Honduras, Hungary, India, Indonesia, Iran, Ireland, Israel, Italy, Ivory Coast, Jamaica, Japan, Jordan, Kenya, Kuwait, Latvia, Luxembourg, Macedonia, Madagascar, Malaysia, Maldives, Mauritania, Mauritius, Mexico, Monaco, Morocco, Myanmar, Nepal, the Netherlands, New Zealand, Nicaragua, Niger, Nigeria, Norway, Oman, Pakistan, Panama, Paraguay, Peru, the Philippines, Poland, Portugal, Qatar, Romania, Russia, Saudi Arabia, Senegal, Seychelles, Sierra Leone, Slovak Republic, Slovenia, Spain, Sri Lanka, Sudan, Suriname, Sweden, Switzerland, Suriname, Syria, Tanzania, Togo, Trinidad and Tobago, Tunisia, Turkey, Uganda, Ukraine, United Arab Emirates, United Kingdom (and dependent territories), United States, Uruguay, Venezuela, Yemen, Yugoslavia, Zaire, Zambia, and Zimbabwe.

The Financial Action Task Force (1988)

The Financial Action Task Force was formed by the seven leading industrialized democracies, the G-7, in 1988 to fight money laundering. The G-7 consist of the United States, the United Kingdom, France, Italy, Japan, Germany, and Canada. Other FATF members include Australia, Austria, Belgium, Luxembourg, the Netherlands, Spain, Sweden and Switzerland. The Organization for Economic Cooperation and Development provides staffing and support for the FATF.

In 1989, the FATF released 40 recommendations to intensify the global war on crime. Some suggestions—including the global criminalization of laundering, global tracing of laundered assets, and the global lifting of secrecy in laundering investigations—were already part of the U.N. Vienna Narcotics Convention. However, the FATF recommendations go further in recommending that predicate laundering offenses be extended to "all serious crimes," including insider trading, environmental offenses, economic fraud, kidnapping, terrorism, negligent laundering and "any economic advantage derived from any serious criminal offense."

The FATF was also more specific in suggesting strategies for global anti-laundering enforcement that mirror legislation proposed or already in effect in the United States. They include:

- imposing both monetary and civil penalties for laundering offenses;

- **voiding contracts** where parties knew or should have known that the contract would make it more difficult to forfeit laundered proceeds;

- imposing a global "know your customer" burden on all financial institutions;

- requiring financial institutions to report "suspicious transactions" to law enforcement authorities;

- imposing a global currency transaction reporting system;

- studying measures to detect or monitor cash crossing national borders;

• monitoring currency flows globally and making such data available to the International Monetary Fund and the Bank for International Settlements;

• encouraging governments to automatically provide information on suspicious transactions to other governments and inter-governmental organizations;

• monitoring electronic money movements, particularly international wire transfers; and

• coordinating the confiscation and forfeiture of tainted assets, including the payment of commissions to informants and inter-governmental organizations.

More recent FATF initiatives, which are summarized each year in an annual report, include seeking to abolish anonymous bank accounts worldwide; imposing stricter licensing requirements for non-bank financial institutions; imposing tighter financial transaction reporting requirements; initiating anti-laundering sting operations globally; and providing for greater transparency in electronic money movement while encouraging national authorities to require such transparency.

In response to this last recommendation, in 1993, the Society for Worldwide Interbank Financial Telecommunications (SWIFT), the largest international electronic funds transfer network, asked its users to identity payors, payees, intermediaries and the purpose of payments in messages they send.

Recommendations from the FATF have generally been adopted by both member and non-member governments. In the United States, for instance, the U.S. Annunzio-Wylie Anti-Money Laundering Act (1992) provides for a recordkeeping procedure for electronic funds transfers. In Austria, the FATF initiative against anonymous accounts was in part responsible for a decision in 1994 to restrict their use.

Council of Europe Laundering Convention (1990)

In 1990, the Council of Europe's "Select Committee of Experts" prepared an anti-laundering and forfeiture treaty based on FATF recommendations. The Convention on Laundering, Search, Seizure and Confiscation of the Proceeds from Crime became effective in 1993. Signatories include Australia, Belgium, Bulgaria, Cyprus, Denmark, Finland, France, Germany, Greece, Iceland, Italy, Luxembourg, the Netherlands, Norway, Portugal, Spain, Sweden, Switzerland and the United Kingdom.

The Laundering Convention provides a more comprehensive set of rules covering all stages of forfeiture than the U.N. Vienna Narcotics Convention. Signatories must enforce asset restraint orders from a requesting state even in civil and administrative proceedings. Once seizure has occurred, applying whatever burden of proof is necessary in the seizing jurisdiction, the burden shifts to claimants to demonstrate that they are innocent bona fide purchasers or lienholders.

The Laundering Convention follows FATF recommendations in providing an optional procedure for signatories to criminalize laundering relating to **all serious criminal activity**. While the Convention allows governments to enter reservations restricting cooperation to certain offenses, most ratifying states have chosen not to do so. For instance, the Convention applies to **all crimes** in Switzerland.

Laundering Convention signatories must also consider new investigative techniques to fight laundering. These including covert observation, continuous monitoring of all transactions in financial institutions, monitoring of communications (including wiretaps), and computerized investigative aids, as permitted under domestic law.

All these recommendations mirror laws in effect or proposals in the United States and other countries. For instance, the Convention's proposal for continuous monitoring of all transactions in financial institutions ties in directly to the Deposit Tracking System proposed in 1993 by the Financial Crimes Enforcement Network. Its proposal for the expansion of wiretapping dovetails with the revelation that the governing body of the European Union was developing a "global surveillance system." (See Chapter 4.)

There appear to be significant contradictions between the language of the Laundering Convention and that of Protocol No. 1 of the European Convention on Human Rights, which guarantees to all "natural and legal persons" the right not to be deprived of their possessions. Most European nations that have ratified the Laundering Convention have also ratified Protocol No. 1. The author's *Asset Protection 2000* (Chapter 4) examines the interaction between these two agreements in greater detail.

Surveillance in Offshore Financial Centers

Jurisdictions commonly acknowledged as offshore financial centers; i.e., that have enacted laws favoring the conduct of financial transactions by non-resident alien investors, are commonly acknowledged to include: Austria, the Bahamas, Barbados, Belize, Bermuda, the British Virgin Islands, the Cayman Islands (Jersey and Guernsey), the Channel Islands (Jersey, Guernsey, and Sark), the Cook Islands, the Czech Republic, Cyprus, Gibraltar, Grenada, Hong Kong, Hungary, the Isle of Man, Liechtenstein, Malaysia, Malta, Mauritius, Montserrat, the Seychelles, Singapore, Sri Lanka, St. Christopher and Nevis, Switzerland, the Turks & Caicos Islands, Vanuatu, and Western Samoa.

Crown Offshore Financial Centers

With the exception of a handful of western European jurisdictions, virtually every offshore financial center is a colony or former colony of the British Crown and has inherited English Common Law. This shared legal heritage lends itself to surveillance in that **legislation, regulation,** the **financial system** and the **judicial system** are interrelated. In offshore financial centers with an English Common Law background, legislation, regulations and judicial decisions in one jurisdiction apply in other jurisdictions, unless dealt with by statute.

For instance, **attorneys** in the United Kingdom became independent financial investigators for the Crown when the Criminal Justice Act (1993) and the Money

Laundering Regulations (1993) came into force. The legislation requires financial institutions and **attorneys** to report **suspected** laundering activities by their clients. The client's right to confidentiality from a financial institution or solicitor (lawyer) is overridden by their duty to report suspicious transactions (Chapter 4).

As with all U.K. legislation, this law may be extended to Crown dependent territories and may also be enforced in Commonwealth jurisdictions. These jurisdictions could adopt legislation reinstating attorney-client confidentiality, but given the role of the Crown in each jurisdiction's constitution and government, such reinstatement may be unlikely. Absent such correcting legislation, it is **unclear** whether attorney-client privilege extends to financial transactions viewed by the attorney as potentially suspicious in any Crown dependent territory or Commonwealth nation.

The Crown. The Crown is not a person or a family. It is a bureaucracy. One organ of the Crown is the hereditary monarch that serves as sovereign; the House of Windsor.

In a Westminster Constitution, the Crown **is** the government. The Statute of Westminster (1931) formalizes a 1,000-year-old evolutionary process through which Crown possessions assumed increasing responsibility for their own local, non-executive governance. Statutes in a Westminster Constitution are made exclusively by one organ: the Crown-in-Parliament. **Parliament** does not exist without the Crown.

The Crown under its inherent **prerogative** authority grants the country a constitution, representing that country's highest law, and standing independently with respect to other constitutions. The Crown remains a party to this constitutional contract, which recognizes the Crown's executive authority. This contract also provides for English Common Law to be inherited, including decisions of the English courts. English Common Law is thus **international law** and applies in jurisdictions that have inherited it unless specifically amended, repudiated, or excluded.

As the Executive Branch of a constitutional monarchy, the Crown must assent to all acts of local legislatures, or **Parliaments**, for the legislation to take effect. The Crown also retains the authority to **legislate** through Letters Patent, Proclamations and Orders in Council. In Crown dependent territories, the Parliament of the United Kingdom, with Crown assent, may also legislate.

The **Commonwealth** is a series of separate and distinct Westminster constitutional contracts creating separate Crowns in each member state. Crown dependent territories are members of the Commonwealth in which the Crown directly oversees external affairs and defense, which encompass matters relating to security, law enforcement, Admiralty jurisdiction, international treaties and diplomacy, constitutional changes, reciprocal enforcement of judgments and intellectual property. The constitutions of dependent territories retain a right of appeal to the Crown's highest court, the Judicial Committee of the Privy Council. Crown dependent territories may amend, but may not repeal, English Common Law. A **Governor** represents the Crown.

Commonwealth status, or "independence," does not represent independence from the Crown. The Crown in its executive role continues to oversee defense, external affairs, law enforcement, etc. Commonwealth constitutions may or may not preserve the right of appeal to the Privy Council. The Crown in a Commonwealth nation is represented by the **Queen's Representative**.

The Queen's Representative in a Commonwealth nation and the Governor of a dependent territory have the constitutional responsibilities to convene and dismiss Parliament, make ministerial and judicial appointments, and assent to legislation. These duties may be carried out in consultation with the **Cabinet** or **Executive Council**, consisting of the Governor or Queen's Representative and ministers, including the Prime Minister. The Constitution or statutes may also grant the Crown or Executive Council the authority to **legislate**. In Crown dependent territories, this authority includes the power to vary or revoke any legislation. These officials also have the implied powers discussed in the following section.

Enforcement and Executive Powers. Emergency powers statutes and executive orders under U.S. law are in theory subject to constitutional restraints (see "Emergency Powers"), but there are **no** similar restraints on the Crown's executive authority in a Westminster Constitution. While a Westminster Constitution will limit the ability of the **local legislature** to enact legislation that would abrogate fundamental rights and freedoms, no such limits are placed on the Crown. Nor is the Crown made accountable to the local legislature. The limits of these executive powers, which include authority over law enforcement and "security of the realm," are **unclear.**

An example of how these powers may be exercised occurred in the 1980s, when a narcotics trafficking scandal involving high government officials in the Crown dependent territory of the Turks & Caicos Islands was uncovered. The Crown **shut down** the offshore financial sector and prohibited it from reopening until laws were amended to provide greater transparency and existing regulatory supervisors were replaced.

The Crown may also enter into treaties **without** the consent of the local legislature. An analogous situation would be for the U.S. President to instruct the State Department to negotiate a treaty and the FBI to enforce its provisions, without obtaining the consent of Congress.

Statute of Elizabeth (1571). Laws in jurisdictions with an English Common Law background provide that transfers of property may be voided if a creditor presents a claim to that property. In the United States, this concept of **fraudulent conveyance** has expanded to encompass transactions designed to avoid creditor claims for civil **tort liability** (including liability for punitive damages). Fraudulent conveyances deemed to violate federal laws or defraud federal agencies or federally-insured financial institutions may result in **criminal liability**.

The basis of fraudulent conveyance in English Common Law is the **Statute of Elizabeth** (1571). This criminal statute makes all property transfers made with the intention of delaying or hindering forfeitures, or delaying, hindering, or defrauding other creditors void or voidable. The court may set aside the transfer and order the assets paid to the creditor. The court order may be reinforced with fines, foreclosures, seizure of substitute property, civil contempt citations and criminal penalties.

"Intent to defraud" is interpreted broadly and has been held to mean merely depriving creditors of timely recourse to property. Although persons seeking to set aside a transaction must demonstrate intent, the courts readily accept circumstantial evidence to prove intent. If a transfer leaves a person insolvent, such evidence may be accepted as intent to defraud. A person may be held to be legally insolvent even with sufficient assets to cover existing or reasonably foreseen debts, if such assets are not readily available to creditors.

Even absent legislation implementing Elizabeth, in jurisdictions with an English Common Law background, its principles must be presumed to apply. Depending on how it is invoked under local law, Elizabeth may provide an even stricter definition of fraudulent conveyance than under U.S. law.

Several Crown offshore financial centers have limited Elizabeth, but such action could violate these jurisdictions' own Constitutions, which limit amendments "inconsistent with the Constitution," which include the inherited English Common Law.

For instance, the Cook Islands International Trusts Act (1984) **repeals** Elizabeth. However, Article 39 of the Cook Islands Constitution states in part:

> **Power to make laws.** (1) Subject to the provisions of this Constitution, Parliament may make laws ... for the peace, order and good government of the Cook Islands ... (4) Except to the extent to which it is inconsistent with this Constitution, no Act and no provision of any Act shall be deemed to be invalid solely on the ground that it is inconsistent with any law in force in the Cook Islands."

Article 77, on the other hand, states in part:

> **Existing law to continue**. Subject to the provisions of this Constitution, (a) The existing law shall, until repealed, and subject to any amendment thereof, continue in force.

These existing laws include 1,000 years of English Common Law.

Article 77 accepts existing law but states that it may be repealed or amended by Parliament. Article 39(4) limits this power "... to the extent to which it is inconsistent with this Constitution." Opponents in jurisdictions that compete with the Cook Islands argue that repeal of the Statute of Elizabeth is unconstitutional in a jurisdiction with an English Common Law background. As the Cook Islands Constitution retains the right of appeal to the Privy Council in London, perhaps this court, the ultimate arbiter of English Common Law, will eventually be called upon to rule on it.

Another effect of Elizabeth and related legislation is to facilitate surveillance and eliminate privacy. Preventing fraudulent transfers provides an effective rationale to construct the global surveillance infrastructure this report documents.

No Solid Economies. Crown offshore financial centers almost universally lack an industrial infrastructure. They depend exclusively on income from tourism and revenues attached to their "tax haven" status. The contrast between these jurisdictions and a non-common-law offshore financial center such as Liechtenstein, the most heavily industrialized country in Europe, is immense.

Organizations such as the International Monetary Fund exert great influence in jurisdictions that lack solid economies, particularly where the organizations coordinate foreign aid efforts. Both the United States and international organizations such as the FATF have stipulated that international aid be contingent on recipients complying in full with the surveillance and enforcement requirements of agreements such as the U.N. Vienna Narcotics Convention and the FATF's 40-point financial transparency program.

Unless and until Crown offshore financial centers develop diversified economies, they will be ill suited to resist the imposition of a surveillance infrastructure by international aid organizations and others. Persons who believe they are escaping global surveillance by investing or doing business in these jurisdictions are mistaken.

Regulation. Privacy and asset protection require reducing government powers over wealth. However, persons seeking less government authority over their assets may substitute one government's power for another. These powers may be more threatening than those left behind.

The Commonwealth of the Cook Islands is an excellent example. Much has been written of the Cook Islands as an asset protection jurisdiction. These discussions have focused on legislation restricting foreign judgments and repealing the Statute of Elizabeth in relation to trusts.

However, a critical review of this legislation, the International Trusts Act 1984, as amended, yields astonishing results. A plain reading of this law and a related statute, the International Companies Act 1981-82, as amended, suggests the following:

- The Minister of Finance, an official appointed by the Crown, may terminate trusts and companies organized or operating under Cook Islands law;

- The Minister may do so without a court proceeding and with no right of appeal; and

- There is no legal recourse against the Minister or other government officials.

The statutes may be interpreted as empowering the Minister to apply such "due process" to confiscate the assets of an international company or trust situated in the Cook Islands. While the Cook Islands Constitution protects certain "fundamental **human** rights and freedoms," no protection appears to be afforded statutory persons such as trusts.

While it is unknown and perhaps unknowable whether such powers will be applied against any **particular** trust, international investors should carefully review the actual laws that apply in the jurisdiction(s) they choose for privacy and asset protection.

Intelligence. The "U.K.-U.S.A. Agreement" signed by the United States, United Kingdom, Canada, Australia, and New Zealand divides the world into "spheres of cryptologic influence" and mandates the exchange of information between the defense intelligence agencies of the signatories. (See "National Security Agency.")

One capability of the U.S. National Security Agency is to monitor all **electronic funds transfers** in or out of the United States. Does the NSA share such data with the Crown intelligence agencies? Do these agencies have similar capabilities in Crown offshore financial centers?

Further, U.S. dollar transactions in Crown offshore financial centers clear through the Federal Reserve. Data from these clearing operations are conveyed to the Financial Crimes Enforcement Network. Do Crown intelligence agencies monitor transactions in the pound sterling and turn such data over to FinCEN?

The exchange of personnel between Crown agencies and international regulatory and enforcement agencies implies a high level of intelligence coordination. Officials from the Bank of England, for instance, are routinely assigned overseas duties in Crown offshore financial centers. So are officials of international aid organizations. For instance, the International Monetary Fund has supplied the Cayman Islands Inspector of Banks and Trusts.

Homogenization. The Crown is both a hereditary monarch and a global organization. The practical effect of its legal heritage, English Common Law, is to **eliminate** conflict of law. The arrangements summarized in "Bilateral Information Exchange and Forfeiture Agreements" and "International Tax and Forfeiture Agreements" are an attempt to avoid conflicting sovereignties and political tensions between different legal systems. The goal is the **homogenization of systems toward a common norm.**

This goal seems analogous to the "one-world government" and "one-world law" documented in books such as Quigley's *The Anglo-American Establishment*. Is the Commonwealth the model for such homogenization, with English Common Law the glue binding it together? Are MLATs and their multilateral counterparts an effort to construct a global surveillance infrastructure to enforce this common norm?

Switzerland

Switzerland markets itself as a laissez-faire democracy with impenetrable financial confidentiality laws; one of the last bastions of capitalism and freedom in an unfree world.

This image is an **illusion**. Switzerland in reality is a socialist state run by cartels. Confidentiality laws can be, and are, frequently set aside. Switzerland has entered fully into the global surveillance infrastructure.

Switzerland has also sacrificed its sovereignty. Under U.S. pressure, it adopted strict laws against insider trading and money laundering. It is also a signatory to numerous treaties authorizing the setting aside of secrecy, including the U.S.-Swiss Mutual Legal Assistance Treaty, the U.S.-Swiss Income Tax Treaty, the Council of Europe Laundering Convention, and the U.N. Vienna Narcotics Convention.

These treaties may not only apply to "mutually recognized crimes," but to all crimes. For instance, while the U.S.-Swiss MLAT generally requires dual criminality, Switzerland has no racketeering statute. Yet RICO appears to apply in Switzerland.

U.S. authorities have considerable success in penetrating Swiss bank secrecy when investigating tax offenses that allegedly involve "organized crime." This has occurred even when such allegations have later been found to be unsupported by evidence. For instance, in *United States v. Sturman*, 951 F.2d 1466 (6th Cir. 1991), U.S. authorities claimed they were investigating the defendant's involvement in organized crime, when in reality a tax investigation was underway. Swiss authorities released the requested records based on this assertion. Using this data, Sturman was convicted of tax evasion.

In *Sturman*, the Federal Appeals Court ruled:

Any misconduct by Government in submitting to Swiss government allegedly false statements linking defendant to organized crime, in order to obtain Swiss bank records pursuant to mutual assistance treaty, was not so serious as to require reversal of defendant's conviction, in that defendant suffered no identifiable constitutional injury.

In addition, while the U.S.-Swiss MLAT does not provide for splitting seized assets, in practice, the Swiss accept such commissions for monies they seize. The United States has paid more than $30 million in forfeiture commissions to the Swiss government.

Even where Swiss secrecy is still upheld, penalties for its violation are not proportional to punishments that can be imposed for violations of U.S. laws such as the Bank Secrecy Act. The stakes are much higher for a U.S. person not complying with BSA reporting requirements than for a Swiss person making an unauthorized release of account records.

Switzerland is also wired into the global surveillance infrastructure. It is well documented that during the 1980s, copies of a "bugged" computer program were sold to several Swiss banks. This program, Inslaw's PROMIS, allegedly contains a "trap door" permitting U.S. intelligence agencies direct access to Swiss bank account information.

Switzerland should not be dismissed out of hand for persons seeking privacy and asset protection. Swiss insurance contracts, for instance, offer privacy and asset protection against non-governmental litigants that may be superior to any instrument in common law. Chapter 4 discusses foreign insurance contracts in greater detail.

Austria

Austria is widely touted as a secrecy haven, but as in Switzerland, secrecy can be lifted for an increasingly long list of alleged crimes. Unlike Switzerland, prosecution of secrecy violations must be initiated by the depositor, not the government. The victim of a secrecy breach has only **six weeks** after it occurs to bring suit. Unless a depositor somehow learns of the breach within that time, he would have no knowledge of it and thus no opportunity to prosecute the case. Even if he did, all documents must be translated into German and attorneys paid in advance. Should the breach lead to seizure of the funds, the depositor might not have funds available to prosecute the case, or other recourse.

Austria is also a signatory of the U.N. Vienna Narcotics Convention, although it has not ratified the Council of Europe Laundering Convention. The U.S.-Austrian Tax Treaty requires assistance not only where tax fraud is suspected (as in Switzerland), but for ordinary tax evasion. Moreover, the U.S.-Austrian MLAT, once ratified, will not require dual criminality to be invoked.

One Austrian relationship often touted as a privacy strategy is the *sparbuch*, or anonymous passbook account. However, the use of such accounts has already been restricted, and their abolition is a priority of the Financial Action Task Force and the European Community. If abolished, will sparbuch holders be permitted to redeem their investments anonymously?

Chapter 4

COUNTER-SURVEILLANCE?

Expectations of Privacy

Global surveillance and forfeiture places many persons at risk merely through the routine exercise of their business or profession. Those who wish to protect their estate must relocate assets to instruments outside their domestic jurisdiction. This requires that they engage in **capital flight**, defined by Lessard & Williamson in *Capital Flight and Third World Debt*, as "capital outflow that is viewed as disadvantageous by the national authorities" (p. 2).

The U.S. government's sweeping *in personam* jurisdiction (i.e., jurisdiction over persons) negates any expectation that capital flight by U.S. persons can be private. Yet without privacy from government, there can be no asset protection from government.

English Common Law

In English Common Law, there is **no** expectation of privacy. Zweigert & Kotz state in *An Introduction to Comparative Law* that: "The English courts have not yet recognized any ...general right to the protection of one's privacy" (vol. 2, p. 399). Indeed, according to the *Washington Post*:

> Britain bristles with video surveillance cameras—more per capita, according to some estimates, than any other country. They scrutinize parking garages, housing developments department stores and offices, all in the interest of fighting crime. They also watch couples intertwined in office stockrooms, elevators and cars; women undressing in department store changing rooms; and husbands and wives in domestic disputes.

Promoters of Crown offshore financial centers may claim that these jurisdictions offer **financial** privacy, referring to the "common law contractual duty of secrecy" due a client and to specific **statutory** guarantees of confidentiality.

According to Campbell in *International Banking Secrecy*, this duty is defined in common law by the decision of the English Court of Appeals in *Tournier v. National Provincial and Union Bank of England* [1924] 1 K.B. 461. While *Tournier* declared that banks have a duty to maintain the privacy of client records, the **sweeping exceptions** to this duty the Court noted tend to **nullify** confidentiality.

Tournier gives banks discretion to release information where disclosure is under compulsion of law; where there is a duty to the public to disclose; where the interests of the bank require disclosure; or where the disclosure is made by the express or implied consent of the customer. *International Banking Secrecy* lists those jurisdictions whose decisional law explicitly refers to *Tournier* as the legal basis for financial privacy as Australia, the Bahamas, British Virgin Islands, Canada, the Cayman Islands, Gibraltar, Hong Kong, Ireland, the Isle of Man, New Zealand and Singapore.

Even where a jurisdiction inheriting English Common Law enacts a statute that establishes **criminal penalties** for persons who fail to preserve secrecy, such statute establishes no civil right. This was made plain by the Cayman Court of Appeal, interpreting the Cayman's Confidential Relationships (Preservation) Law in *Bertoli v. Malone* (1990-91 CILR 58):

> The ... Law ... established no civil right. It relied on the common law principle that a duty of confidentiality did not exist where there was disclosure under compulsion of law and it recognized that the circumstances under which this compulsion might be exerted could ... be changed without derogation from the principle.
>
> Consequently, any breach of confidentiality to which the appellants could lay claim could only derive from the common law position with respect to the limits and qualifications of the contractual duty of secrecy implied in relation to banker and customer ... **The appellants never had a right to confidentiality in respect of information required in criminal proceedings.**

U.S. Common Law

U.S. Common Law defines a narrow expectation of privacy under the Bill of Rights. That expectation does not include any reasonable belief that capital flight will be private.

> The right of the people to be secure in their persons, houses, papers and effects, against unreasonable searches and seizures, shall not be violated, and no warrants shall issue, but upon probable cause... (Fourth Amendment)
>
> No person shall ... be compelled in any criminal case to be a witness against himself (Fifth Amendment).

Attorneys Ellen Alderman and Carolyn Kennedy define the extraordinarily narrow bounds of this expectation under U.S. Common Law in *The Right to Privacy*. Wherever he is, a person may exercise his Fifth Amendment "right to silence," although, "We have no reasonable expectation that our physical appearance, voice, handwriting, or fingerprints will remain private" (Alderman & Kennedy, p. 25). Moreover,

> The Supreme Court has rejected the notion that an encounter with police is so inherently intimidating that people cannot be expected to walk away. The Court has long held that a refusal to cooperate with the police does not justify detaining or arresting someone. Furthermore, the Court assumes that we know this.
>
> Therefore, the Court has declared that ... police officers may approach an individual without any suspicion whatever, ask potentially incriminating questions, and request to search the individual's luggage "so long as the officers do not convey a message that compliance with their requests is required." It is up to the individual to simply walk away if he does not want his bags searched (Alderman & Kennedy, p. 34).

provides absolutely no protection for the contents of private papers of any kind."
United States v. Doe, 465 U.S. 605, 618 (1984). Records prepared voluntarily or by compulsion for a non-testimonial purpose (e.g., records maintained for tax purposes), if subpoenaed, **must** be disclosed to the government under threat of contempt.

Nor may a person refuse to release to the government **foreign** records or **foreign** property under his control. *Doe v. United States*, 487 U.S. 201 (1988) and *United States v. Sellers, et al.*, 848 F.Supp. 73 (E.D.La. 1994). A court may also require U.S. custodians to release or have released such records or property, even if the records or property are not in the custodian's possession. Consent is compelled. If refused, the individual or custodian may be held in contempt of court, fined and/or imprisoned. *United States v. Bank of Nova Scotia*, 691 F.2d 1384 (11th Cir. 1982), *cert. denied*, 462 U.S. 1119 (1983). Indeed, U.S. courts have imposed sanctions even when non-compliance for the court order is based upon a foreign court order not to produce the requested documents. *In re Marc Rich & Co.*, 707 F.2d 663 (2d Cir. 1984).

Additional circumstances under which U.S. courts may assert *in personam* jurisdiction include, according to *International Estate Planning*, include:

(1) physical presence before the court or in its territorial jurisdiction; (2) consent to jurisdiction or his **implied** consent; (3) domicile; i.e., his permanent home; (4) contacts, even minimal contacts; 5) intentionally obtaining benefits; or (6) having an "effect" in the territorial jurisdiction of the court. Sec. 9.04

Indeed, the courts have ruled that a U.S. person investing outside the United States abandons virtually all constitutional protection relating to the disclosure of information relating to such investments or their confiscation. Such investors "assume the risk" of depositing their money in a foreign country. Since "traditional domestic investigatory methods" are relatively ineffective abroad, the public interest in combating international crime justifies a lesser standard of protection. *In re Air Crash in Bali, Indonesia on April 22, 1974*, 684 F.2d 1301 (9th Cir. 1982).

Even a foreign person residing in a foreign nation has no legitimate expectation that U.S. law enforcement will not forcibly enter his home or office, seize his property, kidnap and/or torture him, and forcibly repatriate him to the United States. This is the case even if such actions violate the foreign person's domestic law and/or U.S. treaty obligations. *United States v. Alvarez-Machain*, 112 S.Ct. 2188 (1992).

Curtilage

A U.S. person's expectation of privacy is restricted to

a certain zone of privacy around the home that we can reasonably expect to reserve for ourselves. That space, along with our house, is protected by the Fourth Amendment. Under the law, this area is known as the "curtilage." To most of us, it is known as our yard ... [unless] we have a really big yard (Alderman & Kennedy, pp. 25-26).

The Supreme Court defines **curtilage** as "the area [that] harbors the intimate activity associated with the sanctity of a man's home and the privacy of life." *United States v. Dunn*, 480 U.S. 294, 300 (1987). **A person may not assert a constitutional right to privacy outside the curtilage.**

The expectation of privacy is thus limited to personal activities **in one's own home** and interactions with others there. A person may therefore refuse consent for a warrantless search of his home unless there is probable cause that evidence of a crime is being destroyed. *Vale v. Louisiana*, 399 U.S. 30 (1970). However, "aerial surveillance did not constitute a Fourth Amendment search, ... [including] using high-tech devices to detect things **not** visible to the naked eye" (Alderman & Kennedy, p. 26).

Even within the curtilage, the act of asserting one's constitutional right to refuse a warrantless search may provide probable cause to obtain a search warrant. In one case, a homeowner was asked by police for permission to search his home. He refused and declined to talk to police until an attorney was present, and became, according to police reports, "nervous" and "loud and aggressive." Police presented this "evidence" to a county magistrate and obtained a search warrant for the home. Based on the results of the search, the homeowner was tried and convicted on criminal charges. A U.S. Federal Appeals Court ruled that while the warrant was improperly issued, police could rely upon it to search the home and that evidence seized in the search was admissible in a criminal trial. *United States v. Hyppolite*, 65 F.3d 1151 (4th Cir. 1995), *cert. denied*, 116 S.Ct. 1158 (1996).

Outside the curtilage, *in personam* jurisdiction reaches U.S. persons in all places, activities and transactions. There is **no** expectation of privacy and **no** restriction on the gathering and maintenance of information and intelligence by the government or informants.

No expectation of privacy extends to documents or other items once they leave the curtilage. For instance,

> The Supreme Court has decided that trash placed out for collection is **not** protected by the Fourth Amendment. Instead, we "knowingly expose it to the public" and "voluntarily turn it over to third parties" ...[Even if trash is shredded,] for constitutional purposes...trash is trash (Alderman & Kennedy, p. 28).

Records maintained outside the curtilage have no expectation of privacy:

> When the Fourth Amendment was drafted, one's "papers" were likely to comprise a record of one's life. They were also likely to be stored ... in the home. Today, our papers are just as likely to comprise a record of our lives ... But ... we have a paper trail that leads right **out the door** and into a multitude of offices and institutions (Alderman & Kennedy, p. 27).

With respect to telephone records, the Supreme Court held:

> "We doubt that people in general entertain any actual expectation of privacy in the [telephone] numbers they dial. [The person appealing] voluntarily con-

veyed information to the telephone company" every time he dialed his phone. Therefore, he "assumed the risk that the company would reveal to police the numbers he dialed" (Alderman & Kennedy, p. 27).

The **contents** of telephonic communications fare little better. Statutes extending an expectation of privacy to such communications are riddled with exceptions (Chapter 2), and technology permits the government to routinely evade these restrictions without detection.

Spencer in *States of Injustice* writes:

> The digitization of telephone networks means that telephone tapping no longer requires a physical connection to be made to the telephone line. Tapping can be performed remotely by sending signals to the exchange switching system, and this can even in principle be done **from another country.** The U.K.'s British Telecom assists the security services and other agencies in this activity (p. 173).

U.S. law prohibits warrantless taps only by **domestic** government agencies. **Foreign** agencies such as MI-5 (Crown Intelligence) may originate warrantless taps and share the contents with U.S. intelligence agencies. According to Bamford in *The Puzzle Palace*, such sharing is mandated by international agreement (p. 372).

A 1997 report from Statewatch reveals that the FBI and European Union (EU) are creating a **global wiretapping system.** EU members, Canada and the FBI have signed a Memorandum of Understanding that calls for real-time access to all telecommunications; access to related call data; information pinpointing the location of cellular telephone users; instant decryption of encrypted communications; and monitoring of communications in jurisdictions that refuse to cooperate in these efforts. The constitutions of many EU nations guarantee telecommunications privacy. How global wiretapping will be reconciled with these guarantees remains to be seen.

The vulnerability of encrypted communications requires further emphasis. According to Computer Crime" in the *FBI Law Enforcement Bulletin:*

> RSA-129 is a 129-digit number created in 1977 by the developers of an encryption system said to be "provably secure." The creators of the code estimated that it would take 40 quadrillion years to factor the number using the methods available in the late 1970s ... In 1994, a mere 17 years later, a group of 600 Internet volunteers cracked the code.

The successful attack on one RSA-129 key does not mean that every such key will be successfully attacked, only that a determined attack can succeed. Moreover, RSA keys can be 1,000 digits long or longer, making them billions of times more secure than RSA-129. But given the rapid progress in computer technology, there is no guarantee they will remain "provably secure."

Similarly, no warrant is required to monitor **correspondence.** While the **contents** of correspondence are protected by statute, it is simple for the government to secretly and illegally open and inspect the contents of any envelope or parcel. Nor is there an expectation of privacy to the envelope or packaging in which correspondence is sent. In a "mail cover," the government may legally record addresses, handwriting styles, etc. **without** obtaining a warrant (Chapter 2).

Affiliations and financial transactions of persons active in U.S. and U.K. political movements are of particular interest to U.S. and Crown intelligence. Among other groups, surveillance is maintained in the United States on "patriot" and "militia" organizations; in the United Kingdom, on the Irish Republican Army and loyalist paramilitary groups. The July 8, 1996 *London Daily Telegraph* asks:

> What proportion of the growing U.S. militia movement is now composed of government informants? A tenth? A fifth? A third? It is hard to tell but events over the past few weeks have shown that the self-styled "patriot" groups are deeply penetrated by the authorities. It is difficult to know whether an armed militia is an authentic group of citizens or a front organization of the federal agencies, or a cross between the two.

Journalist Larry O'Hara, in *Turning Up the Heat: MI-5 After the Cold War*, presents evidence suggesting that MI-5, the CIA, and the FBI share intelligence gathered from "controlled" addresses and build lists of persons sympathetic to or affiliated with such organizations, or who subscribe to their publications (pp. 69-70). O'Hara says it is "unquestionable" that such movements are "full of spook assets" (p. 71).

Common law governments have developed an elaborate surveillance infrastructure to monitor personal affiliations, credit relationships and financial transactions. This infrastructure includes thousands of laws requiring the retrieval of all domestic financial transactions and an array of paid and unpaid informants gathering such intelligence. Its existence **cannot** be challenged on constitutional grounds. See, e.g., *California Bankers Association v. Shultz*, 416 U.S. 21 (1974).

According to the Feb. 24, 1994 issue of *Intelligence Newsletter*, the most sophisticated financial intelligence agency is the **Financial Crimes Enforcement Network (FinCEN)** (Chapter 2). FinCEN collects and analyzes data **globally** to unearth financial transactions of criminals and suspected criminals. Appendix B contains Forms 4789, 4790, and 8300, the core of FinCEN's cash transactions database.

Databases accessible to FinCEN include those maintained by the IRS; FBI; Drug Enforcement Administration; Secret Service; Customs Service; Postal Service; Census Bureau; CIA; National Security Agency (and thus Crown intelligence); Defense Intelligence Agency; Bureau of Alcohol, Tobacco, and Firearms; the Immigration and Naturalization Service; National Security Council; the Federal Deposit Insurance Corporation; the Comptroller of the Currency; the Federal Reserve; and the State Department's Bureau of Intelligence and Research.

Private databases to which FinCEN has access include Dun and Bradstreet; LEXIS-NEXIS (real estate ownership, court decisions, and public filings); Metromail (nationwide name, address, and telephone file, Postal Service address forwarding data, and change of address records filed with major publishers); and Prentice-Hall Online (nationwide name, address, and telephone file, Postal Service address forwarding data, and change of address records filed with major publishers); and Prentice-Hall Online (officers, directors and partners of U.S. corporations and limited partnerships, Uniform Commercial Code filings, bankruptcy filings, tax liens, judgments, and notices of default or foreclosure).

Outside the United States, FinCEN has an information sharing agreement with Interpol that gives it access to Interpol's worldwide criminal tracking data. Other nations have developed **financial intelligence units** and have information exchange agreements with FinCEN. They include TRACFIN (France), NCIN (the Crown of the United Kingdom) and AUSTRAC (Australia). FinCEN is building similar alliances with authorities in Japan, Italy, Switzerland and more than two dozen other jurisdictions, many of them offshore financial centers.

FinCEN's proposed "Deposit Tracking System" will instantaneously track transactions in every U.S. bank and credit card account and create a continuously updated financial dossier on every person with a U.S. bank account or credit card.

FinCEN may be avoided only through cash transactions and foreign investing. However, it is a crime to structure cash transactions to avoid FinCEN (e.g., to engage in a series of related cash transactions below the $10,000 reporting threshold). There is no requirement that the cash be associated with any crime for a structuring conviction to occur. *United States v. Scanio*, 900 F.2d 485 (2d Cir. 1990). Cash or other property involved in transactions designed to avoid FinCEN are subject to confiscation, as the property itself, even if legitimately earned, is defined as the **object of a crime**. *United States v. $145,139*, 18 F.3d 73 (2d Cir.) *cert. denied*, *Etim v. United States*, 115 S.Ct. 72 (1994). Indeed, according to Pratt & Petersen, "Civil Forfeiture in the Second Circuit,"

> Through the Byzantine world of [civil] forfeiture law, Congress and the courts have implicitly created a rebuttable presumption that the possession of large amounts of cash is *per se* evidence of illegal activity (p. 666).

U.S. persons who have signature or other authority over a "foreign bank, brokerage, or other financial account" must report such accounts to FinCEN annually. Failure to do so is an offense subject to confiscation of the account or equivalent property and five years imprisonment and a $500,000 fine for **each** incident of non-filing.

Attorney-Client Privilege

Even **privileged** professional relationships have little or no expectation of privacy. Professionals who must disclose client information to the government almost on demand include accountants, **attorneys**, brokers, physicians—virtually every regulated business or profession. **U.S. persons should not rely on "attorney-client privilege" or any other promise of confidentiality from domestic advisors to formulate a capital flight strategy for asset protection.**

According to "Protect Yourself and Your Fees," a publication written for attorneys practicing in the United States:

> The enactment and expansion of forfeiture and money laundering statutes ... have spread before prosecutors a smorgasbord of opportunities to insert themselves into fee transactions between lawyer and client ... **There may simply be no way for an attorney to accept a fee** in certain circumstances without putting himself or herself, the client, or the fee at risk (p. 30).

Attorneys who allegedly violate these statutes or represent clients in forfeiture cases risk having their fees confiscated. This may result in

> a lawyer [advising] his client to accept an agreement entailing a harsher prison sentence but no forfeiture—even where contrary to the client's interests—in an effort to preserve the lawyer's fee (D. Smith, Sec. 13.04).

In "What Every Practitioner Needs to Know About Criminal Exposure in the Everyday Practice of Law," former federal prosecutors Axelrod *et al.* write that attorneys practicing in the United States may face "criminal liability [even] on the provision of routine legal services" (p. 66). Attorneys should "conduct client conferences as if each client is an undercover agent or a government informant (as he or she may be)" (p. 69).

Federal statutes attorneys may violate in preparing a flight capital strategy include: aiding and abetting (18 U.S.C. 2); conspiracy (to defraud the United States) (18 U.S.C. 371); bankruptcy fraud (18 U.S.C. 152); mail fraud (18 U.S.C. 1341); obstruction of justice (18 U.S.C. 1503, 1505); false statements (18 U.S.C. 1001) and money laundering (18 U.S.C. 1956, 1957). Most of these offenses also constitute "predicate offenses" under the racketeering (RICO) statutes (18 U.S.C. 1961, et seq.).

Criminal convictions against attorneys have resulted from their efforts to facilitate cash or other domestic or foreign financial transactions without filing required disclosure reports (Axelrod, *et al.*, p. 65) or merely providing erroneous advice regarding compliance and reporting requirements. *Wallace v. United States*, 281 F.2d 656 (1960) *(reversed on procedural grounds)*. Attorneys are also subject to "sting" operations authorized by U.S. (and now U.K.) legislation that may lure them into violating laundering laws.

To avoid criminal liability, attorneys must insert language in asset protection instruments to insure compliance with U.S forfeiture orders. Rosen's *Asset Protection Planning*, written for attorneys who prepare such instruments, recommends language defining circumstances under which trustees of "asset protection trusts" are to convey trust assets to U.S. regulatory agencies (Sec. V(B)).

According to Axelrod, *et al.*, the reality that attorneys may be held criminally accountable in their representation of clients seeking asset protection has devastated attorney-client privilege:

> Meticulous recordkeeping provides the attorney's only protection. Lawyers ... who suspect that clients may be withholding information should carefully document their inquiries and the clients' responses ... Ethics rules ordinarily permit

counsel to use such information in their own defense, even if it otherwise would be privileged ... Most of the lawyer's file is vulnerable to a grand jury subpoena when counsel is suspected of criminal activity (pp. 28-29, 69).

Other circumstances in which attorney-client privilege may be lost under U.S. law include where: (1) the attorney is a participant in his client's illegal activity, even if the attorney is not aware of such participation; (2) **the attorney becomes an informant against his client**; (3) pre-existing documents are turned over to an attorney; (4) the court subpoenas a client's name and address or the client's fee arrangements; (5) the client testifies that he acted on the advice of his attorney; (6) the client reviews privileged documents prior to testimony; (7) **testimony is gathered through electronic eavesdropping of conversations between attorney and client**, if the intrusion relates only to particular charges against the client; or (8) a bankruptcy trustee is deemed to have control over and power to waive the privilege. Many of these exceptions and others are discussed in Larkin in "Attorney-Client Privilege."

The informant exception to attorney-client privilege deserves special emphasis. To receive immunity from criminal prosecution and/or to obtain lucrative commissions, attorneys may become informants against their clients or other attorneys. According to Wisotsky in *A Society of Suspects*, the U.S. Department of Justice has "publicly defended using attorneys as informants as a 'perfectly valid' law enforcement tool" (p. 12).

Attorneys or other informants providing information leading to most forfeitures are eligible for commissions up to 25 percent of the amount confiscated, with a maximum commission of $150,000 (Chapter 2). Burnham's *Above the Law* documents the Department of Justice's misuse of informants and "secret deals, political fixes, and misadventures."

The situation is similar in other jurisdictions inheriting English Common Law. In the United Kingdom, for instance, it is a crime for all persons, **including attorneys**, not to inform NCIN of any suspicion of illegal financial transactions. Radmore, *et al.* state, "It is provided ... that any disclosure ... will not be treated as a breach of the solicitor's duty of confidence." (p. 156). This principle applies in all common law jurisdictions. **Persons doing business in Crown offshore financial centers should assume all financial transactions are monitored by NCIN and the results shared with FinCEN.**

Investments

Many persons concerned with the virtually **unlimited** scope of *in personam* jurisdiction seek protection from governments through certain investments domiciled in the United States, Crown offshore financial centers or in Switzerland. Promoters claim such investments avoid surveillance and forfeitures. **These claims are false.**

Investments regulated by the Crown or the State, such as bank accounts, securities accounts, insurance contracts, mutual funds, and other regulated investments with regulated companies are particularly vulnerable. For instance, the U.S. Supreme Court has held that a person establishing a bank account "takes the risk, in revealing his affairs to another, that the information will be conveyed by the person to the government." *United States v. Miller*, 425 U.S. 435, 442 (1976). Once he conveys financial information to a third party, he may not object to its disclosure, "even on the understanding that the communication was confidential." *SEC v. Jerry T. O'Brien, Inc.*, 467 U.S. 735, 736 (1984).

In the Crown offshore financial center of the Isle of Man, an insurance company claims that its single-premium variable benefit life assurance policy "offers immediate law suit and privacy benefits. Assets held within a life insurance policy cannot normally be claimed as settlement by a creditor." Many purchasers believe that this protection extends to government surveillance and/or forfeiture. **It does not**, although some promoters allow investors to believe otherwise.

Even unregistered common law instruments remain regulated by common law. Trusts in the offshore financial center of Jersey need not be registered with the Crown. However, the choice of law of a Jersey trust is necessarily that of Jersey. As Jersey law is common law, such a trust could not repel a confiscation order.

U.S. **retirement assets** are also vulnerable, despite the apparent protection provided by the Employee Retirement Income Security Act (ERISA) to ERISA-qualified pension plans (but **not** to Individual Retirement Accounts). Claims by the IRS take precedence over the ERISA exemptions, particularly where a bankruptcy petition is filed after a tax lien. *Ameritrust v. Derakhshan*, 92 CV-0931 (N.D. Ohio 1993). U.S. courts under the relation-back theory of forfeiture would likely honor claims by government that "tainted" assets in ERISA-qualified plans became subject to confiscation at the time such assets were contributed.

Social Security payments are subject to termination for crimes committed by the recipient, including payments to the recipient's innocent spouse. This is true even if conduct for which payments are terminated was legal at the time it occurred. *Ex post facto* laws that impose penalties for acts committed before a statute is enacted prohibiting them are prohibited by the U.S. Constitution and the Universal Declaration of Human Rights, but a termination of Social Security payments in this situation has been upheld by the U.S. Supreme Court. *Fleming v. Nestor*, 363 U.S. 603 (1960).

Contracts With the Government

The foregoing discussion is not intended to discourage persons who risk confiscation of their property in the ordinary course of their business or profession, or who merely wish to preserve family assets from formulating a flight capital strategy for privacy and asset protection. Indeed, such a strategy, properly executed, is the **only** way to protect at least a portion of an estate.

Most attorneys practicing in the United States approach asset protection as a way to protect their clients from lawsuits, not from government. They will help erect legal barriers between assets and unknown future creditors. However, given sufficient funding by a "determined creditor" (i.e., the government), many if not all such legal barriers may be circumvented. Creating these barriers may require complex plans with high annual maintenance fees and extensive reporting to the IRS and other agencies. (See Forms 926, 1041, 3520, 3520-A, 5471, and 8621 in Appendix B). Depending on the plan's structure and the nature of its income, filing requirements for other forms may be triggered, including Forms 1042, 1065, and 8804.)

Limited partnerships, corporations and other "statutory entities" have been widely promoted in recent years as providing asset protection and privacy. These benefits are **greatly exaggerated**.

An Act is required to create a "statutory entity" such as a corporation or limited partnership, in any jurisdiction. The Act provides benefits to the entity, which may include limited liability from the entity's creditors, the ability to issue securities, and recognition before the jurisdiction's courts. To obtain these benefits, the entity must comply with obligations of the Act and conduct itself in strict accordance with its own Memoranda of Association, Articles of Incorporation, etc.

Failure to comply with these requirements may result in unlimited liability to creditors or the entity being dissolved. In some offshore financial centers (e.g., the Cook Islands), this may be done administratively, without a judicial hearing, with no right of appeal, and with no recourse against the government.

Persons who create, operate or invest in such entities enter into a contract with the government. The contract exists only because the government allows it to exist, and can be redefined by statute anytime. **A government cannot declare an individual not to exist, but it can strip a corporation or other statutory entity from its register**.

In some jurisdictions, statutes may extend limited privacy and/or asset protection benefits to statutory entities, although these benefits may be withdrawn anytime. In other jurisdictions, such protections are expressly denied.

For instance, U.S. statutes that provide limited privacy rights for natural persons, such as the Privacy Act (1974) and the Right to Financial Privacy Act (1978) specifically exclude corporations and other statutory entities from coverage (Chapter 2).

A financial newsletter recently promoted a "Complete Wealth Protection Program" through which buyers would learn "the sure-fire way to hermetically seal your cash and assets against **any and every threat**." The program promotes instruments such as limited partnerships and "asset protection trusts." Many attendees interpret the "any and every threat" claim literally.

However, these instruments offer **no protection** against government surveillance and/or confiscation. Moreover, buyers have no constitutional grounds on which to object to disclosure of records relating to their purchase. **Persons seeking asset protection from government should avoid such programs and the instruments they promote.**

Corporation Acts

The asset protection and privacy advantages of corporations are essentially **non-existent.** Corporation Acts create this statutory entity and define its benefits and responsibilities. These benefits generally include **limitations of personal liability**: 1) for shareholders, primarily from creditors of the corporation in its unwinding or bankruptcy; and 2) for officers and directors, from claims against them while working within the narrow scope of their authority.

There is no limitation of personal liability when the officers and/or directors of a corporation exceed their authority (*ultra vires*). *Ultra vires* actions include **recklessness, negligence** and **breach of duty**. Even if a Corporation Act stipulates that officers and directors are not liable for their "lawful acts," a person acting in a reckless or negligent manner may not convince a court he was acting lawfully.

For instance, an officer or director is **personally liable** to shareholders if his *ultra vires* acts bring loss to the corporation and to anyone who suffers an injury or loss due to such acts. Similarly, a majority shareholder is **personally liable** to a minority shareholder, if the majority shareholder (particularly if also an officer or director) adversely affected the corporation by *ultra vires* actions.

Nor is personal liability limited if a corporation is deemed not to have an independent existence. For instance, a creditor may claim that the officers and directors of a corporation act for their own benefit, not that of the corporation. Unless the officers and directors can document that virtually **every** decision made in that capacity benefited or could benefit the corporation, the corporation may be deemed a sham. Proving independent existence is particularly challenging for small businesses organized as corporations. One person typically holds **all** the shares **and** serves as the sole officer and director. It may be difficult to prove that a sole shareholder-officer-director is acting on behalf of the corporation, not for his own benefit.

Rights extended corporations exist only under statute. For instance, in *United States v. Raniere*, No. 95-162 (AJL), D.N.J. (July 24, 1995) the custodian of corporate documents was an officer of a company subject of an IRS summons. The court ruled that the fifth amendment privilege against self-incrimination did not operate to protect him from producing the corporate records. Further, corporations organized in the United States are excluded from all federal privacy legislation and must file an annual **balance sheet** with their tax returns. Payments of **dividends** by a corporation must also be disclosed to the IRS along with the Social Security Number of the recipient.

Some states, such as Nevada, permit corporations to issue **bearer shares** that are widely touted by promoters as providing significant asset protection and privacy. These claims are **not** true. **As long as the corporation remains under U.S. jurisdiction, no real privacy is possible using this technique.** An investigator may obtain ownership information through a subpoena of the corporation's tax return, on which 50 percent or greater shareholders and the names and Social Security numbers of persons receiving dividend payments must be disclosed. Shareholders may also be identified in public records.

Limited Partnership Acts

The asset protection and privacy benefits of limited partnerships are also greatly exaggerated, particularly in relation to claims by and disclosure to **governments**. This is particularly true of a form of limited partnership recently used as an estate planning technique to hold family interests—the so-called "Family Limited Partnership."

Limited Partnership Acts define limited partnerships, which consist of limited partners with liability limited to their initial investment and at least one general partner who assumes unlimited liability for the partnership's activities. They are distinguished from **general partnerships** in which **all** partners have unlimited liability. **A partnership agreement** establishes a limited partnership, with the agreement stipulating specific objectives for the partnership.

Limited partnerships were unknown in English law until authorized by statute in 1907. However, the concept of limited liability for investors in a cooperative venture has a long history in **civil law**, and the first U.S. limited partnership statutes were derived from the French Code.

State Limited Partnership Acts are adapted from the Uniform Limited Partnership Act (1916), Revised Uniform Limited Partnership Act (1976), and/or the 1985 amendments to the Revised Act. Under these Acts, a limited partner is not liable beyond his original contribution if the business activities carried out by the limited partnership fail, and the partnership is unwound. Other provisions of limited partnership law are generally derived from **general partnership** law, as defined by state partnership acts adapted from the U.S. Uniform Partnership Act.

However, a limited partner may become liable beyond his contribution if he assumes a management role in the partnership; the partnership is not in substantial compliance with statutory requirements; or he also serves as a general partner.

Such liability may include criminal and quasi-criminal sanctions, such as fines and punitive damages, and be **joint and several** against both the partnership and individual partners. This means that a partner with a relatively small investment, but with deep pockets, may be forced to pay an entire judgment for which other partners are primarily liable. Even partners who do not conspire to conduct an illegal act may be criminally liable if "intent" is not required to obtain a conviction. *Ex Parte Casperson*, P.2d 88 (1945).

Charging Orders. All partnerships, limited or general, are presumed to have a business purpose. The Uniform Partnership Act defines a partnership as "an association of two or more persons to carry on as co-owners a business for profit."

To prevent disruption to an **ongoing partnership business**, the English Partnership Act (1890) provides:

Where the judgment or order is against a partner or partners individually, no writ of execution can issue against any of the partnership property, but the creditor may obtain an order charging that partner's interest in the partnership.

This **charging order** concept, which applies to interests in both general and limited partnerships, exists in any jurisdiction inheriting English Common Law. Limited partnership interests held by a trustee in a Crown offshore financial center could potentially be reached with a charging order issued or recognized by that jurisdiction's courts.

The charging order is widely misunderstood. The order requires that any distributions from the partnership to the liable partner be made to the creditor, up to the amount of judgment. A partnership cannot be **forced** to make a distribution.

Promoters often claim that a creditor's inability to force distributions permits a debtor partner to indefinitely avoid creditor claims. But the Uniform Limited Partnership Act provides that the charging order remedy "shall not be deemed exclusive of others which may exist" and that a court may make "all other orders, directions, and inquiries which the circumstances of the case may require." **Such orders may include garnishment, execution and foreclosure of the debtor partner's partnership interest.** *Klein v. Klein*, 81 A.2d 775 (1981).

These measures may be imposed if the court finds the charging order is unlikely to result in the creditor being paid in a reasonable time and if stronger measures will not adversely affect innocent, unrelated, non-debtor partners or interfere with the limited partnership's ongoing business. **Such measures may be enforced even if the partnership agreement prohibits sale or assignment.** *Tupper v. Kroc*, 494 P.2d 1275 (1975).

According to the 1991 opinion of the California Appeals Court in *Helman v. Anderson*, 233 Cal.App.3d 840, 284 Cal.Rptr. 830 (1991), all that is necessary for judicial foreclosure to occur is that a debt exist and that the foreclosure not "unduly interfere with partnership business." **Consent by non-liable partners is unnecessary, unless they can show that foreclosure would cause such interference.** This makes the judicial foreclosure and subsequent sale of limited partnership interests potentially as common as other foreclosures.

A few courts have declared that the charging order is the exclusive remedy of a judgment creditor against a liable partner's limited partnership interest. **However, this limitation presumes the partnership is conducting a business.** For instance, in *Evans v. Galardi,* 546 P.2d 313 (1976), the court authorized only a charging order because the partnership was a viable business and the creditor could not demonstrate that the charging order would not satisfy the debt.

If the limited partnership is used to hold family interests, including investment assets and perhaps the family residence, it is difficult to argue that an ongoing business will be disrupted. The partnership is designed exclusively to provide tax advantages and asset protection and lacks a trade or business purpose. **Such an entity may not**

even meet the statutory definition of "partnership." What stops the court from applying whatever measures are necessary to recover from the debtor partner(s)?

Other techniques may also be available to collect against a debtor partner. For instance, a bankrupt partner's partnership interest is part of his bankruptcy estate, and thus may be sold by the bankruptcy trustee. *In re Priestly*, 93 B.R. 253 (Bankr. D.N.M. 1988).

Creditors may also seek to recharacterize the limited partnership as another entity. For instance, a common technique to minimize estate tax is to transfer minority limited partnership interests to children, grandchildren or others. However, the IRS may claim that the limited partners have control over their investments and the partnership management as do shareholders in a corporation, and tax the partnership as a corporation. The burden of proof is entirely upon representatives of the estate to demonstrate that the IRS valuation is too high.

Even in a limited partnership carrying out an ongoing business, fraud by the general partner(s) may result in the seizure of assets contributed by innocent partners. In one case, a federal prosecutor seized the assets of a limited partnership because of alleged tax fraud by the general partners. *United States v. Regan*, 858 F.2d 115 (2d Cir. 1988).

Because of the reputation of limited partnerships as being resistant to creditor attack, some creditors will not attack them. In practice, limited partnerships that are carrying out an actual business with diverse ownership may make it more difficult and expensive for a creditor to recover against a debtor partner's partnership interest. However, under U.S. law, limited partnership interests are generally considered **securities**. The more limited partners, the more likely the partnership must comply with disclosure and other requirements of U.S. securities laws.

Even without disclosures required under securities laws, there is little privacy associated with a limited partnership under U.S. law. The names of all general and limited partners must be disclosed to the IRS, and tax paid by the partners on the actual (or imputed) income of the partnership. Names of the general and limited partners are generally on file at the county seat or with the Secretary of State.

Hybrid Limited Partnership-Foreign Trust Structures

In recent years, some attorneys have created structures that combine a U.S. limited partnership with a trust formed in a foreign jurisdiction. The trust is formed in a jurisdiction with laws favoring the preservation of trust assets with respect to creditor claims. In theory, creditors can recover assets only in the foreign jurisdiction.

However, the construction of such structures contradicts their intended use. The U.S. partnership provides U.S. jurisdiction over the combined structure.

In addition, the partnership assets themselves generally remain within U.S. jurisdiction. While in theory **liquid** assets can be transferred outside the United States in the event of creditor attack, the reality is that U.S. courts can issue *ex parte* orders freezing U.S. assets before legal proceedings even begin. Should partnership assets are removed from U.S. jurisdiction once an attack begins, it will be difficult for the general partner(s) to argue that they had by intention and documentation nothing to do with such relocation.

An even more fundamental problem of this combination is that the contracts in this structure conflict. The **same people** have control over the **same assets** in **separate capacities**. The limited partners generally transfer their limited partnership interest to the trustee of the trust. These former limited partners–ordinarily husband and wife–continue to serve as the general partner(s) of the limited partnership. They are also the settlors (grantors), and often the beneficiaries, of the trust.

The effect is not unlike the "Shell Game." Under which shell is the limited partner? The General Partner? The trustee? The settlor? These competing contracts and capacities may lead an astute creditor may challenge the entire structure as a sham. Which contact applies, and when? Who owns what? Which law applies?

Further, the general partner(s)–the husband and/or the wife–generally serve in this capacity **only** until a challenge to the partnership comes about. If this occurs, the partnership agreement typically calls for the trustees, in their capacity as majority limited partners, to dismiss the general partners and dissolve the partnership. What is the business purpose of a partnership that exists only until it undergoes a creditor attack? Such an agreement stands on its head the traditional concept in limited partnership law that the general partners can only be dismissed under very narrow circumstances; fraud, for instance.

A trust formed in an offshore financial center **without** an intervening domestic structure, with assets transferred outside U.S. jurisdiction, will be much less expensive to create and far more likely to withstand creditor attacks. U.S. courts have no jurisdiction over the assets of the trust or its foreign trustee. Any attorney in any Crown offshore financial center can form such a structure for a modest fee.

Tenancy by the Entireties

No discussion of contracts with the government would be complete without a discussion of perhaps the most popular example of "do-it-yourself" asset protection— the use of a common law contract recognized in many states to protect the interests of a married couple in real, and in some cases personal, property.

Tenancy by the entireties is ownership of property, real or personal, tangible and intangible, by a **husband and wife** together. Neither may sell any part of the property so held without the other's consent; each holds an indivisible half interest. The survivor of the marriage is entitled to the entire property.

Most states recognize this form of joint ownership for real property; a few recognize it for personal property as well. Entireties ownership provides creditor protection **for the entire homestead** for an obligation created by **one spouse**. Entireties ownership resembles joint tenancy, but is distinguishable because without statutory authorization or an end to the entireties estate, the property cannot be divided. In states that recognize entireties ownership, it is usually deemed a common law contract that **automatically exists** from the conveyance of property to husband and wife, even if the deed fails to mention it.

In general, a creditor, **even the federal government**, has no greater right than the liable spouse to alienate the property against the wishes of the non-liable spouse. *United States v. 15621 SW 209th Ave.,* 894 F.2d 1511 (11th Cir. 1990). This has been the result even under statutes that specify that forfeiture shall occur "irrespective of any provision of state law." *United States v. 2525 Leroy Lane,* 910 F.2d 343 (6th Cir. 1990).

However, in the event of civil forfeiture, the non-liable spouse has no claim unless the forfeiture statute provides for an **innocent owner** defense, since in a civil forfeiture, "the innocence of the owner is irrelevant." *United States v. Sandini,* 816 F.2d 869 (3rd Cir. 1987). Many forfeiture statutes lack such a provision, such as the one upheld by the Supreme Court in *Bennis v. Michigan,* 116 S.Ct. 994 (1996). Moreover, proving innocent ownership can be an **onerous burden** (Chapter 2).

Further, not all federal circuits recognize tenancy by the entireties as binding "irrespective of any provision of state law." In *United States v. Davenport* (7th Cir., 96-1299, Feb. 11, 1997), the IRS sought to seize a residence owned as entireties property in Illinois, displacing an innocent spouse. Relying on Section 7403(a) of the Internal Revenue Code (Title 26), which "grants no exemption to sale where an innocent party holds an interest in the subject property," the Federal Appeals Court overruled a lower court decision and held that the IRS could seize the property.

Another important exception occurred in a recent Florida bankruptcy case, in which the court ruled that a bankruptcy trustee could liquidate a debtor's interest in alleged entireties property, for the benefit of creditors of only one spouse. *In Re Juan E. Planas,* 199 B.R. 211 (S.D. Fla. 1996). The court ruled as it did in part due to the entireties interest not being recorded properly, and the result may have differed if another factual situation existed. Nonetheless, the decision illustrates the elusive protection of this common law contract.

Entireties ownership is also transitory. Death of the non-liable spouse, or divorce, dissolves the entireties estate and ends any asset protection.

Tenancy by the entireties should not be confused with state **homestead** statutes, which are entirely ineffective against **federal forfeitures**. In 1983, the Supreme Court ruled that the Texas homestead law was preempted by revenue laws permitting a person's home to be seized to satisfy a federal tax lien. *United States v. Rodgers,* 103 S.Ct. 2132. This ruling, cited in hundreds of forfeiture cases, makes **useless** any effort to apply state homestead laws to protect property from federal forfeiture.

Privacy

Persons relying on above ground structures and government-regulated contracts for asset protection also face an even more fundamental problem: **the government can (and does) change the law.**

Schindler's List

The stakes are the ultimate: life or death. Don't say it can't happen: It has. The movie *Schindler's List* provided a sobering reminder. After conquering Poland in 1939, the Nazis required all Jews to register with the authorities. Most did. With this information, the Nazis relocated Jews to the ghettos, seized their property and sent them to death camps. Jews who obeyed the Nazi laws lost everything, including their lives.

The only survivors were those who left Nazi jurisdiction or who violated the Nazi laws, didn't register and illegally hid their wealth in offshore financial centers so it couldn't be confiscated—or that tiny minority who entered into oral contracts with persons such as Oskar Schindler, not relying on the Nazi courts to enforce these contracts, but on the good faith and credit of those individuals.

The *Schindler's List* yardstick is: will this technique or structure protect wealth from a despotic government? This approach demands personal and financial privacy.

This requirement poses an insurmountable problem for U.S. persons who seek asset protection. As noted previously, U.S. Common Law defines **no** expectation of financial privacy. Indeed, it may constitute money laundering for U.S. persons to seek financial privacy and/or protect their assets from government.

The following remarks are for informational purposes only; the author **does not** endorse any asset protection scheme that requires conduct that could be defined as criminal. Its brevity is **un**intentional; for persons who do not wish to do business with the State, options are limited. None are perfect; some may be closed down.

Cash

It remains possible to conduct private financial transactions using cash. Yet as noted earlier, it is a crime to use cash to avoid FinCEN.

Certain transactions subject to the U.S. Bank Secrecy Act must be reported to the IRS, Treasury and/or Customs Department. A transaction or two or more **related** transactions exceeding $10,000 in cash (and in certain cases, other monetary instruments) is reportable. **Any declaration that separate transactions are related makes them treated as a single transaction.**

U.S. **trades, businesses** and **financial institutions** are subject to these requirements. The terms "trade or business" and "financial institutions" are defined broadly. Chapter 2 discusses the Bank Secrecy Act in greater detail.

Two significant **exceptions** to cash reporting apply. The General Instructions for IRS Currency Transaction Reporting Form 8300 for trades and businesses, "Exceptions," state:

> Cash is not required to be reported if it is received ... in a transaction that occurs entirely outside the United States ... [or] in a transaction that is not in the course of a person's trade or business.

For the full text of the general instructions for Form 8300, see Appendix B.

IRS Publication 1544, "Reporting Cash Payments of Over $10,000 (Received in a Trade or Business") provides an example of the second excepted transaction:

> If you own a jewelry store and sell your automobile for more than $10,000 in cash, you would not submit a Form 8300 for that transaction.

Therefore, cash transactions of any size between parties not engaging in a "trade or business" appear non-reportable.

Funding

Moving money internationally leaves a "paper trail" and is **not** private. Once funds are abroad, they may be reclaimed in much greater privacy.

Small amounts of cash and monetary instruments may be moved privately across U.S. borders. U.S. law requires any person transporting, causing to transport, or mailing more than $10,000 in cash or certain cash equivalents, or an equivalent amount of foreign currency, across a U.S. border to declare that fact on Customs Form 4790, "Report of International Transportation of Currency or Monetary Instruments." While making an **unrelated** series of such transactions, each under $10,000, may not constitute "structuring" under the Bank Secrecy Act, this limit makes relocating **significant** assets in this manner impractical.

Form 4790 states:

> **Who Must File**. Each person who physically transports, mails, or ships, or causes to be physically transported, mailed, shipped, or received currency or other monetary instruments in an aggregate amount exceeding $10,000 on any one occasion from the United States to any place outside the United States, or into the United States from any place outside the United States. A transfer of funds through normal banking procedures, which does not involve the physical transportation of currency or monetary instruments, is not required to be reported.

"Monetary instruments" are:

coin or currency of the United States or of any other country, travelers' checks, money orders, investment securities in bearer form or otherwise in such form that title thereto passes upon delivery, and negotiable instruments (except warehouse receipts and bills of lading) in bearer form or in such form that title thereto passes upon delivery.

U.S. Customs strictly enforces these reporting provisions. Customs may seize **all** unreported cash or cash equivalents, including the balance of monies under the reporting limit. *United States v. $11,580,* 454 F.Supp. 376 (M.D. Fla. 1978). Completing Form 4790 inaccurately subjects all assets listed on it to confiscation, no matter how minor the inaccuracy. *United States v. $173,081.04,* 652 F.Supp. 1468 (W.D. Tex. 1987), *modified* 835 F.2d 1141 (5th Cir. 1988), *cert. denied,* 109 S.Ct. 133 (1988). Structuring cross-border cash movements to avoid reporting is a crime and subjects all assets involved in the violation to confiscation. *United States v. Morales-Vasquez,* 919 F.2d 258 (5th Cir. 1990).

Many foreign recipients will not accept cash payments from unknown persons, and may be required to notify government authorities when cash is received.

When moving money, **avoid** U.S. $100s. Counterfeit $100s are widespread, including the newest series with the enlarged portrait. Some hotels, banks and merchants outside the United States refuse $100s. Use $50s or smaller denominations or another currency.

"Monetary instruments" subject to Bank Secrecy Act reporting requirements do not include

> bank checks, travelers' checks and money orders made payable to the order of a named person, which have not been endorsed or which bear restrictive endorsements.

A **restrictive endorsement** is one where a third-party payee is named in the endorsement. The third-party payee may or may not be willing to accept such payment.

A check made payable **directly** to a foreign recipient will eventually "disappear" in the sense that the paper or electronic trail ages. However, banks in all jurisdictions keep records of cleared checks, and a trail is also created through the clearing process.

Certain **valuables** can be used to transport wealth internationally. For instance, numismatic coins and jewelry are not monetary instruments. Once removed from domestic jurisdiction, the valuables may be stored for safekeeping or converted to cash and/or securities.

Accounts receivable can be marketed internationally and funds paid conveyed to a foreign recipient. Names of companies willing to purchase receivables at a discount (**factoring companies**) are published in sources such as *The International Her-*

ald Tribune and the *Financial Times*. This strategy may produce taxable and reportable income.

All non-cash U.S. dollar transactions, wherever they occur, clear through the Federal Reserve. Therefore foreign investments denominated in currencies other than the U.S. dollar more effectively avoid U.S. *in rem* jurisdiction. Such jurisdiction may be exercised as dollar-denominated transactions clear or against property deemed to have facilitated such transactions.

The mere transfer to or through a U.S. bank of the alleged proceeds of a crime or property deemed to facilitate a crime may subject the entire transfer to confiscation. This is true even if neither sender nor recipient are subject to U.S. jurisdiction, and the seized funds represent the proceeds of activity outside U.S. territorial jurisdiction. *United States v. Daccaret*, 6.F.3d 37 (2d Cir. 1993).

The same methods used to fund foreign investments may also be used to reclaim them. **Overseas travel expenses** other than airline travel to or from any point in the United States can also be funded with offshore monies in relative privacy by using a debit card drawn on a non-U.S. financial institution. **Accounts payable** may be settled with offshore monies.

Non-Reportable Foreign Investments

U.S. law requires U.S. persons holding more than $10,000 in one or more "foreign financial accounts" to report their presence on Schedule B, line 11(a) of their federal income tax return, and file a separate information return to Treasury. Schedule B must be completed for the purpose of reporting foreign accounts, even if interest and dividend income is less than the threshold for completing it. "Willful" non-compliance may result in criminal prosecution.

Treasury Form TD F 90-22.1, the "Foreign Bank Account Reporting Form," is submitted to a Treasury Department intelligence center in Detroit and its data conveyed to FinCEN. Instructions for this form read, in part:

> A. **Who Must File a Report.** Each United States person who has a financial interest in or signature authority or other authority over bank, securities, or other financial accounts in a foreign country, which exceeds $10,000 in aggregate value at any time during the calendar year, must report that relationship each calendar year by filing Form TD F 90-22.1 with the Department of the Treasury on or before June 30, of the succeeding year...

> F. **Bank, Financial Account.** The term "bank account" means a savings, demand, checking, deposit, loan, or any other account maintained with a financial institution or other person engaged in the business of banking. It includes certificates of deposit. The term "securities account" means an account maintained with a financial institution or other person who buys, sells, holds, or trades stock or other securities for the benefit of another. The term "other financial account" means any other account maintained with a financial institution or other person who accepts deposits, exchanges or transmits funds, or

acts as a broker or dealer for future transactions in any commodity on (or subject to the rules of) a commodity exchange or association.

Checking "yes" on line 11a and completing Form TD F 90-22.1 raises an unavoidable red flag; a person identifies himself as engaging in international financial transactions. The head of the IRS International Compliance Office has stated that tax returns indicating foreign transactions are **always** reviewed to determine if they warrant further investigation. In a lawsuit where tax returns are subpoenaed, the disclosure of offshore investments may also raise intense interest.

Several types of investments and holdings appear to be excluded from reporting if they are purchased **without** opening a "bank, securities, or other financial account" or using such an account to maintain custody. They include (1) real estate; (2) safekeeping arrangements; (3) insurance policies; and (4) securities.

However, even a mere book entry in a foreign corporation is an "other financial account" within the meaning of Instruction F if the foreign entity transmits or disburses funds or otherwise functions as a bank on behalf of the holder of the "account." *United States v. Clines*, 958 F.2d 1182 (11th Cir. 1992).

Real estate. A U.S. person's holdings of real property in a foreign country are not a "foreign bank, securities, or other financial account" as defined in the instructions for Schedule B of IRS Form 1040 or Treasury Form TD F 90-22.1. However, real estate holdings are generally a matter of public record in the jurisdiction in which they are made. Nor are they investments that can easily be liquidated.

Safekeeping. Valuables or documents purchased outside the United States and placed directly into a non-U.S. **safety deposit box** or **private vault** likewise do not constitute a "foreign bank, securities, or other financial account." Safety deposit boxes are available at many foreign banks. Opening an account may be required to rent one. Such an account may become known to global intelligence agencies such as FinCEN. To avoid having to personally visit the box each time valuables are to be added or removed, the boxholder may give an attorney or other trusted intermediary a limited Power of Attorney or other legal authority necessary to perform this function.

Non-bank safekeeping is also available in many jurisdictions. Such depositories, not being financial institutions, are subject to fewer recordkeeping and disclosure requirements. Some vaults permit anonymous safekeeping arrangements.

Materials held in a safety deposit box or private vault are not ordinarily insured against theft or other loss. Supplemental insurance may be available, but will compromise privacy.

Insurance contracts. Foreign insurance policies do not **appear** to be "foreign bank, securities, or other financial accounts" and are thus **apparently** exempted from annual reporting by U.S. persons. However, U.S. persons purchasing foreign insurance contracts must make a one-time filing of IRS Form 720 and pay a 1-percent excise tax. Under U.S. law, income accumulating within a life insurance contract, single-premium or variable annuity is tax-deferred and non-reportable. This status may not last. Proposals to eliminate tax-free deferral in annuity contacts are before the U.S. Congress.

Insurance contracts are **regulated** contracts issued by **regulated** institutions. In common law jurisdictions, these contracts are subject to confiscation by under Mutual Legal Assistance treaties, other treaties or Crown prerogative. In most civil law countries, confiscation can only occur after a criminal conviction unless otherwise permitted by treaty.

Foreign annuity contracts may be held in a U.S. retirement plan. A **domestic** annuity may be rolled over into a **foreign** annuity in a tax-free exchange. The annuity certificate must remain in the United States. **This makes the contract subject to U.S. *in rem* jurisdiction and essentially eliminates its privacy and asset protection features.** A properly worded contract may make it possible to deal with this problem if a receptive U.S. custodian can be found.

No laws prohibit U.S. investors from buying foreign insurance contracts. No jurisdiction is established if a foreign insurance company merely answers an unsolicited inquiry or accepts an unsolicited investment. Foreign insurance companies will ordinarily respond to inquiries from both U.S. and non-U.S. addresses. All will accept investments in U.S. dollars. Policies denominated in U.S. dollars and other currencies are available.

Most foreign insurance companies will not divulge information without the policyholder's written permission, except in a criminal investigation. However, many U.S. persons purchase foreign insurance policies through domestic referrer networks. These networks are not parties to the annuity contract, receive fees, and maintain lists. The use or misuse of these lists is undeterminable. The lists are also subject to discovery in civil litigation or government surveillance.

Securities. Foreign stocks, bonds, or other securities purchased **directly** from a foreign issuer, without opening an account, do not **appear** to be reportable by a U.S. person as a "foreign bank, securities, or other financial account." They **appear** to remain non-reportable so long as a foreign bank or brokerage account is not used to maintain custody. Purchasing securities in this manner also makes it impossible for governments to enforce a confiscation order through an intermediary. The securities may be kept in a safety deposit box, private vault or other secure location.

Bearer securities are private. An issuer will recognize the person having physical possession of its bearer securities as their owner without further inquiry. Some jurisdictions require issuers to request positive identification of persons redeeming bearer securities, including a taxpayer identification number. Failure to present positive identification may result in the withholding of a portion of principal, interest and dividends, or both.

Non-dividend paying bearer shares and **zero-coupon bonds** avoid presenting shares or coupons to receive dividends or interest payments. Bearer securities valued at more than $10,000 must be declared at U.S. borders.

For persons subject to U.S. taxation, income or gain from securities is taxable, but may be deferrable. The amount of the issuer's security that is held and the nature of the issuer's income or gain determine deferral. U.S. taxpayers are not required to report unrealized capital gains on securities. Annual income deemed earned from zero-coupon bonds is reportable and taxable as are dividends received.

To understand the different tax treatment afforded foreign investments under U.S. law, consider the accounts, shares and mutual funds offered by a foreign bank. A more favorable U.S. tax regime applies to shares (registered or bearer) issued by a foreign bank than shares of mutual funds managed by that bank. This difference is relevant only when (and if) the shares are sold (or deemed sold). Purchasing shares of the bank or its mutual funds provides much greater privacy than opening an account with the bank.

U.S. investors in foreign mutual funds can defer taxation on reinvested dividends and capital gains until the shares are sold. An interest charge applies to tax-deferred gains in the shares. Such gains are taxed at the highest income tax rate applicable to the year in which it is allocated, without taking into account the taxpayer's actual marginal rate.

No law prohibits U.S. investors from buying foreign securities, but managers of most foreign mutual funds discourage direct investment by U.S. persons to avoid U.S. jurisdiction. However, no U.S. jurisdiction is established if an offshore fund merely answers an unsolicited inquiry or accepts an unsolicited investment. Inquiries made from non-U.S. addresses and from non-U.S. entities (e.g., foreign corporations) often receive more favorable consideration.

Asset Protection Trusts

Trusts are contracts under English Common Law. **Privacy** provided by a trust is determined by whether the jurisdiction in which the trust is created requires registration of the trusts; permits the use of a non-commercial trustee; and guarantees confidentiality in all matters relating to the trust. **Asset protection** by a trust is determined by whether the jurisdiction has repealed the Statute of Elizabeth; prohibits the enforcement of foreign judgments; and has a custodial infrastructure sufficient that assets conveyed to the trust may be maintained in the trust jurisdiction, not in another jurisdiction where less favorable law might be applied.

As trusts are English Common Law instruments, they are recognized almost exclusively in jurisdictions that have inherited this body of law. A few civil law jurisdictions also recognize trusts.

The Statute of Elizabeth is English Common Law. Only those jurisdictions that are independent from the U.K. Parliament and the Crown of the United Kingdom have constitutions permitting **repeal** of English Common Law, such as the Statute of Elizabeth, or permit an argument supporting repeal. Crown dependent territories may **modify** English Common Law, and thus the Statute of Elizabeth, but not repeal it.

Currently, no jurisdiction meets these criteria. The Cook Islands comes closest in its pioneering legislation barring foreign civil judgments and repealing the Statute of Elizabeth in reference to trusts formed under the International Trusts Act (1984). However, this law assigns enormous power to Crown administrative agencies, which appear to have statutory authority to confiscate trust assets without a judicial hearing.

Moreover, no custodial infrastructure exists in the Cook Islands in which to maintain trust assets. Non-commercial trustees are recognized, but typically formed in association with a Cook Islands international company, which is also subject to immense interference by Crown officials. All matters relating to trusts are secret, but the trust instrument must be registered.

Repeal of Elizabeth may also violate the Cook Islands Constitution, although the Constitution supports an argument that English Common Law can be repealed. The final determination may ultimately be made by the Cook Islands' highest court, the Judicial Committee of the Queen's Privy Council in **London**. The problem is not unique to the Cook Islands. Any jurisdiction that inherits English Common Law may find it difficult or impossible to repeal this 400-year-old body of law.

Even if the Cook Islands Parliament amends its trust law to correct these deficiencies, the Cook Islands remain members of the Commonwealth. Its Westminster Constitution acknowledges the **Crown's executive authority**. Amending the Act would remove **parliamentary** authority, but not **prerogative** authority, for the Crown to exercise its powers against trusts or trust property. The only way for the Cook Islands or any Commonwealth jurisdiction to eliminate the Crown's prerogative authority may be to become a constitutional republic.

A fundamental problem for U.S. persons setting up trusts in foreign jurisdictions are the tax penalties their creation may trigger. Amendments in 1996 to the Internal Revenue Code stipulate that all assets conveyed to a foreign trust are subject to a 35 percent excise tax on unrealized appreciation.

To avoid the tax, the trust must qualify as a "domestic trust" for U.S. tax purposes. This requires that a court within the United States be able to exercise primary jurisdiction over the administration of the trust **and** that one or more U.S. fiduciaries have the authority to control all substantial decisions of the trust. Authority over the trust is placed squarely within U.S. jurisdiction, making it **much less** attractive as an asset protection measure. Trusts that fail to meet this definition are deemed converted to a foreign trust and are subject to the 35 percent tax.

Civil Law

As discussed in the author's *Asset Protection 2000*, the historical and cultural conditions that led to the evolution of the civil law were entirely different from those of common law. **Any** investment in a civil law jurisdiction has a **much** higher probability of repelling common-law forfeiture than in a common law jurisdiction.

The problem of *in personam* jurisdiction remains. To avoid it, investors must structure their investments so that their compelled consent with a disclosure or repatriation order is ignored by the party holding the funds. If this is accomplished before any claims are made against the investor and/or his property, U.S. courts may not be able to hold the investor accountable criminally or civilly, although the courts could potentially forfeit substitute untainted property subject to U.S. jurisdiction. Speaking in the context of the "anti-duress" provisions of certain trusts, Rosen in "Uses and Abuses of Offshore Trusts in Asset Protection Planning" states:

> The U.S. Supreme Court in both *United States v. Rylander*, 460 U.S. 752 (1983) and *United States v. Bryan*, 339 U.S. 323 (1950), has held that a person cannot be held in contempt for failing to do that which is not within his power to do--unless he created the impossibility. The settlor-debtor should not be deemed to have created the impossibility where the trust containing a properly constructed duress provision has been established far in advance of the origination of the creditor's claim. The lack of a nexus in time between the establishment of the trust and the claim that compliance is impossible will substantially overcome an argument that the settlor-debtor was responsible for the resulting impossibility.

Most civil law jurisdictions do **not** recognize the concept of a trust. However, many investments and instruments **indigenous** to civil law exist. Each must be evaluated independently. Most elude lawyers trained only in common law.

The asset protection opportunities in civil law investments stem from the civil law itself. Civil law jurisdictions recognize the doctrine of **forced heirship.** This doctrine provides that the bulk of an individual's property must pass on death to his descendants immediately and unconditionally, in equal shares *per stirpes*, **regardless of his wishes.** Each beneficiary receives what their immediate ancestors were to receive, or did receive. For instance, when a person with three children and a deceased spouse dies, most of his property is split in thirds between the children. If only two children were living, the deceased child's share is split between his descendants.

Forced heirship is a **draconian** result where the individual does not wish his property to flow to his heirs. **However, where this is the individual's intent, forced heirship may avoid creditor claims, including claims by a foreign government, in an estate settlement.**

Civil law jurisdictions recognize a much smaller number of **torts** than in U.S. and English Common Law and the concept of punitive damages is virtually unknown. While civil law jurisdictions recognize the concept of fraudulent conveyance, for debts other than direct obligations such determination is generally much less sweeping than under the Statute of Elizabeth.

The most basic opportunities in civil law jurisdictions do not require the use of any "structures." A German bank account, for instance, while reportable under U.S. law, provides asset protection from **government** that is superior to any common law instrument. The assets in the account can be claimed by an individual's heirs without going through a probate proceeding if the individual makes a Power of Attorney designation before his death. However, if the account owner is a U.S. person, a U.S. court could order that person to repatriate the assets to U.S. jurisdiction.

Liechtenstein

For individuals seeking asset protection within a civil law structure with the potential to solve the dilemma of *in personam* jurisdiction, **the Principality of Liechtenstein** offers perhaps the most adaptable law in the world. Liechtenstein's **indigenous** civil law structures–in particular the **Anstalt** (Family Establishment) and the **Stiftung** (Family Foundation)–provide opportunities for asset protection, estate planning and privacy. Liechtenstein law also recognizes **trusts**. Proper counsel is essential in setting up these entities, which should be individually tailored.

Liechtenstein is the world's oldest offshore financial center and is the **only** jurisdiction whose company law (1926) was created to protect capital from **government confiscation**. It is also a jurisdiction where the constitution protects **statutory entities** formed by **non-resident aliens**. In this regard, Liechtenstein, a constitutional monarchy with its own Crown, provides much more protection than Crown offshore financial centers inheriting English Common Law.

Articles 123-128 of the Company Law allow for termination of these entities if formed for unlawful or **immoral** purposes or if there are important **defects** in the Articles. There exists substantial judicial remedy: Article 34 of the Constitution states that, "The inviolability of private property is guaranteed; confiscation shall only take place in such cases as are laid down by the law." Indeed, Articles 27, 28, 32 and 42 appear to afford Constitutional protections to the users of such entities. Further, these Articles appear to provide judicial recourse against the Liechtenstein **government.** Such rights are in marked contrast to U.S. law and the laws of most Crown offshore financial centers, which **exclude** statutory entities and non-resident aliens from **any** constitutional rights or protections.

Asset protection opportunities are specifically written into law for both Family Establishments and Family Foundations. Article 567 of the Company Law provides:

> In the case of Family Foundations, the Founder may determine at the same time that the creditors of the specifically designated third party beneficiaries shall not withdraw from these [beneficiaries] their beneficial interest acquired without valuable consideration by way of injunction, levy of execution and writ or bankruptcy proceedings.

These entities also permit flexible estate planning. Unlike trust laws in most English Common Law jurisdictions, there is no rule against their perpetual existence.

Secure Communications

Secure telephonic communications can help preserve the privacy of offshore investments.

The most practical strategy to avoid telephone surveillance is to use public phones. Some public phones are monitored, but their sheer number assures that most are not. Public phones in locations where **international** calls are common (e.g., airports) may also be monitored. To reduce the cost of calls from public phones, prepaid calling cards are available. They may be purchased with cash, anonymously, with calling time paid for in advance and are sold in currency exchanges, convenience stores and supermarkets.

Using a pre-paid calling card from a home or office phone may compromise its privacy advantages if a court orders the connection of a **dialed number recorder** ("pen register") to the line(s). The DNR records each digit pressed or dialed for all outgoing calls. Long-distance billing records record only long-distance numbers dialed, but the DNR records local access numbers, passwords and other confidential information entered from a telephone. The government must obtain a warrant to install a DNR, but need not demonstrate probable cause of criminal activity; only "the likelihood that a crime has been committed." The only way to defeat a DNR is to use a public phone or other phone on which the device is not installed.

Monitoring the **contents** of telephonic communication may be discouraged or defeated using a telephone and/or personal computer equipped with **digital encryption** software. Private digital financial transactions using encrypted e-mail are now available, although the author cannot vouch for the integrity of those offering such transactions. The most popular and most tested digital encryption software is **Pretty Good Privacy**, or PGP. Software engineer Phil Zimmermann created PGP because he was concerned about continuing efforts by governments to outlaw effective encryption. PGP is available from many sites on the Internet or on computer bulletin boards. A commercial version is also available.

Recall, however, the comments earlier relative to the ease with which intelligence agencies may be able to break even the strongest encryption algorithms. The possibility of dialing information being captured by a dialed number recorder remains. Further, the use of encrypted communications may encourage surveillance.

Warning: U.S. persons should not export PGP or similar programs. Effective encryption programs are considered "munitions" by the U.S. government. Persons who export munitions without a license are subject to fines, imprisonment and forfeiture. This is despite that PGP is already available worldwide through the Internet.

Alternative Travel Documents and Citizenship

Alternative travel documents are useful if a primary passport is withdrawn; for identification purposes in international investing; and if they provide citizenship or legal residency privileges. Residing permanently in the nation where the document is issued may subject the holder to its laws. The most practical documents are therefore from countries that provide citizenship, but classify the holder as a foreign resident, exempting that person from tax and military obligations, among other responsibilities.

The most economical way to obtain an alternative travel document is to take advantage of **ancestry**. Ireland, for instance, grants citizenship to anyone with one or more grandparents born in Ireland. Many countries offer "economic citizenship" to persons who make substantial investments. Once a person has obtained an alternative travel document, he can give up his citizenship and obtain alternative citizenship.

The cover story of the November 21, 1994 *Forbes* magazine characterized affluent Americans giving up U.S. citizenship as "The New Refugees." *Forbes* concluded that there is very little such persons can do **other than give up their citizenship** to preserve their estate.

Tax exiles include Michael Dingman, chairman of Abex and a Ford Motor Co. director, now a citizen and resident of the Bahamas. John (Ippy) Dorrance III, a billionaire and heir to the Campbell's Soup fortune, is a citizen of Ireland, and splits his residency between there, the Bahamas, and the United States. Kenneth Dart, an heir to Dart Container and the $1 billion family fortune, is a citizen of Belize and works in the Cayman Islands.

For wealthy Americans, giving up U.S. citizenship makes estate planning (asset protection for family wealth) much simpler, much less expensive, and much more effective. The first question estate planners should ask their clients is: "Are you willing to give up U.S. citizenship?" The United States is the **only** country that imposes significant income and estate taxes on the worldwide income and assets of every citizen, even those living outside U.S. territorial boundaries. Giving up U.S. citizenship may **eliminate** this liability.

While the IRS may seek income and estate taxes for 10 years after a person gives up their U.S. citizenship, these "anti-expatriation" rules are widely misunderstood, particularly in light of 1996 amendments. These rules apply **only** to the net combined amount of U.S. source income and income "effectively connected" with a U.S. trade or business. According to Isenbergh, *International Taxation*, "These rules create a tax base consisting of income arising in the United States plus income artificially shifted outside the United States" (Sec. 2.7.2).

Historically, the IRS had the burden of proof to demonstrate that one of the principal reasons for giving up citizenship was to reduce U.S. taxes. The IRS did not need to prove that tax avoidance was the exclusive or even principal purpose for expatriating, but only one such purpose. *Kronenberg v. Commissioner*, 64 T.C. 428 (1975). The 1996 amendments establish a presumption that persons expatriating after February 5, 1995 do so for tax avoidance purposes and are subject to the anti-expatriation regime **if** they have income exceeding certain thresholds **or** a net worth exceeding $500,000 **and** fail to demonstrate "an abiding connection by birth, marriage, or domicile, to a country other than the United States" (Isenbergh, Sec. 2.6.1).

Persons who expatriate from the United States for tax purposes after February 5, 1995 are also **forbidden** to come back and visit. Name of persons deemed to have expatriated for tax purposes are now published in the *Federal Register*. The list is circulated to U.S. embassies and consulates worldwide. **A former U.S. citizen who has renounced their citizenship can no longer obtain a U.S. entrance visa.**

Various strategies remain to structure one's affairs in advance of expatriation to avoid the anti-expatriation regime. A discussion of these strategies is beyond the scope of this book. Readers are referred to Isenbergh's treatise or to an attorney with a practice focusing on expatriation.

REFERENCES

"A-Bomb Birthplace Helps Target Cash; Needles in Haystack Don't Want to be Found," *Money Laundering Alert*, Sept. 1990

"ABA Task Force Pushes for Freeze on OTS' Powers," *National Law Journal*, Feb. 22, 1993

Alderman & Kennedy, *The Right to Privacy* (New York: Knopf, 1995)

Allen, *Constitutional Criminal Procedure: An Examination of the Fourth, Fifth, and Sixth Amendments, and Related Areas,* 3d ed. (Boston: Little-Brown, 1991)

"Anti-Money Laundering: World Wide Network," *Intelligence Newsletter* (Paris: Indigo Publications), no. 236, Mar. 10, 1994

"Asset Seizure," Associated Press, June 23, 1993

Axelrod, Price, & Thornton, "What Every Practitioner Needs to Know About Criminal Exposure in the Everyday Practice of Law," *Criminal Justice*, vol. 8, no. 3, p. 27 (Fall 1993).

Bamford, *The Puzzle Palace* (Boston: Houghton-Mifflin, 1982)

"Bankers Convicted of Violating Sec. 1956 Offenses & Bank Fraud," *Money Laundering Law Report*, Aug. 1994

Benson, *The Law That Never Was* (vols. 1 & 2) (S. Holland, Ill.: B. Benson, 1990)

Black's Law Dictionary, 6th ed. (St Paul, Minn.: West Publishing Co., 1991)

Bradbury, *Report on the Death of Donald Scott* (Ventura, Cal.: Office of the District Attorney, 1993)

Brazil & Berry, "Tainted Cash or Easy Money,?" *The Orlando Sentinel*, June 14-17, 1992

"Broward Sheriff Sorts Through Fiscal Mess," United Press, Sept. 5, 1993

Brown, *The Flight of International Capital: A Contemporary History* (New York: Croom Helm/Methuen, 1987)

Burnham, *Above the Law* (New York: Simon & Schuster, 1995)

Burnham, *A Law Unto Itself: Power, Politics and the IRS* (New York: Random House, 1989)

Campbell, *International Banking Secrecy* (London: Sweet & Maxwell, 1992)

Chambost, *Bank Accounts—A World Guide to Confidentiality* (Wiley, 1983)

"Coke Cop Pleads Guilty, " United Press, June 10, 1993

Comisky, Feld, & Harris, *Tax Fraud and Evasion* (vol. 2) (Boston: Warren, Gorham, & Lamont, 1997)

"Death on the Rock: Double Bind," *Intelligence* (Paris: Schmidt/AIMS), no. 23, Oct. 9, 1995

"Endangered Rat," Associated Press, May 24, 1994

European Union and FBI Launch Global Surveillance System (London: Statewatch, 1997)

Explanatory Report on the Council of Europe's Convention on Laundering, Search, Seizure and Confiscation of the Proceeds from Crime (Strasbourg: Council of Europe, 1991)

"FinCEN: Financial Vacuum Cleaner," *Intelligence Newsletter* (Paris: Indigo Publications); no. 235, Feb. 24, 1994

Fischer, *The Law of Financial Privacy* (Boston: Warren, Gorham, & Lamont, 1983-)

Gilmore, "Mutual Legal Assistance and the Privy Council: A Consideration of the Eisenberg Case," *Commonwealth Law Bulletin*, vol. 17, July 1991, p. 1028

International Estate Planning (New York: Matthew Bender & Co., 1994)

Internal Revenue Service Receivables (Washington, DC: General Accounting Office, 1992)

"IRS Likely to Increase Use of Money Laundering and Related Statutes," *Journal of Taxation*, Nov. 1990

Kacareb, "An In-Depth Analysis of the New Money Laundering Statutes," *Akron Tax Journal*, Spring 1991

Langer & Kleinfeld, *Practical International Tax Planning* (4th ed.) (New York: Practising Law Institute, 1995)

Larkin, "Attorney-Client Privilege" in *Federal Testimonial Privileges* (New York: Boardman-Callaghan, 1991)

Lessard & Williamson, (eds.), *Capital Flight and Third World Debt* (Washington, D.C.: Institute for International Economics, 1987)

Madsen, *Handbook of Personal Data Protection* (New York: Stockton Press, 1992)

McClean, *International Judicial Assistance* (Oxford: Clarendon Press, 1992)

Merryman & Clark, *Comparative Law: Western European and Latin American Legal Systems, Cases and Materials* (Indianapolis: Bobbs-Merrill Co., 1978)

Miller & Selva, "Drug Enforcement's Double Edged Sword: An Assessment of Asset Forfeiture Programs," *Justice Quarterly*, vol. 11, June 1994, p. 313

"Money Laundering Experts Team Up On and Off the Job," *Bank Management*, March 1991

Nilsson, "The Council of Europe Laundering Convention: A Recent Example of a Developing International Criminal Law," *Criminal Law Forum* (Spring 1991)

Parlour (ed.), *Butterworths Guide to International Money Laundering* (London: Butterworths, 1995).

Pratt & Petersen, "Civil Forfeiture in the Second Circuit," *St. John's Law Review*, vol. 65, p. 653 (1991)

President's Commission on Organized Crime, *The Cash Connection: Organized Crime, Financial Institutions, and Money Laundering* (Washington, D.C.: U.S. Government Printing Office, 1984)

"Protect Yourself and Your Fees," *Criminal Justice*, vol. 6, no. 4, p. 30 (Winter 1992)

Quigley, *The Anglo-American Establishment* (New York: Books in Focus, 1981)

Radmore, Bhattacharyya, & Laddie, "Money Laundering Prevention—Effect of the New Law on Solicitors," *The Company Lawyer*, vol. 16, no. 5, p. 155 (1995)

Raikoff & Goldstein, *RICO: Civil and Criminal Law and Strategy* (New York: New York Law Publishing, 1995)

Ristau & Abbell, *International Judicial Assistance (Criminal)* (Washington, D.C.: International Law Institute, 1984-)

Rosen, *Asset Protection Planning* (Washington, D.C., Tax Management, Inc., 1994-)

Rosen, "Uses and Abuses of Offshore Trusts in Asset Protection Planning," *Journal of Asset Protection*, September-October 1995

Rothfedder, *Privacy for Sale* (New York: Simon & Schuster, 1993)

Schneider & Flaherty, "Presumed Guilty: The Law's Victims in the War on Drugs," *The Pittsburgh Press*, Aug. 11-16, 1991

Senator et al., "The Financial Crimes Enforcement Network AI System (FAIS): Identifying Potential Money Laundering From Reports of Large Cash Transactions," *Artificial Intelligence*, Winter 1995

Scultz, "FBI Said to See Compiled Lists for Use in Its Field Investigations," *DM News,* April 20, 1992, p. 1

Sermet, *The European Convention on Human Rights and Property Rights* (Strasbourg: Council of Europe, 1992)

Smith, D. *Prosecution and Defense of Forfeiture Cases* (New York: Matthew Bender & Co., 1995)

Smith, G. W. L., "The Legal System of the United Kingdom (British Dependencies)," *Modern Legal Systems Cyclopedia* (Buffalo, N.Y.: William S. Hein, 1992)

"Spotting and Handling Suspicious Transactions," *ABA Banking Journal*, Jan. 1991

Strafer, "Money Laundering: The Crime of the '90s," *American Criminal Law Review*, vol. 27, p. 149 (1989)

"Statement of Harlan Vander Zee," U.S. House of Representatives, Government Operations Committee, Sept. 30, 1992 (Washington, D.C.: Government Printing Office, 1992).

"Study Shows Government Snitches Controlling Agents," Reuters, Feb. 12, 1995

"The New Refugees," *Forbes*, vol. 154, no. 12, Nov. 21, 1994, p. 131

"The Pinocchio Papers," Los Angeles Times, July 21, 1993

"35 Arrested Despite Bumbling Ways of Informant," *Pittsburgh Press*, August 14, 1991

"When Money Laundering Meets the Environment," *ABA Banking Journal,* July 1992

Wisotsky, *A Society of Suspects* (Washington, D.C.: Cato Institute, 1992)

"You Can Survive a Compliance Exam," *ABA Banking Journal*, Oct. 1991

"You Know Who You Are, and So Do We," *Forbes*, April 11, 1994

Zeldin, "How to Set Up a Money Laundering Compliance Program," *Business Crimes Bulletin*, Feb. 1994

Zweigert & Kotz, *An Introduction to Comparative Law* (2 vols.) (Oxford: Clarendon Press, 1987)

APPENDIX A:
A GUIDE TO CITATIONS USED IN THIS BOOK

Privacy 2000 cites court cases decided mainly in the U.S. federal court system. Non-attorneys who wish to review these cases may find the following remarks helpful.

The listing of a case and its location in a "reporter" is a **citation**. Federal reporters are found in law libraries and also in many public libraries. Any law librarian can assist you in retrieving these reporters and looking up the cases cited.

A citation such as *United States v. One 1963 Cadillac,* 250 F.Supp. 183 (W.D.Mo. 1966) has three parts: 1) the case name; 2) the volume number (250) and page number (183) of the reporter in which the case is found ("F.Supp."); and 3) the federal district and year in which the case was decided (western district of Missouri). Where a cited case is also quoted, the citation contains the page number on which the quotation is found after the page reference for the case; e.g., *United States v. One 1963 Cadillac,* 250 F.Supp. 183, **185** (W.D.Mo. 1966)

The reporter for all published decisions of U.S. District Courts is the *Federal Supplement*, abbreviated "F.Supp." Published decisions of the Federal Circuit Courts of Appeal are located in the *Federal Reporter, Second Series* and the *Federal Reporter, Third Series* ("F.2d" and "F.3d") respectively.

There are three reporting services for decisions of the U.S. Supreme Court: 1) *United States Reports* ("U.S."); 2) *Supreme Court Reports* ("S.Ct."); and 3) *United States Supreme Court, Lawyer's Edition, Second Series* ("L.Ed.2d"). Citations in this book for cases decided by the U.S. Supreme Court are from *United States Reports* and *Supreme Court Reports*.

Appeals are noted in a separate citation connected to the original citation; e.g. *United States v. Hennsel*, 699 F.2d 18 (1st Cir.), *cert. denied*, 461 U.S. 958 (1983). "Cert. denied" indicates that the decision was appealed to the Supreme Court, but that the Court declined to review it (*certiorari denied*). The reasons for the denial, if any are given, are found at the volume and page number after the abbreviation. Remember that the later opinion is the controlling opinion in Common Law.

Other reporters cited include the *Tax Court Reporter* ("T.C."), the *Bankruptcy Reporter* ("B.R."), *U.S. Treaties in Force* (U.S.T.), the *Cayman Islands Law Review* ("CILR"), and various state law reporters.

APPENDIX B:
U.S. GOVERNMENT REPORTING FORMS

The forms reproduced in this Appendix apply to foreign investments made by persons subject to the U.S. tax or cash reporting laws or (in the case of Customs Form 4790) who cross a U.S. border. The forms are:

Form 720 (Quarterly Federal Excise Tax Return)

Form 926 (Return by a U.S. Transferor of Property to a Foreign Corporation, Foreign Estate or Trust, or Foreign Partnership

Form 1041 (U.S. Income Tax Return for Estates and Trusts)

Form 3520 (Creation of or Transfers to Certain Foreign Trusts)

Form 3520-A (Annual Return of Foreign Trust With U.S. Beneficiaries)

Form 4789 (Currency Transaction Report)

Form 4790 (Report of International Transportation of Currency or Monetary Instruments)

Form 5471 (Annual Information Return of U.S. Persons With Respect to Certain Foreign Corporations)

Form 8300 (Receipt of Cash Payments Over $10,000 Received in a Trade or Business)

Publication 1544 (Reporting Cash Payments of Over $10,000)

Form 8362 (Currency Transaction Report by Casinos)

Form 8621 (Return of a Shareholder of a Passive Foreign Investment Company or Qualified Electing Fund)

Form TD F 90-22.1 (Annual Report of Foreign Bank and Financial Accounts)

Form TD F 90-22.47 (Suspicious Activity Report)

Form 720
(Rev. January 1997)
Department of the Treasury
Internal Revenue Service

Quarterly Federal Excise Tax Return

▶ For Paperwork Reduction Act Notice, see the separate instructions.

OMB No. 1545-0023

If you are not using a preprinted label, enter your name, address, employer identification number, and calendar quarter of return. See the separate instructions.

Name

Number, street, and room or suite no. (If you have a P.O. box, see page 2.)

City, state, and ZIP code (If you have a foreign address, see page 2.)

Quarter ending

Employer identification number

FOR IRS USE ONLY

T	
FF	
FD	
FP	
I	
T	

Check here if this is a final return ▶ ☐ or a one-time filing ▶ ☐ (See instructions.)

Part I   **Caution:** *Taxes that do not apply after December 31, 1996, are marked with an asterisk.*

IRS No.	Environmental Taxes (Attach Form 6627 for all environmental taxes.)			Tax	IRS No.
98	Ozone-depleting chemicals (ODCs)				98
19	ODC tax on imported products				19
IRS No.	**Communications and Air Transportation Taxes**			**Tax**	**IRS No.**
22	Toll telephone service, teletypewriter exchange service, and local telephone service				22
*26	Transportation of persons by air				26
*28	Transportation of property by air				28
*27	Use of international air travel facilities				27
IRS No.	**Fuel Taxes**	**Number of gallons**	**Rate**	**Tax**	**IRS No.**
	(a) Diesel fuel, tax on removal at terminal rack		$.243		
60	(b) Diesel fuel, tax on taxable events other than removal at terminal rack, including tax on previously untaxed liquids blended with previously taxed diesel fuel		.243		60
71	Dyed diesel fuel used in trains		.0555		71
78	Dyed diesel fuel used in certain intercity or local buses		.073		78
61	Special motor fuels		.183		61
79	Other alcohol fuels		(See instructions.)		79
	(a) Gasoline, tax on removal at terminal rack		.183		
62	(b) Gasoline, tax on taxable events other than removal at terminal rack		.183		62
	(c) Gasoline, tax on failure to blend or later separation		(See instructions.)		
58	Gasoline removed or entered for gasohol production containing at least 10% alcohol		.14333		58
73	Gasoline removed or entered for gasohol production containing at least 7.7% alcohol but less than 10% alcohol		.15321		73
74	Gasoline removed or entered for gasohol production containing at least 5.7% alcohol but less than 7.7% alcohol		.16142		74
59	Gasohol containing at least 10% alcohol		.129		59
75	Gasohol containing at least 7.7% alcohol but less than 10% alcohol		.14142		75
76	Gasohol containing at least 5.7% alcohol but less than 7.7% alcohol		.15222		76
69	Aviation fuel (other than gasoline)		.043**		69
14	Aviation gasoline		.043**		14
77	Aviation fuel (other than gasoline) for use in commercial aviation		.043		77
101	Compressed natural gas (taxed at $.4854 per thousand cubic feet)				101

**Applicable after December 31, 1996.

Cat. No. 10175Y

Form **720** (Rev. 1-97)

Form 720 (Rev. 1-97) Page **2**

Part I (continued)

IRS No.	Retail Tax			Rate	Tax	IRS No.
33	Truck, trailer, and semitrailer chassis and bodies, and tractors			12% of sales price		33

IRS No.	Ship Passenger Tax		Number of persons	Rate	Tax	IRS No.
29	Transportation by water			$3 per person		29

IRS No.	Other Excise Tax		Amount of obligations	Rate	Tax	IRS No.
31	Obligations not in registered form			$ .01		31

IRS No.	Luxury Tax			Rate	Tax	IRS No.
92	Passenger vehicles (See instructions.)			8% of sales price over $36,000**		92

IRS No.	Manufacturers Taxes	Number of tons	Sales price	Rate	Tax	IRS No.
36	Coal—Underground mined			$1.10 per ton		36
37				4.4% of sales price		37
38	Coal—Surface mined			$ .55 per ton		38
39				4.4% of sales price		39
66	Highway-type tires (See instructions.)					66
40	Gas guzzler tax (Attach Form 6197.)					40

IRS No.	Vaccine Taxes	Number of doses	Rate	Tax	IRS No.
81	DPT vaccine		$4.56		81
82	DT vaccine		.06		82
83	MMR vaccine		4.44		83
84	Polio vaccine		.29		84

IRS No.	Foreign Insurance Taxes	Premiums paid	Rate	Tax	IRS No.
	Policies issued by foreign insurers (See instructions.)				
	Casualty insurance and indemnity bonds		$ .04		
30	Life insurance, sickness and accident policies, and annuity contracts		.01		30
	Reinsurance		.01		

1 Total. Add all amounts in Part I. (Complete Schedule A unless one-time filing.) ▶ $

Part II

IRS No.		Rate	Tax	IRS No.
41	Sport fishing equipment	10% of sales price		41
42	Electric outboard motors and sonar devices	3% of sales price		42
44	Bows and arrows	11% of sales price		44

IRS No.		Number of gallons	Rate	Tax	IRS No.
64	Inland waterways fuel use tax		$ .243		64
51	Alcohol sold as but not used as fuel (See instructions.)		.54/.40		51

IRS No.	Floor Stocks Taxes	Number of gallons	Rate	Tax	IRS No.
20	Ozone-depleting chemicals (floor stocks) (Attach Form 6627.)				20
87	Aviation fuel (See instructions.)		.175		87

2 Total. Add all amounts in Part II. ▶ $

Part III

3	Total tax. Add line 1, Part I, and line 2, Part II	3	
4	Adjustments and claims (See instructions. Complete Schedule C.)	4	
5	Net tax after adjustments and claims. Combine lines 3 and 4. (If no entry on line 4, enter amount from line 3.)	5	
6	Deposits you made for the quarter ▶	6	
7	Overpayment from previous quarter ▶	7	
8	Total of lines 6 and 7 ▶	8	
9	**Balance Due.** If line 5 is greater than line 8, enter the difference. This amount must be paid with the return. Attach check or money order for full amount payable to "Internal Revenue Service." Write your EIN, "Form 720," and the quarter on it ▶	9	
10	**Overpayment.** If line 8 is greater than line 5, enter the difference. If you have an entry that is less than zero on line 5, combine line 5 and line 8. Check if you want the overpayment: ☐ **Applied to your next return, or** ☐ **Refunded to you.**	10	

Sign Here

Under penalties of perjury, I declare that I have examined this return, including accompanying schedules and statements, and to the best of my knowledge and belief, it is true, correct, and complete.

▶ Signature | Date | ▶ Title

(Please type or print name below signature.) | Telephone number ( )

![IRS Logo] **Department of the Treasury**
Internal Revenue Service

Instructions for Form 720
(Revised October 1996)
Quarterly Federal Excise Tax Return

Section references are to the Internal Revenue Code unless otherwise noted.

Paperwork Reduction Act Notice.— We ask for the information on these forms to carry out the Internal Revenue laws of the United States. You are required to give us the information. We need it to ensure that you are complying with these laws and to allow us to figure and collect the right amount of tax.

You are not required to provide the information requested on a form that is subject to the Paperwork Reduction Act unless the form displays a valid OMB control number. Books or records relating to a form or its instructions must be retained as long as their contents may become material in the administration of any Internal Revenue law. Generally, tax returns and return information are confidential, as required by Code section 6103.

The time needed to complete and file these forms and related schedules will vary depending on individual circumstances. The estimated average times are:

Form	Recordkeeping	Learning about the law or the form	Preparing and sending the form to the IRS
720	24 hr., 9 min.	2 hr., 17 min.	6 hr., 25 min.
Sch. A	1 hr., 55 min.		2 min.
Sch. C Part I	1 hr., 55 min.		2 min.
Part II	14 hr., 21 min.		14 min.
Part III	14 min.		

If you have comments concerning the accuracy of these time estimates or suggestions for making this form and related schedules simpler, we would be happy to hear from you. You can write to the Tax Forms Committee, Western Area Distribution Center, Rancho Cordova, CA 95743-0001. **DO NOT** send the tax form to this office. Instead, see **Where To File** below.

Changes To Note

1. Beginning January 1, 1997, **all** taxpayers will file Form 720 with the Internal Revenue Service Center, Cincinnati, Ohio (no matter where you filed before). See **Where To File** on this page.

2. A floor stocks tax on aviation fuel (other than gasoline) is imposed on fuel held on the first moment of August 27, 1996. See page 4 for payment information.

3. The expired environmental taxes (IRS Nos. 53, 16, 54, and 17) have been deleted from Form 720.

4. If your total deposits of social security, Medicare, and withheld income taxes were more than $50,000 in 1995, you must make electronic deposits for **all** depository tax liabilities that occur after June 30, 1997. See page 5.

General Instructions

Purpose of Form

Use Form 720 and attachments to report and pay the excise taxes listed on the form.

When To File

Except as otherwise provided in the instructions, you must file a return for each quarter of the calendar year as follows:

Quarter covered	All excise taxes other than ODCs, comm., and air trans. due by	ODCs, comm., and air trans. due by
Jan., Feb., Mar.	Apr. 30	May 31
Apr., May, June	July 31	Aug. 31
July, Aug., Sept.	Oct. 31	Nov. 30
Oct., Nov., Dec.	Jan. 31	Feb. 28

Report the floor stocks tax on aviation fuel (other than gasoline), IRS No. 87, on the return for the 1st quarter of 1997.

The filing date for the floor stocks tax on ozone-depleting chemicals (ODCs), IRS No. 20, is August 31, 1997, which is a return for the 2nd quarter of 1997.

If any due date for filing a return falls on a Saturday, Sunday, or legal holiday, you may file the return on the next business day.

If you are reporting two or more excise taxes and they are due on different dates, use the later filing date. **File only one return each quarter.**

Where To File

After December 31, 1996, file Form 720 with:

Internal Revenue Service Center
Cincinnati, OH 45999–0009

How To File

If you are not reporting a tax that you normally report, enter a zero on the appropriate line in Part I or II (Form 720). Also, if you have no tax to report, write "None" on lines 3 and 5, page 2, Part III, and sign the return.

If you have adjustments to Part I or Part II (Form 720) taxes, do not enter adjustments in the "tax" column. See **Schedule C—Adjustments and Claims** on page 6.

Special Rules—One-Time Filings

If you import for personal use a gas guzzling automobile or a passenger vehicle subject to the luxury tax, you may be eligible to make a one-time filing of Form 720 and Form 6197. You may make a one-time filing to report the gas guzzler tax or the luxury tax if you meet all three of the following conditions:

1. You do not use the vehicle in the course of any trade or business;

2. You do not import gas guzzling automobiles or luxury passenger vehicles in the course of your trade or business; and

3. You are not required to file Form 720 reporting excise taxes for the calendar quarter, except for one-time filings.

The following rules apply if you are making a one-time filing:

1. File the return for the quarter in which you incur liability for the tax. See **When To File** on this page.

2. Pay the tax with the return. No deposits are required.

3. If you are an individual and do not have an employer identification number (EIN), enter your social security number (SSN) on Form 720 on the line for the EIN.

4. Check the one-time filing box above Part I on page 1 of Form 720.

Final Return

File a final return if you have been filing a Form 720 and you: **(1)** go out of business, **(2)** stop collecting and paying air transportation and communications taxes reportable on Form 720, or **(3)** will not owe for excise taxes that are reportable on Form 720 in future quarters. For example, if you are only filing to report zero tax and you will no longer owe excise tax in future quarters, check the final return box above Part I on page 1 of Form

Cat. No. 64240C

720. The IRS will then stop mailing Package 720 to you each quarter.

Records

Keep copies of your tax return, records, and accounts of all transactions to show that the correct tax has been paid. Keep records to support all adjustments claimed and all exemptions at least 4 years from the latest of the following dates: **(1)** when the tax became due, **(2)** when you paid the tax, **(3)** when you claimed an adjustment, or **(4)** when you filed a claim for a refund. Always keep your records available for IRS inspection.

Penalties and Interest

Avoid penalties and interest by filing returns and depositing and paying taxes when due. The law provides penalties for filing a return late; depositing taxes late; paying taxes late; willfully failing to collect and pay tax, keep records, or file a return; negligence; and fraud. These penalties are in addition to the interest charge on late payments. The penalty for filing a return late will not be imposed if you can show that the failure to file a timely return is due to reasonable cause. Those filing after the due date must attach an explanation to the return to show reasonable cause.

Trust fund recovery penalty.— If communications and air transportation taxes are collected but not paid over to the IRS or are willfully not collected, the trust fund recovery penalty may apply. The penalty is 100% of these taxes. The penalty may apply to you if these taxes cannot be immediately recovered from the business. The penalty may be imposed on all persons who are determined by the IRS to be **responsible** for collecting, accounting for, and paying over these taxes, and who acted **willfully** in not doing so.

A **responsible person** can be an officer or employee of a corporation, a partner or employee of a partnership, an employee of a sole proprietorship, or an accountant. A responsible person may also include one who signs checks for the business or otherwise has authority to cause the spending of business funds. **Willfully** means voluntarily, consciously, and intentionally. A responsible person acts willfully if he or she knows the required actions are not being taken.

Additional Information

- **Pub. 510,** Excise Taxes for 1997, has more information on the taxes reported on Form 720. Pub. 510 contains definitions and examples that will help you prepare Form 720 and the attachments.
- **Pub. 378,** Fuel Tax Credits and Refunds, has more information on how to file for these credits and refunds.

Specific Instructions

Name and Address

The first time you file Form 720, enter the required information. After that, the IRS will mail you a Package 720 with a preprinted label every quarter. Use the preprinted label on your form. Include the suite, room, or other unit number after the street address on the label. If you did not receive a label, type or print your name, address, and quarter ending date (month and year).

P.O. box.— If the Post Office does not deliver mail to the street address and you have a P.O. box, show the box number instead of the street address.

Foreign address.— If your address is outside the United States or its possessions or territories, instead of providing "city, state, and ZIP code," enter the city, province or state, and name of the country. Do not abbreviate the country name. Include the postal code, if any, in the appropriate location.

Employer Identification Number (EIN)

If the EIN on the label is wrong or you did not receive a label, enter the correct number. (If you are a one-time filer, you do not need an EIN. See **Special Rules—One-Time Filings** on page 1.) If you do not have an EIN, you must apply for one. Get **Form SS-4,** Application for Employer Identification Number. Form SS-4 has information on how to apply for an EIN. If the EIN has not been received by the filing date of Form 720, write "Applied for" in the space for the EIN.

Part I

Environmental Taxes

Form 6627, Environmental Taxes, is used to figure the environmental taxes on ODCs, IRS No. 98; imported products that used ODCs as materials in the manufacture or production of the product, IRS No. 19; and the floor stocks tax on ODCs, IRS No. 20. Attach Form 6627 to Form 720 each quarter. The tax rates for these taxes are shown on Form 6627 and its instructions.

Communications and Air Transportation Taxes

Who must file.— The person receiving the payment for communications or air transportation services is required to collect and pay over the tax and file the return.

Communications services (IRS No. 22).— Enter the amount of tax collected or considered collected for the quarter. The tax is 3% of amounts paid for toll telephone service, teletypewriter exchange service, and local telephone service.

Note: *The following taxes apply to amounts paid on or after August 27, 1996, for transportation beginning on or after August 27, 1996, and before January 1, 1997. No tax applies to amounts paid before August 27, 1996, and, unless extended by future legislation, these taxes will not apply to amounts paid for transportation beginning after December 31, 1996.*

Transportation of persons by air (IRS No. 26).— Enter the amount of tax collected or considered collected for the quarter. The tax is 10% of amounts paid for taxable transportation of persons by air, including amounts paid for related seating or sleeping accommodations.

Transportation of property by air (IRS No. 28).— Enter the amount of tax collected or considered collected for the quarter. The tax is 6.25% of amounts paid for transportation of property by air.

International air travel facilities (IRS No. 27).— Enter the amount of tax collected or considered collected for the quarter. The tax is $6 per person.

Fuel Taxes

Enter the number of gallons subject to tax for each fuel. The fuels subject to tax and the tax rates are listed on Form 720.

Diesel fuel (IRS No. 60).— If you are liable for the diesel fuel tax on removal at the terminal rack, report these gallons on line **(a)** of IRS No. 60. If you are liable for the diesel fuel tax on events other than removal at the terminal rack, report these gallons on line **(b)** of IRS No. 60. Include on line **(b)** the tax on previously untaxed liquids that are blended with previously taxed diesel fuel.

Multiply the total number of gallons subject to tax on lines **(a)** and **(b)** by $.243 and make one entry in the tax column.

If you are reporting gallons that may again be subject to tax, you may need to file a "first taxpayer's report" with Form 720. See Regulations section 48.4081-7.

Dyed diesel fuel used in trains (IRS No. 71).— Dyed diesel fuel used in a diesel-powered train is taxed at $.0555 a gallon.

Dyed diesel fuel used in certain intercity or local buses (IRS No. 78).— Dyed diesel fuel used in certain intercity or local buses is taxed at $.073 a gallon.

Special motor fuels (IRS No. 61).— Any liquid other than gasoline, kerosene, gas oil, fuel oil, or diesel fuel sold for use or used in a motor vehicle or motorboat (other than a commercial fishing boat) is taxed at $.183 a gallon.

Other alcohol fuels (IRS No. 79).— Report the tax for the following fuels on this line.

Fuel	Tax Rate per Gallon
Qualified ethanol	$ .1290
Qualified methanol	.1230

Page 2

Qualified methanol and ethanol produced from natural gas	.1130
Gasoline sold for gasohol production containing at least 10% alcohol (methanol)	.13666
Gasoline sold for gasohol production containing at least 7.7% alcohol but less than 10% alcohol (methanol)	.14821
Gasoline sold for gasohol production containing at least 5.7% alcohol but less than 7.7% alcohol (methanol)	.15779
Gasohol containing at least 10% alcohol (methanol)	.1230
Gasohol containing at least 7.7% alcohol but less than 10% alcohol (methanol)	.1368
Gasohol containing at least 5.7% alcohol but less than 7.7% alcohol (methanol)	.1488
Special motor fuels/alcohol mixture containing ethanol	.1290
Special motor fuels/alcohol mixture containing methanol	.1230
Diesel/alcohol mixture containing ethanol	.1890
Diesel sold for diesel/alcohol mixture containing ethanol	.2100
Diesel/alcohol mixture containing methanol	.1830
Diesel sold for diesel/alcohol mixture containing methanol	.2033
Aviation fuel/alcohol mixture containing ethanol	.084
Aviation fuel sold for aviation/alcohol mixture containing ethanol	.09333
Aviation fuel/alcohol mixture containing methanol	.078
Aviation fuel sold for aviation/alcohol mixture containing methanol	.08666

Gasoline (IRS No. 62).— If you are liable for the gasoline tax on removal at the terminal rack, report these gallons on line **(a)** of IRS No. 62. If you are liable for the gasoline tax on events other than removal at the terminal rack, report these gallons on line **(b)** of IRS No. 62. If you are liable for the additional tax on failure to blend or later separation, report these gallons on line **(c)** of IRS No. 62.

Multiply the total number of gallons subject to tax on lines **(a)** and **(b)** by $.183. Multiply the total number of gallons subject to tax on line **(c)** by the appropriate rate (see below). Combine the tax for lines **(a), (b),** and **(c),** and make one entry in the tax column.

If you are reporting gallons that may again be subject to tax, you may need to file a "first taxpayer's report" with Form 720. See Regulations section 48.4081-7.

Additional tax on failure to blend or later separation.— Anyone who purchases gasoline for gasohol production at one of the reduced rates (IRS No. 58, 73, and 74) and fails to blend the gasoline with alcohol is subject to an additional tax. Anyone who purchases gasohol at one of the reduced rates (IRS No. 59, 75, and 76) and later separates the gasoline from the mixture is subject to an additional tax. The additional tax rates per gallon of gasoline are:

Type of Mixture	Rate of Tax
At least 10% alcohol	$ .03967
At least 7.7% alcohol but less than 10% alcohol	.02979
At least 5.7% alcohol but less than 7.7% alcohol	.02158

Report the number of gallons on line **(c)** of IRS No. 62.

Compressed natural gas (IRS No. 101).— Tax is imposed on compressed natural gas (CNG) that is sold for use or used as fuel in a motor vehicle or motorboat. The rate of tax is $.4854 per thousand cubic feet (determined at standard temperature and pressure). See Regulations section 48.4041-21 to determine liability for, and exemptions from, the tax on CNG.

Retail Tax

Truck, trailer, and semitrailer chassis and bodies, and tractors (IRS No. 33).— The tax is 12% (.12) of the sales price on the first retail sale of each unit. The sales price of a vehicle includes certain related parts and accessories sold on or in connection with the sale of the vehicle. It applies to trucks that have a gross vehicle weight (GVW) over 33,000 pounds. It also applies to trailer and semitrailer chassis and bodies for use with a trailer or semitrailer with a GVW over 26,000 pounds. Tractors mainly used for highway transportation with a trailer or semitrailer are taxable regardless of GVW.

See Pub. 510 for more information.

Ship Passenger Tax

Transportation by water (IRS No. 29).— A tax is imposed on the operator of commercial ships. The tax is $3 for each passenger on a commercial passenger ship that has berth or stateroom accommodations for at least 17 passengers if the trip is over 1 or more nights. A voyage extends "over 1 or more nights" if it is longer than 24 hours. The tax also applies to passengers on any commercial ship that transports passengers engaged in gambling aboard the ship beyond the territorial waters of the United States. Enter the number of passengers for the quarter on the line for IRS No. 29.

Other Excise Tax

Obligations not in registered form (IRS No. 31).— For obligations issued during the quarter, enter the principal amount of the obligation multiplied by the number of calendar years (or portion thereof) during the period beginning on the issue date and ending on the maturity date on the line for IRS No. 31.

Luxury Tax

Passenger vehicles (IRS No. 92).— The tax is imposed on the first retail sale of any passenger vehicle and is equal to 9% of the sales price to the extent the price exceeds $34,000. The first retail sale includes the use or lease of a vehicle. The tax must be paid by the seller of the vehicle.

The tax generally applies to passenger vehicles having an unloaded vehicle weight of 6,000 pounds or less. The tax also applies to trucks and vans having a gross vehicle weight (the weight of the vehicle plus its maximum load) of 6,000 pounds or less. Limousines are taxable regardless of weight. The tax does not apply to taxicabs and other passenger vehicles used by the purchaser exclusively in the business of transporting persons or property for compensation or hire, to law enforcement vehicles, public safety or public works vehicles, or emergency medical service vehicles. Add the tax on each sale during the quarter and enter the total on the line for IRS No. 92.

See Pub. 510 for more information.

Manufacturers Taxes

Caution: *Do not include the excise tax on coal in the sales price when determining which tax rate to use.*

Underground mined coal (IRS Nos. 36 and 37).— The tax on underground mined coal is the lower of $1.10 per ton or 4.4% of the sales price. Enter on the line for IRS No. 36 the number of tons of underground mined coal sold at $25 or more per ton. Enter on the line for IRS No. 37 the total sales price for all sales of underground mined coal sold at a selling price of less than $25 per ton.

Surface mined coal (IRS Nos. 38 and 39).— The tax on surface mined coal is the lower of $.55 per ton or 4.4% of the sales price. Enter on the line for IRS No. 38 the number of tons of surface mined coal sold at $12.50 or more per ton. Enter on the line for IRS No. 39 the total sales price for all sales of surface mined coal sold at a selling price of less than $12.50 per ton.

Highway-type tires (IRS No. 66).— The tax applies only to highway-type tires and is as follows:

1. For tires weighing more than 40 pounds but not more than 70 pounds— $.15 a pound for each pound over 40 pounds.

2. For tires weighing more than 70 pounds but not more than 90 pounds— $4.50 PLUS $.30 a pound for each pound over 70 pounds.

3. For tires weighing more than 90 pounds—$10.50 PLUS $.50 a pound for each pound over 90 pounds.

Figure the tax for each tire sold and enter the total for the quarter on the line for IRS No. 66.

Gas guzzler tax (IRS No. 40).— Use Form 6197, Gas Guzzler Tax, to figure the liability for this tax and attach it each quarter to Form 720. The tax rates for the gas guzzler tax are shown on Form 6197.

Vaccine tax (IRS Nos. 81, 82, 83, and 84).— Enter the number of doses of each vaccine on Form 720. The taxable vaccines are: DPT (diphtheria, pertussis, and tetanus); DT (diphtheria-tetanus);

MMR (measles, mumps, and rubella); and polio.

Foreign Insurance Taxes

Policies issued by foreign insurers (IRS No. 30).— Enter the amount of premiums paid during the quarter on policies issued by foreign insurers. Multiply the premiums paid by the rates listed on Form 720 and enter the total for the three types of insurance on the line for IRS No. 30.

Treaty-based return positions under section 6114.— Foreign insurers and reinsurers who take the position that a treaty of the United States overrules, or otherwise modifies, an Internal Revenue law of the United States, must disclose such position. This disclosure must be made once a year on a statement filed with the 1st quarter Form 720, which is due before May 1 of each year. The statement must report the payments of premiums that are exempt from the excise tax on policies issued by foreign insurers for the previous calendar year.

You may be able to use **Form 8833,** Treaty-Based Return Position Disclosure Under Section 6114 or 7701(b), as a disclosure statement.

How to file.— Send the Form 720 with the attached statement to: Internal Revenue Service, P.O. Box 21086, Philadelphia, PA 19114. At the top of Form 720, write "Section 6114 Treaty." You need an EIN to file Form 720. If you do not have an EIN, get Form SS-4 for instructions on how to apply for one. Provided you have no other transactions reportable on Form 720, check the one-time filing box on page 1. If this is your final return, check the final return box. Write "None" on lines 1, 3, and 5; and sign the return.

Part II

Sport fishing equipment (IRS No. 41).— The tax on sport fishing equipment is 10% (.10) of the sales price. The tax is paid by the manufacturer, producer, or importer. Taxable articles include fishing rods and poles (and component parts), reels, fly fishing lines (and other lines not over 130 pounds test), fishing spears, spear guns, spear tips, terminal tackle, fishing supplies and accessories, and any parts or accessories sold on or in connection with these articles. Add the tax on each sale during the quarter and enter the total on the line for IRS No. 41.

Electric outboard motors and sonar devices (IRS No. 42).— The tax on an outboard motor or a sonar device for finding fish is 3% (.03) of its sale price. The tax is paid by the manufacturer, producer, or importer. The tax is limited to $30 for each sonar device. Sonar devices for finding fish do not include graph recorders, digital types, meter readouts, or combination graph recorders or combination meter readouts. Add the tax on each sale during the quarter and enter the total on the line for IRS No. 42.

Bows and arrows (IRS No. 44).— The tax on the sales price of bows and arrows is 11% (.11). The tax is paid by the manufacturer, producer, or importer. It applies to bows having a draw weight of 10 pounds or more and to arrows 18 inches or more in overall length. Arrows less than 18 inches are taxable if they are suitable for use with a bow that has a draw weight of 10 pounds or more. The tax is also imposed on the sale of any part or accessory suitable for inclusion in or attachment to a taxable bow or arrow and any quiver suitable for use with taxable arrows. The tax on parts and accessories does not apply to an article on which the tax on bows and arrows has been previously imposed. Add the tax on each sale during the quarter and enter the total on the line for IRS No. 44.

Inland waterways fuel use (IRS No. 64).— Enter the number of gallons subject to tax. The tax is $.243 per gallon.

Alcohol sold as but not used as fuel (IRS No. 51).— Alcohol, either mixed or straight, designated for use as fuel is eligible for a credit. **Form 6478,** Credit for Alcohol Used as Fuel, is used to figure the credit. An excise tax is imposed if the credit was determined and any person later either **(1)** uses a mixture or straight alcohol for a purpose other than fuel, **(2)** separates the alcohol from the mixture, or **(3)** mixes the straight alcohol. The tax for each gallon of alcohol that is at least 190 proof is $.54 a gallon if ethanol; $.60 a gallon if methanol; and $.64 a gallon if the alcohol benefited from the small ethanol producer credit. The tax for each gallon of alcohol that is at least 150 proof but less than 190 proof is $.40 a gallon if ethanol; $.45 a gallon if methanol; and $.50 a gallon if the alcohol benefited from the small ethanol producer credit.

Floor Stocks Taxes

Ozone-depleting chemicals floor stocks tax (IRS No. 20).— Use Form 6627 to figure the liability for this tax. Enter the amount from Form 6627, Part III, line 4, column (d) on the line for IRS No. 20. Attach Form 6627 to Form 720 for the 2nd quarter of 1997. Deposit the payment by June 30, 1997, at an authorized depositary. See **How To Make Deposits** on this page.

Aviation fuel floor stocks tax (IRS No. 87).— A floor stocks tax is imposed on any person that holds perviously-taxed aviation fuel (other than gasoline) on the first moment of August 27, 1996. The rate of the floor stocks tax is $.175 per gallon. The floor stocks tax payment is due by March 1, 1997.

The floor stocks tax does not apply to aviation fuel held for use in foreign trade or in military aircraft. Also, the floor stocks tax does not apply if the aggregate amount of aviation fuel held by a person or related group of persons on August 27, 1996, is not more than 2,000 gallons. Aviation fuel held for an exempt use is not taken into account for purposes of calculating the 2,000 gallons.

Part III

Report the total adjustments and claims from Part III, line 13 of Schedule C on line 4 of Form 720. See the **Schedule C** instructions on page 6.

You may have the overpayment refunded or applied to your next return. Enter on line 7 of your next return the amount you want to have applied to that return.

Caution: *If you owe other Federal tax, interest, or penalty, the overpayment on line 10 will be applied to the unpaid amounts.*

Payment of Taxes

Generally, semimonthly deposits of excise taxes are required. However, no deposit is required for the situations listed below; the taxes are payable with the return.

● The net liability for taxes listed in Part I (Form 720) does not exceed $2,000 for the quarter.

● The gas guzzler tax and/or the luxury tax is being paid on a one-time filing. See **Special Rules—One-Time Filings** on page 1.

● The liability is for taxes listed in Part II (Form 720), except for the floor stocks taxes, which require a single deposit. See **Floor Stocks Taxes** on this page.

● The tax liability is for the removal of a batch of gasohol from an approved refinery by bulk transfer, if the refiner elects to treat itself for that removal as not registered under section 4101. See Regulations section 48.4081-3.

How To Make Deposits

Deposit Federal excise tax payments with a **Form 8109,** Federal Tax Deposit Coupon, at an authorized depositary or the Federal Reserve bank serving the area in which you are located. But see **Federal tax deposits by electronic funds transfer** on page 5. See the instructions in the coupon book for additional information. If you do not have a coupon book, contact your IRS district office.

To avoid a penalty, make your deposits timely and do not mail your deposits directly to the IRS. Records of your deposits will be sent to the IRS for crediting to your business accounts.

Generally, if any due date for making a deposit falls on a Saturday, Sunday, or legal holiday, you may make the deposit on the next business day.

Semimonthly period.— A semimonthly period is the first 15 days of a month (the first semimonthly period) or the 16th through the last day of a month (the second semimonthly period).

Computation of net tax liability.— Net tax liability for a semimonthly period is the liability for the period plus or minus any adjustments for the period. Liability for a semimonthly period may be figured by dividing the net tax liability for the month by 2, provided this method of computation is used for all semimonthly periods in the calendar quarter.

Federal tax deposits by electronic funds transfer (EFT).— If your total deposits of social security, Medicare, and withheld income taxes were more than $50,000 in 1995, you must make electronic deposits for **all** depository tax liabilities that occur after June 30, 1997. If you are an employer required to use EFT, you must also deposit your Form 720 taxes through EFT. If you were required to deposit by electronic funds transfer in prior years, continue to do so in 1997. The **Electronic Federal Tax Payment System (EFTPS)** must be used to make electronic deposits. If you are required to make deposits by electronic funds transfer and fail to do so, you may be subject to a 10% penalty. Taxpayers who are not required to make electronic deposits may voluntarily participate in EFTPS. For information on EFTPS, call 1-800-555-4477 or 1-800-945-8400. (These numbers are for EFTPS information only.)

If you are first required to make EFT deposits in 1997, your first EFT deposit will be due for a deposit obligation incurred for a return period beginning on or after July 1, 1997. For example, under the 9-day rule, a deposit for the second semimonthly period for June 1997 is due July 9, 1997. If you were not subject to EFT prior to July 1, 1997, the July 9 deposit may be made by paper coupon. The deposit due July 24 will be the first EFT deposit required.

When To Make Deposits

Taxes that are required to be deposited are grouped into classes as follows: **(1)** 9-day-rule taxes, **(2)** 14-day-rule taxes, **(3)** 30-day-rule taxes, and **(4)** alternative method taxes. If you are depositing more than one tax in a class, combine all the taxes in the class and make one deposit for the semimonthly period.

9-day rule.— The deposit of tax for a semimonthly period is due by the 9th day following that period. Generally, this is the 24th day of a month and the 9th day of the following month. The 9-day rule applies to all taxes in Part I of Form 720 except for:

- Gasoline and diesel fuel tax (IRS Nos. 14, 60, 62, 58, 73, 74, 59, 75, and 76), if deposits by qualified persons are made by transfer between accounts in the same depositary. See **14-day rule.**
- ODCs tax (IRS Nos. 19 and 98). See **30-day rule.**
- Communications and air transportation taxes (IRS Nos. 22, 26, 27, and 28), if deposits are based on amounts billed or tickets sold, rather than on amounts actually collected. See **Alternative method** on this page.
- One-time filers of luxury and gas guzzler tax. See **Special Rules—One-Time Filings** on page 1.

14-day rule (IRS Nos. 14, 60, 62, 58, 73, 74, 59, 75, and 76).— Deposits of the gasoline and diesel fuel tax for a semimonthly period by an independent refiner or any person whose average daily production of crude oil for the preceding calendar quarter that did not exceed 1,000 barrels may be made by the 14th day following the semimonthly period. The deposits must be made by transfer between accounts with the same Government depositary. If the 14th day is a Saturday, Sunday, or legal holiday, the due date is the immediately **preceding** day that is not a Saturday, Sunday, or legal holiday. The 14-day rule does not apply to dyed diesel fuel used in trains (IRS No. 71) or to dyed diesel fuel used in certain intercity or local buses (IRS No. 78).

30-day rule (IRS Nos. 19 and 98).— The deposit of tax for a semimonthly period is due by the last day of the second following semimonthly period. Generally, this is the 15th day of the following month and the last day of the following month.

Alternative method (IRS Nos. 22, 26, 27, and 28).— Deposits of communications and air transportation taxes may be based on amounts billed or tickets sold during a semimonthly period instead of on taxes actually collected during the period. Under the alternative method, the tax included in amounts billed or tickets sold during a semimonthly period is considered collected during the first 7 days of the second following semimonthly period. The deposit of tax is due by the 3rd banking day after the 7th day of that period.

Example. The tax included in amounts billed or tickets sold for the period August 16, 1996, to August 31, 1996, is considered collected from September 16, 1996, to September 22, 1996, and must be deposited by September 25, 1996.

To use the alternative method, you must keep a separate account of the tax included in amounts billed or tickets sold during the month and report on Form 720 the tax included in amounts billed or tickets sold and not the amount of tax that is actually collected. For example, amounts billed in December, January, and February are considered collected during January, February, and March and are reported on Form 720 as the tax for the 1st quarter of the calendar year.

Special rules for deposits of taxes in September 1996.— If you are required to make deposits, an additional deposit is due in September as shown in the chart on page 6. The special rule does not apply to air transportation taxes or other taxes not required to be deposited. See Regulations section 40.6302(c)-5T for special rules for figuring the net tax liability for this period.

Amount To Deposit

Deposits of taxes for a semimonthly period must not be less than the net tax liability for that period unless one of the safe harbor rules applies. The safe harbor rules apply separately to deposits under the 9-day rule, 14-day rule, 30-day rule, and the alternative method.

Under the alternative method, the deposit of tax for any semimonthly period must not be less than the net amount of tax that is considered collected during the semimonthly period. The net amount of tax that is considered collected during the semimonthly period must be either **(1)** the net amount of tax reflected in the separate account for the corresponding semimonthly period of the previous month or **(2)** one-half of the net amount of tax reflected in the separate account for the preceding month.

Safe harbor rules.— There are two safe harbor rules: one based on look-back quarter liability and one based on current liability.

The look-back quarter safe harbor rule applies to persons who filed a Form 720 for the look-back quarter (the 2nd calendar quarter preceding the current quarter). Persons who filed for the look-back quarter are considered to meet the semimonthly deposit requirement if the deposit for each semimonthly period in the current quarter is not less than 1/6 (16.67%) of the net tax liability reported for the look-back quarter. For the semimonthly period for which the additional deposit is required, the additional deposit must be not less than 12.23% (11.12% non-EFT) of the net tax liability reported for the look-back quarter, and the total deposit for that semimonthly period must be not less than 16.67% of the net tax liability reported for the look-back quarter. This rule does not apply for the 1st and 2nd quarters beginning on or after the effective date of an increase in the rate of tax unless the deposit of taxes for each semimonthly period in the calendar quarter is not less than 1/6 (16.67%) of the tax liability you would have had for the look-back quarter if the increased rate of tax had been in effect for that look-back quarter.

The current liability safe harbor rule applies to all filers of Form 720. Filers are considered to meet the semimonthly deposit requirement if the deposit for the semimonthly period is at least 95% of the net tax liability for the semimonthly period. For the semimonthly period for which the additional deposit is required, the additional deposit must be not less than 69.67% (63.34% non-EFT) of the net tax liability for the semimonthly period, and the total deposit for that semimonthly period must be not less than 95% of the net liability for the semimonthly period.

The following requirements must be satisfied for the safe harbor rules to apply:

1. Each deposit must be timely made at an authorized Government depositary; and

2. Any underpayment for the current quarter must be paid by the due date of the return. However, if the due date of the return is extended because you report taxes with different return due dates, you must deposit on the earlier due date any underpayment for taxes ordinarily reported on the earlier date.

The IRS may withdraw the right to make deposits of tax using safe harbor rules from any person not complying with the rules as stated above.

Schedule A—Excise Tax Liability

Complete Schedule A to record net tax liabilities for Part I taxes for each semimonthly period in a quarter even if your net liability is under $2,000. See **Computation of net tax liability** on page 5.

If you are reporting more than one type of tax on lines 1, 2, 3, or 4, add the net liability for each tax for each semimonthly period and enter the total in the applicable box. See **When To Make Deposits** on page 5 for details on the types of taxes.

Line 1.— Report in boxes **A–F** the net liability for the 9-day-rule taxes.

Use line 1 for communications and air transportation taxes based on actual collections.

Line 2.— Report in boxes **G–L** the net liability for 30-day-rule taxes.

Line 3.— Report in boxes **M–R** the amount of tax based on billings or tickets sold for communications taxes (IRS No. 22) or air transportation taxes (IRS Nos. 26, 27, and 28). The amount of tax to report for a semimonthly period is the amount that is considered collected during that period. For example, the amounts billed for communications services from December 1, 1996, to December 15, 1996, are considered collected during the period January 1, 1997, to January 7, 1997, and are reported for the 1st quarter of 1997 on Schedule A in box **M**, not the 4th quarter of 1996.

If you report based on actual collections, use line 1.

Line 4.— Report in boxes **S–X** the net liability for 14-day-rule taxes.

If you do not use the 14-day rule, report your gasoline or diesel fuel tax liability on line 1.

Reporting tax liability under the special September rule.— An additional reporting is required under the special September rule (for the period shown in the chart on this page) as follows:

- *9-day-rule taxes.* Enter the tax liability for the period beginning September 16 and ending September 25/26 below box **F**.
- *14-day-rule taxes.* Enter the tax liability for the period beginning September 16 and ending September 25/26 below box **X**.
- *ODCs.* Enter the tax liability for ODCs for the period beginning August 16 and ending September 10/11 below box **K**.
- *Communications based on amounts billed.* Enter the tax included in amounts billed during the period beginning September 1 and ending September 10/11 above box **M** on the **4th quarter return.**

For the remaining days in the September period, report the liability as follows:

- *9-day-rule taxes.* Enter the liability for the period beginning September 26/27 and ending September 30 in box **F**.
- *14-day-rule taxes.* Enter the liability for the period beginning September 26/27 and ending September 30 in box **X**.
- *ODCs.* Enter the liability for the period beginning September 11/12 and ending September 15 in box **K**. Leave box **J** blank. Enter the liability for the period beginning September 16 and ending September 30 in box **L**.
- *Communications based on amounts billed.* Enter the tax included in the amounts billed for the period beginning September 11/12 and ending September 15 in box **M** of the **4th quarter return.** Enter the tax included in amounts billed during the period beginning September 16 and ending September 30 in box **N** of the **4th quarter return.**

Schedule C—Adjustments and Claims

Note: *If you are not required to file Form 720 but you are due a refund of excise tax, you must use* **Form 8849***, Claim for Refund of Excise Taxes, to make your claim.*

Caution: *See Pub. 378 for claim requirements that set dollar amounts and dates for filing your claim.*

To make adjustments or claims, complete Schedule C. Enter on line 4 of Form 720 the total from Part III, line 13, of Schedule C. You cannot claim any amounts on Schedule C that you took or will take as a credit on Form 4136 or as a refund on Form 8849 or Form 843.

Use Form 843 to request an abatement or refund of interest under section 6404(e) (due to IRS errors or delays) or an abatement of a penalty or addition to tax as a result of erroneous IRS written advice.

Complete all information requested for each claim you have. Your adjustment or claim will be disallowed if you do not follow the required procedures or do not provide all the required information.

If you bought fuel taxed at a rate that is different from the rate on the form, attach an explanation of the amount of credit you are claiming.

Line 3

Off-highway business use.— You must have used the gasoline for a business use other than in a highway vehicle registered (or required to be registered) for highway use.

For gasoline you use in aviation, use line 7. For other nontaxable uses of gasoline, use line 11.

Line 4

Off-highway business use.— You must have used the gasohol for a business use other than in a highway vehicle registered (or required to be registered) for highway use. The rate per gallon is based on the percentage of alcohol in the mixture.

For other nontaxable uses of gasohol, use line 11.

Line 5

5a. Heating oil.— You must have used the diesel fuel as heating oil.

5b. Off-highway business use.— You must have used the diesel fuel for a business use other than in a highway vehicle registered (or required to be registered) for highway use.

5c. Qualified local and school buses.— You must have used the diesel fuel in a qualified local bus or in a bus that

---

Additional deposit of taxes in September 1996

Type	For the Period Beginning on	Ending on	Due Date
All Part I taxes:*			
EFT**	Sept. 16	Sept. 26	Sept. 30
Non-EFT	Sept. 16	Sept. 25	Sept. 27
ODCs (IRS Nos. 98 and 19):			
EFT	Aug. 16	Sept. 11	Sept. 30
Non-EFT	Aug. 16	Sept. 10	Sept. 27
Communications (IRS No. 22) (based on amounts billed):			
EFT	Sept. 1	Sept. 11	Sept. 30
Non-EFT	Sept. 1	Sept. 10	Sept. 27

* Except ODCs and communications taxes based on amounts billed, which are listed separately.

** See **Federal tax deposits by electronic funds transfer (EFT)** on page 5.

Note: *For the remaining days in September, be sure to make your deposits by the regular due date.*

transports students and school employees.

For diesel fuel you used in certain intercity or local buses or diesel-powered trains, use line 10. For other nontaxable uses of diesel fuel, use line 11.

5d. Sales by registered ultimate vendors.— You must attach the following information:

1. Your UV registration number issued to you by the IRS;

2. The name and TIN of each farmer, custom harvester, or governmental unit that bought diesel fuel from you and the number of gallons that you sold to each; and

3. A statement that you have:
- Not included the amount of tax in the sales price and have not collected the amount of tax from your buyer; **or**
- Repaid the amount of the tax to your buyer; **or**
- Obtained the written consent from your buyer to take the claim.

Line 6

6a. Special motor fuels— Off-highway business use.— If you bought taxed special motor fuels, you may make a claim for the tax included in the price of special motor fuels you used for off-highway business use. You must have used the special motor fuels for a business use other than in a highway vehicle registered (or required to be registered) for highway use.

For other nontaxable uses of special motor fuels, use line 11.

6c. Compressed natural gas (CNG).— If you bought taxed CNG, you may make a claim for the tax included in the price of CNG you used for off-highway business use. You must have used the CNG for a business use other than in a highway vehicle registered (or required to be registered) for highway use. The tax rate shown on line 6c is per thousand cubic feet (MCF).

For other nontaxable uses of CNG, use line 11.

Line 7

7a. Used in foreign trade or in certain helicopters.— You may make a claim for the $.193 per gallon of tax included in the price of gasoline.

7b. Used in commercial aviation.— You may make a claim for $.15 per gallon of the tax included in the price of gasoline.

Line 8

8a. Used in foreign trade, on a farm, or in certain helicopters.— You may make a claim for $.218 per gallon of tax included in the price of aviation fuel.

8b. Used in commercial aviation (other than foreign trade).— You may file a claim for $.175 per gallon of the tax included in the price of the aviation fuel.

Line 9

If you bought gasoline taxed at the full rate, have not claimed a refund, and used that gasoline to make gasohol, you may make a claim for each gallon of gasoline you used to make gasohol. The rate per gallon is based on the percentage of alcohol in the mixture.

Line 10

You must have used the diesel fuel for train or certain intercity or local bus use.

For other bus uses that qualify for a full refund of the tax, use line 5c.

Line 11

Enter the claim amount for the IRS No. listed or use the blank line(s) for any claim not described.

You must attach any additional information as required by regulations, a detailed description of the transaction, how you figured the claim amount, and any other information you believe will support the claim. Also, be sure to include your name and EIN on each sheet you attach.

Form **926**
(Rev. April 1996)
Department of the Treasury
Internal Revenue Service

Return by a U.S. Transferor of Property to a Foreign Corporation, Foreign Estate or Trust, or Foreign Partnership

OMB No. 1545-0026

Name of transferor

Identifying number (see instructions)

Number, street, and room or suite no. (If a P.O. box, see instructions.)

Date of transfer (month, day, year)

City or town, state, and ZIP code

Place of organization or creation if a corporation, partnership, estate, or trust

Part I — Foreign Transferee Information

1. Name of transferee

2. Identifying number, if any

3. Address (including country)

4a. Check type of foreign transferee: ☐ Corporation ☐ Estate ☐ Trust ☐ Partnership

  b. Place of organization or creation

  c. If an estate or trust, enter name and address of fiduciary

  d. If stock or securities are transferred to a corporation or partnership, enter the percentage of the transferor's interest in the stock of the transferee corporation or the partnership after the transfer . . . . ▶ %

  e. If stock or securities of a domestic corporation are transferred to a foreign corporation by a U.S. person, other than the domestic corporation, enter the percentage of the total voting power or the total value, whichever is greater, of the transferee foreign corporation owned by all U.S. transferors immediately after the transfer . . . . ▶ %

5. Name and address of each: (a) partner if a partnership or (b) beneficiary if an estate or trust (attach additional sheets, if needed)

Name	Address

Part II — Transfers Exempt from Excise Tax (See instructions.)

6a. Is the transfer to an exempt transferee? . . . . ☐ Yes ☐ No

  b. Check this box if you are making an election under section 1057 . . . . ☐

  c. Is the transfer a transfer described in section 367? . . . . ☐ Yes ☐ No

  d. If "No," have you made an election to apply principles similar to the principles of section 367? . . . ☐ Yes ☐ No

  e. If stock or securities are being transferred to a foreign corporation, have you attached an agreement to recognize gain on a later disposition by the transferee? . . . . ☐ Yes ☐ No

  f. If the answer to 6c, 6d, or 6e is "Yes," attach the information required under section 6038B. If the answer to 6d is "Yes," also attach a statement explaining the application of principles similar to the principles of section 367 to the transfer.

7. Attach a statement summarizing all facts relating to the transfer and a copy of the plan under which the transfer was made.

Part III — Figuring the Excise Tax (Complete only for transfers subject to the excise tax.) (Attach additional sheets if needed.)

(a) Description of property transferred	(b) Number of items transferred	(c) Fair market value on the date of transfer	(d) Cost or other basis (See section 1011)	(e) Amount of gain recognized at the time of transfer	(f) Excess (Column (c) less sum of columns (d) and (e)— enter zero if no excess)

8. Total 8

9. Excise tax. Multiply line 8 by 35% (see instructions) 9

Please Sign Here

Under penalties of perjury, I declare that I have examined this return, including accompanying schedules and statements, and to the best of my knowledge and belief it is true, correct, and complete. Declaration of preparer (other than taxpayer) is based on all information of which preparer has any knowledge.

▶ Signature   Date   ▶ Title

Paid Preparer's Use Only

Preparer's signature ▶	Date	Check if self-employed ▶ ☐	Preparer's social security no.
Firm's name (or yours if self-employed), and address ▶		EIN ▶	
		ZIP code ▶	

For Paperwork Reduction Act Notice, see instructions on back.   Cat. No. 16982D   Form **926** (Rev. 4-96)

Paperwork Reduction Act Notice

We ask for the information on this form to carry out the Internal Revenue laws of the United States. You are required to give us the information. We need it to ensure that you are complying with these laws and to allow us to figure and collect the right amount of tax.

You are not required to provide the information requested on a form that is subject to the Paperwork Reduction Act unless the form displays a valid OMB control number. Books or records relating to a form or its instructions must be retained as long as their contents may become material in the administration of any Internal Revenue law. Generally, tax returns and return information are confidential, as required by Code section 6103.

The time needed to complete and file this form will vary depending on individual circumstances. The estimated average time is:

Recordkeeping	7 hr., 39 min.
Learning about the law or the form	3 hr., 11 min.
Preparing and sending the form to the IRS	3 hr., 26 min.

If you have comments concerning the accuracy of these time estimates or suggestions for making this form simpler, we would be happy to hear from you. You can write to the Western Area Distribution Center, Rancho Cordova, CA 95743-0001. **DO NOT** send the tax form to this office. Instead, see **When and where to file** below.

General Instructions

Section references are to the Internal Revenue Code unless otherwise noted.

Purpose of form.—Use Form 926 to report transfers of property to a foreign corporation, a foreign estate or trust, or a foreign partnership and to pay any excise tax due under section 1491 and to report information required by section 6038B.

Who must file.—A U.S. citizen or resident, a domestic corporation or partnership, or an estate or trust (other than a foreign estate or trust) must file Form 926 to report the information described below. For purposes of section 367(a), in the case of a transfer by a domestic or foreign partnership, a U.S. person (as defined in Temporary Regulations section 1.367(a)-1T(d)(1)) that is a partner in the partnership must generally report the information discussed below. See Temporary Regulations section 1.367(a)-1T(c)(3).

a. A transfer of property to a foreign corporation (as paid-in surplus or a contribution of capital).

b. Any transfer to a foreign partnership, or foreign estate or trust.

c. Information required by section 6038B. A U.S. person must report section 6038B information if **(a)** the U.S. person transfers property to a foreign corporation and the transfer is described in section 367(a) or (d) or **(b)** the U.S. person transfers property to a foreign entity and, prior to the transfer, elects to apply principles similar to the principles of section 367 to the transfer.

When and where to file.—Generally, on the day you make the transfer, file Form 926 with the Internal Revenue Service Center where you file your income tax return.

If section 6038B applies, also file Form 926 and attachments with your income tax return for the tax year of the transfer.

Other forms that may be required.—Persons filing this form may have to file **Form TD F 90-22.1,** Report of Foreign Bank and Financial Accounts, **Form 3520,** Creation of or Transfers to Certain Foreign Trusts, and **Form 3520-A,** Annual Return of Foreign Trust with U.S. Beneficiaries.

A U.S. transferor that is required to enter into a gain recognition agreement under section 367(a), 367(e)(1), 367(e)(2), or section 1492(2)(B) (with respect to an election to apply principles similar to the principles of section 367 to a transfer described in section 1491) must file **Form 8838,** Consent To Extend the Time To Assess Tax Under Section 367-Gain Recognition Agreement (or a similar statement).

Specific Instructions

Address.—Include the suite, room, or other unit number after the street address. If the Post Office does not deliver mail to the street address and the transferor has a P.O. box, show the box number instead of the street address.

Identifying number.—Use the social security number for an individual. Use the employer identification number for any other entity.

Part I

Foreign transferee information.—Line 4d.— The transferor must determine his or her interest in the transferee foreign corporation or partnership by applying the rules of attribution under section 958. The transferor must state separately his or her percentage interest in the combined voting power and value of the stock of the foreign corporation. If the percentages differ, attach an explanation to Form 926. See Notice 87-85, 1987-2 C.B. 395.

Line 4e.—The transfer of stock or securities of a domestic corporation by a U.S. person to a transferee foreign corporation is taxable under section 367(a)(1) if all U.S. transferors own in the aggregate 50% or more (applying the attribution rules of section 958) of either the total voting power or the total value of the stock of the transferee foreign corporation immediately after the transfer. See Notice 94-46, 1994-1 C.B. 356.

Part II

Transfers exempt from excise tax.—A transfer is exempt from the excise tax if **(a)** property is transferred to an exempt transferee; **(b)** the transferor makes an election under section 1057; **(c)** the transfer is described in section 367; or **(d)** the transferor makes an election to apply principles similar to the principles of section 367.

Exempt transferee.—If property is transferred to an organization (other than an organization described in section 401(a)) exempt from tax under section 501(a), the transfer is not subject to the excise tax. You must file Form 926 and attach the following to it:

• If the organization is exempt from income tax, attach a copy of the IRS's determination letter.

• If the organization meets the tests of exemption from income tax but its exemption has not been established, attach a statement to establish the exemption. The statement must contain:

a. A description of the character of the transferee and the reason it was organized.

b. The activities of the transferee.

c. The source and disposition of its income.

d. A written statement indicating whether or not any of the transferee's income is credited to surplus or may benefit any private shareholder or individual.

e. All of the facts about the transferee's operations that affect its right to an exemption from taxation.

Also attach a copy of the charter or articles of incorporation, the by-laws, and the latest financial statement showing assets, liabilities, receipts, and disbursements of the transferee.

Transfers for which an election is being made under section 1057.—The excise tax does not apply if an election is made under section 1057. Section 1057 allows transferors to elect to treat the transfer as a taxable exchange.

Transfers described in section 367.—Section 367 applies to transfers described in section 332, 351, 354, 355, 356, or 361 when a U.S. person transfers property to a foreign corporation. For transfers described in section 367(a), see Temporary Regulations section 1.367-1T(c). See sections 367(a)(2) through (6) for rules and exceptions. Section 367(d) contains rules for transfers of intangibles. To meet the requirements of section 367(a) or (d), attach the information required by Temporary Regulations section 1.6038B-1T(c) or (d), respectively.

Transfers for which the transferor elects to apply principles similar to the principles of section 367.—An exception applies for transferors who elect, before the transfer, to apply principles similar to those of section 367 to the transfer. The transferor must comply with all the requirements of section 367, including the reporting of information under section 6038B. Attach a statement explaining how the principles of section 367 apply to the transfer.

Agreement to recognize gain upon later disposition by transferee.—Under certain circumstances, stock or securities of a domestic or foreign corporation may be transferred to a foreign corporation in a nonrecognition exchange. If permitted, nonrecognition treatment may be conditional upon the transferor's agreement to recognize gain on the amount realized if the foreign corporation disposes of (or is treated as disposing of) the stock or securities while the agreement is in force. See Temporary Regulations section 1.367-3T(g), as modified by Notices 87-85 and 94-46.

Reporting Requirements of Section 6038B

Attach the information required by the regulations under section 6038B to Form 926. If a U.S. person is treated as having made an indirect transfer to a foreign corporation because the U.S. person held interests in a corporation, partnership, trust or estate that made a direct transfer to a foreign corporation, then the corporation, partnership, or grantor trust may satisfy the section 6038B reporting requirements for all of its U.S. interest holders by filing a single Form 926 with the section 6038B information attached for each of them. A husband, wife, and minor children may file a joint Form 926 to report section 6038B information.

Section 6038B information and applicable penalties.—Penalties may apply if information required under section 6038B is not filed in the manner and at the time required by the regulations. The penalty is 25% of the gain realized on the transfer. The penalty may be waived if the failure is due to reasonable cause and not willful neglect. The statute of limitations for the transfer does not begin until the information is filed.

Part III

Figuring the Amount of the Excise Tax

Separately compute the excise tax for each block of stock or securities that has a separately identifiable basis. Do not offset appreciation in one block by depreciation in another block regardless of whether the stock or securities are from the same or different corporations. (Rev. Rul. 71-433, 1971-2 C.B. 325.)

Payment of Tax

Full payment of the excise tax must be sent with Form 926. Make your check or money order payable to the "Internal Revenue Service."

Who Must Sign

Form 926 must be signed and dated by the transferor or joint transferors. If the transferor is a partnership, one of the partners must sign. If the transferor is a fiduciary, the fiduciary or officer representing the fiduciary must sign. If the transferor is a corporation, the president, vice-president, treasurer, assistant treasurer, chief accounting officer, or other authorized officer (such as a tax officer) must sign.

Anyone who prepares Form 926 but does not charge the transferor should not sign. Anyone who is paid to prepare the return must sign it and fill in the Paid Preparer's Use Only area.

The paid preparer must complete the required preparer information and:

• Sign the return, by hand, in the space provided for the preparer's signature (signature stamps and labels are not acceptable).

• Give a copy of the return to the transferor.

Form **1041** Department of the Treasury—Internal Revenue Service
U.S. Income Tax Return for Estates and Trusts **1996**

For calendar year 1996 or fiscal year beginning , 1996, and ending , 19   OMB No. 1545-0092

A Type of entity:	Name of estate or trust (If a grantor type trust, see page 7 of the instructions.)	**C** Employer identification number
☐ Decedent's estate		
☐ Simple trust		**D** Date entity created
☐ Complex trust		
☐ Grantor type trust	Name and title of fiduciary	**E** Nonexempt charitable and split-interest trusts. check applicable boxes (see page 8 of the instructions):
☐ Bankruptcy estate–Ch. 7		
☐ Bankruptcy estate–Ch. 11	Number, street, and room or suite no. (If a P.O. box, see page 7 of the instructions.)	
☐ Pooled income fund		☐ Described in section 4947(a)(1)
B Number of Schedules K-1 attached (see instructions) ▶	City or town, state, and ZIP code	☐ Not a private foundation
		☐ Described in section 4947(a)(2)

F Check applicable boxes: ☐ Initial return ☐ Final return ☐ Amended return   **G** Pooled mortgage account (see page 9 of the instructions):
☐ Change in fiduciary's name ☐ Change in fiduciary's address   ☐ Bought ☐ Sold Date:

Income

1	Interest income	1
2	Dividends	2
3	Business income or (loss) (attach Schedule C or C-EZ (Form 1040))	3
4	Capital gain or (loss) (attach Schedule D (Form 1041))	4
5	Rents, royalties, partnerships, other estates and trusts, etc. (attach Schedule E (Form 1040))	5
6	Farm income or (loss) (attach Schedule F (Form 1040))	6
7	Ordinary gain or (loss) (attach Form 4797)	7
8	Other income. List type and amount	8
9	**Total income.** Combine lines 1 through 8 ▶	9

Deductions

10	Interest. Check if Form 4952 is attached ▶ ☐	10
11	Taxes	11
12	Fiduciary fees	12
13	Charitable deduction (from Schedule A, line 7)	13
14	Attorney, accountant, and return preparer fees	14
15a	Other deductions NOT subject to the 2% floor (attach schedule)	15a
b	Allowable miscellaneous itemized deductions subject to the 2% floor	15b
16	**Total.** Add lines 10 through 15b	16
17	Adjusted total income or (loss). Subtract line 16 from line 9. Enter here and on Schedule B, line 1 ▶	17
18	Income distribution deduction (from Schedule B, line 17) (attach Schedules K-1 (Form 1041))	18
19	Estate tax deduction (including certain generation-skipping taxes) (attach computation)	19
20	Exemption	20
21	**Total deductions.** Add lines 18 through 20 ▶	21

Tax and Payments

22	Taxable income. Subtract line 21 from line 17. If a loss, see page 13 of the instructions	22
23	**Total tax** (from Schedule G, line 8)	23
24	**Payments: a** 1996 estimated tax payments and amount applied from 1995 return	24a
b	Estimated tax payments allocated to beneficiaries (from Form 1041-T)	24b
c	Subtract line 24b from line 24a	24c
d	Tax paid with extension of time to file: ☐ Form 2758 ☐ Form 8736 ☐ Form 8800	24d
e	Federal income tax withheld. If any is from Form(s) 1099, check ▶ ☐	24e
	Other payments: **f** Form 2439 ....; **g** Form 4136 ....; Total ▶	24h
25	**Total payments.** Add lines 24c through 24e, and 24h ▶	25
26	Estimated tax penalty (see page 13 of the instructions)	26
27	**Tax due.** If line 25 is smaller than the total of lines 23 and 26, enter amount owed	27
28	**Overpayment.** If line 25 is larger than the total of lines 23 and 26, enter amount overpaid	28
29	Amount of line 28 to be: **a** Credited to 1997 estimated tax ▶ ; **b** Refunded ▶	29

Please Sign Here

Under penalties of perjury, I declare that I have examined this return, including accompanying schedules and statements, and to the best of my knowledge and belief, it is true, correct, and complete. Declaration of preparer (other than fiduciary) is based on all information of which preparer has any knowledge.

▶ ▶
Signature of fiduciary or officer representing fiduciary Date   EIN of fiduciary if a financial institution (see page 4 of the instructions)

Paid Preparer's Use Only

Preparer's signature ▶	Date	Check if self-employed ▶ ☐	Preparer's social security no.
Firm's name (or yours if self-employed) and address ▶		EIN ▶	
		ZIP code ▶	

For Paperwork Reduction Act Notice, see page 1 of the separate instructions. Cat. No. 11370H   Form **1041** (1996)

Form 1041 (1996) Page **2**

Schedule A — Charitable Deduction. Do not complete for a simple trust or a pooled income fund.

1	Amounts paid for charitable purposes from gross income	1
2	Amounts permanently set aside for charitable purposes from gross income	2
3	Add lines 1 and 2	3
4	Tax-exempt income allocable to charitable contributions (see page 14 of the instructions)	4
5	Subtract line 4 from line 3	5
6	Capital gains for the tax year allocated to corpus and paid or permanently set aside for charitable purposes	6
7	**Charitable deduction.** Add lines 5 and 6. Enter here and on page 1, line 13	7

Schedule B — Income Distribution Deduction

1	Adjusted total income (from page 1, line 17) (see page 14 of the instructions)	1
2	Adjusted tax-exempt interest	2
3	Total net gain from Schedule D (Form 1041), line 17, column (a) (see page 15 of the instructions)	3
4	Enter amount from Schedule A, line 6	4
5	Long-term capital gain for the tax year included on Schedule A, line 3	5
6	Short-term capital gain for the tax year included on Schedule A, line 3	6
7	If the amount on page 1, line 4, is a capital loss, enter here as a positive figure	7
8	If the amount on page 1, line 4, is a capital gain, enter here as a negative figure	8
9	**Distributable net income (DNI).** Combine lines 1 through 8. If zero or less, enter -0-	9
10	If a complex trust, enter accounting income for the tax year as determined under the governing instrument and applicable local law	10
11	Income required to be distributed currently	11
12	Other amounts paid, credited, or otherwise required to be distributed	12
13	Total distributions. Add lines 11 and 12. If greater than line 10, see page 15 of the instructions	13
14	Enter the amount of tax-exempt income included on line 13	14
15	Tentative income distribution deduction. Subtract line 14 from line 13	15
16	Tentative income distribution deduction. Subtract line 2 from line 9. If zero or less, enter -0-	16
17	**Income distribution deduction.** Enter the smaller of line 15 or line 16 here and on page 1, line 18	17

Schedule G — Tax Computation (see page 16 of the instructions)

1	Tax: a ☐ Tax rate schedule or ☐ Schedule D (Form 1041)	1a
	b Other taxes	1b
	c Total. Add lines 1a and 1b	1c
2a	Foreign tax credit (attach Form 1116)	2a
b	Check: ☐ Nonconventional source fuel credit ☐ Form 8834	2b
c	General business credit. Enter here and check which forms are attached: ☐ Form 3800 or ☐ Forms (specify) ▶	2c
d	Credit for prior year minimum tax (attach Form 8801)	2d
3	**Total credits.** Add lines 2a through 2d	3
4	Subtract line 3 from line 1c	4
5	Recapture taxes. Check if from: ☐ Form 4255 ☐ Form 8611	5
6	Alternative minimum tax (from Schedule I, line 41)	6
7	Household employment taxes. Attach Schedule H (Form 1040)	7
8	**Total tax.** Add lines 4 through 7. Enter here and on page 1, line 23	8

Other Information

		Yes	No
1	Did the estate or trust receive tax-exempt income? If "Yes," attach a computation of the allocation of expenses. Enter the amount of tax-exempt interest income and exempt-interest dividends ▶ $		
2	Did the estate or trust receive all or any part of the earnings (salary, wages, and other compensation) of any individual by reason of a contract assignment or similar arrangement?		
3	At any time during calendar year 1996, did the estate or trust have an interest in or a signature or other authority over a bank, securities, or other financial account in a foreign country? See page 17 of the instructions for exceptions and filing requirements for Form TD F 90-22.1. If "Yes," enter the name of the foreign country ▶		
4	During the tax year, did the estate or trust receive a distribution from, or was it the grantor of, or transferor to, a foreign trust? If "Yes," see page 17 of the instructions for other forms the estate or trust may have to file		
5	Did the estate or trust receive, or pay, any seller-financed mortgage interest? If "Yes," see page 17 of the instructions for required attachment		
6	If this is a complex trust making the section 663(b) election, check here (see page 17 of the instructions) ▶ ☐		
7	To make a section 643(e)(3) election, attach Schedule D (Form 1041), and check here (see page 17) ▶ ☐		
8	If the decedent's estate has been open for more than 2 years, check here ▶ ☐		

Form 1041 (1996) Page **3**

Schedule I — Alternative Minimum Tax (see pages 18 through 22 of the instructions)

Part I—Estate's or Trust's Share of Alternative Minimum Taxable Income

1	Adjusted total income or (loss) (from page 1, line 17)	1
2	Net operating loss deduction. Enter as a positive amount	2
3	Add lines 1 and 2	3
4	**Adjustments and tax preference items:**	

a	Interest	4a	
b	Taxes	4b	
c	Miscellaneous itemized deductions (from page 1, line 15b)	4c	
d	Refund of taxes	4d	( )
e	Depreciation of property placed in service after 1986	4e	
f	Circulation and research and experimental expenditures	4f	
g	Mining exploration and development costs	4g	
h	Long-term contracts entered into after February 28, 1986	4h	
i	Amortization of pollution control facilities	4i	
j	Installment sales of certain property	4j	
k	Adjusted gain or loss (including incentive stock options)	4k	
l	Certain loss limitations	4l	
m	Tax shelter farm activities	4m	
n	Passive activities	4n	
o	Beneficiaries of other trusts or decedent's estates	4o	
p	Tax-exempt interest from specified private activity bonds	4p	
q	Depletion	4q	
r	Accelerated depreciation of real property placed in service before 1987	4r	
s	Accelerated depreciation of leased personal property placed in service before 1987	4s	
t	Intangible drilling costs	4t	
u	Other adjustments	4u	

5	Combine lines 4a through 4u	5
6	Add lines 3 and 5	6
7	Alternative tax net operating loss deduction (see page 21 of the instructions for limitations)	7
8	Adjusted alternative minimum taxable income. Subtract line 7 from line 6. Enter here and on line 13	8

Note: *Complete Part II before going to line 9.*

9	Income distribution deduction from line 27	9	
10	Estate tax deduction (from page 1, line 19)	10	
11	Add lines 9 and 10		11
12	Estate's or trust's share of alternative minimum taxable income. Subtract line 11 from line 8		12

If line 12 is:
- $22,500 or less, stop here and enter -0- on Schedule G, line 6. The estate or trust is not liable for the alternative minimum tax.
- Over $22,500, but less than $165,000, go to line 28.
- $165,000 or more, enter the amount from line 12 on line 34 and go to line 35.

(continued on page 4)

Form 1041 (1996) Page **4**

Part II—Income Distribution Deduction on a Minimum Tax Basis

13	Adjusted alternative minimum taxable income (from line 8)	13
14	Adjusted tax-exempt interest (other than amounts included on line 4p)	14
15	Total net gain from Schedule D (Form 1041), line 17, column (a). If a loss, enter -0-	15
16	Capital gains for the tax year allocated to corpus and paid or permanently set aside for charitable purposes (from Schedule A, line 6)	16
17	Capital gains paid or permanently set aside for charitable purposes from current year's income (see page 21 of the instructions)	17
18	Capital gains computed on a minimum tax basis included on line 8	18 ( )
19	Capital losses computed on a minimum tax basis included on line 8. Enter as a positive amount	19
20	Distributable net alternative minimum taxable income (DNAMTI). Combine lines 13 through 19	20
21	Income required to be distributed currently (from Schedule B, line 11)	21
22	Other amounts paid, credited, or otherwise required to be distributed (from Schedule B, line 12)	22
23	Total distributions. Add lines 21 and 22	23
24	Tax-exempt income included on line 23 (other than amounts included on line 4p)	24
25	Tentative income distribution deduction on a minimum tax basis. Subtract line 24 from line 23	25
26	Tentative income distribution deduction on a minimum tax basis. Subtract line 14 from line 20	26
27	**Income distribution deduction on a minimum tax basis.** Enter the smaller of line 25 or line 26. Enter here and on line 9	27

Part III—Alternative Minimum Tax

28	Exemption amount		28 $22,500
29	Enter the amount from line 12	29	
30	Phase-out of exemption amount	30 $75,000	
31	Subtract line 30 from line 29. If zero or less, enter -0-	31	
32	Multiply line 31 by 25% (.25)		32
33	Subtract line 32 from line 28. If zero or less, enter -0-		33
34	Subtract line 33 from line 29		34
35	If line 34 is: • $175,000 or less, multiply line 34 by 26% (.26). • Over $175,000, multiply line 34 by 28% (.28) and subtract $3,500 from the result		35
36	Alternative minimum foreign tax credit (see page 21 of instructions)		36
37	Tentative minimum tax. Subtract line 36 from line 35		37
38	Regular tax before credits (see page 22 of instructions)	38	
39	Section 644 tax included on Schedule G, line 1b	39	
40	Add lines 38 and 39		40
41	**Alternative minimum tax.** Subtract line 40 from line 37. If zero or less, enter -0-. Enter here and on Schedule G, line 6		41

Printed on recycled paper

SCHEDULE K-1 (Form 1041)	**Beneficiary's Share of Income, Deductions, Credits, etc.**	OMB No. 1545-0092
Department of the Treasury Internal Revenue Service	for the calendar year 1996, or fiscal year beginning ...., 1996, ending ...., 19 .... ▶ Complete a separate Schedule K-1 for each beneficiary.	**1996**

Name of trust or decedent's estate

☐ Amended K-1
☐ Final K-1

Beneficiary's identifying number ▶	Estate's or trust's EIN ▶
Beneficiary's name, address, and ZIP code	Fiduciary's name, address, and ZIP code

(a) Allocable share item		(b) Amount	(c) Calendar year 1996 Form 1040 filers enter the amounts in column (b) on:
1	Interest	1	Schedule B, Part I, line 1
2	Dividends	2	Schedule B, Part II, line 5
3a	Net short-term capital gain	3a	Schedule D, line 5, column (g)
b	Net long-term capital gain	3b	Schedule D, line 13, column (g)
4a	Annuities, royalties, and other nonpassive income before directly apportioned deductions	4a	Schedule E, Part III, column (f)
b	Depreciation	4b	Include on the applicable line of the appropriate tax form
c	Depletion	4c	
d	Amortization	4d	
5a	Trade or business, rental real estate, and other rental income before directly apportioned deductions (see instructions)	5a	Schedule E, Part III
b	Depreciation	5b	Include on the applicable line of the appropriate tax form
c	Depletion	5c	
d	Amortization	5d	
6	Income for minimum tax purposes	6	
7	Income for regular tax purposes (add lines 1 through 3b, 4a, and 5a)	7	
8	Adjustment for minimum tax purposes (subtract line 7 from line 6)	8	Form 6251, line 12
9	Estate tax deduction (including certain generation-skipping transfer taxes)	9	Schedule A, line 27
10	Foreign taxes	10	Form 1116 or Schedule A (Form 1040), line 8
11	Adjustments and tax preference items (itemize):		
a	Accelerated depreciation	11a	Include on the applicable line of Form 6251
b	Depletion	11b	
c	Amortization	11c	
d	Exclusion items	11d	1997 Form 8801
12	Deductions in the final year of trust or decedent's estate:		
a	Excess deductions on termination (see instructions)	12a	Schedule A, line 22
b	Short-term capital loss carryover	12b	Schedule D, line 5, column (f)
c	Long-term capital loss carryover	12c	Schedule D, line 13, column (f)
d	Net operating loss (NOL) carryover for regular tax purposes	12d	Form 1040, line 21
e	NOL carryover for minimum tax purposes	12e	See the instructions for Form 6251, line 20
f	....	12f	Include on the applicable line of the appropriate tax form
g	....	12g	
13	Other (itemize):		
a	Payments of estimated taxes credited to you	13a	Form 1040, line 53
b	Tax-exempt interest	13b	Form 1040, line 8b
c	....	13c	
d	....	13d	
e	....	13e	Include on the applicable line of the appropriate tax form
f	....	13f	
g	....	13g	
h		13h	

For Paperwork Reduction Act Notice, see page 1 of the Instructions for Form 1041. Cat. No. 11380D Schedule K-1 (Form 1041) 1996

Instructions for Beneficiary Filing Form 1040

Note: *The fiduciary's instructions for completing Schedule K-1 are in the Instructions for Form 1041.*

General Instructions

Purpose of Form

The fiduciary of a trust or decedent's estate uses Schedule K-1 to report your share of the trust's or estate's income, credits, deductions, etc. **Keep it for your records. Do not file it with your tax return.** A copy has been filed with the IRS.

Tax Shelters

If you receive a copy of **Form 8271,** Investor Reporting of Tax Shelter Registration Number, see the instructions for Form 8271 to determine your reporting requirements.

Errors

If you think the fiduciary has made an error on your Schedule K-1, notify the fiduciary and ask for an amended or a corrected Schedule K-1. Do not change any items on your copy. Be sure that the fiduciary sends a copy of the amended Schedule K-1 to the IRS.

Beneficiaries of Generation-Skipping Trusts

If you received **Form 706-GS(D-1),** Notification of Distribution From a Generation-Skipping Trust, and paid a generation-skipping transfer (GST) tax on **Form 706-GS(D),** Generation-Skipping Transfer Tax Return for Distributions, you can deduct the GST tax paid on income distributions on Schedule A (Form 1040), line 8. To figure the deduction, see the instructions for Form 706-GS(D).

Specific Instructions

Lines 3a and 3b

If there is an attachment to this Schedule K-1 reporting a disposition of a passive activity, see the instructions for **Form 8582,** Passive Activity Loss Limitations, for information on the treatment of dispositions of interests in a passive activity.

Lines 5b through 5d

The deductions on lines 5b through 5d may be subject to the passive loss limitations of Internal Revenue Code section 469, which generally limits deductions from passive activities to the income from those activities. The rules for applying these limitations to beneficiaries have not yet been issued. For more details, see **Pub. 925,** Passive Activity and At-Risk Rules.

Line 11d

If you pay alternative minimum tax in 1996, the amount on line 11d will help you figure any minimum tax credit for 1997. See the 1997 **Form 8801,** Credit for Prior Year Minimum Tax—Individuals, Estates, and Trusts, for more information.

Line 13a

To figure any underpayment and penalty on **Form 2210,** Underpayment of Estimated Tax by Individuals, Estates, and Trusts, treat the amount entered on line 13a as an estimated tax payment made on January 15, 1997.

Lines 13c through 13h

The amount of gross farming and fishing income is included on line 5a. This income is also separately stated on line 13 to help you determine if you are subject to a penalty for underpayment of estimated tax. Report the amount of gross farming and fishing income on Schedule E (Form 1040), line 41.

 Printed on recycled paper

1996

Department of the Treasury
Internal Revenue Service

Instructions for Form 1041 and Schedules A, B, D, G, I, J, and K-1

U.S. Income Tax Return for Estates and Trusts

Section references are to the Internal Revenue Code unless otherwise noted.

Paperwork Reduction Act Notice

We ask for the information on this form to carry out the Internal Revenue laws of the United States. You are required to give us the information. We need it to ensure that you are complying with these laws and to allow us to figure and collect the right amount of tax.

You are not required to provide the information requested on a form that is subject to the Paperwork Reduction Act unless the form displays a valid OMB control number. Books or records relating to a form or its instructions must be retained as long as their contents may become material in the administration of any Internal Revenue law. Generally, tax returns and return information are confidential, as required by Code section 6103.

The time needed to complete and file this form and related schedules will vary depending on individual circumstances. The estimated average times are:

	Form 1041	Schedule D	Schedule J	Schedule K-1
Recordkeeping	40 hr., 53 min.	16 hr., 1 min.	39 hr., 28 min.	8 hr., 22 min.
Learning about the law or the form	18 hr., 37 min.	1 hr., 47 min.	1 hr., 5 min.	1 hr., 12 min.
Preparing the form	34 hr., 58 min.	2 hr., 8 min.	1 hr., 47 min.	1 hr., 23 min.
Copying, assembling, and sending the form to the IRS	4 hr., 17 min.			

If you have comments concerning the accuracy of these time estimates or suggestions for making this form and related schedules simpler, we would be happy to hear from you. You can write to the Tax Forms Committee, Western Area Distribution Center, Rancho Cordova, CA 95743-0001. **DO NOT** send the tax form to this address. Instead, see **Where To File** on page 3.

Contents	Page
Changes To Note	1
Unresolved Tax Problems	1
How To Get Forms and Publications	1
General Instructions	2
Purpose of Form	2
Income Taxation of Trusts and Decedents' Estates	2
Definitions	2
Who Must File	2
Electronic Filing	3
When To File	3
Period Covered	3
Where To File	3
Who Must Sign	4
Accounting Methods	4
Accounting Periods	4
Rounding Off to Whole Dollars	4
Estimated Tax	4
Interest and Penalties	4
Other Forms That May Be Required	5
Attachments	5
Additional Information	5

Contents	Page
Of Special Interest to Bankruptcy Trustees and Debtors-in-Possession	5
Specific Instructions	7
Name of Estate or Trust	7
Address	7
Type of Entity	7
Number of Schedules K-1 Attached	8
Employer Identification Number	8
Date Entity Created	8
Nonexempt Charitable and Split-Interest Trusts	8
Initial Return, Amended Return, Final Return; or Change in Fiduciary's Name or Address	9
Pooled Mortgage Account	9
Income	9
Deductions	10
Tax and Payments	13
Schedule A—Charitable Deductions	14
Schedule B—Income Distribution Deduction	14
Schedule G—Tax Computation	16

Contents	Page
Other Information	17
Schedule I—Alternative Minimum Tax	18
Schedule D (Form 1041)—Capital Gains and Losses	22
Schedule J (Form 1041)—Accumulation Distribution for a Complex Trust	23
Schedule K-1 (Form 1041)—Beneficiary's Share of Income, Deductions, Credits, etc.	25

Changes To Note

- Three new optional filing methods for certain grantor type trusts are available for tax years beginning after 1995. The optional methods are alternatives to the filing of Form 1041 for these trusts. If the trustee elects an optional method, he or she generally must file a final Form 1041 for the tax year that immediately precedes the first tax year for which the trustee elects to report under one of the optional methods. For details, see page 7.

- For tax years beginning in 1996, the requirement to file a return for a bankruptcy estate applies only if gross income is at least $5,900.

Unresolved Tax Problems

The Problem Resolution Program is for taxpayers that have been unable to resolve their problems with the IRS. If the estate or trust has a tax problem it cannot clear up through normal channels, write to the estate's or trust's local IRS District Director, or call the local IRS office and ask for Problem Resolution assistance. Persons who have access to TTY/TDD equipment may call 1-800-829-4059 to ask for help from Problem Resolution. This office cannot change the tax law or technical decisions. But it can help clear up problems that resulted from previous contacts.

How To Get Forms and Publications

By personal computer.— If you subscribe to an on-line service, ask if IRS information is available and, if so, how to access it. You can get information through IRIS, the Internal Revenue Information Services, on FedWorld, a government bulletin board. Tax forms, instructions, publications, and other IRS information are available through IRIS.

IRIS is accessible directly using your modem by calling 703-321-8020. On the Internet, telnet to iris.irs.ustreas.gov or, for file transfer protocol services, connect to ftp.irs.ustreas.gov. If you are using the World Wide Web, connect to http://www.irs.ustreas.gov. FedWorld's help desk offers technical assistance on accessing IRIS (not tax help) during regular business hours at 703-487-4608. The IRIS menus offer information on available file formats and software needed to read and print files. You must print the forms to use them; they are not designed to be filled in on-screen.

Tax forms, instructions, and publications are also available on CD-ROM, including prior-year forms starting with the 1991 tax year. For ordering information and software requirements, contact the Government Printing Office's Superintendent of Documents (202-512-1800) or Federal Bulletin Board (202-512-1387).

By phone and in person.— To order forms and publications, call 1-800-TAX-FORM (1-800-829-3676). You can also get most forms and publications at your local IRS office.

General Instructions

Purpose of Form

The fiduciary of a domestic decedent's estate, trust, or bankruptcy estate uses Form 1041 to report: **(a)** the income, deductions, gains, losses, etc. of the estate or trust; **(b)** the income that is either accumulated or held for future distribution or distributed currently to the beneficiaries; **(c)** any income tax liability of the estate or trust; and **(d)** employment taxes on wages paid to household employees.

Income Taxation of Trusts and Decedents' Estates

A trust (except a grantor type trust) or a decedent's estate is a separate legal entity for Federal tax purposes. A decedent's estate comes into existence at the time of death of an individual. A trust may be created during an individual's life (inter vivos) or at the time of his or her death under a will (testamentary). If the trust instrument contains certain provisions, then the person creating the trust (the grantor) is treated as the owner of the trust's assets. Such a trust is a grantor type trust.

A trust or decedent's estate figures its gross income in much the same manner as an individual. Most deductions and credits allowed to individuals are also allowed to estates and trusts. However, there is one major distinction. A trust or decedent's estate is allowed an income distribution deduction for distributions to beneficiaries. To figure this deduction, the fiduciary must complete Schedule B. The income distribution deduction determines the amount of the distribution that is taxed to the beneficiaries.

For this reason, a trust or decedent's estate sometimes is referred to as a "pass-through" entity. The beneficiary, and not the trust or decedent's estate, pays income tax on his or her distributive share of income. Schedule K-1 (Form 1041) is used to notify the beneficiaries of the amounts to be included on their income tax returns.

Before preparing Form 1041, the fiduciary must figure the accounting income of the estate or trust under the will or trust instrument and applicable local law to determine the amount, if any, of income that is required to be distributed because the income distribution deduction is based, in part, on that amount.

Definitions

Beneficiary

A beneficiary is an heir, a legatee, or a devisee.

Distributable Net Income (DNI)

The income distribution deduction allowable to estates and trusts for amounts paid, credited, or required to be distributed to beneficiaries is limited to distributable net income (DNI). This amount, which is figured on Schedule B, line 9, is also used to determine how much of an amount paid, credited, or required to be distributed to a beneficiary will be includible in his or her gross income.

Income and Deductions in Respect of a Decedent

When completing Form 1041, you must take into account any items that are income in respect of a decedent (IRD).

In general, income in respect of a decedent is income that a decedent was entitled to receive but that was not properly includible in the decedent's final Form 1040 under the decedent's method of accounting.

IRD includes: **(a)** all accrued income of a decedent who reported his or her income on a cash method of accounting; **(b)** income accrued solely because of the decedent's death in the case of a decedent who reported his or her income on the accrual method of accounting; and **(c)** income to which the decedent had a contingent claim at the time of his or her death.

Some examples of IRD of a decedent who kept his or her books on a cash method are:

- Deferred salary payments that are payable to the decedent's estate.
- Uncollected interest on U.S. savings bonds.
- Proceeds from the completed sale of farm produce.

- The portion of a lump sum distribution to the beneficiary of a decedent's IRA that equals the balance in the IRA at the time of the owner's death. This includes unrealized appreciation and income accrued to that date, less the aggregate amount of the owner's nondeductible contributions to the IRA. Such amounts are included in the beneficiary's gross income in the tax year that the distribution is received.

The IRD has the same character it would have had if the decedent lived and received such amount.

The following deductions and credits, when paid by the decedent's estate, are allowed on Form 1041 even though they were not allowable on the decedent's final Form 1040:

- Business expenses deductible under section 162.
- Interest deductible under section 163.
- Taxes deductible under section 164.
- Investment expenses described in section 212 (in excess of 2% of AGI).
- Percentage depletion allowed under section 611.
- Foreign tax credit.

For more information, see section 691.

Income Required To Be Distributed Currently

Income required to be distributed currently is income that is required to be distributed in the year it is received. The fiduciary must be under a duty to distribute the income currently, even if the actual distribution is not made until after the close of the trust's tax year. See Regulations section 1.651(a)-2.

Fiduciary

A fiduciary is a trustee of a trust; or an executor, executrix, administrator, administratrix, personal representative, or person in possession of property of a decedent's estate.

Note: *Any reference in these instructions to "you" means the fiduciary of the estate or trust.*

Trust

A trust is an arrangement created either by a will or by an inter vivos declaration by which trustees take title to property for the purpose of protecting or conserving it for the beneficiaries under the ordinary rules applied in chancery or probate courts.

Who Must File

Decedent's Estate

The fiduciary (or one of the joint fiduciaries) must file Form 1041 for the estate of a domestic decedent that has:

1. Gross income for the tax year of $600 or more, or

2. A beneficiary who is a nonresident alien.

Trust

The fiduciary (or one of the joint fiduciaries) must file Form 1041 for a domestic trust taxable under section 641 that has:

1. Any taxable income for the tax year, or

2. Gross income of $600 or more (regardless of taxable income), or

3. A beneficiary who is a nonresident alien.

Two or more trusts are treated as one trust if such trusts have substantially the same grantor(s) and substantially the same primary beneficiary(ies), and a principal purpose of such trusts is avoidance of tax. This provision applies only to that portion of the trust that is attributable to contributions to corpus made after March 1, 1984.

If you are a fiduciary of a nonresident alien estate or foreign trust with U.S. source income, file **Form 1040NR,** U.S. Nonresident Alien Income Tax Return.

Bankruptcy Estate

The bankruptcy trustee or debtor-in-possession must file Form 1041 for the estate of an individual involved in bankruptcy proceedings under chapter 7 or 11 of title 11 of the United States Code if the estate has gross income for the tax year of $5,900 or more. See **Of Special Interest To Bankruptcy Trustees and Debtors-in-Possession** on page 5 for other details.

Qualified Settlement Funds

The trustee of a designated or qualified settlement fund must file **Form 1120-SF,** U.S. Income Tax Return for Settlement Funds, rather than Form 1041. See Regulations section 1.468B-5.

Electronic and Magnetic Media Filing

Qualified fiduciaries or transmitters may be able to file Form 1041 and related schedules electronically or on magnetic media. Tax return data may be filed electronically using telephone lines or on magnetic media using magnetic tape or floppy diskette.

If you wish to do this, **Form 9041,** Application for Electronic/Magnetic Media Filing of Business and Employee Benefit Plan Returns, must be filed. If Form 1041 is filed electronically or on magnetic media, **Form 8453-F,** U.S. Estate or Trust Income Tax Declaration and Signature for Electronic and Magnetic Media Filing, must also be filed. For more details, get **Pub. 1437,** Procedures for Electronic and Magnetic Media Filing of U.S. Income Tax Returns for Estates and Trusts, Form 1041, and **Pub. 1438,** File Specifications, Validation Criteria, and Record Layouts for Electronic and Magnetic Media Filing of Estate and Trust Returns, Form 1041. To order these forms and publications, or for more information on electronic and magnetic media filing of Form 1041, call the Magnetic Media Unit at the Philadelphia Service Center at (215) 516-7533 (not a toll-free number), or write to:

Internal Revenue Service Center
Attention: Magnetic Media Unit–DP 115
11601 Roosevelt Blvd.
Philadelphia, PA 19154

When To File

For calendar year estates and trusts, file Form 1041 and Schedules K-1 on or before April 15, 1997. For fiscal year estates and trusts, file Form 1041 by the 15th day of the 4th month following the close of the tax year. If the due date falls on a Saturday, Sunday, or legal holiday, file on the next business day. For example, an estate that has a tax year that ends on June 30, 1996, must file Form 1041 by October 15, 1997.

Extension of Time To File

Estates.— Use **Form 2758,** Application for Extension of Time To File Certain Excise, Income, Information, and Other Returns, to apply for an extension of time to file.

Trusts.— Use **Form 8736,** Application for Automatic Extension of Time To File U.S. Return for a Partnership, REMIC, or for Certain Trusts, to request an automatic 3-month extension of time to file.

If more time is needed, file **Form 8800,** Application for Additional Extension of Time To File U.S. Return for a Partnership, REMIC, or for Certain Trusts, for an additional extension of up to 3 months. To obtain this additional extension of time to file, you must show reasonable cause for the additional time you are requesting. Form 8800 must be filed by the extended due date for Form 1041.

Period Covered

File the 1996 return for calendar year 1996 and fiscal years beginning in 1996 and ending in 1997. If the return is for a fiscal year or a short tax year, fill in the tax year space at the top of the form.

The 1996 Form 1041 may also be used for a tax year beginning in 1997 if:

1. The estate or trust has a tax year of less than 12 months that begins and ends in 1997; and

2. The 1997 Form 1041 is not available by the time the estate or trust is required to file its tax return. However, the estate or trust must show its 1997 tax year on the 1996 Form 1041 and incorporate any tax law changes that are effective for tax years beginning after December 31, 1996.

Where To File

For all estates and trusts, except charitable and split-interest trusts and pooled income funds:

If you are located in	Please mail to the following Internal Revenue Service Center
New Jersey, New York (New York City and counties of Nassau, Rockland, Suffolk, and Westchester)	Holtsville, NY 00501
New York (all other counties), Connecticut, Maine, Massachusetts, New Hampshire, Rhode Island, Vermont	Andover, MA 05501
Florida, Georgia, South Carolina	Atlanta, GA 39901
Indiana, Kentucky, Michigan, Ohio, West Virginia	Cincinnati, OH 45999
Kansas, New Mexico, Oklahoma, Texas	Austin, TX 73301
Alaska, Arizona, California (counties of Alpine, Amador, Butte, Calaveras, Colusa, Contra Costa, Del Norte, El Dorado, Glenn, Humboldt, Lake, Lassen, Marin, Mendocino, Modoc, Napa, Nevada, Placer, Plumas, Sacramento, San Joaquin, Shasta, Sierra, Siskiyou, Solano, Sonoma, Sutter, Tehama, Trinity, Yolo, and Yuba), Colorado, Idaho, Montana, Nebraska, Nevada, North Dakota, Oregon, South Dakota, Utah, Washington, Wyoming	Ogden, UT 84201
California (all other counties), Hawaii	Fresno, CA 93888
Illinois, Iowa, Minnesota, Missouri, Wisconsin	Kansas City, MO 64999
Alabama, Arkansas, Louisiana, Mississippi, North Carolina, Tennessee	Memphis, TN 37501
Delaware, District of Columbia, Maryland, Pennsylvania, Virginia, any U.S. possession, or foreign country	Philadelphia, PA 19255

For a charitable or split-interest trust described in section 4947(a) and a pooled income fund defined in section 642(c)(5):

If you are located in	Please mail to the following Internal Revenue Service Center
Alabama, Arkansas, Florida, Georgia, Louisiana, Mississippi, North Carolina, South Carolina, Tennessee	Atlanta, GA 39901
Arizona, Colorado, Kansas, New Mexico, Oklahoma, Texas, Utah, Wyoming	Austin, TX 73301
Indiana, Kentucky, Michigan, Ohio, West Virginia	Cincinnati, OH 45999
Alaska, California, Hawaii, Idaho, Nevada, Oregon, Washington	Fresno, CA 93888
Connecticut, Maine, Massachusetts, New Hampshire, New York, Rhode Island, Vermont	Holtsville, NY 00501
Illinois, Iowa, Minnesota, Missouri, Montana, Nebraska, North Dakota, South Dakota, Wisconsin	Kansas City, MO 64999

Delaware, District of Columbia, Maryland, New Jersey, Pennsylvania, Virginia, any U.S. possession, or foreign country	Philadelphia, PA 19255

Who Must Sign

The fiduciary, or an authorized representative, must sign Form 1041.

A financial institution that submitted estimated tax payments for trusts for which it is the trustee must enter its EIN in the space provided for the EIN of the fiduciary. Do not enter the EIN of the trust. For this purpose, a financial institution is one that maintains a Treasury Tax and Loan account. If you are an attorney or other individual functioning in a fiduciary capacity, leave this space blank. DO NOT enter your individual social security number (SSN).

If you, as fiduciary, fill in Form 1041, leave the Paid Preparer's space blank. If someone prepares this return and does not charge you, that person should not sign the return.

Generally, anyone who is paid to prepare a tax return must sign the return and fill in the other blanks in the Paid Preparer's Use Only area of the return.

The person required to sign the return must complete the required preparer information and:

- Sign it in the space provided for the preparer's signature. A facsimile signature is acceptable if certain conditions are met. See Regulations section 1.6695-1(b)(4)(iv) for details.
- Give you a copy of the return in addition to the copy to be filed with the IRS.

Accounting Methods

Figure taxable income using the method of accounting regularly used in keeping the estate's or trust's books and records. Generally, permissible methods include the cash method, the accrual method, or any other method authorized by the Internal Revenue Code. In all cases, the method used must clearly reflect income.

Generally, the estate or trust may change its accounting method (for income as a whole or for any material item) only by getting consent on **Form 3115,** Application for Change in Accounting Method. For more information, get **Pub. 538,** Accounting Periods and Methods.

Accounting Periods

For a decedent's estate, the moment of death determines the end of the decedent's tax year and the beginning of the estate's tax year. As executor or administrator, you choose the estate's tax period when you file its first income tax return. The estate's first tax year may be any period of 12 months or less that ends on the last day of a month. If you select the last day of any month other than December, you are adopting a fiscal tax year.

To change the accounting period of an estate, get **Form 1128,** Application To Adopt, Change, or Retain a Tax Year.

Generally, a trust must adopt a calendar year. The following trusts are exempt from this requirement:

- A trust that is exempt from tax under section 501(a);
- A charitable trust described in section 4947(a)(1); and
- A trust that is treated as wholly owned by a grantor under the rules of sections 671 through 679.

Rounding Off to Whole Dollars

You may show the money items on the return and accompanying schedules as whole-dollar amounts. To do so, drop amounts less than 50 cents and increase any amounts from 50 to 99 cents to the next dollar.

Estimated Tax

Generally, an estate or trust must pay estimated income tax for 1997 if it expects to owe, after subtracting any withholding and credits, at least $500 in tax, and it expects the withholding and credits to be less than the smaller of:

1. 90% of the tax shown on the 1997 tax return, or
2. 100% of the tax shown on the 1996 tax return (110% of that amount if the estate's or trust's adjusted gross income on that return is more than $150,000, and less than $2/3$ of gross income for 1996 or 1997 is from farming or fishing).

However, if a return was not filed for 1996 or that return did not cover a full 12 months, item 2 does not apply.

Exceptions

Estimated tax payments are not required from:

1. An estate of a domestic decedent or a domestic trust that had no tax liability for the full 12-month 1996 tax year;
2. A decedent's estate for any tax year ending before the date that is 2 years after the decedent's death; or
3. A trust that was treated as owned by the decedent if the trust will receive the residue of the decedent's estate under the will (or if no will is admitted to probate, the trust primarily responsible for paying debts, taxes, and expenses of administration) for any tax year ending before the date that is 2 years after the decedent's death.

For more information, get **Form 1041-ES,** Estimated Income Tax for Estates and Trusts.

Section 643(g) Election

Fiduciaries of trusts that pay estimated tax may elect under section 643(g) to have any portion of their estimated tax payments allocated to any of the beneficiaries.

The fiduciary of a decedent's estate may make a section 643(g) election only for the final year of the estate.

See the instructions for line 24b for more details.

Interest and Penalties

Interest

Interest is charged on taxes not paid by the due date, even if an extension of time to file is granted.

Interest is also charged on the failure-to-file penalty, the accuracy-related penalty, and the fraud penalty. The interest charge is figured at a rate determined under section 6621.

Late Filing of Return

The law provides a penalty of 5% a month, or part of a month, up to a maximum of 25%, for each month the return is not filed. The penalty is imposed on the net amount due. If the return is more than 60 days late, the minimum penalty is the smaller of $100 or the tax due. The penalty will not be imposed if you can show that the failure to file on time was due to reasonable cause. If the failure is due to reasonable cause, attach an explanation to the return.

Late Payment of Tax

Generally, the penalty for not paying tax when due is 1/2 of 1% of the unpaid amount for each month or part of a month it remains unpaid. The maximum penalty is 25% of the unpaid amount. The penalty is imposed on the net amount due. Any penalty is in addition to interest charges on late payments.

Note: *If you include interest or either of these penalties with your payment, identify and enter these amounts in the bottom margin of Form 1041, page 1. Do not include the interest or penalty amount in the balance of tax due on line 27.*

Failure To Supply Schedule K-1

The fiduciary must provide Schedule K-1 (Form 1041) to each beneficiary who receives a distribution of property or an allocation of an item of the estate. A penalty of $50 (not to exceed $100,000 for any calendar year) will be imposed on the fiduciary for each failure to furnish Schedule K-1 to each beneficiary unless reasonable cause for each failure is established.

Underpaid Estimated Tax

If the fiduciary underpaid estimated tax, get **Form 2210,** Underpayment of Estimated Tax by Individuals, Estates, and Trusts, to figure any penalty. Enter the amount of any penalty on line 26, Form 1041.

Trust Fund Recovery Penalty

This penalty may apply if certain excise, income, social security, and Medicare taxes that must be collected or withheld are not collected or withheld, or these taxes are not paid to the IRS. These taxes are generally reported on Forms 720, 941, 943, or 945. The trust fund recovery penalty may be imposed on all persons who are determined by the IRS to have been **responsible** for collecting, accounting for, and paying over these taxes, and who acted willfully in not doing so. The penalty is equal to the unpaid trust fund tax. See the instructions for Form 720, **Pub. 15 (Circular E),** Employer's Tax Guide, or **Pub. 51 (Circular A),** Agricultural Employer's Tax Guide, for more details, including the definition of responsible persons.

Other Penalties

Other penalties can be imposed for negligence, substantial underpayment of tax, and fraud. Get **Pub. 17,** Your Federal Income Tax, for details on these penalties.

Other Forms That May Be Required

Forms W-2 and **W-3,** Wage and Tax Statement; and Transmittal of Wage and Tax Statements.

Form 56, Notice Concerning Fiduciary Relationship.

Form 706, United States Estate (and Generation-Skipping Transfer) Tax Return; or **Form 706-NA,** United States Estate (and Generation-Skipping Transfer) Tax Return, Estate of nonresident not a citizen of the United States.

Form 706-GS(D), Generation-Skipping Transfer Tax Return For Distributions.

Form 706-GS(D-1), Notification of Distribution From a Generation-Skipping Trust.

Form 706-GS(T), Generation-Skipping Transfer Tax Return for Terminations.

Form 720, Quarterly Federal Excise Tax Return. Use Form 720 to report environmental excise taxes, communications and air transportation taxes, fuel taxes, luxury tax on passenger vehicles, manufacturers' taxes, ship passenger tax, and certain other excise taxes.

Caution: *See Trust Fund Recovery Penalty on page 4.*

Form 940 or **Form 940-EZ,** Employer's Annual Federal Unemployment (FUTA) Tax Return. The estate or trust may be liable for FUTA tax and may have to file Form 940 or 940-EZ if it paid wages of $1,500 or more in any calendar quarter during the calendar year (or the preceding calendar year) or one or more employees worked for the estate or trust for some part of a day in any 20 different weeks during the calendar year.

Form 941, Employer's Quarterly Federal Tax Return. Employers must file this form quarterly to report income tax withheld on wages and employer and employee social security and Medicare taxes. Agricultural employers must file **Form 943,** Employer's Annual Tax Return for Agricultural Employees, instead of Form 941, to report income tax withheld and employer and employee social security and Medicare taxes on farmworkers.

Caution: *See Trust Fund Recovery Penalty on page 4.*

Form 945, Annual Return of Withheld Federal Income Tax. Use this form to report income tax withheld from nonpayroll payments, including pensions, annuities, IRAs, gambling winnings, and backup withholding.

Caution: *See Trust Fund Recovery Penalty on page 4.*

Form 1040, U.S. Individual Income Tax Return.

Form 1040NR, U.S. Nonresident Alien Income Tax Return.

Form 1041-A, U.S. Information Return—Trust Accumulation of Charitable Amounts.

Forms 1042 and **1042-S,** Annual Withholding Tax Return for U.S. Source Income of Foreign Persons; and Foreign Person's U.S. Source Income Subject to Withholding. Use these forms to report and transmit withheld tax on payments or distributions made to nonresident alien individuals, foreign partnerships, or foreign corporations to the extent such payments or distributions constitute gross income from sources within the United States that is not effectively connected with a U.S. trade or business. For more information, see sections 1441 and 1442, and **Pub. 515,** Withholding of Tax on Nonresident Aliens and Foreign Corporations.

Forms 1099-A, B, INT, MISC, OID, R, and **S.**—You may have to file these information returns to report abandonments, acquisitions through foreclosure, proceeds from broker and barter exchange transactions, interest payments, medical and dental health care payments, miscellaneous income, original issue discount, distributions from pensions, annuities, retirement or profit-sharing plans, individual retirement arrangements, insurance contracts, and proceeds from real estate transactions.

Also, use these returns to report amounts received as a nominee on behalf of another person, except amounts reported to beneficiaries on Schedule K-1 (Form 1041).

Form 8275, Disclosure Statement. File Form 8275 to disclose items or positions, except those contrary to a regulation, that are not otherwise adequately disclosed on a tax return. The disclosure is made to avoid parts of the accuracy-related penalty imposed for disregard of rules or substantial understatement of tax. Form 8275 is also used for disclosures relating to preparer penalties for understatements due to unrealistic positions or disregard of rules.

Form 8275-R, Regulation Disclosure Statement, is used to disclose any item on a tax return for which a position has been taken that is contrary to Treasury regulations.

Forms 8288 and **8288-A,** U.S. Withholding Tax Return for Dispositions by Foreign Persons of U.S. Real Property Interests; and Statement of Withholding on Dispositions by Foreign Persons of U.S. Real Property Interests. Use these forms to report and transmit withheld tax on the sale of U.S. real property by a foreign person. Also, use these forms to report and transmit tax withheld from amounts distributed to a foreign beneficiary from a "U.S. real property interest account" that a domestic estate or trust is required to establish under Regulations section 1.1445-5(c)(1)(iii).

Form 8300, Report of Cash Payments Over $10,000 Received in a Trade or Business. Generally, this form is used to report the receipt of more than $10,000 in cash or foreign currency in one transaction (or a series of related transactions).

Attachments

If you need more space on the forms or schedules, attach separate sheets. Use the same size and format as on the printed forms. **But show the totals on the printed forms.**

Attach these separate sheets after all the schedules and forms. Enter the estate's or trust's employer identification number on each sheet.

Do not file a copy of the decedent's will or the trust instrument unless the IRS requests it.

Additional Information

The following publications may assist you in preparing Form 1041.

Pub. 550, Investment Income and Expenses; and

Pub. 559, Survivors, Executors, and Administrators.

Of Special Interest to Bankruptcy Trustees and Debtors-in-Possession

Taxation of Bankruptcy Estates of an Individual

A bankruptcy estate is a separate taxable entity created when an individual debtor files a petition under either chapter 7 or 11 of title 11 of the U.S. Code. The estate is administered by a trustee or a debtor-in-possession. If the case is later dismissed by the bankruptcy court, the debtor is treated as if the bankruptcy petition had never been filed. This provision does NOT apply to partnerships or corporations.

Who Must File

Every trustee (or debtor-in-possession) for an individual's bankruptcy estate under chapter 7 or 11 of title 11 of the U.S. Code must file a return if the bankruptcy estate has gross income of $5,900 or more for tax years beginning in 1996.

Failure to do so may result in an estimated Request for Administrative Expenses being filed by the IRS in the bankruptcy proceeding or a motion to compel filing of the return.

Note: *The filing of a tax return for the bankruptcy estate does not relieve the individual debtor of his or her (or their) individual tax obligations.*

Employer Identification Number

Every bankruptcy estate of an individual required to file a return must have its own employer identification number (EIN). You may apply for one on **Form SS-4,** Application for Employer Identification Number. The social security number (SSN) of the individual debtor cannot be used as the EIN for the bankruptcy estate.

Accounting Period

A bankruptcy estate is allowed to have a fiscal year. The period can be no longer than 12 months.

When To File

File Form 1041 on or before the 15th day of the 4th month following the close of the tax year. Use Form 2758 to apply for an extension of time to file.

Disclosure of Return Information

Under section 6103(e)(5), tax returns of individual debtors who have filed for bankruptcy under chapters 7 or 11 of title 11 are, upon written request, open to inspection by or disclosure to the trustee.

The returns subject to disclosure to the trustee are those for the year the bankruptcy begins and prior years. Use **Form 4506,** Request for Copy or Transcript of Tax Form, to request copies of the individual debtor's tax returns.

If the bankruptcy case was not voluntary, disclosure cannot be made before the bankruptcy court has entered an order for relief, unless the court rules that the disclosure is needed for determining whether relief should be ordered.

Transfer of Tax Attributes From the Individual Debtor to the Bankruptcy Estate

The bankruptcy estate succeeds to the following tax attributes of the individual debtor:

1. Net operating loss (NOL) carryovers;
2. Charitable contributions carryovers;
3. Recovery of tax benefit items;
4. Credit carryovers;
5. Capital loss carryovers;
6. Basis, holding period, and character of assets;
7. Method of accounting;
8. Unused passive activity losses;
9. Unused passive activity credits; and
10. Unused section 465 losses.

Income, Deductions, and Credits

Under section 1398(c), the taxable income of the bankruptcy estate generally is figured in the same manner as an individual. The gross income of the bankruptcy estate includes any income included in property of the estate as defined in Bankruptcy Code section 541. Also included is gain from the sale of property. To figure gain, the trustee or debtor-in-possession must determine the correct basis of the property.

To determine whether any amount paid or incurred by the bankruptcy estate is allowable as a deduction or credit, or is treated as wages for employment tax purposes, treat the amount as if it were paid or incurred by the individual debtor in the same trade or business or other activity the debtor engaged in before the bankruptcy proceedings began.

Administrative expenses.— The bankruptcy estate is allowed a deduction for any administrative expense allowed under section 503 of title 11 of the U.S. Code, and any fee or charge assessed under chapter 123 of title 28 of the U.S. Code, to the extent not disallowed under an Internal Revenue Code provision (e.g., section 263, 265, or 275).

Administrative expense loss.— When figuring a net operating loss, nonbusiness deductions (including administrative expenses) are limited under section 172(d)(4) to the bankruptcy estate's nonbusiness income. The excess nonbusiness deductions are an administrative expense loss that may be carried back to each of the 3 preceding tax years and forward to each of the 7 succeeding tax years of the bankruptcy estate. The amount of an administrative expense loss that may be carried to any tax year is determined after the net operating loss deductions allowed for that year. An administrative expense loss is allowed only to the bankruptcy estate and cannot be carried to any tax year of the individual debtor.

Carryback of net operating losses and credits.— If the bankruptcy estate itself incurs a net operating loss (apart from losses carried forward to the estate from the individual debtor), it can carry back its net operating losses not only to previous tax years of the bankruptcy estate, but also to tax years of the individual debtor prior to the year in which the bankruptcy proceedings began. Excess credits, such as the foreign tax credit, also may be carried back to pre-bankruptcy years of the individual debtor.

Exemption.— For tax years beginning in 1996, a bankruptcy estate is allowed a personal exemption of $2,550.

Standard deduction.— For tax years beginning in 1996, a bankruptcy estate that does not itemize deductions is allowed a standard deduction of $3,350.

Discharge of indebtedness.— In a title 11 case, gross income does not include amounts that normally would be included in gross income resulting from the discharge of indebtedness. However, any amounts excluded from gross income must be applied to reduce certain tax attributes in a certain order. Attach **Form 982,** Reduction of Tax Attributes Due to Discharge of Indebtedness, to show the reduction of tax attributes.

Tax Rate Schedule

Figure the tax for the bankruptcy estate using the tax rate schedule shown below. Enter the tax on Form 1040, line 38.

If taxable income is:

Over—	But not over—	The tax is:	Of the amount over—
$0	$20,050	15%	$0
20,050	48,450	$3,007.50 + 28%	20,050
48,450	73,850	10,959.50 + 31%	48,450
73,850	131,875	18,833.50 + 36%	73,850
131,875	------	39,722.50 + 39.6%	131,875

Prompt Determination of Tax Liability

To request a prompt determination of the tax liability of the bankruptcy estate, the trustee or debtor-in-possession must file a written application for the determination with the IRS District Director for the district in which the bankruptcy case is pending. The application must be submitted in duplicate and executed under the penalties of perjury. The trustee or debtor-in-possession must submit with the application an **exact copy** of the return (or returns) filed by the trustee with the IRS for a completed tax period, and a statement of the name and location of the office where the return was filed. The envelope should be marked, "Personal Attention of the Special Procedures Function (Bankruptcy Section). DO NOT OPEN IN MAILROOM."

The IRS will notify the trustee or debtor-in-possession within 60 days from receipt of the application whether the return filed by the trustee or debtor-in-possession has been selected for examination or has been accepted as filed. If the return is selected for examination, it will be examined as soon as possible. The IRS will notify the trustee or debtor-in-possession of any tax due within 180 days from receipt of the application or within any additional time permitted by the bankruptcy court.

See Rev. Proc. 81-17, 1981-1 C B 688.

Special Filing Instructions for Bankruptcy Estates

Use Form 1041 only as a transmittal for Form 1040. In the top margin of Form 1040 write "Attachment to Form 1041 DO NOT DETACH." Attach Form 1040 to Form 1041. Complete only the identification area at the top of Form 1041. Enter the name of the individual debtor in the following format: "John Q Public Bankruptcy Estate." Beneath enter the name of the trustee in the following format: "Avery Snow, Trustee." In item D, enter the date the petition was filed or the date of conversion to a chapter 7 or 11 case. Enter on Form 1041, line 23, any tax due from line 51 of Form 1040. Complete lines 24 through 29 of Form 1041, and sign and date it.

Specific Instructions

Name of Estate or Trust

Copy the exact name of the estate or trust from the **Form SS-4,** Application for Employer Identification Number, that you used to apply for the employer identification number (EIN).

If a grantor type trust (discussed below), write the name, identification number, and address of the grantor(s) or other person(s) in parentheses after the name of the trust.

Address

Include the suite, room, or other unit number after the street address.

If the Post Office does not deliver mail to the street address and the fiduciary has a P.O. box, show the box number instead of the street address.

If you change your address after filing Form 1041, use **Form 8822,** Change of Address, to notify the IRS.

A. Type of Entity

Check the appropriate box that describes the entity for which you are filing the return.

Note: *There are special filing requirements for grantor type trusts and bankruptcy estates (discussed below).*

Decedent's Estate

An estate of a deceased person is a taxable entity separate from the decedent. It generally continues to exist until the final distribution of the assets of the estate is made to the heirs and other beneficiaries. The income earned from the property of the estate during the period of administration or settlement must be accounted for and reported by the estate.

Simple Trust

A trust may qualify as a simple trust if:

1. The trust instrument requires that all income must be distributed currently;

2. The trust instrument does not provide that any amounts are to be paid, permanently set aside, or used for charitable purposes; and

3. The trust does not distribute amounts allocated to the corpus of the trust.

Complex Trust

A complex trust is any trust that does not qualify as a simple trust as explained above.

Grantor Type Trust

A grantor type trust is a legal trust under applicable state law that is not recognized as a separate taxable entity for income tax purposes because the grantor or other substantial owners have not relinquished complete dominion and control over the trust.

Generally, for transfers made in trust after March 1, 1986, the grantor is treated as the owner of any portion of a trust in which he or she has a reversionary interest in either the income or corpus therefrom, if, as of the inception of that portion of the trust, the value of that interest is more than 5% of the value of that portion. Also, the grantor is treated as holding any power or interest that was held by either the grantor's spouse at the time that the power or interest was created or who became the grantor's spouse after the creation of that power or interest.

Report on Form 1041 the part of the income that is taxable to the trust. Do not report on Form 1041 the income that is taxable to the grantor or another person. Instead, attach a separate sheet to report the following:

- The income of the trust that is taxable to the grantor or another person under sections 671 through 678;
- The name, identifying number, and address of the person(s) to whom the income is taxable; and
- Any deductions or credits applied to this income.

The income taxable to the grantor or another person under sections 671 through 678 and the deductions and credits applied to the income must be reported on the income tax return that person files.

Family estate trust.— A family estate trust is also known as a family, family estate, pure, equity, equity pure, prime, or constitutional trust.

In most cases, the grantor transfers property to the trust or assigns to the trust the income for services the grantor performs. The trust instrument usually provides:

- Evidence of ownership, such as certificates of beneficial interest in the trust.
- That the grantor is a trustee and executive officer.
- That the trust pays the living expenses for the grantor and the grantor's family.
- That the corpus and undistributed income are distributed to the owners after the trust is terminated.

Generally, a family estate trust is treated as a grantor type trust. For more information, see Rev. Rul. 75-257, 1975-2 C.B. 251.

Mortgage pools.— The trustee of a mortgage pool, such as the Federal National Mortgage Association, collects principal and interest payments on each mortgage and makes distributions to the certificate holders. Each pool is considered a grantor type trust, and each certificate holder is treated as the owner of an undivided interest in the entire trust under the grantor trust rules. Certificate holders must report their proportionate share of the mortgage interest and other items of income on their individual tax returns.

Pre-need funeral trusts.— The purchasers of pre-need funeral services are the grantors and the owners of pre-need funeral trusts established under state laws. See Rev. Rul. 87-127, 1987-2 C.B. 156.

Nonqualified deferred compensation plans.— Taxpayers may adopt and maintain grantor trusts in connection with nonqualified deferred compensation plans (sometimes referred to as "rabbi trusts"). Rev. Proc. 92-64, 1992-2 C.B. 422, provides a "model grantor trust" for use in rabbi trust arrangements. The procedure also provides guidance for requesting rulings on the plans that use these trusts.

Optional filing methods for certain grantor type trusts.— Generally, for a trust all of which is treated as owned by one or more grantors or other persons, the trustee may use one of the following 3 optional methods to report instead of filing Form 1041:

Method 1. For a trust treated as owned by one grantor or by one other person, the trustee must give all payers of income during the tax year the name and taxpayer identification number (TIN) of the grantor or other person treated as the owner of the trust and the address of the trust. This method may be used only if the owner of the trust provides the trustee with a signed **Form W-9,** Request for Taxpayer Identification Number and Certification. In addition, unless the grantor or other person treated as owner of the trust is the trustee or a co-trustee of the trust, the trustee must give the grantor or other person treated as owner of the trust a statement that **(a)** shows all items of income, deduction, and credit of the trust; **(b)** identifies the payer of each item of income; **(c)** explains how the grantor or other person treated as owner of the trust takes those items into account when figuring the grantor's or other person's taxable income or tax; and **(d)** informs the grantor or other person treated as the owner of the trust that those items must be included when figuring taxable income and credits on his or her income tax return.

Method 2. For a trust treated as owned by one grantor or by one other person, the trustee must give all payers of income during the tax year the name, address, and TIN of the trust. The trustee also must file with the IRS the appropriate Forms 1099 to report the income or gross proceeds paid to the trust during the tax year that shows the trust as the payer and the grantor or other person treated as owner as the payee. The trustee must report each type of income in the aggregate and each item of gross proceeds separately. In addition, unless the grantor or other person treated as owner of the trust is the trustee or a co-trustee of the trust, the trustee must give the grantor or other person treated as owner of the trust a statement that **(a)** shows all items of income, deduction, and credit of the trust; **(b)** explains how the grantor or other person treated as owner of the trust takes those items into account when figuring the grantor's or other person's taxable income or tax; and **(c)** informs the grantor or other person treated as the owner of the trust that those items must be included when figuring taxable income and credits on his or her income tax return. This statement satisfies the requirement to give the recipient copies of the Forms 1099 filed by the trustee.

Method 3. For a trust treated as owned by two or more grantors or other persons, the trustee must give all payers of income during the tax year the name, address, and TIN of the trust. The trustee also must file with the IRS the appropriate Forms 1099 to report the income or gross proceeds paid to the trust by all payers during the tax year attributable to the part of the trust treated as owned by each grantor or other person, showing the trust as the payer and each grantor or other person treated as owner of the trust as the payee. The trustee must report each type of income in the aggregate and each item of gross proceeds separately. In addition, the trustee must give each grantor or other person treated as owner of the trust a statement that **(a)** shows all items of income, deduction, and credit of the trust attributable to the part of the trust treated as owned by the grantor or other person; **(b)** explains how the grantor or other person treated as owner of the trust takes those items into account when figuring the grantor's or other person's taxable income or tax; and **(c)** informs the grantor or other person treated as the owner of the trust that those items must be included when figuring taxable income and credits on his or her income tax return. This statement satisfies the requirement to give the recipient copies of the Forms 1099 filed by the trustee.

Exceptions.—The following trusts cannot report using the optional filing methods:

1. A common trust fund (as defined in section 584(a)).

2. A foreign trust or a trust that has any of its assets located outside the United States.

3. A qualified subchapter S trust (as defined in section 1361(d)(3)).

4. A trust all of which is treated as owned by one grantor or one other person whose tax year is other than a calendar year.

5. A trust all of which is treated as owned by one or more grantors or other persons, one of which is not a U.S. person.

6. A trust all of which is treated as owned by one or more grantors or other persons if at least one grantor or other person is an exempt recipient for information reporting purposes, unless at least one grantor or other person is not an exempt recipient and the trustee reports without treating any of the grantors or other persons as exempt recipients.

A trustee who previously had filed Form 1041 for any tax year ending before January 1, 1996 (and who previously had not filed a final Form 1041 under the simplified filing rule in effect prior to January 1, 1996), or who files a Form 1041 for any later tax year, can change to one of the optional methods by filing a final Form 1041 for the tax year that immediately precedes the first tax year for which the trustee elects to report under one of the optional methods. On the front of the final Form 1041, the trustee must write "Pursuant to section 1.671-4(g), this is the final Form 1041 for this grantor trust," and check the "Final return" box in item F. For more details on changing reporting methods, including changes from one optional method to another, see Regulations section 1.671-4(g).

Backup withholding.— Generally, a grantor trust is considered a payor of reportable payments received by the trust for purposes of backup withholding. If the trust has 10 or fewer grantors, a reportable payment made to the trust is treated as a reportable payment of the same kind made to the grantors on the date the trust received the payment. If the trust has more than 10 grantors, a reportable payment made to the trust is treated as a payment of the same kind made by the trust to each grantor in an amount equal to the distribution made to each grantor on the date the grantor is paid or credited. The trustee must withhold 31% of reportable payments made to any grantor who is subject to backup withholding. For more information, see section 3406 and Temporary Regulations section 35a.9999-2, Q&A 20.

Bankruptcy Estate

A chapter 7 or 11 bankruptcy estate is a separate and distinct taxable entity from the individual debtor for Federal income tax purposes. See **Of Special Interest to Bankruptcy Trustees and Debtors-in-Possession** on page 5.

For more information, see section 1398 and **Pub. 908**, Bankruptcy Tax Guide.

Pooled Income Fund

A pooled income fund is a split-interest trust with a remainder interest for a public charity and a life income interest retained by the donor or for another person. The property is held in a pool with other pooled income fund property and does not include any tax-exempt securities. The income for a retained life interest is figured using the yearly rate of return earned by the trust. See section 642(c) and the related regulations for more information.

If you are filing for a pooled income fund, attach a statement to support the following:

● The calculation of the yearly rate of return.

● The computation of the deduction for distributions to the beneficiaries.

● The computation of any charitable deduction.

You do not have to complete Schedules A or B of Form 1041.

If the fund has accumulations of income, file Form 1041-A unless the fund is required to distribute all of its net income to beneficiaries currently.

You must also file **Form 5227**, Split-Interest Trust Information Return, for the pooled income fund.

B. Number of Schedules K-1 Attached

Every trust or decedent's estate claiming an income distribution deduction on page 1, line 18, must enter the number of Schedules K-1 (Form 1041) that are attached to Form 1041.

C. Employer Identification Number

Every estate or trust must have an EIN. To apply for one, use Form SS-4. You may get this form from the IRS or the Social Security Administration. See **Pub. 583**, Starting a Business and Keeping Records, for more information.

If you are filing a return for a mortgage pool, such as one created under the mortgage-backed security programs administered by the Federal National Mortgage Association ("Fannie Mae") or the Government National Mortgage Association ("Ginnie Mae"), the EIN stays with the pool if that pool is traded from one financial institution to another.

D. Date Entity Created

Enter the date the trust was created, or, if a decedent's estate, the date of the decedent's death.

E. Nonexempt Charitable and Split-Interest Trusts

Section 4947(a)(1) Trust

Check this box if the trust is a nonexempt charitable trust within the meaning of section 4947(a)(1). A nonexempt charitable trust is a trust that is not exempt from tax under section 501(a); all of the unexpired interests are devoted to one or more charitable purposes described in section 170(c)(2)(B); and for which a deduction was allowed under section 170 (for individual taxpayers) or similar Code section for personal holding companies, foreign personal holding companies, or estates or trusts (including a deduction for estate or gift tax purposes).

Not a Private Foundation

Check this box if the charitable trust is not treated as a private foundation under section 509. For more information, see Regulations section 53.4947-1.

If a nonexempt charitable trust is not treated as though it were a private foundation, the fiduciary must file **Form 990 (or Form 990-EZ),** Return of Organization Exempt From Income Tax, and **Schedule A (Form 990),** Organization Exempt Under Section 501(c)(3), in addition to Form 1041 if the trust's gross receipts are normally more than $25,000.

If a nonexempt charitable trust is not treated as though it were a private foundation, and it has no taxable income under Subtitle A, it can file either Form 990 or Form 990-EZ instead of Form 1041 to meet its section 6012 filing requirement.

Section 4947(a)(2) Trust

Check this box if the trust is a split-interest trust described in section 4947(a)(2). A split-interest trust is a trust that is not exempt from tax under section 501(a); has some unexpired interests that are devoted to purposes other than religious, charitable, or similar purposes described in section 170(c)(2)(B); and has amounts transferred in trust after May 26, 1969, for which a deduction was allowed under section 170 (for individual taxpayers) or similar Code section for personal holding companies, foreign personal holding companies, or estates or trusts (including a deduction for estate or gift tax purposes).

The fiduciary of a split-interest trust must also file Form 5227 (for amounts transferred in trust after May 26, 1969); and Form 1041-A if the trust's governing instrument does not require that all of the trust's income be distributed currently.

If a split-interest trust has any unrelated business taxable income, however, it must file Form 1041 to report all of its income and to pay any tax due.

Nonexempt Charitable Trust Treated as a Private Foundation

If a nonexempt charitable trust is treated as though it were a private foundation under section 509, then the fiduciary must file **Form 990-PF,** Return of Private Foundation, in addition to Form 1041.

If a nonexempt charitable trust is subject to any of the private foundation excise taxes, then it must also file **Form 4720,** Return of Certain Excise Taxes on Charities and Other Persons Under Chapters 41 and 42 of the Internal Revenue Code. Any private foundation taxes paid by the trust cannot be taken as a deduction on Form 1041.

If a nonexempt charitable trust is treated as though it were a private foundation, and it has no taxable income under Subtitle A, it may file Form 990-PF instead of Form 1041 to meet its section 6012 filing requirement.

F. Initial Return, Amended Return, Final Return; or Change in Fiduciary's Name or Address

Amended Return

If you are filing an amended Form 1041, check the "Amended return" box. Complete the entire return, correct the appropriate lines with the new information, and refigure the estate's or trust's tax liability. If the total tax on line 23 is larger on the amended return than on the original return, you generally should pay the difference with the amended return. However, you should adjust this amount if there is any increase or decrease in the total payments shown on line 25. On an attached sheet explain the reason for the amendments and identify the lines and amounts being changed on the amended return.

If the amended return results in a change to income, or a change in distribution of any income or other information provided to a beneficiary, an amended Schedule K-1 (Form 1041) must also be filed with the amended Form 1041 and given to each beneficiary. Check the "Amended K-1" box at the top of the amended Schedule K-1.

Final Return

Check this box if this is a final return because the estate or trust has terminated. Also, check the "Final K-1" box at the top of Schedule K-1.

If, on the final return, there are excess deductions, an unused capital loss carryover, or a net operating loss carryover, see the discussion in the Schedule K-1 instructions on page 27. Figure the deductions on an attached sheet.

G. Pooled Mortgage Account

If you bought a pooled mortgage account during the year, and still have that pool at the end of the tax year, check the "Bought" box and enter the date of purchase. If you sold a pooled mortgage account that was purchased during this, or a previous, tax year, check the "Sold" box and enter the date of sale. If you neither bought nor sold a pooled mortgage account, skip this item.

Income

Special Rule for Blind Trust

If you are reporting income from a qualified blind trust (under the Ethics in Government Act of 1978), do not identify the payer of any income to the trust but complete the rest of the return as provided in the instructions. Also write "Blind Trust" at the top of page 1.

Line 1—Interest Income

Report the estate's or trust's share of all taxable interest income that was received during the tax year. Examples of taxable interest include interest from:
- Accounts (including certificates of deposit and money market accounts) with banks, credit unions, and thrifts.
- Notes, loans, and mortgages.
- U.S. Treasury bills, notes, and bonds.
- U.S. savings bonds.
- Original issue discount.
- Income received as a regular interest holder of a real estate mortgage investment conduit (REMIC).

For taxable bonds acquired after 1987, amortizable bond premium is treated as an offset to the interest income instead of as a separate interest deduction. See Pub. 550.

For the year of the decedent's death, Forms 1099-INT issued in the decedent's name may include interest income earned after the date of death that should be reported on the income tax return of the decedent's estate. When preparing the decedent's final income tax return, report on line 1 of Schedule B (Form 1040) or Schedule 1 (Form 1040A) the total interest shown on Form 1099-INT. Under the last entry on line 1, subtotal all the interest reported on line 1. Below the subtotal, write "Form 1041" and the name and address shown on Form 1041 for the decedent's estate. Also, show the part of the interest reported on Form 1041 and subtract it from the subtotal.

Line 2—Dividends

Report the estate's or trust's share of all ordinary dividends received during the tax year.

For the year of the decedent's death, Forms 1099-DIV issued in the decedent's name may include dividends earned after the date of death that should be reported on the income tax return of the decedent's estate. When preparing the decedent's final income tax return, report on line 5 of Schedule B (Form 1040) or Schedule 1 (Form 1040A) the total dividends shown on Form 1099-DIV. Under the last entry on line 5, subtotal all the dividends reported on line 5. Below the subtotal, write "Form 1041" and the name and address shown on Form 1041 for the decedent's estate. Also, show the part of the dividends reported on Form 1041 and subtract it from the subtotal.

Note: *Report capital gain distributions on Schedule D (Form 1041), line 10.*

Line 3—Business Income or (Loss)

If the estate or trust operated a business, report the income and expenses on **Schedule C (Form 1040),** Profit or Loss From Business (or **Schedule C-EZ (Form 1040),** Net Profit From Business). Enter the net profit or (loss) from Schedule C (or Schedule C-EZ) on line 3.

Line 4—Capital Gain or (Loss)

Enter the gain from Schedule D (Form 1041), Part III, line 17, column (c); or the loss from Part IV, line 18.

Note: *Do not substitute Schedule D (Form 1040) for Schedule D (Form 1041).*

Line 5—Rents, Royalties, Partnerships, Other Estates and Trusts, etc.

Use **Schedule E (Form 1040)**, Supplemental Income and Loss, to report the estate's or trust's share of income or (losses) from rents, royalties, partnerships, S corporations, other estates and trusts, and REMICs. Enter the net profit or (loss) from Schedule E on line 5. See the instructions for Schedule E (Form 1040) for reporting requirements.

If the estate or trust received a Schedule K-1 from a partnership, S corporation, or other flow-through entity, use the corresponding lines on Form 1041 to report the interest, dividends, capital gains, etc., from the flow-through entity.

Line 6—Farm Income or (Loss)

If the estate or trust operated a farm, use **Schedule F (Form 1040)**, Profit or Loss From Farming, to report farm income and expenses. Enter the net profit or (loss) from Schedule F on line 6.

Line 7—Ordinary Gain or (Loss)

Enter from line 20, **Form 4797**, Sales of Business Property, the ordinary gain or loss from the sale or exchange of property other than capital assets and also from involuntary conversions (other than casualty or theft).

Line 8—Other Income

Enter other items of income not included on lines 1 through 7. List the type and amount on an attached schedule if the estate or trust has more than one item.

Items to be reported on line 8 include:

- Unpaid compensation received by the decedent's estate that is income in respect of a decedent.
- Any part of a total distribution shown on **Form 1099-R**, Distributions From Pensions, Annuities, Retirement or Profit-Sharing Plans, IRAs, Insurance Contracts, etc., that is treated as ordinary income. For more information, see the separate instructions for **Form 4972**, Tax on Lump-Sum Distributions.

Deductions

Amortization, Depletion, and Depreciation

A trust or decedent's estate is allowed a deduction for amortization, depletion, and depreciation only to the extent the deductions are not apportioned to the beneficiaries.

For a decedent's estate, the depreciation deduction is apportioned between the estate and the heirs, legatees, and devisees on the basis of the estate's income allocable to each.

For a trust, the depreciation deduction is apportioned between the income beneficiaries and the trust on the basis of the trust income allocable to each, unless the governing instrument (or local law) requires or permits the trustee to maintain a depreciation reserve. If the trustee is required to maintain a reserve, the deduction is first allocated to the trust, up to the amount of the reserve. Any excess is allocated among the beneficiaries in the same manner as the trust's accounting income. See Regulations section 1.167(h)-1(b).

For mineral or timber property held by a decedent's estate, the depletion deduction is apportioned between the estate and the heirs, legatees, and devisees on the basis of the estate's income from such property allocable to each.

For mineral or timber property held in trust, the depletion deduction is apportioned between the income beneficiaries and the trust based on the trust income from such property allocable to each, unless the governing instrument (or local law) requires or permits the trustee to maintain a reserve for depletion. If the trustee is required to maintain a reserve, the deduction is first allocated to the trust, up to the amount of the reserve. Any excess is allocated among the beneficiaries in the same manner as the trust's accounting income. See Regulations section 1.611-1(c)(4).

The deduction for amortization is apportioned between an estate or trust and its beneficiaries under the same principles for apportioning the deductions for depreciation and depletion.

An estate or trust is not allowed to make an election under section 179 to expense certain tangible property.

The deduction for the amortization of reforestation expenditures under section 194 is allowed only to an estate.

The estate's or trust's share of amortization, depletion, and depreciation should be reported on the appropriate lines of Schedule C (or C-EZ), E, or F (Form 1040), the net income or loss from which is shown on line 3, 5, or 6 of Form 1041. If the deduction is not related to a specific business or activity, then report it on line 15a.

Allocation of Deductions for Tax-Exempt Income

Generally, no deduction that would otherwise be allowable is allowed for any expense (whether for business or for the production of income) that is allocable to tax-exempt income. Examples of tax-exempt income include:

- Certain death benefits (section 101);
- Interest on state or local bonds (section 103);
- Compensation for injuries or sickness (section 104); and
- Income from discharge of indebtedness in a title 11 case (section 108).

Exception. State income taxes and business expenses that are allocable to tax-exempt interest are deductible.

Expenses that are directly allocable to tax-exempt income are allocated only to tax-exempt income. A reasonable proportion of expenses indirectly allocable to both tax-exempt income and other income must be allocated to each class of income.

Deductions That May Be Allowable for Estate Tax Purposes

Administration expenses and casualty and theft losses deductible on Form 706 may be deducted, to the extent otherwise deductible for income tax purposes, on Form 1041 if the fiduciary files a statement waiving the right to deduct the expenses and losses on Form 706. The statement must be filed before the expiration of the statutory period of limitations for the tax year the deduction is claimed. See Pub. 559 for more information.

Accrued Expenses

Generally, an accrual basis taxpayer can deduct accrued expenses in the tax year that: **(a)** all events have occurred that determine the liability; and **(b)** the amount of the liability can be figured with reasonable accuracy. However, all the events that establish liability are treated as occurring only when economic performance takes place. There are exceptions for recurring items. See section 461(h).

Limitations on Deductions

At-Risk Loss Limitations

Generally, the amount the estate or trust has "at risk" limits the loss it can deduct for any tax year. Use **Form 6198**, At-Risk Limitations, to figure the deductible loss for the year and file it with Form 1041. For more information, get **Pub. 925**, Passive Activity and At-Risk Rules.

Passive Activity Loss and Credit Limitations

Section 469 and the regulations thereunder generally limit losses from passive activities to the amount of income derived from all passive activities. Similarly, credits from passive activities are generally limited to the tax attributable to such activities. These limitations are first applied at the estate or trust level.

Generally, an activity is a passive activity if it involves the conduct of any trade or business, and the taxpayer does not materially participate in the activity. Passive activities do not include working interests in oil and gas properties. See section 469(c)(3).

For a grantor trust, material participation is determined at the grantor level.

Generally, rental activities are passive activities, whether or not the taxpayer materially participates. However, certain taxpayers who materially participate in real property trades or businesses are not subject to the passive activity limitations on losses from rental real estate activities in which they materially participate. For more details, see section 469(c)(7).

Note: *Material participation standards for estates and trusts had not been established by regulations at the time these instructions went to print.*

For tax years of an estate ending less than 2 years after the decedent's date of death, up to $25,000 of deductions and deduction equivalents of credits from rental real estate activities in which the decedent actively participated is allowed. Any excess losses and/or credits are suspended for the year and carried forward.

If the estate or trust distributes an interest in a passive activity, the basis of the property immediately before the distribution is increased by the passive activity losses allocable to the interest, and such losses cannot be deducted. See section 469(j)(12).

Note: *Losses from passive activities are first subject to the at-risk rules. When the losses are deductible under the at-risk rules, the passive activity rules then apply.*

Portfolio income is not treated as income from a passive activity, and passive losses and credits generally may not be applied to offset it. Portfolio income generally includes interest, dividends, royalties, and income from annuities. Portfolio income of an estate or trust must be accounted for separately.

See **Form 8582,** Passive Activity Loss Limitations, to figure the amount of losses allowed from passive activities. See **Form 8582-CR,** Passive Activity Credit Limitations, to figure the amount of credit allowed for the current year.

Transactions Between Related Taxpayers

Under section 267, a trust that uses the accrual method of accounting may only deduct business expenses and interest owed to a related party in the year the payment is included in the income of the related party. For this purpose, a related party includes:

1. A grantor and a fiduciary of any trust;
2. A fiduciary of a trust and a fiduciary of another trust, if the same person is a grantor of both trusts;
3. A fiduciary of a trust and a beneficiary of such trust;
4. A fiduciary of a trust and a beneficiary of another trust, if the same person is a grantor of both trusts; and
5. A fiduciary of a trust and a corporation more than 50% in value of the outstanding stock of which is owned, directly or indirectly, by or for the trust or by or for a person who is a grantor of the trust.

Line 10—Interest

Enter the amount of interest (subject to limitations) paid or incurred by the estate or trust on amounts borrowed by the estate or trust, or on debt acquired by the estate or trust (e.g., outstanding obligations from the decedent) that is not claimed elsewhere on the return.

If the proceeds of a loan were used for more than one purpose (e.g., to purchase a portfolio investment and to acquire an interest in a passive activity), the fiduciary must make an interest allocation according to the rules in Temporary Regulations section 1.163-8T.

Do not include interest paid on indebtedness incurred or continued to purchase or carry obligations on which the interest is wholly exempt from income tax.

Personal interest is not deductible. Examples of personal interest include interest paid on:
- Revolving charge accounts.
- Personal notes for money borrowed from a bank, credit union, or other person.
- Installment loans on personal use property.
- Underpayments of Federal, state, or local income taxes.

Interest that is paid or incurred on indebtedness allocable to a trade or business (including a rental activity) should be deducted on the appropriate line of Schedule C (or C-EZ), E, or F (Form 1040), the net income or loss from which is shown on line 3, 5, or 6 of Form 1041.

Types of interest to include on line 10 are:

1. Any investment interest (subject to limitations);
2. Any qualified residence interest; and
3. Any interest payable under section 6601 on any unpaid portion of the estate tax attributable to the value of a reversionary or remainder interest in property, or an interest in a closely held business for the period during which an extension of time for payment of such tax is in effect.

Investment interest.— Generally, investment interest is interest (including amortizable bond premium on taxable bonds acquired after October 22, 1986, but before January 1, 1988) that is paid or incurred on indebtedness that is properly allocable to property held for investment. Investment interest does not include any qualified residence interest, or interest that is taken into account under section 469 in figuring income or loss from a passive activity.

Generally, net investment income is the excess of investment income over investment expenses. Investment expenses are those expenses (other than interest) allowable after application of the 2% floor on miscellaneous itemized deductions.

The amount of the investment interest deduction may be limited. Use **Form 4952,** Investment Interest Expense Deduction, to figure the allowable investment interest deduction.

If you must complete Form 4952, check the box on line 10 and attach Form 4952. Then, add the deductible investment interest to the other types of deductible interest and enter the total on line 10.

Qualified residence interest.— Interest paid or incurred by an estate or trust on indebtedness secured by a qualified residence of a beneficiary of an estate or trust is treated as qualified residence interest if the residence would be a qualified residence (i.e., the principal residence or the second residence selected by the beneficiary) if owned by the beneficiary. The beneficiary must have a present interest in the estate or trust or an interest in the residuary of the estate or trust. See **Pub. 936,** Home Mortgage Interest Deduction, for an explanation of the general rules for deducting home mortgage interest.

See section 163(h)(3) for a definition of qualified residence interest and for limitations on indebtedness.

Line 11—Taxes

Enter any deductible taxes paid or incurred during the tax year that are not deductible elsewhere on Form 1041.

Deductible taxes include:
- State and local income or real property taxes.
- The generation-skipping transfer (GST) tax imposed on income distributions.

Do not deduct:
- Federal income taxes.
- Estate, inheritance, legacy, succession, and gift taxes.
- Federal duties and excise taxes.
- State and local sales taxes. Instead, treat these taxes as part of the cost of the property.

Line 12—Fiduciary Fees

Enter the deductible fees paid or incurred to the fiduciary for administering the estate or trust during the tax year.

Note: *Fiduciary fees deducted on Form 706 cannot be deducted on Form 1041.*

Line 15a—Other Deductions NOT Subject to the 2% Floor

Attach your own schedule, listing by type and amount, all allowable deductions that are not deductible elsewhere on Form 1041.

Do not include any losses on worthless bonds and similar obligations and nonbusiness bad debts. Report these losses on Schedule D (Form 1041).

Do not deduct medical or funeral expenses on Form 1041. Medical expenses of the decedent paid by the estate may be deductible on the decedent's income tax return for the year incurred. See section 213(c). Funeral expenses are deductible ONLY on Form 706.

The following are examples of deductions that are reported on line 15a.

Bond premium(s).— For taxable bonds acquired before October 23, 1986, if the fiduciary elected to amortize the premium, report the amortization on this line. For tax-exempt bonds, the amortization cannot be deducted. In all cases where the fiduciary has made an election to amortize the premium, the basis must be reduced by the amount of amortization.

For more information, see section 171 and Pub. 550.

If you claim a bond premium deduction for the estate or trust, figure the deduction on a separate sheet and attach it to Form 1041.

Casualty and theft losses.— Use **Form 4684,** Casualties and Thefts, to figure any deductible casualty and theft losses.

Deduction for clean-fuel vehicles.— Section 179A allows a deduction for part of the cost of qualified clean-fuel vehicle property. Get **Pub. 535,** Business Expenses, for more details.

Net operating loss deduction (NOLD).— An estate or trust is allowed the net operating loss deduction (NOLD) under section 172.

If you claim an NOLD for the estate or trust, figure the deduction on a separate sheet and attach it to this return.

Estate's or trust's share of amortization, depreciation, and depletion not claimed elsewhere.— If you cannot deduct the amortization, depreciation, and depletion as rent or royalty expenses on Schedule E (Form 1040), or as business or farm expenses on Schedule C, C-EZ, or F (Form 1040), itemize the fiduciary's share of the deductions on an attached sheet and include them on line 15a. Itemize each beneficiary's share of the deductions and report them on the appropriate line of Schedule K-1 (Form 1041).

Line 15b—Allowable Miscellaneous Itemized Deductions Subject to the 2% Floor

Miscellaneous itemized deductions are deductible only to the extent that the aggregate amount of such deductions exceeds 2% of adjusted gross income (AGI).

Miscellaneous itemized deductions do not include deductions for:
- Interest under section 163.
- Taxes under section 164.
- The amortization of bond premium under section 171.
- Estate taxes attributable to income in respect of a decedent under section 691(c).

For other exceptions, see section 67(b).

For estates and trusts, the AGI is figured by subtracting the following from total income on line 9 of page 1:

1. The administration costs of the estate or trust (the total of lines 12, 14, and 15a to the extent they are costs incurred in the administration of the estate or trust) that would not have been incurred if the property were NOT held by the estate or trust;
2. The income distribution deduction (line 18);
3. The amount of the exemption (line 20);
4. The deduction for clean-fuel vehicles claimed on line 15a; and
5. The net operating loss deduction claimed on line 15a.

For those estates and trusts whose income distribution deduction is limited to the actual distribution, and NOT the DNI (i.e., the income distribution is less than the DNI), when computing the AGI, use the amount of the actual distribution.

For those estates and trusts whose income distribution deduction is limited to the DNI (i.e., the actual distribution exceeds the DNI), the DNI must be figured taking into account the allowable miscellaneous itemized deductions (AMID) after application of the 2% floor. In this situation there are two unknown amounts: **(a)** the AMID; and **(b)** the DNI.

The following example illustrates how an algebraic equation can be used to solve for these unknown amounts:

The Malcolm Smith Trust, a complex trust, earned $20,000 of dividend income, $20,000 of capital gains, and a fully deductible $5,000 loss from XYZ partnership (chargeable to corpus) in 1996. The trust instrument provides that capital gains are added to corpus. 50% of the fiduciary fees are allocated to income and 50% to corpus. The trust claimed a $2,000 deduction on line 12 of Form 1041. The trust incurred $1,500 of miscellaneous itemized deductions (chargeable to income), which are subject to the 2% floor. There are no other deductions. The trustee made a discretionary distribution of the accounting income of $17,500 to the trust's sole beneficiary.

Because the actual distribution can reasonably be expected to exceed the DNI, the trust must figure the DNI, taking into account the allowable miscellaneous itemized deductions, to determine the amount to enter on line 15b.

The trust also claims an exemption of $100 on line 20.

To compute line 15b, use the equation below:

$AMID$ = total miscellaneous itemized deductions $- (.02(AGI))$

In the above example:

$AMID = 1,500 - (.02(AGI))$

In all situations, use the following equation to compute the AGI:

AGI = (line 9) $-$ (the total of lines 12, 14, and 15a to the extent they are costs incurred in the administration of the estate or trust that would not have been incurred if the property were NOT held by the estate or trust) $-$ (line 18) $-$ (line 20).

Note: *There are no other deductions claimed by the trust on line 15a that are deductible in arriving at AGI.*

In the above example:

$AGI = 35,000 - 2,000 - DNI - 100$

Since the value of line 18 is not known because it is limited to the DNI, you are left with the following:

$AGI = 32,900 - DNI$

Substitute the value of AGI in the equation:

$AMID = 1,500 - (.02(32,900 - DNI))$

The equation cannot be solved until the value of DNI is known. The DNI can be expressed in terms of the AMID. To do this, compute the DNI using the known values. In this example, the DNI is equal to the total income of the trust (less any capital gains allocated to corpus; or plus any capital loss from line 4); less total deductions from line 16 (excluding any miscellaneous itemized deductions); less the AMID.

Thus, DNI = (line 9) $-$ (line 17, column (b) of Schedule D (Form 1041)) $-$ (line 16) $-$ (AMID)

Substitute the known values:

$DNI = 35,000 - 20,000 - 2,000 - AMID$
$DNI = 13,000 - AMID$

Substitute the value of DNI in the equation to solve for AMID:

$AMID = 1,500 - (.02(32,900 - (13,000 - AMID)))$
$AMID = 1,500 - (.02(32,900 - 13,000 + AMID))$
$AMID = 1,500 - (658 - 260 + .02\ AMID)$
$AMID = 1,102 - .02\ AMID$
$1.02\ AMID = 1,102$
$AMID = 1,080$
$DNI = 11,920$ (i.e., $13,000 - 1,080$)
$AGI = 20,980$ (i.e., $32,900 - 11,920$)

Note: *The income distribution deduction is equal to the smaller of the distribution ($17,500) or the DNI ($11,920).*

Enter the value of AMID on line 15b (the DNI should equal line 9 of Schedule B) and complete the rest of Form 1041 according to the instructions.

If the 2% floor is more than the deductions subject to the 2% floor, no deductions are allowed.

Line 18—Income Distribution Deduction

If the estate or trust was required to distribute income currently or if it paid, credited, or was required to distribute any other amounts to beneficiaries during the tax year, complete Schedule B to determine the estate's or trust's income distribution deduction. However, if you are filing for a pooled income fund, do not complete Schedule B. Instead, attach a statement to support the computation of the income distribution deduction. If the estate or trust claims an income distribution deduction, complete and attach:

- Parts I and II of Schedule I to refigure the deduction on a minimum tax basis; AND
- Schedule K-1 (Form 1041) for each beneficiary to which a distribution was made or required to be made.

Cemetery perpetual care fund.— On line 18, deduct the amount, not more than $5 per gravesite, paid for maintenance of cemetery property. To the right of the entry space for line 18, enter the number of gravesites. Also write "Section 642(i) trust" in parentheses after the trust's name at the top of Form 1041. You do not have to complete Schedules B of Form 1041 and K-1 (Form 1041).

Line 19—Estate Tax Deduction (Including Certain Generation-Skipping Transfer Taxes)

If the estate or trust includes income in respect of a decedent (IRD) in its gross income, and such amount was included in the decedent's gross estate for estate tax purposes, the estate or trust is allowed to deduct in the same tax year that portion of the estate tax imposed on the decedent's estate that is attributable to the inclusion of the IRD in the decedent's estate. For an example of the computation, see Regulations section 1.691(c)-1 and Pub. 559.

If any amount properly paid, credited, or required to be distributed by an estate or trust to a beneficiary consists of IRD received by the estate or trust, do not include such amounts in determining the estate tax deduction for the estate or trust. Figure the deduction on a separate sheet. Attach the sheet to your return. Also, a deduction is allowed for the GST tax imposed as a result of a taxable termination, or a direct skip occurring as a result of the death of the transferor. See section 691(c)(3). Enter the estate's or trust's share of these deductions on line 19.

Line 20—Exemption

Decedents' estates.— A decedent's estate is allowed a $600 exemption.

Trusts.— A trust whose governing instrument requires that all income be distributed currently is allowed a $300 exemption, even if it distributed amounts other than income during the tax year. All other trusts are allowed a $100 exemption. See Regulations section 1.642(b)-1.

Tax and Payments

Line 22—Taxable Income

Net operating loss.— If line 22 is a loss, the estate or trust may have a net operating loss (NOL). Do not include the deductions claimed on lines 13, 18, and 20 when figuring the amount of the NOL. An NOL generally may be carried back to the 3 prior tax years and forward to the following 15 tax years. Complete Schedule A of **Form 1045,** Application for Tentative Refund, to figure the amount of the NOL that is available for carryback or carryover. Use Form 1045 or file an amended return to apply for a refund based on an NOL carryback. For more information, get **Pub. 536,** Net Operating Losses.

On the termination of the estate or trust, any unused NOL carryover that would be allowable to the estate or trust in a later tax year, but for the termination, is allowed to the beneficiaries succeeding to the property of the estate or trust. See the instructions for Schedule K-1, lines 12d and 12e.

Excess deductions on termination.— If the estate or trust has for its final year deductions (excluding the charitable deduction and exemption) in excess of its gross income, the excess is allowed as an itemized deduction to the beneficiaries succeeding to the property of the estate or trust. However, an unused NOL carryover that is allowed to beneficiaries (as explained in the above paragraph) cannot also be treated as an excess deduction. If the final year of the estate or trust is also the last year of the NOL carryover period, the NOL carryover not absorbed in that tax year by the estate or trust is included as an excess deduction. See the instructions for Schedule K-1, line 12a.

Line 24a—1996 Estimated Tax Payments and Amount Applied From 1995 Return

Enter the amount of any estimated tax payment you made with Form 1041-ES for 1996 plus the amount of any overpayment from the 1995 return that was applied to the 1996 estimated tax.

If the estate or trust is the beneficiary of another trust, and received a payment of estimated tax that was credited to the trust (as reflected on the Schedule K-1 issued to the trust), then report this amount separately with the notation "section 643(g)" in the space next to line 24a.

Note: *Do not include on Form 1041 estimated tax paid by an individual before death. Instead, include the payments on the decedent's final Form 1040.*

Line 24b—Estimated Tax Payments Allocated to Beneficiaries

The trustee (or executor, for the final year of the estate) may elect under section 643(g) to have any portion of its estimated tax treated as a payment of estimated tax made by a beneficiary or beneficiaries. The election is made on **Form 1041-T,** Allocation of Estimated Tax Payments to Beneficiaries, which must be filed by the 65th day after the close of the trust's tax year. Form 1041-T shows the amounts to be allocated to each beneficiary. This amount is reported on the beneficiary's Schedule K-1, line 13a.

Failure to file Form 1041-T by the due date (March 6, 1997, for calendar year estates and trusts) will result in an invalid election. An invalid election will require the filing of amended Schedules K-1 for each beneficiary who was allocated a payment of estimated tax. Attach Form 1041-T to your return ONLY if you have not yet filed it. If you have already filed Form 1041-T, do not attach a copy to your return.

Line 24d—Tax Paid With Extension of Time To File

If you filed either Form 2758 (for estates only), Form 8736, or Form 8800 to request an extension of time to file Form 1041, enter the amount that you paid with the extension request and check the appropriate box(es).

Line 24e—Federal Income Tax Withheld

Use line 24e to claim a credit for any Federal income tax withheld (and not repaid) by: **(a)** an employer on wages and salaries of a decedent received by the decedent's estate; **(b)** a payer of certain gambling winnings (e.g., state lottery winnings); or **(c)** a payer of distributions from pensions, annuities, retirement or profit-sharing plans, IRAs, insurance contracts, etc., received by a decedent's estate or trust. Attach a copy of **Form W-2, Form W-2G,** or **Form 1099-R.**

Backup withholding.— If the estate or trust received a 1996 Form 1099 showing Federal income tax withheld (i.e., backup withholding) on interest income, dividends, or other income, check the box and include the amount withheld on income retained by the estate or trust in the total for line 24e.

Report on Schedule K-1 (Form 1041), line 13, any credit for backup withholding on income distributed to the beneficiary.

Line 24f—Credit From Regulated Investment Companies

Attach copy B of **Form 2439,** Notice to Shareholder of Undistributed Long-Term Capital Gains.

Line 24g—Credit for Federal Tax on Fuels

Include any credit for Federal excise taxes paid on fuels that are ultimately used for nontaxable purposes (e.g., an off-highway business use) and any credit for a diesel-powered car, van, or light truck purchased before August 21, 1996. Attach **Form 4136,** Credit for Federal Tax Paid on Fuels. Get **Pub. 378,** Fuel Tax Credits and Refunds, for more information.

Line 26—Underpayment of Estimated Tax

If line 27 is at least $500 and more than 10% of the tax shown on Form 1041, or the estate or trust underpaid its 1996 estimated tax liability for any payment period, it may owe a penalty. See Form 2210 to determine whether the estate or trust owes a penalty and to figure the amount of the penalty.

Note: *The penalty may be waived under certain conditions. Get Pub. 505, Tax Withholding and Estimated Tax, for details.*

Line 27—Tax Due

You must pay the tax in full when the return is filed. Make the check or money order payable to "Internal Revenue Service." Write the EIN and "1996 Form 1041" on the payment. Enclose, but do not attach, the payment with Form 1041.

Line 29a—Credit to 1997 Estimated Tax

Enter the amount from line 28 that you want applied to the estate's or trust's 1997 estimated tax.

Schedule A—Charitable Deduction

General Instructions

Generally, any part of the gross income of an estate or trust (other than a simple trust) that, under the terms of the will or governing instrument, is paid (or treated as paid) during the tax year for a charitable purpose specified in section 170(c) is allowed as a deduction to the estate or trust. It is not necessary that the charitable organization be created or organized in the United States.

Trusts that claim a charitable deduction must also file Form 1041-A. See Form 1041-A for exceptions.

A pooled income fund, nonexempt private foundation, or trust with unrelated business income should attach a separate sheet to Form 1041 instead of using Schedule A of Form 1041 to figure the charitable deduction.

Election to treat contributions as paid in the prior tax year.— The fiduciary of an estate or trust may elect to treat as paid during the tax year any amount of gross income received during that tax year or any prior tax year that was paid in the next tax year for a charitable purpose.

To make the election, the fiduciary must file a statement with Form 1041 for the tax year in which the contribution is treated as paid. This statement must include:

1. The name and address of the fiduciary;
2. The name of the estate or trust;
3. An indication that the fiduciary is making an election under section 642(c)(1) for contributions treated as paid during such tax year;
4. The name and address of each organization to which any such contribution is paid; and
5. The amount of each contribution and date of actual payment or, if applicable, the total amount of contributions paid to each organization during the next tax year, to be treated as paid in the prior tax year.

The election must be filed by the due date (including extensions) for Form 1041 for the next tax year.

For more information about the charitable deduction, see section 642(c) and related regulations.

Specific Instructions

Line 1—Amounts Paid for Charitable Purposes From Gross Income

Enter amounts that were paid for a charitable purpose out of the estate's or trust's gross income, including any capital gains that are attributable to income under the governing instrument or local law. Include amounts paid during the tax year from gross income received in a prior tax year, but only if no deduction was allowed for any prior tax year for these amounts. Do not include any capital gains for the tax year allocated to corpus and paid or permanently set aside for charitable purposes. Instead, enter these amounts on line 6.

Line 2—Amounts Permanently Set Aside for Charitable Purposes From Gross Income

Estates, and certain trusts, may claim a deduction for amounts permanently set aside for a charitable purpose from gross income. Such amounts must be permanently set aside during the tax year or be used exclusively for religious, charitable, scientific, literary, or educational purposes, or for the prevention of cruelty to children or animals, or for the establishment, acquisition, maintenance, or operation of a public cemetery not operated for profit.

For a trust to qualify, the trust may not be a simple trust, and the set aside amounts must be required by the terms of a trust instrument that was created on or before October 9, 1969.

Further, the trust instrument must provide for an irrevocable remainder interest to be transferred to or for the use of an organization described in section 170(c); OR the trust must have been created by a grantor who was at all times after October 9, 1969, under a mental disability to change the terms of the trust.

Also, certain testamentary trusts that were established by a will that was executed on or before October 9, 1969, may qualify. See Regulations section 1.642(c)-2(b).

Do not include any capital gains for the tax year allocated to corpus and paid or permanently set aside for charitable purposes. Instead, enter these amounts on line 6.

Line 4—Tax-Exempt Income Allocable to Charitable Contributions

Any estate or trust that pays or sets aside any part of its income for a charitable purpose must reduce the deduction by the portion allocable to any tax-exempt income. If the governing instrument specifically provides as to the source from which amounts are paid, permanently set aside, or to be used for charitable purposes, the specific provisions control. In all other cases, determine the amount of tax-exempt income allocable to charitable contributions by multiplying line 3 by a fraction, the numerator of which is the total tax-exempt income of the estate or trust, and the denominator of which is the gross income of the estate or trust. Do not include in the denominator any losses allocated to corpus.

Line 6—Capital Gains for the Tax Year Allocated to Corpus and Paid or Permanently Set Aside for Charitable Purposes

Enter the total of all capital gains for the tax year that are:
- Allocated to corpus; and
- Paid or permanently set aside for charitable purposes.

Schedule B—Income Distribution Deduction

General Instructions

If the estate or trust was required to distribute income currently or if it paid, credited, or was required to distribute any other amounts to beneficiaries during the tax year, complete Schedule B to determine the estate's or trust's income distribution deduction. However, if you are filing for a pooled income fund, do not complete Schedule B. Instead, attach a statement to support the computation of the income distribution deduction.

Note: *Use Schedule I to compute the DNI and income distribution deduction on a minimum tax basis.*

Separate share rule.— If a single trust has more than one beneficiary, and if different beneficiaries have substantially separate and independent shares, their shares are treated as separate trusts for the sole purpose of determining the DNI allocable to the respective beneficiaries. If the separate share rule applies, figure the DNI allocable to each beneficiary on a separate sheet and attach the sheet to this return. Any deduction or loss that is applicable solely to one separate share of the trust is not available to any other share of the same trust. For more information, see section 663(c) and related regulations.

Specific Instructions

Line 1—Adjusted Total Income

If the amount on line 17 of page 1 is a loss that is attributable wholly or in part to the capital loss limitation rules under section 1211(b) (line 4), then enter as a negative amount on line 1, Schedule B, the smaller of the loss from line 17 on page 1, or the loss from line 4 on page 1. If the line 17 loss is not attributable to the capital loss on line 4, enter zero.

If you are filing for a simple trust, subtract from adjusted total income any extraordinary dividends or taxable stock dividends included on page 1, line 2, and determined under the governing instrument and applicable local law to be allocable to corpus.

Line 2—Adjusted Tax-Exempt Interest

To figure the adjusted tax-exempt interest:

Step 1. Add tax-exempt interest income on line 4 of Schedule A, any expenses allowable under section 212 allocable to tax-exempt interest, and any interest expense allocable to tax-exempt interest.

Step 2. Subtract the Step 1 total from the amount of tax-exempt interest (including exempt-interest dividends) received.

Section 212 expenses that are directly allocable to tax-exempt interest are allocated only to tax-exempt interest. A reasonable proportion of section 212 expenses that are indirectly allocable to both tax-exempt interest and other income must be allocated to each class of income.

Figure the interest expense allocable to tax-exempt interest according to the guidelines in Rev. Proc. 72-18, 1972-1 C.B. 740.

See Regulations sections 1.643(a)-5 and 1.265-1 for more information.

Line 3

Include all capital gains, whether or not distributed, that are attributable to income under the governing instrument or local law. For example, if the trustee distributed 50% of the current year's capital gains to the income beneficiaries (and reflects this amount in column (a), line 17 of Schedule D (Form 1041)), but under the governing instrument all capital gains are attributable to income, then include 100% of the capital gains on line 3. If the amount on Schedule D (Form 1041), line 17, column (a) is a net loss, enter zero.

Line 5

In figuring the amount of long-term capital gain for the tax year included on Schedule A, line 3, the specific provisions of the governing instrument control if the instrument specifically provides as to the source from which amounts are paid, permanently set aside, or to be used for charitable purposes. In all other cases, determine the amount to enter by multiplying line 3 of Schedule A by a fraction, the numerator of which is the amount of long-term capital gains that are included in the accounting income of the estate or trust (i.e., not allocated to corpus) AND are distributed to charities, and the denominator of which is all items of income (including the amount of such long-term capital gains) included in the DNI.

Line 6

Figure line 6 in a similar manner as line 5.

Line 10—Accounting Income

If you are filing for a decedent's estate or a simple trust, skip this line. If you are filing for a complex trust, enter the income for the tax year determined under the terms of the governing instrument and applicable local law. Do not include extraordinary dividends or taxable stock dividends determined under the governing instrument and applicable local law to be allocable to corpus.

Lines 11 and 12

Do not include any:

- Amounts deducted on prior year's return that were required to be distributed in the prior year.
- Amount that is properly paid or credited as a gift or bequest of a specific amount of money or specific property. (To qualify as a gift or bequest, the amount must be paid in three or fewer installments.) An amount that can be paid or credited only from income is not considered a gift or bequest.
- Amount paid or permanently set aside for charitable purposes or otherwise qualifying for the charitable deduction.

Line 11—Income Required To Be Distributed Currently

Line 11 is to be completed by all simple trusts as well as complex trusts, and decedent's estates, that are required to distribute income currently, whether it is distributed or not. The determination of whether trust income is required to be distributed currently depends on the terms of the governing instrument and the applicable local law.

The line 11 distributions are referred to as first tier distributions and are deductible by the estate or trust to the extent of the DNI. The beneficiary includes such amounts in his or her income to the extent of his or her proportionate share of the DNI.

Line 12—Other Amounts Paid, Credited, or Otherwise Required To Be Distributed

Line 12 is to be completed ONLY by a decedent's estate or complex trust. These distributions consist of any other amounts paid, credited, or required to be distributed and are referred to as second tier distributions. Such amounts include annuities to the extent not paid out of income, discretionary distributions of corpus, and distributions of property in kind.

If Form 1041-T was filed to elect to treat estimated tax payments as made by a beneficiary, the payments are treated as paid or credited to the beneficiary on the last day of the tax year and must be included on line 12.

Unless a section 643(e)(3) election is made, the value of all noncash property actually paid, credited, or required to be distributed to any beneficiaries is the smaller of:

1. The estate's or trust's adjusted basis in the property immediately before distribution, plus any gain or minus any loss recognized by the estate or trust on the distribution (basis of beneficiary), or
2. The fair market value (FMV) of such property.

If a section 643(e)(3) election is made by the fiduciary, then the amount entered on line 12 will be the FMV of the property.

A fiduciary of a complex trust may elect to treat any amount paid or credited to a beneficiary within 65 days following the close of the tax year as being paid or credited on the last day of that tax year. To make this election, see the instructions for Question 6 on page 17.

The beneficiary includes the amounts on line 12 in his or her income only to the extent of his or her proportionate share of the DNI.

Complex trusts.— If the second tier distributions exceed the DNI allocable to the second tier, the trust may have an accumulation distribution. See the line 13 instructions below.

Line 13—Total Distributions

If line 13 is more than line 10 and you are filing for a complex trust, complete **Schedule J (Form 1041)** and file it with Form 1041 unless the trust has no previously accumulated income.

Line 14—Adjustment for Tax-Exempt Income

In figuring the income distribution deduction, the estate or trust is not allowed a deduction for any item of the DNI that is not included in the gross income of the estate or trust. Thus, for purposes of figuring the allowable income distribution deduction, the DNI (line 9) is figured without regard to any tax-exempt interest.

If tax-exempt interest is the only tax-exempt income included in the total distributions (line 13), and the DNI (line 9) is less than or equal to line 13, then enter on line 14 the amount from line 2.

If tax-exempt interest is the only tax-exempt income included in the total distributions (line 13), and the DNI is more than line 13 (i.e., the estate or trust made a distribution that is less than the DNI), then figure the adjustment by multiplying line 2 by a fraction, the numerator of which is the total distributions (line 13), and the denominator of which is the DNI (line 9). Enter the result on line 14.

If line 13 includes tax-exempt income other than tax-exempt interest, figure line 14 by subtracting the total of the following from tax-exempt income included on line 13:

1. The charitable contribution deduction allocable to such tax-exempt income, and
2. Expenses allocable to tax-exempt income.

Expenses that are directly allocable to tax-exempt income are allocated only to tax-exempt income. A reasonable proportion of expenses indirectly allocable to both tax-exempt income and other income must be allocated to each class of income.

Line 17—Income Distribution Deduction

The income distribution deduction determines the amount of income that will be taxed to the beneficiaries. The total amount of income for regular tax purposes that is reflected on line 7 of the individual beneficiaries' Schedules K-1 should equal the amount claimed on line 17.

Schedule G—Tax Computation

Line 1a

Tax rate schedule.— For tax years beginning in 1996, figure the tax using the Tax Rate Schedule below. Enter the tax on line 1a and check the "Tax rate schedule" box.

1996 Tax Rate Schedule

If taxable income is:			
Over—	But not over—	Its tax is:	Of the amount over—
$0	$1,600	15%	$0
1,600	3,800	$240.00 + 28%	1,600
3,800	5,800	856.00 + 31%	3,800
5,800	7,900	1,476.00 + 36%	5,800
7,900	-----	2,232.00 + 39.6%	7,900

Schedule D.— If the estate or trust had a net capital gain and taxable income of more than $3,800, complete Part VI of Schedule D (Form 1041), enter the tax from line 45 of Schedule D, and check the "Schedule D" box.

Line 1b—Other Taxes

Include any additional tax from the following:
- **Form 4972**, Tax on Lump-Sum Distributions.
- Section 644 tax on trusts.

Section 644 tax.— If the trust sells or exchanges property at a gain within 2 years after receiving it from a transferor, a section 644 tax may be due. The tax may be due if both **1** and **2** below apply:

1. There is an includible gain (defined below) recognized by the trust; and

2. At the time the trust received the property, the property had an FMV higher than its adjusted basis.

The trustee is authorized by section 6103(e)(1)(A)(ii) to inspect the transferor's income tax return to the extent necessary to figure the section 644 tax if the transferor refuses to make a disclosure to the trustee.

Includible gain is the smaller of **1** or **2** below:

1. The gain recognized by the trust on the sale or exchange of the property; or

2. The amount by which the FMV of the property at the time of the initial transfer to the trust exceeds the adjusted basis of the property immediately after the transfer.

Figure the tax on the includible gain by subtracting the transferor's actual tax for the tax year of the sale or exchange from the transferor's tax for the year of the sale or exchange refigured to include the includible gain minus any deductions allocable to the gain.

See section 644 for additional information, including character rules, special rules, exceptions, installment sale rules, and the interest due on the tax if the transferor and the trust have different tax years.

If the section 644 tax is the only tax due on line 1b, enter the amount of the tax on line 1b and write "Section 644 tax" to the left of the amount column on line 1b. If there is more than one tax, include the amount of the section 644 tax in the total tax entered on line 1b.

Attach the section 644 tax computation to the return. When figuring the trust's taxable income, exclude the amount of any includible gain minus any deductions allocable to the gain.

Line 2a—Foreign Tax Credit

Attach **Form 1116**, Foreign Tax Credit (Individual, Estate, Trust, or Nonresident Alien Individual), if you elect to claim credit for income or profits taxes paid or accrued to a foreign country or a U.S. possession. The estate or trust may claim credit for that part of the foreign taxes not allocable to the beneficiaries (including charitable beneficiaries). Enter the estate's or trust's share of the credit on line 2a. See **Pub. 514**, Foreign Tax Credit for Individuals, for details.

Line 2b

Nonconventional Source Fuel Credit

If the estate or trust can claim any section 29 credit for producing fuel from a nonconventional source, figure the credit on a separate sheet and attach it to the return. Include the credit on line 2b.

Qualified Electric Vehicle Credit

Use **Form 8834**, Qualified Electric Vehicle Credit, if the estate or trust can claim a credit for the purchase of a new qualified electric vehicle. Include the credit on line 2b.

Line 2c—General Business Credit

Complete this line if the estate or trust is claiming any of the credits listed below. Use the appropriate credit form to figure the credit. If the estate or trust is claiming only one credit, enter the form number and the amount of the credit in the space provided.

If the estate or trust is claiming more than one credit (not including the empowerment zone employment credit), a credit from a passive activity (other than the low-income housing credit or the empowerment zone employment credit), or a credit carryforward, also complete **Form 3800**, General Business Credit, to figure the total credit and enter the amount from Form 3800 on line 2c. Also, be sure to check the box for Form 3800.

Do not include any amounts that are allocated to a beneficiary. Credits that are allocated between the estate or trust and the beneficiaries are listed in the instructions for Schedule K-1, line 13, on page 27. Generally, these credits are apportioned on the basis of the income allocable to the estate or trust and the beneficiaries.

- Investment credit (Form 3468).
- Work opportunity credit (Form 5884).
- Credit for alcohol used as fuel (Form 6478).
- Credit for increasing research activities (Form 6765).
- Low-income housing credit (Form 8586).
- Enhanced oil recovery credit (Form 8830).
- Disabled access credit (Form 8826).
- Renewable electricity production credit (Form 8835).
- Empowerment zone employment credit (Form 8844).
- Indian employment credit (Form 8845).
- Credit for employer social security and Medicare taxes paid on certain employee tips (Form 8846).
- Orphan drug credit (Form 8820).
- Credit for contributions to selected community development corporations (Form 8847).

Line 2d—Credit for Prior Year Minimum Tax

An estate or trust that paid alternative minimum tax in a previous year may be eligible for a minimum tax credit in 1996. See **Form 8801**, Credit for Prior Year Minimum Tax—Individuals, Estates, and Trusts.

Line 5—Recapture Taxes

Recapture of investment credit.— If the estate or trust disposed of investment credit property or changed its use before the end of its useful life or recovery period, get **Form 4255**, Recapture of Investment Credit, to figure the recapture tax allocable to the estate or trust.

Recapture of low-income housing credit.— If the estate or trust disposed of property (or there was a reduction in the qualified basis of the property) on which the low-income housing credit was claimed, get **Form 8611**, Recapture of Low-Income Housing Credit, to figure any recapture tax allocable to the estate or trust.

Recapture of qualified electric vehicle credit.— If the estate or trust claimed the qualified electric vehicle credit in a prior tax year for a vehicle that ceased to qualify for the credit, part or all of the credit may have to be recaptured. See Pub. 535 for details. If the estate or trust owes any recapture tax, include it on line 5 and write "QEV" on the dotted line to the left of the entry space.

Recapture of the Indian employment credit.— Generally, if the estate or trust terminates a qualified employee less than 1 year after the date of initial employment, any Indian employment credit allowed for a prior tax year by reason of wages paid or incurred to that employee must be recaptured. See Form 8845 for details. If the estate or trust owes any recapture tax, include it on line 5 and write "45A" on the dotted line to the left of the entry space.

Line 7—Household Employment Taxes

If **any** of the following apply, get **Schedule H (Form 1040),** Household Employment Taxes, and its instructions, to see if the estate or trust owes these taxes.

1. The estate or trust paid **any one** household employee cash wages of $1,000 or more in 1996. When figuring the amount of cash wages paid, combine cash wages paid by the estate or trust with cash wages paid to the household employee in the same calendar year by the household of the decedent or beneficiary for whom the administrator, executor, or trustee of the estate or trust is acting.

2. The estate or trust withheld Federal income tax during 1996 at the request of any household employee.

3. The estate or trust paid **total** cash wages of $1,000 or more in **any** calendar **quarter** of 1995 or 1996 to household employees.

Line 8—Total Tax

Interest on tax deferred under the installment method for certain nondealer real property installment obligations.— If an obligation arising from the disposition of real property to which section 453A applies is outstanding at the close of the year, the estate or trust must include the interest due under section 453A(c) in the amount to be entered on line 8 of Schedule G, Form 1041, with the notation "Section 453A(c) interest." Attach a schedule showing the computation.

Form 4970, Tax on Accumulation Distribution of Trusts.— Include on this line any tax due on an accumulation distribution from a trust. To the left of the entry space, write "From Form 4970" and the amount of the tax.

Form 8697, Interest Computation Under the Look-Back Method for Completed Long-Term Contracts.— Include the interest due under the look-back method of section 460(b)(2). To the left of the entry space, write "From Form 8697" and the amount of interest due.

Form 5329, Additional Taxes Attributable to Qualified Retirement Plans (Including IRAs), Annuities, and Modified Endowment Contracts.— If the estate or trust fails to receive the minimum distribution under section 4974, use Form 5329 to pay the excise tax. To the left of the entry space, write "From Form 5329" and the amount of the tax.

Other Information

Question 1

If the estate or trust received tax-exempt income, figure the allocation of expenses between tax-exempt and taxable income on a separate sheet and attach it to the return. Enter only the deductible amounts on the return. Do not figure the allocation on the return itself. For more information, see the instructions for **Allocation of Deductions for Tax-Exempt Income** on page 10.

Report the amount of tax-exempt interest income received or accrued in the space provided below Question 1.

Also, include any exempt-interest dividends the estate or trust received as a shareholder in a mutual fund or other regulated investment company.

Question 2

All salaries, wages, and other compensation for personal services must be included on the return of the person who earned the income, even if the income was irrevocably assigned to a trust by a contract assignment or similar arrangement.

The grantor or person creating the trust is considered the owner if he or she keeps "beneficial enjoyment" of or substantial control over the trust property. The trust's income, deductions, and credits are allocable to the owner.

If you checked "Yes" for Question 2, see the **Grantor Type Trust** instructions on page 7.

Question 3

Check the "Yes" box and enter the name of the foreign country if either **1** or **2** below applies.

1. At any time during the year the estate or trust had an interest in or signature or other authority over a bank, securities, or other financial account in a foreign country.

Exception. Check "No" if either of the following applies to the estate or trust:
- The combined value of the accounts was $10,000 or less during the whole year; OR
- The accounts were with a U.S. military banking facility operated by a U.S. financial institution.

2. The estate or trust owns more than 50% of the stock in any corporation that owns one or more foreign bank accounts.

Get **Form TD F 90-22.1,** Report of Foreign Bank and Financial Accounts, to see if the estate or trust is considered to have an interest in or signature or other authority over a bank, securities, or other financial account in a foreign country.

If you checked "Yes" for Question 3, file Form TD F 90-22.1 by June 30, 1997, with the Department of the Treasury at the address shown on the form.

Form TD F 90-22.1 is not a tax return, so do not file it with Form 1041.

You may order Form TD F 90-22.1 by calling 1-800-829-3676 (1-800-TAX-FORM).

Question 4

If the estate or trust received a distribution from a foreign trust after August 20, 1996, it must provide additional information. For this purpose, a loan of cash or marketable securities generally is considered to be a distribution. See **Pub. 553,** Highlights of 1996 Tax Changes, for details.

If the estate or trust was the grantor of, or the transferor to, a foreign trust that existed during the tax year, it may have to file **Form 3520,** Creation of or Transfers to Certain Foreign Trusts, **Form 3520–A,** Annual Return of Foreign Trust With U.S. Beneficiaries, or **Form 926,** Return by a U.S. Transferor of Property to a Foreign Corporation, Foreign Estate or Trust, or Foreign Partnership.

Question 5

An estate or trust claiming an interest deduction for qualified residence interest (as defined in section 163(h)(3)) on seller-provided financing, must include on an attachment to the 1996 Form 1041 the name, address, and taxpayer identifying number of the person to whom the interest was paid or accrued (i.e., the seller).

If the estate or trust received or accrued such interest, it must provide identical information on the person liable for such interest (i.e., the buyer). This information does not need to be reported if it duplicates information already reported on Form 1098.

Question 6

To make the section 663(b) election for a complex trust to treat any amount paid or credited to a beneficiary within 65 days following the close of the tax year as being paid or credited on the last day of that tax year, check the box. For the election to be valid, you must file Form 1041 by the due date (including extensions). Once made, the election is irrevocable.

Question 7

To make the section 643(e)(3) election to recognize gain on property distributed in kind, check the box and see the instructions for Schedule D (Form 1041).

Question 8

If the decedent's estate has been open for more than 2 years, check the box and attach an explanation for the delay in closing the estate.

Schedule I—Alternative Minimum Tax

General Instructions

Use Schedule I to compute:
1. The estate's or trust's alternative minimum taxable income;
2. The income distribution deduction on a minimum tax basis; and
3. The estate's or trust's alternative minimum tax (AMT).

Who Must Complete

- Complete Schedule I, Parts I and II, if the decedent's estate or trust is required to complete Schedule B.
- Complete Schedule I, Parts I and III, if the decedent's estate's or trust's share of alternative minimum taxable income (Part I, line 12) exceeds $22,500.

Recordkeeping

Schedule I contains adjustments and tax preference items that are treated differently for regular tax and AMT purposes. If you, as fiduciary for the estate or trust, completed a form to figure an item for regular tax purposes, you may have to complete it a second time for AMT purposes. Generally, the difference between the amounts on the two forms is the AMT adjustment or tax preference item to enter on Schedule I. Except for Form 1116, any additional form completed for AMT purposes does not have to be filed with Form 1041.

For regular tax purposes, some deductions and credits may result in carrybacks or carryforwards to other tax years. Examples are: investment interest expense; a net operating loss deduction; a capital loss; and the foreign tax credit. Because these items may be refigured for the AMT, the carryback or carryforward amount may be different for regular and AMT purposes. Therefore, you should keep records of these different carryforward and carryback amounts for the AMT and regular tax. The AMT carryforward will be important in completing Schedule I for 1997.

Credit for Prior Year Minimum Tax

Estates and trusts that paid alternative minimum tax in 1995, or had a minimum tax credit carryforward, may be eligible for a minimum tax credit in 1996. See Form 8801.

Partners, Shareholders, etc.

An estate or trust that is a partner in a partnership or a shareholder in an S corporation must take into account its share of items of income and deductions that enter into the computation of its adjustments and tax preference items.

Allocation of Deductions to Beneficiaries

The distributable net alternative minimum taxable income (DNAMTI) of the estate or trust does not include amounts of depreciation, depletion, and amortization that are allocated to the beneficiaries, just as the distributable net income (DNI) of the estate or trust does not include these items for regular tax purposes.

Report separately on line 11 of Schedule K-1 (Form 1041) any adjustments or tax preference items attributable to depreciation, depletion, and amortization that were allocated to the beneficiaries.

Optional Write-Off Period Under Section 59(e)

The estate or trust may elect under section 59(e) to use an optional 10-year (60-month for intangible drilling and development expenditures and 3-year for circulation expenditures) write-off period for certain expenditures. If this election is made, the optional write-off period is used for regular tax purposes and there is no AMT adjustment. This election can be made for the following items:

- Circulation expenditures (section 173).
- Research and experimental expenditures (section 174).
- Intangible drilling and development expenditures (section 263(c)).
- Development expenditures for mines and natural deposits (section 616).
- Mining exploration expenditures (section 617(a)).

The election must be made in the year the expenditure was made and may be revoked only with IRS consent. See section 59(e) for more details.

Specific Instructions

Part I—Estate's or Trust's Share of Alternative Minimum Taxable Income

Line 1—Adjusted Total Income or (Loss)

Enter the amount from line 17 of page 1. If the adjusted total income includes the amount of the alcohol fuel credit as required under section 87, reduce the adjusted total income by the credit included in income.

Line 2—Net Operating Loss Deduction

Enter any net operating loss deduction (NOLD) from line 15a of page 1 as a positive amount.

Line 4a—Interest

In determining the alternative minimum taxable income, qualified residence interest (other than qualified housing interest defined in section 56(e)) is not allowed.

If you completed Form 4952 for regular tax purposes, you may have an adjustment on this line. Refigure your investment interest expense on another Form 4952 as follows:

Step 1. On line 1 of Form 4952, add any interest expense allocable to specified private activity bonds issued after August 7, 1986, to the other interest expense. For a definition of "specified private activity bonds," see the instructions for line 4p.

Step 2. On line 2, enter the AMT disallowed investment interest expense from 1995.

Step 3. When completing Part II of Form 4952, refigure gross income from property held for investment, any net gain from the disposition of property held for investment, and any investment expenses, taking into account all AMT adjustments and tax preference items that apply. Include any interest income and investment expenses from private activity bonds issued after August 7, 1986.

To figure the adjustment for line 4a, subtract the total interest allowable for AMT purposes from the interest deduction claimed on line 10 of page 1. If the total interest expense allowed for AMT purposes is more than that allowed for regular tax purposes, enter the difference as a negative amount on line 4a.

Line 4b—Taxes

Enter any state, local, or foreign real property taxes; state or local personal property taxes; and state, local, or foreign income taxes that were included on line 11 of page 1.

Line 4d—Refund of Taxes

Enter any refunds received in 1996 of taxes described for line 4b above that were deducted in a tax year after 1986.

Line 4e—Depreciation of Property Placed in Service After 1986

Caution: *Do not include on this line any depreciation adjustment from:* **(a)** an activity for which you are not at risk; **(b)** a partnership or an S corporation if the basis limitations under section 704(d) or 1366(d) apply; **(c)** a tax shelter farm activity; or **(d)** a passive activity. Instead, take these depreciation adjustments into account when figuring the adjustments on line 4l, 4m, or 4n, whichever applies.

For AMT purposes, the depreciation deduction for tangible property placed in service after 1986 (or after July 31, 1986, if an election was made) must be refigured under the alternative depreciation system (ADS) described in section 168(g).

For property, other than residential rental and nonresidential real property, use the 150% declining balance method (switching to the straight line method in the first tax year when that method gives a better result). However, use the straight line method if that method was used for regular tax purposes. Generally, ADS depreciation is figured over the class life of the property. For tangible personal property not assigned a class life, use 12 years. See **Pub. 946,** How To Depreciate Property, for a discussion of class lives.

For residential rental and nonresidential real property, use the straight line method over 40 years.

Use the same convention that was used for regular tax purposes.

See Rev. Proc. 87-57, 1987-2 C.B. 687, or Pub. 946 for the optional tables for the alternative minimum tax, using the 150% declining balance method.

Do not make an adjustment for motion picture films, videotapes, sound recordings, or property depreciated under the unit-of-production method or any other method not expressed in a term of years. (See section 168(f)(1), (2), (3), or (4).)

When refiguring the depreciation deduction, be sure to report any adjustment from depreciation that was allocated to the beneficiary for regular tax purposes separately on line 11 of Schedule K-1 (Form 1041).

To figure the adjustment, subtract the depreciation for AMT purposes from the depreciation for regular tax purposes.

If the depreciation figured for AMT purposes exceeds the depreciation allowed for regular tax purposes, enter the adjustment as a negative amount.

Line 4f—Circulation and Research and Experimental Expenditures

Caution: *Do not make this adjustment for expenditures for which you elected the optional 3-year write-off period (10-year for research and experimental expenditures) under section 59(e) for regular tax purposes.*

Circulation expenditures.— Circulation expenditures deducted under section 173(a) for regular tax purposes must be amortized for AMT purposes over 3 years beginning with the year the expenditures were paid or incurred.

Research and experimental expenditures.— Research and experimental expenditures deducted under section 174(a) for regular tax purposes generally must be amortized for AMT purposes over 10 years beginning with the year the expenditures were paid or incurred. However, do not make an adjustment for expenditures paid or incurred in connection with an activity in which the estate or trust materially participated under the passive activity rules.

Enter the difference between the amount allowed for AMT purposes and the amount allowed for regular tax purposes. If the amount for AMT purposes exceeds the amount allowed for regular tax purposes, enter the difference as a negative amount.

See section 56(b)(2)(B) for a discussion of the rules for losses on properties for which a deduction was allowed under section 173(a) or 174(a).

Line 4g—Mining Exploration and Development Costs

Caution: *Do not make this adjustment for costs for which you elected the optional 10-year write-off period under section 59(e) for regular tax purposes.*

Expenditures for the development or exploration of a mine or certain other mineral deposits (other than an oil, gas, or geothermal well) deducted under sections 616(a) and 617(a) for regular tax purposes must be amortized for AMT purposes over 10 years beginning with the year the expenditures were paid or incurred.

Enter the difference between the amount allowed for AMT purposes and the amount allowed for regular tax purposes. If the amount allowed for AMT purposes exceeds the amount deducted for regular tax purposes, enter the difference as a negative amount.

See section 56(a)(2)(B) for a discussion of the rules for losses sustained on properties for which a deduction was allowed under section 616(a) or 617(a).

Line 4h—Long-Term Contracts Entered Into After February 28, 1986

For AMT purposes, the percentage of completion method of accounting described in section 460(b) generally must be used. This rule generally does not apply to home construction contracts (as defined in section 460(e)(6)).

Note: *Contracts described in section 460(e)(1) are subject to the simplified method of cost allocation of section 460(b)(4).*

Enter the difference between the amount reported for regular tax purposes and the AMT amount. If the AMT amount is less than the amount figured for regular tax purposes, enter the difference as a negative amount.

Line 4i—Amortization of Pollution Control Facilities

The amortization deduction under section 169 is not allowed for AMT purposes. Instead, the deduction is determined under the ADS described in section 168(g) using the Asset Depreciation Range class life for the facility under the straight line method.

To figure the adjustment, subtract the amortization deduction taken for regular tax purposes from the depreciation deduction determined under the ADS.

If the deduction allowed for AMT purposes is more than the amount allowed for regular tax purposes, enter the difference as a negative amount.

Line 4j—Installment Sales of Certain Property

For either of the following kinds of dispositions in which the estate or trust used the installment method for regular tax purposes, refigure the income for AMT purposes without regard to the installment method:

1. Any disposition after March 1, 1986, of property used or produced in a farming business that was held primarily for sale to customers.

2. Any nondealer disposition of property that occurred after August 16, 1986, but before the first day of your tax year that began in 1987, if an obligation that arose from the disposition was an installment obligation to which the proportionate disallowance rule applied.

Enter the difference between the income that was reported for regular tax purposes and the income for AMT purposes. If the AMT amount is less than that reported for the regular tax, enter the difference as a negative amount.

Line 4k—Adjusted Gain or Loss (Including Incentive Stock Options)

Adjusted gain or loss.— If the estate or trust sold or exchanged property during the year, or had a casualty gain or loss to business or income-producing property, it may have an adjustment. The gain or loss on the disposition of certain assets is refigured for AMT purposes. Use this line if the estate or trust reported a gain or loss on Form 4797, Schedule D (Form 1041), or Form 4684 (Section B). When figuring the adjusted basis for those forms, take into account any AMT adjustments made this year, or in previous years, for items related to lines 4e, 4f, 4g, and 4i of Schedule I. For example, to figure the adjusted basis for AMT purposes, reduce the cost of an asset only by the depreciation allowed for AMT purposes.

Enter the difference between the gain or loss reported for regular tax purposes, and that figured for AMT purposes. If the AMT gain is less than the gain reported for regular tax purposes, enter the adjustment as a negative amount. If the AMT loss is more than the loss allowed for regular tax purposes, enter the adjustment as a negative amount.

Incentive stock options (ISOs).— For regular tax purposes, no income is recognized when an incentive stock option (as defined in section 422(b)) is granted or exercised. However, this rule does not apply for AMT purposes. Instead, the estate or trust must generally include the excess, if any, of:

1. The fair market value of the option (determined without regard to any lapse restriction) at the first time its rights in the option become transferable or when these rights are no longer subject to a substantial risk of forfeiture, over

2. The amount paid for the option.

Increase the AMT basis of any stock acquired through the exercise of an incentive stock option by the amount of the adjustment.

If the estate or trust acquired stock by exercising an incentive stock option and disposed of that stock in the same year, the tax treatment for regular and AMT purposes is the same.

See section 83 for more details.

Line 4l—Certain Loss Limitations

Caution: *If the loss is from a passive activity, use line 4n instead. If the loss is from a tax shelter farm activity (that is not passive), use line 4m.*

Refigure your allowable losses for AMT purposes from activities for which you are not at risk and basis limitations applicable to interests in partnerships and stock in S corporations, by taking into account your AMT adjustments and tax preference

Page 19

items. See sections 59(h), 465, 704(d), and 1366(d).

Enter the difference between the loss reported for regular tax purposes and the AMT loss. If the AMT loss is more than the loss reported for regular tax purposes, enter the adjustment as a negative amount.

Line 4m—Tax Shelter Farm Activities

Note: *Use this line only if the tax shelter farm activity is not a passive activity. Otherwise, use line 4n.*

For AMT purposes, no loss is allowed from any tax shelter farm activity as defined in section 58(a)(2).

An excess farm loss from one farm activity cannot be netted against income from another farm activity. Any disallowed loss (for AMT purposes) is carried forward until offset by income from the same activity or when the entire activity is sold.

Include any other adjustment or tax preference item and your prior year AMT unallowed loss when refiguring the farm loss. For example, if depreciation must be refigured for AMT purposes, include the adjustment on this line. DO NOT include it again on line 4e, 4r, or 4s.

Determine your tax shelter farm activity gain or loss for AMT purposes using the same rules you used for regular tax purposes except that any AMT loss is allowed only to the extent that a taxpayer is insolvent (see section 58(c)(1)). An AMT loss may not be used in the current tax year to offset gains from other tax shelter farm activities. Instead, it must be suspended and carried forward indefinitely until either you have a gain in a subsequent tax year from that same tax shelter farm activity or the activity is disposed of.

Line 4n—Passive Activities

For AMT purposes, the rules described in section 469 apply, except that in applying the limitations, minimum tax rules apply.

Refigure passive activity gains and losses on an AMT basis. Refigure a passive activity gain or loss by taking into account all AMT adjustments or tax preference items that pertain to that activity.

You may complete a second Form 8582 to determine the passive activity losses allowed for AMT purposes, but do not send this AMT Form 8582 to the IRS.

Note: *The amount of any passive activity loss that is not deductible (and is therefore carried forward) for AMT purposes is likely to differ from the amount (if any) that is carried forward for regular tax purposes. Therefore, it is essential that you retain adequate records for both AMT and regular tax purposes.*

Enter the difference between the loss reported on page 1, and the AMT loss, if any.

Caution: *Do not enter again elsewhere on this schedule any AMT adjustment or tax preference item included on this line.*

Publicly traded partnerships (PTPs).— If the estate or trust had a loss from a PTP, refigure the loss using any AMT adjustments and tax preference items.

Line 4o—Beneficiaries of Other Trusts or Decedent's Estates

If the estate or trust is the beneficiary of another estate or trust, enter the adjustment for minimum tax purposes from line 8, Schedule K-1 (Form 1041).

Line 4p—Tax-Exempt Interest From Specified Private Activity Bonds

Enter the interest earned from specified private activity bonds reduced (but not below zero) by any deduction that would have been allowable if the interest were includible in gross income for regular tax purposes. Specified private activity bonds are any qualified bonds (as defined in section 141) issued after August 7, 1986. See section 57(a)(5) for more information.

Exempt-interest dividends paid by a regulated investment company are treated as interest from specified private activity bonds to the extent the dividends are attributable to interest received by the company on the bonds, minus an allocable share of the expenses paid or incurred by the company in earning the interest.

Line 4q—Depletion

Refigure the depletion deduction for AMT purposes by using only the income and deductions allowed for the AMT when refiguring the limit based on taxable income from the property under section 613(a) and the limit based on taxable income, with certain adjustments, under section 613A(d)(1). Also, the depletion deduction for mines, wells, and other natural deposits under section 611 is limited to the property's adjusted basis at the end of the year, as refigured for the AMT, unless the estate or trust is an independent producer or royalty owner claiming percentage depletion for oil and gas wells. Figure this limit separately for each property. When refiguring the property's adjusted basis, take into account any AMT adjustments made this year or in previous years that affect basis (other than the current year's depletion).

Enter on line 4q the difference between the regular tax and AMT deduction. If the AMT deduction is more than the regular tax deduction, enter the difference as a negative amount.

Line 4r—Accelerated Depreciation of Real Property Placed in Service Before 1987

For AMT purposes, use the straight line method to figure depreciation. Use a recovery period of 19 years for 19-year real property and 15 years for low-income housing. Enter the excess of depreciation claimed for regular tax purposes over depreciation refigured using the straight line method. Figure this amount separately for each property and include on line 4r only positive amounts.

Line 4s—Accelerated Depreciation of Leased Personal Property Placed in Service Before 1987

For leased personal property other than recovery property, enter the amount by which the regular tax depreciation using the pre-1987 rules exceeds the depreciation allowable using the straight line method.

For leased 10-year recovery property and leased 15-year public utility property, enter the amount by which the depreciation deduction determined for regular tax purposes is more than the deduction allowable using the straight line method with a half-year convention, no salvage value, and the following recovery period:

10-year property .... 15 years
15-year public utility property .... 22 years

Figure this amount separately for each property and include on line 4s only positive amounts.

Line 4t—Intangible Drilling Costs

Caution: *Do not make this adjustment for costs for which you elected the optional 60-month write-off under section 59(e) for regular tax purposes.*

Except as provided below, intangible drilling costs (IDCs) from oil, gas, and geothermal wells are a tax preference item to the extent that the excess IDCs exceed 65% of the net income from the wells. Figure the tax preference item for all geothermal properties separately from the preference for all oil and gas properties.

Excess IDCs are figured by taking the amount of your IDCs allowed for regular tax purposes under section 263(c) (not including any section 263(c) deduction for nonproductive wells) minus the amount that would have been allowed if that amount had been amortized over a 120-month period starting with the month the well was placed in production.

Note: *Cost depletion can be substituted for the amount allowed using amortization over 120 months.*

Net income is determined by taking the gross income from all oil, gas, and geothermal wells reduced by the deductions allocable to those properties (determined without regard to excess IDCs). When figuring net income, use only income and deductions allowed for the AMT.

Exception. The preference for IDCs from oil and gas wells does not apply to taxpayers who are independent producers (i.e., not integrated oil companies as defined in section 291(b)(4)). However, this benefit may be limited. First, figure the IDC preference as if this exception did not apply. Then, for purposes of this exception, complete Schedule I through line 6, including the IDC preference. If the amount of the IDC preference exceeds 40% of the amount figured for line 6, enter the excess on line 4t (the benefit of this exception is limited). If the amount of the

IDC preference is equal to or less than 40% of the amount figured for line 6, do not enter an amount on line 4t (the benefit of this exception is not limited).

Line 4u—Other Adjustments

Include on this line:

- **Patron's adjustment.**—Distributions the estate or trust received from a cooperative may be includible in income. Unless the distributions are nontaxable, include on line 4u the total AMT patronage dividend adjustment reported to the estate or trust from the cooperative.
- **Related adjustments.**—AMT adjustments and tax preference items may affect deductions that are based on an income limit other than AGI or modified AGI (e.g., farm conservation expenses). Refigure these deductions using the income limit as modified for the AMT. Include the difference between the regular tax and AMT deduction on line 4u. If the AMT deduction is more than the regular tax deduction, include the difference as a negative amount.

Note: *Do not make an adjustment on line 4u for an item you refigured on another line of Schedule I (e.g., line 4q).*

Line 7—Alternative Tax Net Operating Loss Deduction (ATNOLD)

For tax years beginning after 1986, the net operating loss (NOL) under section 172(c) is modified for alternative tax purposes by **(a)** adding the adjustments made under sections 56 and 58 (subtracting if the adjustments are negative); and **(b)** reducing the NOL by any item of tax preference under section 57 (except the appreciated charitable contribution preference item).

When figuring an NOL from a loss year prior to 1987, the rules in effect before enactment of the Tax Reform Act (TRA) of 1986 apply. The NOL under section 172(c) is reduced by the amount of the tax preference items that were taken into account in figuring the NOL. In addition, the NOL is figured by taking into account only itemized deductions that were alternative tax itemized deductions for the tax year and that were a modification to the NOL under section 172(d). See sections 55(d) and 172 as in effect before the TRA of 1986.

If this estate or trust is the beneficiary of another estate or trust that terminated in 1996, include any AMT NOL carryover that was reported on line 12e of Schedule K-1 (Form 1041).

The ATNOLD may be limited. To figure the ATNOLD limitation, first figure AMTI without regard to the ATNOLD. For this purpose, figure a tentative amount for line 4q of Schedule I by treating line 7 as if it were zero. Then, figure a tentative amount for line 6 of Schedule I. The ATNOLD limitation is 90% of the tentative line 6 amount. Enter on line 7 the smaller of the ATNOLD or the ATNOLD limitation. Any alternative tax NOL not used because of the ATNOLD limitation can be carried back or forward. See section 172(b) for details. The treatment of alternative tax NOLs does not affect your regular tax NOL.

Note: *If you elected under section 172(b)(3) to forego the carryback period for regular tax purposes, the election will also apply for the AMT.*

Part II—Income Distribution Deduction on a Minimum Tax Basis

Line 13—Adjusted Alternative Minimum Taxable Income

If the amount on line 8 of Schedule I is less than zero, and the negative number is attributable wholly or in part to the capital loss limitation rules under section 1211(b), then enter as a negative number the smaller of **(a)** the loss from line 8; or **(b)** the loss from line 4 on page 1.

Line 14—Adjusted Tax-Exempt Interest

To figure the adjusted tax-exempt interest (including exempt-interest dividends received as a shareholder in a mutual fund or other regulated investment company), subtract the total of **(a)** any tax-exempt interest from line 4 of Schedule A of Form 1041 figured for AMT purposes; and **(b)** any section 212 expenses allowable for AMT purposes allocable to tax-exempt interest from the amount of tax-exempt interest received. DO NOT subtract any deductions reported on lines 4a through 4c. Section 212 expenses that are directly allocable to tax-exempt interest are allocated only to tax-exempt interest. A reasonable proportion of section 212 expenses that are indirectly allocable to both tax-exempt interest and other income must be allocated to each class of income.

Line 17

Enter any capital gains that were paid or permanently set aside for charitable purposes from the current year's income included on line 3 of Schedule A.

Lines 18 and 19

Capital gains and losses must take into account any basis adjustments from line 4k, Part I.

Line 24—Adjustment for Tax-Exempt Income

In figuring the income distribution deduction on a minimum tax basis, the estate or trust is not allowed a deduction for any item of DNAMTI (line 20) that is not included in the gross income of the estate or trust figured on an AMT basis. Thus, for purposes of figuring the allowable income distribution deduction on a minimum tax basis, the DNAMTI is figured without regard to any tax-exempt interest (except for amounts from line 4p).

If tax-exempt interest is the only tax-exempt income included in the total distributions (line 23), and the DNAMTI (line 20) is less than or equal to line 23, then enter on line 24 the amount from line 14.

If tax-exempt interest is the only tax-exempt income included in the total distributions (line 23), and the DNAMTI is more than line 23 (i.e., the estate or trust made a distribution that is less than the DNAMTI), then figure the adjustment by multiplying line 14 by a fraction, the numerator of which is the total distributions (line 23), and the denominator of which is the DNAMTI (line 20). Enter the result on line 24.

If line 23 includes tax-exempt income other than tax-exempt interest (except for amounts from line 4p), figure line 24 by subtracting the total expenses allocable to tax-exempt income that are allowable for AMT purposes from tax-exempt income included on line 23.

Expenses that are directly allocable to tax-exempt income are allocated only to tax-exempt income. A reasonable proportion of expenses indirectly allocable to both tax-exempt income and other income must be allocated to each class of income.

Line 27—Income Distribution Deduction on a Minimum Tax Basis

Allocate the income distribution deduction figured on a minimum tax basis among the beneficiaries in the same manner as income was allocated for regular tax purposes. Report each beneficiary's share on line 6 of Schedule K-1 (Form 1041).

Part III—Alternative Minimum Tax Computation

Line 36—Alternative Minimum Foreign Tax Credit

To figure the AMT foreign tax credit:

1. Complete and attach Form 1116, with the notation at the top, "Alt Min Tax" for each type of income specified at the top of Form 1116.

2. Complete Part I, entering income, deductions, etc., attributable to sources outside the United States computed on a minimum tax basis.

3. Complete Part III. On line 9, do not enter any taxes taken into account in a tax year beginning after 1986 that are treated under section 904(c) as paid or accrued in a tax year beginning before 1987. On line 10 of Form 1116, enter the alternative minimum tax foreign tax credit carryover, and on line 17 of Form 1116, enter the alternative minimum taxable income from line 12 of Schedule I. On line 19 of Form 1116, enter the amount from line 35 of Schedule I.

Complete Part IV. The foreign tax credit from line 32 of the AMT Form 1116 is limited to the tax on line 35 of Schedule I, less 10% of what would have been the tax on line 35 of Schedule I, if line 7 of Schedule I had been zero and the exception for intangible drilling costs does not apply (see the instructions for line 4t on page 20). If Schedule I, line 7, is zero or blank, and the estate or trust has no intangible drilling costs (or the exception does not apply), enter on Schedule I, line 36, the smaller of Form 1116, line 32; or

Page 21

90% of Schedule I, line 35. If line 7 has an entry (other than zero), or the exception for intangible drilling costs applies, for purposes of this line refigure what the tax would have been on Schedule I, line 35, if line 7 were zero and the exception did not apply. Multiply that amount by 10% and subtract the result from line 35. Enter on Schedule I, line 36, the smaller of that amount or the amount from Form 1116, line 32.

If the AMT foreign tax credit is limited, any unused amount can be carried back or forward in accordance with section 904(c).

Note: *The election to forego the carryback period for regular tax purposes also applies for the AMT.*

Line 38—Regular Tax Before Credits

Enter the tax from line 1a of Schedule G, reduced by the amount of any foreign tax credit entered on line 2a of Schedule G. DO NOT deduct any foreign tax credit that was allocated to the beneficiaries.

Schedule D (Form 1041)—Capital Gains and Losses

General Instructions

Use Schedule D (Form 1041) to report gains and losses from the sale or exchange of capital assets by an estate or trust.

To report sales or exchanges of property other than capital assets, including the sale or exchange of property used in a trade or business and involuntary conversions (other than casualties and thefts), see Form 4797 and related instructions.

If property is involuntarily converted because of a casualty or theft, use Form 4684.

Capital Asset

Each item of property held by the estate or trust (whether or not connected with its trade or business) is a capital asset except:
- Inventoriable assets or property held primarily for sale to customers;
- Depreciable or real property used in a trade or business;
- Certain copyrights, literary, musical, or artistic compositions, letters or memoranda, or similar property;
- Accounts or notes receivable acquired in the ordinary course of a trade or business for services rendered or from the sale of inventoriable assets or property held primarily for sale to customers; and
- Certain U.S. Government publications not purchased at the public sale price.

You may find additional helpful information in the following publications:
- **Pub. 544,** Sales and Other Dispositions of Assets; and
- **Pub. 551,** Basis of Assets.

Short-Term or Long-Term

Separate the capital gains and losses according to how long the estate or trust held or owned the property. The holding period for short-term capital gains and losses is 1 year or less. The holding period for long-term capital gains and losses is more than 1 year. Property acquired by a decedent's estate from the decedent is considered as held for more than 1 year.

When you figure the length of the period the estate or trust held property, begin counting on the day after the estate or trust acquired the property and include the day the estate or trust disposed of it. Use the trade dates for the date of acquisition and sale of stocks and bonds traded on an exchange or over-the-counter market.

Section 643(e)(3) Election

For noncash property distributions, a fiduciary may elect to have the estate or trust recognize gain or loss in the same manner as if the distributed property had been sold to the beneficiary at its fair market value (FMV). The distribution deduction is the property's FMV. This election applies to all distributions made by the estate or trust during the tax year and, once made, may be revoked only with the consent of the IRS.

Note that section 267 does not allow a deduction for any loss from the sale of property on which a trust makes a section 643(e)(3) election. In addition, when a trust distributes depreciable property, section 1239 applies to deny capital gains treatment on the gain to the trust if the trust makes a section 643(e)(3) election.

Section 644 Tax on Trusts

If a trust sells or exchanges property at a gain within 2 years after receiving it from a transferor, a special tax may be due. **Do not report includible gains under section 644 on Schedule D.** The tax on these gains is reported separately on Form 1041. For more information, see the instructions for Schedule G, line 1b, on page 16.

Related Persons

A trust cannot deduct a loss from the sale or exchange of property directly or indirectly between any of the following:
- A grantor and a fiduciary of a trust;
- A fiduciary and a fiduciary or beneficiary of another trust created by the same grantor;
- A fiduciary and a beneficiary of the same trust; or
- A trust fiduciary and a corporation of which more than 50% in value of the outstanding stock is owned directly or indirectly by or for the trust or by or for the grantor of the trust.

Items for Special Treatment

The following items may require special treatment:

- Exchange of "like-kind" property.
- Wash sales of stock or securities (including contracts or options to acquire or sell stock or securities) (section 1091).
- Gain or loss on options to buy or sell (section 1234).
- Certain real estate subdivided for sale that may be considered a capital asset (section 1237).
- Gain on disposition of stock in an Interest Charge Domestic International Sales Corporation (section 995(c)).
- Gain on the sale or exchange of stock in certain foreign corporations (section 1248).
- Sales of stock received under a qualified public utility dividend reinvestment plan. See Pub. 550 for details.
- Transfer of appreciated property to a political organization (section 84).
- Distributions received from an employee pension, profit sharing, or stock bonus plan. See Form 4972.
- Disposition of market discount bonds (section 1276).
- Section 1256 contracts and straddles are reported on **Form 6781,** Gains and Losses From Section 1256 Contracts and Straddles.

Specific Instructions

Lines 1 and 7

Short-term and long-term capital gains and losses.— Enter all sales of stocks, bonds, etc.

Redemption of stock to pay death taxes.— If stock is redeemed under the provisions of section 303, list and identify it on line 7 and give the name of the decedent and the IRS office where the estate tax or generation-skipping transfer tax return was filed.

If you are reporting capital gain from a lump-sum distribution, see the instructions for Form 4972 for information about the death benefit exclusion and the Federal estate tax.

Column (d)—Sales Price

Enter either the gross sales price or the net sales price from the sale. On sales of stocks and bonds, report the gross amount as reported to the estate or trust on Form 1099-B or similar statement. However, if the estate or trust was advised that gross proceeds less commissions and option premiums were reported to the IRS, enter that net amount in column (d).

Column (e)—Cost or Other Basis

Basis of trust property.— Generally, the basis of property acquired by gift is the same as the basis in the hands of the donor. If the fair market value (FMV) of the property at the time it was transferred to the trust is less than the transferor's basis, then the FMV is used for determining any loss on disposition.

If the property was transferred to the trust after 1976, and a gift tax was paid under Chapter 12, then increase the donor's basis as follows:

Multiply the amount of the gift tax paid by a fraction, the numerator of which is the net appreciation in value of the gift (discussed below), and the denominator of which is the amount of the gift. For this purpose, the **net appreciation in value of the gift** is the amount by which the FMV of the gift exceeds the donor's adjusted basis.

Basis of decedent's estate property.— Generally, the basis of property acquired by a decedent's estate is the FMV of the property at the date of the decedent's death, or the alternate valuation date if the executor elected to use an alternate valuation under section 2032.

See Pub. 551 for a discussion of the valuation of qualified real property under section 2032A.

Basis of property for bankruptcy estates.— Generally, the basis of property held by the bankruptcy estate is the same as the basis in the hands of the individual debtor.

Adjustments to basis.— Before figuring any gain or loss on the sale, exchange, or other disposition of property owned by the estate or trust, adjustments to the property's basis may be required.

Some items that may increase the basis include:

1. Broker's fees and commissions.
2. Reinvested dividends that were previously reported as income.
3. Reinvested capital gains that were previously reported as income.
4. Costs that were capitalized.
5. Original issue discount that has been previously included in income.

Some items that may decrease the basis include:

1. Nontaxable distributions that consist of return of capital.
2. Deductions previously allowed or allowable for depreciation.
3. Casualty or theft loss deductions.

See Pub. 551 for additional information.

See section 852(f) for treatment of load charges incurred in acquiring stock in a regulated investment company.

Carryover basis.— Carryover basis determined under repealed section 1023 applies to property acquired from a decedent who died after December 31, 1976, and before November 7, 1978, only if the executor elected it on a **Form 5970-A**, Election of Carryover Basis, that was filed on time.

Lines 2 and 8

Installment sales.— If the estate or trust sold property at a gain during the tax year, and will receive a payment in a later tax year, report the sale on the installment method and file **Form 6252**, Installment Sale Income, unless you elect not to do so.

Also, use Form 6252 to report any payment received in 1996 from a sale made in an earlier tax year that was reported on the installment method.

To elect out of the installment method, report the full amount of the gain on a timely filed return (including extensions).

Exchange of "like-kind" property.— Generally, no gain or loss is recognized when property held for productive use in a trade or business or for investment is exchanged solely for property of a like-kind to be held either for productive use in a trade or business or for investment. However, if a trust exchanges like-kind property with a related person (see **Related Persons** on page 22), and before 2 years after the date of the last transfer that was part of the exchange the related person disposes of the property, or the trust disposes of the property received in exchange from the related person, then the original exchange will not qualify for nonrecognition. See section 1031(f) for exceptions.

Complete and attach **Form 8824**, Like-Kind Exchanges, to Form 1041 for each exchange.

Line 10—Capital Gain Distributions

Enter as a long-term capital gain on line 10, capital gain distributions paid during the year, regardless of how long the estate or trust held its investment. Also enter any amounts shown on Form 2439 that represent the estate's or trust's share of the undistributed capital gains of a regulated investment company. Include on Form 1041, line 24f, the tax paid by the company as shown on Form 2439. Add to the basis of the stock the excess of the amount included in income over the credit if the amount is not distributed.

Line 15, Column (a)—Beneficiaries' Net Short-Term Capital Gain or Loss

Enter the amount of net short-term capital gain or loss allocable to the beneficiary or beneficiaries. Except in the final year, include only those short-term capital losses that are taken into account in determining the amount of gain from the sale or exchange of capital assets that is paid, credited, or required to be distributed to any beneficiary during the tax year. See Regulations section 1.643(a)-3 for more information about allocation of capital gains and losses.

Except in the final year, if the losses from the sale or exchange of capital assets are more than the gains, all of the losses are allocated to the estate or trust and none are allocated to the beneficiaries.

Line 15, Column (b)—Estate's or Trust's Net Short-Term Capital Gain or Loss

Enter the amount of the net short-term capital gain or loss allocable to the estate or trust. Include any capital gain paid or permanently set aside for a charitable purpose specified in section 642(c).

Line 15, Column (c)—Total

Enter the total of the amounts entered in columns (a) and (b). The amount in column (c) should be the same as the amount on line 6.

Line 16—Net Long-Term Capital Gain or Loss

Allocate the net long-term capital gain or loss on line 16 in the same manner as the net short-term capital gain or loss on line 15.

Part IV—Capital Loss Limitation

If the sum of all the capital losses is more than the sum of all the capital gains, then these capital losses are allowed as a deduction only to the extent of the smaller of the net loss or $3,000.

Part V—Capital Loss Carryovers From 1996 to 1997

For any year (including the final year) in which capital losses exceed capital gains, complete Part V to figure the capital loss carryover. A capital loss carryover may be carried forward indefinitely. Capital losses keep their character as either short-term or long-term when carried over to the following year.

Part VI—Tax Computation Using Maximum Capital Gains Rate

Line 37c

If the estate or trust received capital gains that were derived from income in respect of a decedent, and a section 691(c)(4) deduction was claimed, then line 37c must be reduced by the portion of the section 691(c)(4) deduction claimed on Form 1041, page 1, line 19.

Line 44

To figure the regular tax, use the 1996 Tax Rate Schedule on page 16.

Line 45

If the tax using the maximum capital gains rate (line 43) is less than the regular tax (line 44), enter the amount from line 45 on line 1a of Schedule G, Form 1041, and check the "Schedule D" box.

Schedule J (Form 1041)— Accumulation Distribution for a Complex Trust

General Instructions

Use Schedule J (Form 1041) to report an accumulation distribution for a complex trust. An accumulation distribution is the excess of amounts properly paid, credited, or required to be distributed (other than income required to be distributed currently) over the DNI of the trust reduced by income required to be distributed currently. To have an accumulation distribution, the distribution must exceed the accounting income of the trust.

Specific Instructions

Part I—Accumulation Distribution in 1996

Line 1—Distribution Under Section 661(a)(2)

Enter the amount from Schedule B of Form 1041, line 12, for 1996. This is the amount properly paid, credited, or required to be distributed other than the amount of income for the current tax year required to be distributed currently.

Line 2—Distributable Net Income

Enter the amount from Schedule B of Form 1041, line 9, for 1996. This is the amount of distributable net income (DNI) for the current tax year determined under section 643(a).

Line 3—Distribution Under Section 661(a)(1)

Enter the amount from Schedule B of Form 1041, line 11, for 1996. This is the amount of income for the current tax year required to be distributed currently.

Line 5—Accumulation Distribution

If line 13, Schedule B of Form 1041 is more than line 10, Schedule B of Form 1041, complete the rest of Schedule J and file it with Form 1041, unless the trust has no previously accumulated income.

Generally, amounts accumulated before a beneficiary reaches age 21 may be excluded by the beneficiary. See sections 665 and 667(c) for exceptions relating to multiple trusts. The trustee reports to the IRS the total amount of the accumulation distribution before any reduction for income accumulated before the beneficiary reaches age 21. If the multiple trust rules do not apply, the beneficiary claims the exclusion when filing **Form 4970,** Tax on Accumulation Distribution of Trusts, as you may not be aware that the beneficiary may be a beneficiary of other trusts with other trustees.

For examples of accumulation distributions that include payments from one trust to another trust, and amounts distributed for a dependent's support, see Regulations section 1.665(b)-1A(b).

Part II—Ordinary Income Accumulation Distribution

Line 6—Distributable Net Income for Earlier Years

Enter the applicable amounts as follows:

Throwback year(s)	Amount from line
1969–1977	Schedule C, Form 1041, line 5
1978–1979	Form 1041, line 61
1980	Form 1041, line 60*
1981–1982	Form 1041, line 58
1983–1995	Schedule B, Form 1041, line 9

For information about throwback years, see the instructions for line 13. For purposes of line 6, in figuring the DNI of the trust for a throwback year, subtract any estate tax deduction for income in respect of a decedent if the income is includible in figuring the DNI of the trust for that year.

Line 7—Distributions Made During Earlier Years

Enter the applicable amounts as follows:

Throwback year(s)	Amount from line
1969–1977	Schedule C, Form 1041, line 8
1978	Form 1041, line 64
1979	Form 1041, line 65
1980	Form 1041, line 64
1981–1982	Form 1041, line 62
1983–1995	Schedule B, Form 1041, line 13

Line 11—Prior Accumulation Distribution Thrown Back to any Throwback Year

Enter the amount of prior accumulation distributions thrown back to the throwback years. Do not enter distributions excluded under section 663(a)(1) for gifts, bequests, etc.

Line 13—Throwback Years

Allocate the amount on line 5 that is an accumulation distribution to the earliest applicable year first, but do not allocate more than the amount on line 12 for any throwback year. An accumulation distribution is thrown back first to the earliest preceding tax year in which there is undistributed net income (UNI). Then, it is thrown back beginning with the next earliest year to any remaining preceding tax years of the trust. The portion of the accumulation distribution allocated to the earliest preceding tax year is the amount of the UNI for that year. The portion of the accumulation distribution allocated to any remaining preceding tax year is the amount by which the accumulation distribution is larger than the total of the UNI for all earlier preceding tax years.

A tax year of a trust during which the trust was a simple trust for the entire year is not a preceding tax year unless **(a)** during that year the trust received outside income or **(b)** the trustee did not distribute all of the trust's income that was required to be distributed currently for that year. In this case, UNI for that year must not be more than the greater of the outside income or income not distributed during that year.

The term "outside income" means amounts that are included in the DNI of the trust for that year but that are not "income" of the trust as defined in Regulations section 1.643(b)-1. Some examples of outside income are: **(a)** income taxable to the trust under section 691; **(b)** unrealized accounts receivable that were assigned to the trust; and **(c)** distributions from another trust that include the DNI or UNI of the other trust. Enter the applicable year at the top of each column for each throwback year.

Line 16—Tax-Exempt Interest Included on Line 13

For each throwback year, divide line 15 by line 6 and multiply the result by the following:

Throwback year(s)	Amount from line
1969–1977	Schedule C, Form 1041, line 2(a)
1978–1979	Form 1041, line 58(a)
1980	Form 1041, line 57(a)
1981–1982	Form 1041, line 55(a)
1983–1995	Schedule B, Form 1041, line 2

Part III—Taxes Imposed on Undistributed Net Income

For the regular tax computation, if there is a capital gain, complete lines 18 through 25 for each throwback year. If the trustee elected the alternative tax on capital gains, complete lines 26 through 31 instead of lines 18 through 25 for each applicable year. If there is no capital gain for any year, or there is a capital loss for every year, enter on line 9 the amount of the tax for each year identified in the instruction for line 18 and do not complete Part III. If the trust received an accumulation distribution from another trust, see Regulations section 1.665(b)-1A.

Note: *The alternative tax on capital gains was repealed for tax years beginning after December 31, 1978. The maximum rate on net capital gain for 1981, 1987, and 1991 through 1995 is not an alternative tax for this purpose.*

Line 18—Regular Tax

Enter the applicable amounts as follows:

Throwback year(s)	Amount from line
1969–1976	Form 1041, page 1, line 24
1977	Form 1041, page 1, line 26
1978–1979	Form 1041, line 27
1980–1984	Form 1041, line 26c
1985–1986	Form 1041, line 25c
1987	Form 1041, line 22c
1988–1995	Schedule G, Form 1041, line 1a

Line 19—Trust's Share of Net Short-Term Gain

For each throwback year, enter the smaller of the capital gain from the two lines indicated. If there is a capital loss or a zero on either or both of the two lines indicated, enter zero on line 19.

Throwback year(s)	Amount from line
1969–1970	Schedule D, Line 10, column 2, or Schedule D, line 12, column 2
1971–1978	Schedule D, line 14, column 2, or Schedule D, line 16, column 2
1979	Schedule D, line 18, column (b) or Schedule D, line 20, column (b)
1980–1981	Schedule D, line 14, column (b) or Schedule D, line 16, column (b)
1982	Schedule D, line 16, column (b) or Schedule D, line 18, column (b)
1983–1995	Schedule D, line 15, column (b) or Schedule D, line 17, column (b)

Line 20—Trust's Share of Net Long-Term Gain

Enter the applicable amounts as follows:

Throwback year(s)	Amount from line
1969–1970	50% of Schedule D, line 13(e)
1971–1977	50% of Schedule D, line 17(e)
1978	Schedule D, line 17(e), or line 31, whichever is applicable, less Form 1041, line 23.
1979	Schedule D, line 25 or line 27, whichever is applicable, less Form 1041, line 23.
1980–1981	Schedule D, line 21, less Schedule D, line 22
1982	Schedule D, line 23, less Schedule D, line 24.
1983–1986	Schedule D, line 22, less Schedule D, line 23.
1987–1995	Schedule D, the smaller of any gain on line 16 or line 17, column (b).

Line 22—Taxable Income

Enter the applicable amounts as follows:

Throwback year(s)	Amount from line
1969–1976	Form 1041, page 1, line 23
1977	Form 1041, page 1, line 25
1978–1979	Form 1041, line 26
1980–1984	Form 1041, line 25
1985–1986	Form 1041, line 24
1987	Form 1041, line 21
1988–1995	Form 1041, line 22

Line 26—Tax on Income Other Than Long-Term Capital Gain

Enter the applicable amounts as follows:

Throwback year(s)	Amount from line
1969	Schedule D, line 20
1970	Schedule D, line 19
1971	Schedule D, line 50
1972–1975	Schedule D, line 48
1976–1978	Schedule D, line 27

Line 27—Trust's Share of Net Short-Term Gain

If there is a loss on any of the following lines, enter zero on line 27 for the applicable throwback year. Otherwise, enter the applicable amounts as follows:

Throwback year(s)	Amount from line
1969–1970	Schedule D, line 10, column 2
1971–1978	Schedule D, line 14, column 2

Line 28—Trust's Share of Taxable Income Less Section 1202 Deduction

Enter the applicable amounts as follows:

Throwback year(s)	Amount from line
1969	Schedule D, line 19
1970	Schedule D, line 18
1971	Schedule D, line 38
1972–1975	Schedule D, line 39
1976–1978	Schedule D, line 21

Part IV—Allocation to Beneficiary

Complete Part IV for each beneficiary. If the accumulation distribution is allocated to more than one beneficiary, attach an additional copy of Schedule J with Part IV completed for each additional beneficiary. Give each beneficiary a copy of his or her respective Part IV information. If more than 5 throwback years are involved, use another Schedule J, completing Parts II and III for each additional throwback year.

If the beneficiary is a nonresident alien individual or a foreign corporation, see section 667(e) about retaining the character of the amounts distributed to determine the amount of the U.S. withholding tax.

The beneficiary uses Form 4970 to figure the tax on the distribution. The beneficiary also uses Form 4970 for the section 667(b)(6) tax adjustment if an accumulation distribution is subject to estate or generation-skipping transfer tax. This is because the trustee may not be the estate or generation-skipping transfer tax return filer.

Schedule K-1 (Form 1041)—Beneficiary's Share of Income, Deductions, Credits, etc.

General Instructions

Use Schedule K-1 (Form 1041) to report the beneficiary's share of income, deductions, and credits from a trust or a decedent's estate.

Who Must File

The fiduciary (or one of the joint fiduciaries) must file Schedule K-1. A copy of each beneficiary's Schedule K-1 is attached to the Form 1041 filed with the IRS and each beneficiary is given a copy of his or her respective Schedule K-1. One copy of each Schedule K-1 must be retained for the fiduciary's records.

Beneficiary's Identifying Number

As a payer of income, you are required under section 6109 to request and provide a proper identifying number for each recipient of income. Enter the beneficiary's number on the respective Schedules K-1 when you file Form 1041. Individuals and business recipients are responsible for giving you their taxpayer identification numbers upon request. You may use **Form W-9,** Request for Taxpayer Identification Number and Certification, to request the beneficiary's identifying number.

Penalty.— Under section 6723, the payer is charged a $50 penalty for each failure to provide a required taxpayer identification number, unless reasonable cause is established for not providing it. Explain any reasonable cause in a signed affidavit and attach it to this return.

Tax Shelter's Identification Number

If the estate or trust is a tax shelter, is involved in a tax shelter, or is considered to be the organizer of a tax shelter, there are reporting requirements under section 6111 for both the fiduciaries and the beneficiaries.

See **Form 8264,** Application for Registration of a Tax Shelter, and **Form 8271,** Investor Reporting of Tax Shelter Registration Number, and their related instructions for information regarding the fiduciary's reporting requirements.

Substitute Forms

You do not need prior IRS approval for a substitute Schedule K-1 (Form 1041) that follows the specifications for filing substitute Schedules K-1 in **Pub. 1167,** Substitute Printed, Computer-Prepared, and Computer-Generated Tax Forms and Schedules, or is an exact copy of an IRS Schedule K-1. You must request IRS approval to use other substitute Schedules K-1. To request approval, write to: Internal Revenue Service, Attention: Substitute Forms Program Coordinator, T:FP:S, 1111 Constitution Avenue, N.W., Washington, DC 20224.

Inclusion of Amounts in Beneficiaries' Income

Simple trust.— The beneficiary of a simple trust must include in his or her gross income the amount of the income required to be distributed currently, whether or not distributed, or if the income required to be distributed currently to all beneficiaries exceeds the distributable net income (DNI), his or her proportionate share of the DNI. The determination of whether trust income is required to be distributed currently depends on the terms of the trust instrument and applicable local law. See Regulations section 1.652(c)-4 for a comprehensive example.

Estates and complex trusts.— The beneficiary of a decedent's estate or complex trust must include in his or her gross income the sum of:

1. The amount of the income required to be distributed currently, or if the income required to be distributed currently to all beneficiaries exceeds the DNI (figured without taking into account the charitable deduction), his or her proportionate share of the DNI (as so figured); and

2. All other amounts properly paid, credited, or required to be distributed, or if the sum of the income required to be distributed currently and other amounts properly paid, credited, or required to be distributed to all beneficiaries exceeds the DNI, his or her proportionate share of the excess of DNI over the income required to be distributed currently.

See Regulations section 1.662(c)-4 for a comprehensive example.

For complex trusts that have more than one beneficiary, and if different beneficiaries have substantially separate and independent shares, their shares are treated as separate trusts for the sole purpose of determining the amount of DNI allocable to the respective beneficiaries. For examples of the application of the separate share rule, see the regulations under section 663(c).

Character of income.— The beneficiary's income is considered to have the same proportion of each class of items entering into the computation of DNI that the total of each class has to the DNI (e.g., half dividends and half interest if the income of the estate or trust is half dividends and half interest).

Allocation of deductions.— Generally, items of deduction that enter into the computation of DNI are allocated among the items of income to the extent such allocation is not inconsistent with the rules set out in section 469 and its regulations, relating to passive activity loss limitations, in the following order.

First, all deductions directly attributable to a specific class of income are deducted from that income. For example, rental expenses, to the extent allowable, are deducted from rental income.

Second, deductions that are not directly attributable to a specific class of income generally may be allocated to any class of income, as long as a reasonable portion is allocated to any tax-exempt income. Deductions considered not directly attributable to a specific class of income under this rule include fiduciary fees, safe deposit box rental charges, and state income and personal property taxes. The charitable deduction, however, must be ratably apportioned among each class of income included in DNI.

Finally, any excess deductions that are directly attributable to a class of income may be allocated to another class of income. In no case can excess deductions from a passive activity be allocated to income from a nonpassive activity, or to portfolio income earned by the estate or trust. Excess deductions attributable to tax-exempt income cannot offset any other class of income.

In no case can deductions be allocated to an item of income that is not included in the computation of DNI, or attributable to corpus.

Except for the final year, and for depreciation or depletion allocations in excess of income (see Rev. Rul. 74-530, 1974-2 C.B. 188), you may not show any negative amounts for any class of income because the beneficiary generally may not claim losses or deductions from the estate or trust.

Gifts and bequests.— Do not include in the beneficiary's income any gifts or bequests of a specific sum of money or of specific property under the terms of the governing instrument that are paid or credited in three installments or less.

Amounts that can be paid or credited only from income of the estate or trust do not qualify as a gift or bequest of a specific sum of money.

Past years.— Do not include in the beneficiary's income any amounts deducted on Form 1041 for an earlier year that were credited or required to be distributed in that earlier year.

Beneficiary's Tax Year

The beneficiary's income from the estate or trust must be included in the beneficiary's tax year during which the tax year of the estate or trust ends. See Pub. 559 for more information, including the effect of the death of a beneficiary during the tax year of the estate or trust.

Specific Instructions

Line 1—Interest

Enter the beneficiary's share of the taxable interest income minus allocable deductions.

Line 2—Dividends

Enter the beneficiary's share of dividend income minus allocable deductions.

Line 3a—Net Short-Term Capital Gain

Enter the beneficiary's share of the net short-term capital gain from line 15, column (a), Schedule D (Form 1041), minus allocable deductions. Do not enter a loss on line 3a. If, for the final year of the estate or trust, there is a capital loss carryover, enter on line 12b the beneficiary's share of short-term capital loss carryover as a loss in parentheses. However, if the beneficiary is a corporation, enter on line 12b the beneficiary's share of all short- and long-term capital loss carryovers as a single item in parentheses. See section 642(h) and related regulations for more information.

Line 3b—Net Long-Term Capital Gain

Enter the beneficiary's share of the net long-term capital gain from line 16, column (a), Schedule D (Form 1041), minus allocable deductions. Do not enter a loss on line 3b. If, for the final year of the estate or trust, there is a capital loss carryover, enter on line 12c the beneficiary's share of the long-term capital loss carryover as a loss in parentheses. (If the beneficiary is a corporation, see the instructions for line 3a.) See section 642(h) and related regulations for more information.

Gains, or losses, from the complete, or partial, disposition of a rental, rental real estate, or trade or business activity that is a passive activity, must be shown on an attachment to Schedule K-1.

Line 4a—Annuities, Royalties, and Other Nonpassive Income

Enter the beneficiary's share of annuities, royalties, or any other income, minus allocable deductions (other than directly apportionable deductions), that is NOT subject to any passive activity loss limitation rules at the beneficiary level. Use line 5a to report income items subject to the passive activity rules at the beneficiary's level.

Lines 4b and 5b—Depreciation

Enter the beneficiary's share of the depreciation deductions attributable to each activity reported on lines 4a and 5a. See the instructions on page 10 for a discussion of how the depreciation deduction is apportioned between the beneficiaries and the estate or trust. Report any AMT adjustment or tax preference item attributable to depreciation separately on line 11a.

Note: *An estate or trust cannot make an election under section 179 to expense certain tangible property.*

Lines 4c and 5c—Depletion

Enter the beneficiary's share of the depletion deduction under section 611 attributable to each activity reported on lines 4a and 5a. See the instructions on page 10 for a discussion of how the depletion deduction is apportioned between the beneficiaries and the estate or trust. Report any tax preference item attributable to depletion separately on line 11b.

Lines 4d and 5d—Amortization

Itemize the beneficiary's share of the amortization deductions attributable to each activity reported on lines 4a and 5a. Apportion the amortization deductions between the estate or trust and the beneficiaries in the same way that the depreciation and depletion deductions are divided. Report any AMT adjustment attributable to amortization separately on line 11c.

Line 5a—Trade or Business, Rental Real Estate, and Other Rental Income

Enter the beneficiary's share of trade or business, rental real estate, and other rental income, minus allocable deductions (other than directly apportionable deductions). To assist the beneficiary in figuring any applicable passive activity loss limitations, also attach a separate schedule showing the beneficiary's share of income derived from each trade or business, rental real estate, and other rental activity.

Lines 5b Through 5d

Caution: *The limitations on passive activity losses and credits under section 469 apply to estates and trusts. Estates and trusts that distribute income to beneficiaries are allowed to apportion depreciation, depletion, and amortization deductions to the beneficiaries. These deductions are referred to as "directly apportionable deductions."*

Rules for treating a beneficiary's income and directly apportionable deductions from an estate or trust and other rules for applying the passive loss and credit limitations to beneficiaries of estates and trusts have not yet been issued.

Any directly apportionable deduction, such as depreciation, is treated by the beneficiary as having been incurred in the same activity as incurred by the estate or trust. However, the character of such deduction may be determined as if the beneficiary incurred the deduction directly.

To assist the beneficiary in figuring any applicable passive activity loss limitations, also attach a separate schedule showing the beneficiary's share of directly apportionable deductions derived from each trade or business, rental real estate, and other rental activity.

Line 6—Income for Minimum Tax Purposes

Enter the beneficiary's share of the income distribution deduction figured on a minimum tax basis from line 27 of Schedule I.

Line 7—Income for Regular Tax Purposes

Enter the beneficiary's share of the income distribution deduction figured on line 17 of Schedule B. This amount should equal the sum of lines 1 through 3b, 4a, and 5a.

Line 9—Estate Tax Deduction (Including Generation-Skipping Transfer Taxes)

If the distribution deduction consists of any income in respect of a decedent, and the estate or trust was allowed a deduction under section 691(c) for the estate tax paid attributable to such income (see the line 19 instructions on page 13), then the beneficiary is allowed an estate tax deduction in proportion to his or her share of the distribution that consists of such income. For an example of the computation, see Regulations section 1.691(c)-2. Figure the computation on a separate sheet and attach it to the return.

Line 10—Foreign Taxes

List on a separate sheet the beneficiary's share of the applicable foreign taxes paid or accrued and the various foreign source figures needed to figure the beneficiary's foreign tax credit. See Pub. 514 and section 901(b)(5) for special rules about foreign taxes.

Lines 11a through 11c

Enter any adjustments or tax preference items attributable to depreciation, depletion, or amortization that were allocated to the beneficiary. For property placed in service before 1987, report separately the accelerated depreciation of real and leased personal property.

Line 11d—Exclusion Items

Enter the beneficiary's share of the adjustment for minimum tax purposes from Schedule K-1, line 8, that is attributable to exclusion items (Schedule I, lines 4a through 4d, 4p, and 4q).

Line 12a—Excess Deductions on Termination

If this is the final return and there are excess deductions on termination (see the instructions for line 22 on page 13), enter the beneficiary's share of the excess deductions on line 12a. Figure the deductions on a separate sheet and attach it to the return.

Excess deductions on termination occur only during the last tax year of the trust or decedent's estate when the total deductions (excluding the charitable deduction and exemption) are greater than the gross income during that tax year. Generally, a deduction based on an NOL carryover is not available to a beneficiary as an excess deduction. However, if the last tax year of the estate or trust is also the last year in which an NOL carryover may be taken (see section 172(b)), the NOL carryover is considered an excess deduction on the termination of the estate or trust to the extent it is not absorbed by the estate or trust during its final tax year. For more information, see Regulations section 1.642(h)-4 for a discussion of the allocation of the carryover among the beneficiaries.

Only the beneficiary of an estate or trust that succeeds to its property is allowed to deduct that entity's excess deductions on termination. A beneficiary who does not have enough income in that year to absorb the entire deduction may not carry the balance over to any succeeding year. An individual beneficiary must be able to itemize deductions in order to claim the excess deductions in determining taxable income.

Lines 12b and 12c—Unused Capital Loss Carryover

Upon termination of the trust or decedent's estate, the beneficiary succeeding to the property is allowed as a deduction any unused capital loss carryover under section 1212. If the estate or trust incurs capital losses in the final year, use Part V of Schedule D (Form 1041) to figure the amount of capital loss carryover to be allocated to the beneficiary.

Lines 12d and 12e—Net Operating Loss (NOL) Carryover

Upon termination of a trust or decedent's estate, a beneficiary succeeding to its property is allowed to deduct any unused NOL (and any AMT NOL) carryover for regular and AMT purposes if the carryover would be allowable to the estate or trust in a later tax year but for the termination. Enter on lines 12d and 12e the unused carryover amounts.

Line 13—Other

Itemize on line 13, or on a separate sheet if more space is needed, the beneficiary's tax information not entered elsewhere on Schedule K-1. This includes the allocable share, if any, of:

- Payment of estimated tax to be credited to the beneficiary (section 643(g));
- Tax-exempt interest income received or accrued by the trust (including exempt-interest dividends from a mutual fund or other regulated investment company);
- Investment income (section 163(d));
- Gross farming and fishing income;
- Credit for backup withholding (section 3406);
- The information a beneficiary will need to figure any investment credit;
- The work opportunity credit;
- The alcohol fuel credit;
- The credit for increasing research activities;
- The low-income housing credit;
- The renewable electricity production credit;
- The empowerment zone employment credit;
- The Indian employment credit;
- The orphan drug credit; and
- The information a beneficiary will need to figure any recapture taxes.

Note: *Upon termination of an estate or trust, any suspended passive activity losses (PALs) relating to an interest in a passive activity cannot be allocated to the beneficiary. Instead, the basis in such activity is increased by the amount of any PALs allocable to the interest, and no losses are allowed as a deduction on the estate's or trust's final Form 1041.*

Form **3520**
(Rev. June 1995)
Department of the Treasury
Internal Revenue Service

U.S. Information Return
Creation of or Transfers to Certain Foreign Trusts
(Under section 6048 of the Internal Revenue Code)
Attach additional sheets if more space is needed.

OMB No. 1545-0159

All information must be in the English language. Show all amounts in U.S. dollars.

Name of U.S. person(s) filing return

Identifying number(s)

Number, street, and room or suite no. (If a P.O. box, see instructions.)

City or town, state, and ZIP code

1   Title of person filing return (check applicable box)
    ☐ Grantor   ☐ Transferor   ☐ Fiduciary of an estate in the case of testamentary trust

2   If fiduciary of an estate, give name and social security number of the decedent.

3   Name of the trust

4   Foreign country under whose laws the trust was created

5   Date trust was created

6   Name and business address of foreign trustee(s)

7   Date of transaction

8   Amount of money and value of property transferred
    $

9	Name of beneficiary	Address of beneficiary	Date of birth (see instructions)	Identifying number (if any)
a				
b				
c				
d				
e				
f				
g				

10   Name and address of the person(s) creating the trust

11   Termination date. If no termination date, attach a statement describing the conditions that will cause the trust to terminate.

12   Is trustee required to distribute all trust income currently? . . . . ☐ Yes   ☐ No
     If "No," attach a statement showing each beneficiary's **(a)** right to receive income or corpus, or both; **(b)** proportionate interest in the income or corpus, or both; and **(c)** any condition governing the time a distribution to the beneficiary may be made, such as a specific date or age. You may attach a copy of the trust instrument instead of the statement.

13   Attach a statement listing the property transferred to the foreign trust in the transaction for which this return is being filed. Include in the statement a detailed description of each item transferred, its adjusted basis and fair market value on the date transferred, and the consideration, if any, paid by the foreign trust for the property.

For Paperwork Reduction Act Notice, see instructions on back.   Cat No. 19594V   Form **3520** (Rev. 6-95)

14 Name and address (Number and street, city, state or province, ZIP or postal code, and country) of person(s) having custody of the books of account and records of the foreign trust

15 Location of the books of account and records if different from above

Signature—Under penalties of perjury, I declare that I have examined this return, including any accompanying reports, schedules, or statements, and to the best of my knowledge and belief, it is true, correct, and complete.

Signature ▶   Title (if any) ▶   Date ▶

Paperwork Reduction Act Notice.—We ask for the information on this form to carry out the Internal Revenue laws of the United States. You are required to give us the information. We need it to ensure that you are complying with these laws and to allow us to figure and collect the right amount of tax.

The time needed to complete and file the form will vary depending on individual circumstances. The estimated average time is:

Recordkeeping . . . . 5 hr., 44 min.
Learning about the law or the form . . . . . 35 min.
Preparing and sending the form to the IRS . . . . . 43 min.

If you have comments concerning the accuracy of these time estimates or suggestions for making this form simpler, we would be happy to hear from you. You can write to the **Internal Revenue Service,** Attention: Tax Forms Committee, PC:FP, Washington, DC 20224. **DO NOT** send the form to this office. Instead, see **When and Where To File** on this page.

General Instructions

Section references are to the Internal Revenue Code.

Who Must File.—Any U.S. person who creates a foreign trust or directly or indirectly transfers money or property to a foreign trust must file Form 3520. However, employers and employees are not required to file if contributions are made to a foreign trust under a plan which provides employee benefits such as pension, profit-sharing, stock bonus, sickness, accident, unemployment, welfare, or a combination of benefits.

If any person is not the actual owner of the money or the property transferred but is merely acting for a U.S. person, the information must be furnished in the name of and by the actual owner of the money or property. A fiduciary of an estate must file information relating to the decedent.

Definitions.—A "U.S. person" means citizen or resident of the United States, a domestic corporation, a domestic partnership, and any estate or trust (other than a foreign estate or trust whose income from sources outside the United States is not effectively connected with the conduct of a trade or business within the United States).

The term "transferor" means any U.S. person other than a person who is the grantor or the fiduciary who transfers money or property to or for the benefit of a foreign trust. It does not refer to a person who transfers money or property to a foreign trust under a sale or exchange made for full and adequate consideration.

When and Where To File.—Unless an extension of time to file is granted, Form 3520 must be filed by the 90th day after a U.S. person creates a foreign trust or transfers any money or property to a foreign trust. The Assistant Commissioner (International) is authorized to grant reasonable extensions of time to file Form 3520. You can request an extension of time by writing to A/C International, 950 L'Enfant Plaza South, SW, Washington, DC 20224.

File Form 3520 with the Internal Revenue Service Center, Philadelphia, PA 19255.

Identifying Number.—Individuals, enter your social security number (SSN). All others, enter your employer identification number (EIN). If the fiduciary of an estate must file **Form 1041,** U.S. Income Tax Return for Estates and Trusts, enter the EIN on the line for identifying number and the decedent's SSN on line 2 of Form 3520.

Beneficiaries.—Attach a statement listing the name, address, identifying number, if any, for each beneficiary who is named in the trust instrument or whose identity can definitely be determined at the time this form must be filed. Also, list the date of birth for each beneficiary who is a U.S. person and whose rights under the trust are determined, in whole or in part, by reference to the beneficiary's age.

Joint Returns.—Two or more persons who jointly create a foreign trust or jointly transfer money or property to a foreign trust may file a joint Form 3520 instead of filing separate Forms 3520.

Multiple Transfers.—If a U.S. person creates more than one foreign trust or transfers money or property to more than one foreign trust, a separate Form 3520 must be filed for each foreign trust. If a U.S. person transfers money or property to a foreign trust at different times, a separate Form 3520 must be filed for each reportable transfer. However, if a U.S. person makes more than one transfer to the same foreign trust during any 90-day period, he or she may elect to file one Form 3520. The form must include all of the information required for each transfer by the 90th day after the earliest transfer made during the 90-day period.

Penalties.—A penalty of 5% of the amount transferred to a foreign trust (but not more than $1,000) is imposed by section 6677 for failure to file on time, or failure to report the required information, unless due to reasonable cause. Criminal penalties for failure to file on time and for filing a false or fraudulent return are provided by sections 7203, 7206, and 7207.

Address.—Include the room, suite, or other unit number after the street address. If the Post Office does not deliver mail to the street address and the transferor has a P.O. box, show the box number instead of the street address.

Signature.—If this form is filed by an individual (including a fiduciary of an estate or trust), it must be signed by that individual. If it is filed by a partnership, one partner must sign. If it is filed by a corporation, it must be signed by the president, vice-president, treasurer, assistant treasurer, or chief accounting officer, or by any other officer (such as a tax officer) who is authorized to sign.

Note: *Persons filing this form may be required to file **Form TD F 90-22.1**, Report of Foreign Bank and Financial Accounts, **Form 926**, Return by a Transferor of Property to a Foreign Corporation, Foreign Estate or Trust, or Foreign Partnership, and **Form 3520-A**, Annual Return of Foreign Trust with U.S. Beneficiaries.*

Form 3520-A
(Rev. August 1995)
Department of the Treasury
Internal Revenue Service

Annual Return of Foreign Trust With U.S. Beneficiaries

▶ Attach additional sheets if more space is needed.

OMB No. 1545-0160

Note: *All information must be written in English.*

For calendar year 19___, or fiscal year beginning ___, 19___, and ending ___, 19___.

Name of United States person(s) filing this return

Identifying number

Number, street, and room or suite no. (If a P.O. box, see instructions on page 4.)

Service center where person filing this return files income tax returns

City or town, state, and ZIP code

1 Title of person filing return (check applicable box): ☐ Grantor ☐ Transferor

2 Are you the sole U.S. grantor or transferor? . . . . ☐ Yes ☐ No
  If "No," attach a list of all other U.S. grantors or transferors showing name, address, and identifying number.

3 Name and address of the foreign trust

4 Country under whose laws the trust was created

5 Date the trust was created

6 Name and business address of foreign trustee

7 **Termination date.** (If no termination date, attach a statement describing the conditions that will cause the trust to terminate.)

8 Name of U.S. beneficiary	Address of U.S. beneficiary	Identifying number, if any	U.S. citizen Yes	No
a				
b				
c				
d				
e				
f				

9 Amendments to trust during this year. Explain (attach statement if necessary):

10 Is trustee required to distribute all trust income currently? . . . .

11 Has the location of the trust changed since its creation? . . . .
   If "Yes," attach explanation.

12 Was Form 3520 filed for this trust? . . . .
   If "Yes," enter date filed ▶

13 Enter date of last transfer of property to trust by grantor or transferor filing this return ▶

14 Has the grantor or transferor filed Form TD F 90-22.1 for this trust? . . . .

15 Did the trust acquire a U.S. beneficiary during the current year? . . . .
   If "Yes," enter amount of deemed accumulation distribution to grantor (see section 679(b) and attach computation) . . . . ▶

16 Attach a statement showing each U.S. beneficiary's **(a)** right to receive income or corpus, or both; **(b)** proportionate interest in the income or corpus, or both; and **(c)** any conditions governing the time a distribution may be made to a U.S. beneficiary, such as a specific date or age. You may attach a copy of the trust instrument instead of the statement. If either the statement or trust instrument was submitted in a prior year, you do not have to resubmit the information unless it has changed. If you previously sent the information and it remains unchanged, enter the year the original information was submitted.

Under penalties of perjury, I declare that I have examined this return, including any accompanying reports, schedules, or statements, and to the best of my knowledge and belief, it is true, correct, and complete.

Signature ▶   Title ▶   Date ▶

For Paperwork Reduction Act Notice, see instructions on page 3.   Cat. No. 19595G   Form **3520-A** (Rev. 8-95)

Form 3520-A (Rev. 8-95) Page 2

Part I — Foreign Trust Income Statement
Show all amounts in U.S. dollars

		(a) Totals from books and records of this foreign trust	(b) Portion to be reported by grantor or transferor
Income			
1	Dividends		
2	Interest		
3	Income from partnerships and other fiduciaries		
4	Gross rents and royalties		
5	Gross profit (loss) from trade or business		
6	Net gain (loss) from capital assets		
7	Ordinary gains and (losses)		
8	Other income (state nature of income) ▶		
9	Total income (add lines 1 through 8)		
Expenses			
10	Interest		
11	Taxes (attach schedule)		
12	Fiduciary's portion of depreciation and depletion (explain depletion) ▶		
13	Charitable contributions		
14	Other expenses ▶		
15	Total expenses (add lines 10 through 14)		
16	Net income (subtract line 15 from line 9)		

Amount from line 16, column (b), should be entered in Schedule E (Form 1040), Form 1065, Form 1041, or Forms 1120 and 1120S (if less than 100% of column (a), attach computations).

Part II — Balance Sheet
Show all amounts in U.S. dollars

		Beginning of Tax Year		End of Tax Year	
		(a) Amount	(b) Total	(c) Amount	(d) Total
Assets					
1	Cash:				
a	Savings and interest-bearing accounts				
b	Other				
2	Net accounts receivable				
3	Notes receivable (attach schedule)				
4	Inventories				
5	Government obligations:				
a	U.S. and instrumentalities				
b	State, subdivisions thereof				
6	Investments in non-Govt. bonds, etc. (attach schedule)				
7	Investments in corporate stocks (attach schedule)				
8	Mortgage loans (number of loans ▶ ....)				
9	Other investments (attach schedule)				
10a	Depreciable (depletable) assets (attach schedule)				
b	Less: accumulated depreciation (depletion)				
11	Land				
12	Other assets (attach schedule)				
13	Total assets				
Liabilities					
14	Accounts payable				
15	Contributions, gifts, grants, etc., payable				
16	Mortgages and notes payable (attach schedule)				
17	Other liabilities (attach schedule)				
18	Total liabilities				
Net Worth					
19	Accumulated trust income				
20	Other (attach schedule)				
21	Total net worth				
22	Total liabilities and net worth (line 18 plus line 21)				

Paperwork Reduction Act Notice

We ask for the information on this form to carry out the Internal Revenue laws of the United States. You are required to give us the information. We need it to ensure that you are complying with these laws and to allow us to figure and collect the right amount of tax.

The time needed to complete and file the form will vary depending on individual circumstances. The estimated average time is:

Recordkeeping . . . . 29 hr., 25 min.
Learning about the law or the form . . . 53 min.
Preparing and sending the form to the IRS . . . . 1 hr., 25 min.

If you have comments concerning the accuracy of these time estimates or suggestions for making the form simpler, we would be happy to hear from you. You can write to the **Internal Revenue Service,** Washington, DC 20224, Attention: Tax Forms Committee, PC:FP. **DO NOT** send the form to this office. Instead, see **When and Where To File** below.

General Instructions

Section references are to the Internal Revenue Code.

Purpose of Form

Form 3520-A is the annual information return of a foreign trust with at least one U.S. beneficiary. The form provides information about the foreign trust, its U.S. beneficiaries, and the U.S. person who created the foreign trust and transferred property to it.

Who Must File

A U.S. person must file Form 3520-A if it has directly or indirectly transferred property to a foreign trust and the trust has a U.S. beneficiary during the tax year. Once such a transfer is made, the U.S. person is required to file Form 3520-A every year as long as the trust has at least one U.S. beneficiary.

The U.S. person who transfers property to a foreign trust is treated as the grantor of the foreign trust when the trust acquires or is treated as acquiring a U.S. beneficiary. As the grantor of the foreign trust, the U.S. person must include in its computation of taxable income and credits against tax those items of income, deductions, and credits against tax attributable to the foreign trust.

A U.S. person is not required to file Form 3520-A if the **(a)** transfer to the foreign trust was made by reason of the death of the transferor, **(b)** transferor recognizes gain on the sale or exchange of assets, **(c)** transfer is to a foreign employee benefit trust qualified under section 404(a)(4) or section 404A, or **(d)** transfer to a foreign trust was made before May 22, 1974.

A U.S. person means a U.S. citizen, a U.S. resident, a domestic corporation, a domestic partnership, and an estate or trust (other than a foreign estate or trust with income from sources outside the United States that is not effectively connected with a trade or business within the United States).

Note: *Two transferors or grantors of the same foreign trust for the same tax year may file a joint Form 3520-A if they filed (or will file) a joint income tax return.*

When and Where To File

File Form 3520-A by the 15th day of the 4th month following the end of the transferor's or grantor's tax year. An extension of time to file may be granted. Get **Form 2758,** Application for Extension of Time To File Certain Excise, Income, Information and Other Returns, for details.

File Form 3520-A with the Internal Revenue Service Center, Philadelphia, PA 19255.

Foreign Trusts Acquiring U.S. Beneficiaries

Any undistributed net income at the end of the preceding year that was earned from the property transferred is considered income (in addition to the grantor's or transferor's other income for the year) to the transferor in the year that the trust acquires the U.S. beneficiary.

Foreign Trusts Treated as Having a U.S. Beneficiary

A trust is treated as having a U.S. beneficiary for the tax year unless under the terms of the trust:

1. None of the income or corpus of the trust may be paid or accumulated during the tax year to or for the benefit of a U.S. person, and

2. None of the income or corpus of the trust could be paid to or for the benefit of a U.S. person if the trust were terminated during the tax year.

Attribution of Ownership

An amount is treated as paid or accumulated to or for the benefit of a U.S. person if such amount is paid or accumulated to or for the benefit of a foreign corporation, foreign partnership, or foreign trust or estate, and

1. More than 50% of the combined voting power of all classes of stock of the foreign corporation entitled to vote are owned or considered as owned by United States shareholders (as defined in section 951(b)),

2. The foreign partnership has at least one partner who is a U.S. person (as defined in section 7701(a)(30)), or

3. The foreign trust or estate has at least one U.S. beneficiary.

Apportionment of Trust Income

If transfers of property to a foreign trust occurred both **(a)** on or before and **(b)** after May 21, 1974, or if transfers were made by the person filing this return and some other person, the income, deductions, and credits from the foreign trust must be apportioned among the transfers. The apportionment must be made in a manner that is reasonable in light of all of the circumstances. See section 671 and the regulations under section 671 for the rules of apportionment. Attach all relevant information including the date, amount, and nature of the property transferred to the foreign trust by the person filing this return and the date, amount, and nature of the property transferred to the foreign trust by all other persons.

Multiple Transfers

If a U.S. person creates more than one foreign trust or transfers money or property to more than one foreign trust, separate returns must be filed for each foreign trust. If more than one U.S. person contributed money or property to a foreign trust with a U.S. beneficiary, each such person must file Form 3520-A.

Definitions

A "transferor" is any U.S. person who directly or indirectly gives, sells, exchanges, transfers or otherwise disposes of money or property to a foreign trust. It does not refer to a transfer made by a U.S. person who is **not** the real owner (such as a bank transferring property for a U.S. person). In this case, the real owner is considered the grantor or transferor.

A "grantor" is a U.S. person who creates or is treated as the owner of any portion of a foreign trust.

A "beneficiary" is a U.S. person who receives, will receive, or may receive money or property, at anytime, from a foreign trust.

Identifying Number and Address

Use social security numbers to identify individuals. Use employer identification numbers to identify estates, trusts, partnerships, and corporations.

Include the suite, room or other unit number after the street address. If the Post Office does not deliver mail to the street address and the U.S. person has a P.O. box, show the box number instead of the street address.

Penalties

A penalty of 5% of the value of the corpus of the trust at the close of the tax year (but not more than $1,000) is imposed by section 6677 for failure to file on time, or failure to report the required information, unless due to reasonable cause. Criminal penalties for failure to file on time and for filing a false or fraudulent return are provided by sections 7203, 7206, and 7207.

Signature

If this return is filed by an individual or a fiduciary, it must be signed by that individual. If it is filed by a partnership, one of the partners must sign. If it is filed by a corporation, it must be signed by the president, vice-president, treasurer, assistant treasurer, chief accounting officer, or by any other corporate officer (such as a tax officer) who is authorized to sign.

Note: *The grantor or transferor is still required to file* **Form 3520,** *United States Information Return-Creation of or Transfers to Certain Foreign Trusts,* **Form TD F 90-22.1,** *Report of Foreign Bank and Financial Accounts, and* **Form 926,** *Return by a U.S. Transferor of Property to a Foreign Corporation, Foreign Estate or Trust, or Foreign Partnership. See these forms for exceptions from filing.*

Form **4789**
(Rev. October 1995)
Department of the Treasury
Internal Revenue Service

Currency Transaction Report

▶ Use this 1995 revision effective October 1, 1995.
▶ For Paperwork Reduction Act Notice, see page 3. ▶ Please type or print.
(Complete all parts that apply—See instructions)

OMB No. 1545-0183

1 Check all box(es) that apply:
a ☐ Amends prior report **b** ☐ Multiple persons **c** ☐ Multiple transactions

Part I — Person(s) Involved in Transaction(s)

Section A—Person(s) on Whose Behalf Transaction(s) Is Conducted

2 Individual's last name or Organization's name	3 First name	4 M.I.
5 Doing business as (DBA)	6 SSN or EIN	
7 Address (number, street, and apt. or suite no.)	8 Date of birth M M D D Y Y	
9 City	10 State	11 ZIP code	12 Country (if not U.S.)	13 Occupation, profession, or business

14 If an individual, describe method used to verify identity:
a ☐ Driver's license/State I.D. **b** ☐ Passport **c** ☐ Alien registration **d** ☐ Other _____
e Issued by: **f** Number:

Section B—Individual(s) Conducting Transaction(s) (if other than above).

If Section B is left blank or incomplete, check the box(es) below to indicate the reason(s):

a ☐ Armored Car Service **b** ☐ Mail Deposit or Shipment **c** ☐ Night Deposit or Automated Teller Machine (ATM)
d ☐ Multiple Transactions **e** ☐ Conducted On Own Behalf

15 Individual's last name	16 First name	17 M.I.
18 Address (number, street, and apt. or suite no.)	19 SSN	
20 City	21 State	22 ZIP code	23 Country (if not U.S.)	24 Date of birth M M D D Y Y

25 If an individual, describe method used to verify identity:
a ☐ Driver's license/State I.D. **b** ☐ Passport **c** ☐ Alien registration **d** ☐ Other _____
e Issued by: **f** Number:

Part II — Amount and Type of Transaction(s). Check all boxes that apply.

26 Cash In $ _____ .00 **27** Cash Out $ _____ .00 **28** Date of Transaction M M D D Y Y

29 ☐ Foreign Currency _____ (Country)
30 ☐ Wire Transfer(s)
31 ☐ Negotiable Instrument(s) Purchased
32 ☐ Negotiable Instrument(s) Cashed
33 ☐ Currency Exchange(s)
34 ☐ Deposit(s)/Withdrawal(s)
35 ☐ Account Number(s) Affected (if any): _____
36 ☐ Other (specify): _____

Part III — Financial Institution Where Transaction(s) Takes Place

37 Name of financial institution	Enter Federal Regulator or BSA Examiner code number from the instructions here. ▶ [ ]
38 Address (number, street, and apt. or suite no.)	39 SSN or EIN
40 City	41 State	42 ZIP code	43 MICR No.

Sign Here ▶

44 Title of approving official	45 Signature of approving official	46 Date of signature M M D D Y Y
47 Type or print preparer's name	48 Type or print name of person to contact	49 Telephone number ( )

Cat. No. 42004W

Form **4789** (Rev. 10-95)

Form 4789 (Rev. 10-95) Page **2**

Multiple Persons
(Complete applicable parts below if box 1b on page 1 is checked.)

Part I Person(s) Involved in Transaction(s)

Section A—Person(s) on Whose Behalf Transaction(s) Is Conducted

2 Individual's last name or Organization's name	3 First name	4 M.I.
5 Doing business as (DBA)	6 SSN or EIN	
7 Address (number, street, and apt. or suite no.)	8 Date of birth M M D D Y Y	
9 City	10 State	11 ZIP code	12 Country (if not U.S.)	13 Occupation, profession, or business

14 If an individual, describe method used to verify identity:
- a ☐ Driver's license/State I.D.
- b ☐ Passport
- c ☐ Alien registration
- d ☐ Other _____
- e Issued by:
- f Number:

Section B—Individual(s) Conducting Transaction(s) (if other than above).

15 Individual's last name	16 First name	17 M.I.
18 Address (number, street, and apt. or suite no.)	19 SSN	
20 City	21 State	22 ZIP code	23 Country (if not U.S.)	24 Date of birth M M D D Y Y

25 If an individual, describe method used to verify identity:
- a ☐ Driver's license/State I.D.
- b ☐ Passport
- c ☐ Alien registration
- d ☐ Other _____
- e Issued by:
- f Number:

~~~~~~

Part I Person(s) Involved in Transaction(s)

Section A—Person(s) on Whose Behalf Transaction(s) Is Conducted

2 Individual's last name or Organization's name	3 First name	4 M.I.
5 Doing business as (DBA)	6 SSN or EIN	
7 Address (number, street, and apt. or suite no.)	8 Date of birth M M D D Y Y	
9 City	10 State	11 ZIP code	12 Country (if not U.S.)	13 Occupation, profession, or business

14 If an individual, describe method used to verify identity:
- a ☐ Driver's license/State I.D.
- b ☐ Passport
- c ☐ Alien registration
- d ☐ Other _____
- e Issued by:
- f Number:

Section B—Individual(s) Conducting Transaction(s) (if other than above).

15 Individual's last name	16 First name	17 M.I.
18 Address (number, street, and apt. or suite no.)	19 SSN	
20 City	21 State	22 ZIP code	23 Country (if not U.S.)	24 Date of birth M M D D Y Y

25 If an individual, describe method used to verify identity:
- a ☐ Driver's license/State I.D.
- b ☐ Passport
- c ☐ Alien registration
- d ☐ Other _____
- e Issued by:
- f Number:

Paperwork Reduction Act Notice.—The requested information has been determined to be useful in criminal, tax, and regulatory investigations and proceedings. Financial institutions are required to provide the information under 31 U.S.C. 5313 and 31 CFR Part 103. These provisions are commonly referred to as the Bank Secrecy Act (BSA) which is administered by the U.S. Department of the Treasury's Financial Crimes Enforcement Network (FinCEN).

The time needed to complete this form will vary depending on individual circumstances. The estimated average time is 19 minutes. If you have comments concerning the accuracy of this time estimate or suggestions for making this form simpler, we would be happy to hear from you. You can write to the **Internal Revenue Service,** Attention: Tax Forms Committee, PC:FP, Washington, DC 20224. **DO NOT** send this form to this office. Instead, see **When and Where To File** below.

Suspicious Transactions

This Currency Transaction Report (CTR) should NOT be filed for suspicious transactions involving $10,000 or less in currency OR to note that a transaction of more than $10,000 is suspicious. Any suspicious or unusual activity should be reported by a financial institution in the manner prescribed by its appropriate federal regulator or BSA examiner. (See Item 37.) If a transaction is suspicious and in excess of $10,000 in currency, then both a CTR and the appropriate referral form must be filed.

Should the suspicious activity require immediate attention, financial institutions should telephone 1-800-800-CTRS. An Internal Revenue Service (IRS) employee will direct the call to the local office of the IRS Criminal Investigation Division (CID). This toll-free number is operational Monday through Friday, from approximately 9:00 am to 6:00 pm Eastern Standard Time. If an emergency, consult directory assistance for the local IRS CID Office.

General Instructions

Who Must File.—Each financial institution (other than a casino, which instead must file Form 8362 and the U.S. Postal Service for which there are separate rules), must file Form 4789 (CTR) for each deposit, withdrawal, exchange of currency, or other payment or transfer, by, through, or to the financial institution which involves a transaction in currency of more than $10,000. Multiple transactions must be treated as a single transaction if the financial institution has knowledge that (1) they are by or on behalf of the same person, and (2) they result in either currency received (Cash In) or currency disbursed (Cash Out) by the financial institution totaling more than $10,000 during any one business day. For a bank, a business day is the day on which transactions are routinely posted to customers' accounts, as normally communicated to depository customers. For all other financial institutions, a business day is a calendar day.

Generally, financial institutions are defined as banks, other types of depository institutions, brokers or dealers in securities, money transmitters, currency exchangers, check cashers, issuers and sellers of money orders and traveler's checks. Should you have questions, see the definitions in 31 CFR Part 103.

When and Where To File.—File this CTR by the 15th calendar day after the day of the transaction with the IRS Detroit Computing Center, ATTN: CTR, P.O. Box 33604, Detroit, MI 48232-5604 or with your local IRS office. Keep a copy of each CTR for five years from the date filed.

A financial institution may apply to file the CTRs magnetically. To obtain an application to file magnetically, write to the IRS Detroit Computing Center, ATTN: CTR Magnetic Media Coordinator, at the address listed above.

Identification Requirements.—All individuals (except employees of armored car services) conducting a reportable transaction(s) for themselves or for another person must be identified by means of an official document(s).

Acceptable forms of identification include a driver's license, military, and military/dependent identification cards, passport, state issued identification card, cedular card (foreign), non-resident alien identification cards, or any other identification document or documents, which contain name and preferably address and a photograph and are normally acceptable by financial institutions as a means of identification when cashing checks for persons other than established customers.

Acceptable identification information obtained previously and maintained in the financial institution's records may be used. For example, if documents verifying an individual's identity were examined and recorded on a signature card when an account was opened, the financial institution may rely on that information. In completing the CTR, the financial institution must indicate on the form the method, type, and number of the identification. Statements such as "known customer" or "signature card on file" are not sufficient for form completion.

Penalties.—Civil and criminal penalties are provided for failure to file a CTR or to supply information or for filing a false or fraudulent CTR. See 31 U.S.C. 5321, 5322 and 5324.

For purposes of this CTR, the terms below have the following meanings:

Currency.—The coin and paper money of the United States or any other country, which is circulated and customarily used and accepted as money.

Person.—An individual, corporation, partnership, trust or estate, joint stock company, association, syndicate, joint venture or other unincorporated organization or group.

Organization.—Person other than an individual.

Transaction In Currency.—The **physical** transfer of currency from one person to another. This does not include a transfer of funds by means of bank check, bank draft, wire transfer or other written order that does not involve the physical transfer of currency.

Negotiable Instruments.—All checks and drafts (including business, personal, bank, cashier's and third-party), money orders, and promissory notes. For purposes of this CTR, all traveler's checks shall also be considered negotiable instruments. All such instruments shall be considered negotiable instruments whether or not they are in bearer form.

Specific Instructions

Because of the limited space on the front and back of the CTR, it may be necessary to submit additional information on attached sheets. Submit this additional information on plain paper attached to the CTR. Be sure to put the individual's or organization's name and identifying number (items 2, 3, 4, and 6 of the CTR) on any additional sheets so that if it becomes separated, it may be associated with the CTR.

Item 1a. Amends Prior Report.—If this CTR is being filed because it amends a report filed previously, check Item 1a. Staple a copy of the original CTR to the amended one, complete Part III fully and only those other entries which are being amended.

Item 1b. Multiple Persons.—If this transaction is being conducted by more than one person or on behalf of more than one person, check Item 1b. Enter information in Part I for one of the persons and provide information on any other persons on the back of the CTR.

Item 1c. Multiple Transactions.—If the financial institution has knowledge that there are multiple transactions, check Item 1c.

PART I - Person(s) Involved in Transaction(s)

Section A **must** be completed. If an individual conducts a transaction on his own behalf, complete Section A; leave Section B BLANK. If an individual conducts a transaction on his own behalf and on behalf of another person(s), complete Section A for each person; leave Section B BLANK. If an individual conducts a transaction on behalf of another person(s), complete Section B for the individual conducting the transaction, and complete Section A for each person on whose behalf the transaction is conducted of whom the financial institution has knowledge.

Section A. Person(s) on Whose Behalf Transaction(s) Is Conducted.—See instructions above.

Items 2, 3, and 4. Individual/Organization Name.—If the person on whose behalf the transaction(s) is conducted is an individual, put his/her last name in Item 2, first name in Item 3 and middle initial in Item 4. If there is no middle initial, leave item 4 BLANK. If the transaction is conducted on behalf of an organization, put its name in Item 2 and leave Items 3 and 4 BLANK.

Item 5. Doing Business As (DBA).—If the financial institution has knowledge of a separate "doing business as" name, enter it in Item 5. For example, Johnson Enterprises DBA PJ's Pizzeria.

Item 6. Social Security Number (SSN) or Employer Identification Number (EIN).—Enter the SSN or EIN of the person identified in Item 2. If none, write NONE.

Items 7, 9, 10, 11 and 12. Address.—Enter the permanent street address including zip code of the person identified in Item 2. Use the Post Office's two letter state abbreviation code. A P.O. Box should not be used by itself and may only be used if there is no street address. If a P.O. Box is used, the name of the apartment or suite number, road or route number where the person resides must also be provided. If the address is outside the U.S., provide the street address, city, province, or state, postal code (if known), and the name of the country.

Item 8. Date of Birth.—Enter the date of birth. Six numerals must be inserted for each date. The first two will reflect the month of birth, the second two the calendar day of birth, and the last two numerals the year of birth. Zero (0) should precede any single digit number. For example, if an individual's birth date is April 3, 1948, Item 8 should read 04 03 48.

Item 13. Occupation, Profession, or Business.—Identify fully the occupation, profession or business of the person on whose behalf the transaction(s) was conducted. For example, secretary, shoe salesman, carpenter, attorney, housewife, restaurant, liquor store, etc. Do not use non-specific terms such as merchant, self-employed, businessman, etc.

Item 14. If an Individual, Describe Method Used To Verify.—If an individual conducts the transaction(s) on his/her own behalf, his/her identity must be verified by examination of an acceptable document (see **General Instructions**). For example, check box **a** if a driver's license is used to verify an individual's identity, and enter the state that issued the license and the number in items **e** and **f**. If the transaction is conducted by an individual on behalf of another individual not present or an organization, enter N/A in item 14.

Section B. Individual(s) Conducting Transaction(s) (if other than above).—Financial institutions should enter as much information as is available. However, there may be instances in which Items 15-25 may be left BLANK or incomplete.

If Items 15-25 are left BLANK or incomplete, check one or more of the boxes provided to indicate the reason(s).

Example: If there are multiple transactions that, if only when aggregated, the financial institution has knowledge the transactions exceed the reporting threshold, and therefore, did not identify the transactor(s), check box **d** for Multiple Transactions.

Items 15, 16, and 17. Individual(s) Name.—Complete these items if an individual conducts a transaction(s) on behalf of another person. For example, if John Doe, an employee of XYZ Grocery Store makes a deposit to the store's account, XYZ Grocery Store should be identified in Section A, and John Doe should be identified in Section B.

Items 18, 20, 21, 22, and 23. Address.—Enter the permanent street address including zip code of the individual. (See Items 7, 9, 10, 11, and 12.)

Item 19. SSN.—If the individual has an SSN, enter it in Item 19. If the individual does not have an SSN, enter NONE.

Item 24. Date of Birth.—Enter the individual's date of birth. See the instructions for item 8.

Item 25. If an Individual, Describe Method Used To Verify.—Enter the method by which the individual's identity is verified (see **General Instructions** and Item 14).

PART II - Amount and Type of Transaction(s)

Complete Part II to identify the type of transaction(s) reported and the amount(s) involved.

Items 26 and 27. Cash In/Cash Out.—In the spaces provided, enter the amount of currency received (Cash In) or disbursed (Cash Out) by the financial institution. If foreign currency is exchanged, use the U.S. dollar equivalent on the day of the transaction.

If less than a full dollar amount is involved, increase that figure to the next highest dollar. For example, if the currency totals $20,000.05, show the total as $20,001.00.

Item 28. Date of Transaction.—Six numerals must be inserted for each date. (See Item 8.)

Determining Whether Transactions Meet the Reporting Threshold

Only cash transactions that, if alone or when aggregated, exceed $10,000 should be reported on the CTR. Transactions shall not be offset against one another.

If there are both Cash In and Cash Out transactions that are reportable, the amounts should be considered separately and not aggregated. However, they may be reported on a single CTR.

If there is a currency exchange, it should be aggregated separately with each of the Cash In and Cash Out totals.

Example 1: A person deposits $11,000 in currency to his savings account and withdraws $3,000 in currency from his checking account.

The CTR should be completed as follows: Cash In $11,000 and no entry for Cash Out. This is because the $3,000 transaction does not meet the reporting threshold.

Example 2: A person deposits $11,000 in currency to his savings account and withdraws $12,000 in currency from his checking account.

The CTR should be completed as follows: Cash In $11,000, Cash Out $12,000. This is because there are two reportable transactions. However, one CTR may be filed to reflect both.

Example 3: A person deposits $6,000 in currency to his savings account and withdraws $4,000 in currency from his checking account. Further, he presents $5,000 in currency to be exchanged for the equivalent in French francs.

The CTR should be completed as follows: Cash In $11,000 and no entry for Cash Out. This is because in determining whether the transactions are reportable, the currency exchange is aggregated with each of the Cash In and the Cash Out amounts. The result is a reportable $11,000 Cash In transaction. The total Cash Out amount is $9,000 which does not meet the reporting threshold; therefore, it is not entered on the CTR.

Example 4: A person deposits $6,000 in currency to his savings account and withdraws $7,000 in currency from his checking account. Further, he presents $5,000 in currency to be exchanged for the equivalent in French francs.

The CTR should be completed as follows: Cash In $11,000, Cash Out $12,000. This is because in determining whether the transactions are reportable, the currency exchange is aggregated with each of the Cash In and Cash Out amounts. In this example, each of the Cash In and Cash Out totals exceed $10,000 and must be reflected on the CTR.

Item 29. Foreign Currency.—If foreign currency is involved, check Item 29 and identify the country. If multiple foreign currencies are involved, identify the country for which the largest amount is exchanged.

Items 30-33.—Check the appropriate item(s) to identify the following type of transaction(s):

30. Wire Transfer(s)
31. Negotiable Instrument(s) Purchased
32. Negotiable Instrument(s) Cashed
33. Currency Exchange(s)

Item 34. Deposits/Withdrawals.—Check this item to identify deposits to or withdrawals from accounts, e.g., demand deposit accounts, savings accounts, time deposits, mutual fund accounts or any other account held at the financial institution. Enter the account number(s) in item 35.

Item 35. Account Numbers Affected (if any).—Enter the account numbers of any accounts affected by the transaction(s) that are maintained at the financial institution conducting the transaction(s). If necessary, use additional sheets of paper to indicate all of the affected accounts.

Example 1: If a person cashes a check drawn on an account held at the financial institution, the CTR should be completed as follows: Indicate Negotable Instrument(s) Cashed and provide the account number of the check.

If the transaction does not affect an account, make no entry.

Example 2: A person cashes a check drawn on another financial institution. In this instance, Negotiable Instrument(s) Cashed would be indicated, but no account at the financial institution has been affected. Therefore, item 35 should be left BLANK.

Item 36. Other (specify).—If a transaction is not identified in Items 30–34, check Item 36 and provide an additional description. For example, a person presents a check to purchase "foreign currency".

Part III - Financial Institution Where Transaction(s) Takes Place

Item 37. Name of Financial Institution and Identity of Federal Regulator or BSA Examiner.—Enter the financial institution's full legal name and identify the federal regulator or BSA examiner, using the following codes:

FEDERAL REGULATOR OR BSA EXAMINER	CODE
Comptroller of the Currency (OCC)	1
Federal Deposit Insurance Corporation (FDIC)	2
Federal Reserve System (FRS)	3
Office of Thrift Supervision (OTS)	4
National Credit Union Administration (NCUA)	5
Securities and Exchange Commission (SEC)	6
Internal Revenue Service (IRS)	7
U.S. Postal Service (USPS)	8

Items 38, 40, 41, and 42. Address.—Enter the street address, city, state, and ZIP code of the financial institution where the transaction occurred. If there are multiple transactions, provide information on the office or branch where any one of the transactions has occurred.

Item 39. EIN or SSN.—Enter the financial institution's EIN. If the financial institution does not have an EIN, enter the SSN of the financial institution's principal owner.

Item 43. MICR Number.—If a depository institution, enter the Magnetic Ink Character Recognition (MICR) number.

Signature

Items 44 and 45. Title and Signature of Approving Official.—The official who reviews and approves the CTR must indicate his/her title and sign the CTR.

Item 46. Date the Form Was Signed.—The approving official must enter the date the CTR is signed. (See Item 8.)

Item 47. Preparer's Name.—Type or print the full name of the individual preparing the CTR. The preparer and the approving official may not necessarily be the same individual.

Items 48 and 49. Contact Person/Telephone Number.—Type or print the name and telephone number of an individual to contact concerning questions about the CTR.

(U.S. Customs Use Only)

Control No.

31 U.S.C. 5316; 31 CFR 103.23 and 103.25

▶ Please type or print.

DEPARTMENT OF THE TREASURY
UNITED STATES CUSTOMS SERVICE

REPORT OF INTERNATIONAL TRANSPORTATION OF CURRENCY OR MONETARY INSTRUMENTS

Form Approved
OMB No. 1515-0079

▶ This form is to be filed with the United States Customs Service

▶ For Paperwork Reduction Act Notice and Privacy Act Notice, see back of form.

Part I — FOR INDIVIDUAL DEPARTING FROM OR ENTERING THE UNITED STATES

1. NAME (Last or family, first, and middle)
2. IDENTIFYING NO. (See instructions)
3. DATE OF BIRTH (Mo./Day/Yr.)
4. PERMANENT ADDRESS IN UNITED STATES OR ABROAD
5. OF WHAT COUNTRY ARE YOU A CITIZEN/SUBJECT?
6. ADDRESS WHILE IN THE UNITED STATES
7. PASSPORT NO. & COUNTRY
8. U.S. VISA DATE
9. PLACE UNITED STATES VISA WAS ISSUED
10. IMMIGRATION ALIEN NO. (If any)
11. CURRENCY OR MONETARY INSTRUMENT WAS: (Complete 11A or 11B)

A. EXPORTED
- Departed From: (City in U.S.)
- Arrived At: (Foreign City/Country)

B. IMPORTED
- From: (Foreign City/Country)
- At: (City in U.S.)

Part II — FOR PERSON SHIPPING, MAILING, OR RECEIVING CURRENCY OR MONETARY INSTRUMENTS

12. NAME (Last or family, first, and middle)
13. IDENTIFYING NO. (See instructions)
14. DATE OF BIRTH (Mo./Day/Yr.)
15. PERMANENT ADDRESS IN UNITED STATES OR ABROAD
16. OF WHAT COUNTRY ARE YOU A CITIZEN/SUBJECT?
17. ADDRESS WHILE IN THE UNITED STATES
18. PASSPORT NO. & COUNTRY
19. U.S. VISA DATE
20. PLACE UNITED STATES VISA WAS ISSUED
21. IMMIGRATION ALIEN NO. (If any)

22. CURRENCY OR MONETARY INSTRUMENTS DATE SHIPPED
    DATE RECEIVED
23. CURRENCY OR MONETARY INSTRUMENTS
    ☐ Shipped To ▶
    ☐ Received From ▶
    NAME AND ADDRESS
24. IF THE CURRENCY OR MONETARY INSTRUMENT WAS MAILED, SHIPPED, OR TRANSPORTED COMPLETE BLOCKS A AND B.
    A. Method of Shipment (Auto, U.S. Mail, Public Carrier, etc.)
    B. Name of Transporter/Carrier

Part III — CURRENCY AND MONETARY INSTRUMENT INFORMATION (SEE INSTRUCTIONS ON REVERSE) (To be completed by everyone)

25. TYPE AND AMOUNT OF CURRENCY/MONETARY INSTRUMENTS — Value in U.S. Dollars

- Coins ☐ A. ▶ $
- Currency ☐ B. ▶
- Other Instruments (Specify Type) _____ ☐ C. ▶
- (Add lines A, B and C) TOTAL AMOUNT ▶ $

26. IF OTHER THAN U.S. CURRENCY IS INVOLVED, PLEASE COMPLETE BLOCKS A AND B. (SEE SPECIAL INSTRUCTIONS)
    A. Currency Name
    B. Country

Part IV — GENERAL - TO BE COMPLETED BY ALL TRAVELERS, SHIPPERS, AND RECIPIENTS

27. WERE YOU ACTING AS AN AGENT, ATTORNEY OR IN CAPACITY FOR ANYONE IN THIS CURRENCY OR MONETARY INSTRUMENT ACTIVITY? (If "Yes" complete A, B and C)   ☐ Yes   ☐ No

PERSON IN WHOSE BEHALF YOU ARE ACTING ▶
- A. Name
- B. Address
- C. Business activity, occupation, or profession

Under penalties of perjury, I declare that I have examined this report, and to the best of my knowledge and belief it is true, correct and complete.

28. NAME AND TITLE
29. SIGNATURE
30. DATE

(Replaces IRS Form 4790 which is obsolete.)

Customs Form 4790 (031695)

GENERAL INSTRUCTIONS

This report is required by Treasury Department regulations (31 Code of Federal Regulations 103).

Who Must File.--Each person who physically transports, mails, or ships, or causes to be physically transported, mailed, shipped or received currency or other monetary instruments in an aggregate amount exceeding $10,000 on any one occasion from the United States to any place outside the United States, or into the United States from any place outside the United States.

A TRANSFER OF FUNDS THROUGH NORMAL BANKING PROCEDURES WHICH DOES NOT INVOLVE THE PHYSICAL TRANSPORTATION OF CURRENCY OR MONETARY INSTRUMENTS IS NOT REQUIRED TO BE REPORTED.

Exceptions.--The following persons are not required to file reports: (1) a Federal Reserve bank, (2) a bank, a foreign bank, or a broker or dealer in securities in respect to currency or other monetary instruments mailed or shipped through the postal service or by common carrier, (3) a commercial bank or trust company organized under the laws of any State or of the United States with respect to overland shipments of currency or monetary instruments shipped to or received from an established customer maintaining a deposit relationship with the bank, in amounts which the bank may reasonably conclude do not exceed amounts commensurate with the customary conduct of the business, industry, or profession of the customer concerned, (4) a person who is not a citizen or resident of the United States in respect to currency or other monetary instruments mailed or shipped from abroad to a bank or broker or dealer in securities through the postal service or by common carrier, (5) a common carrier of passengers in respect to currency or other monetary instruments in the possession of its passengers, (6) a common carrier of goods in respect to shipments of currency or monetary instruments not declared to be such by the shipper, (7) a travelers' check issuer or its agent in respect to the transportation of travelers' checks prior to their delivery to selling agents for eventual sale to the public, nor by (8) a person engaged as a business in the transportation of currency, monetary instruments and other commercial papers with respect to the transportation of currency or other monetary instruments overland between established offices of banks or brokers or dealers in securities and foreign persons.

WHEN AND WHERE TO FILE:

A. Recipients.--Each person who receives currency or other monetary instruments shall file Form 4790, within 30 days after receipt, with the Customs officer in charge at any port of entry or departure or by mail with the Commissioner of Customs, Attention: Currency Transportation Reports, Washington DC 20229.

B. Shippers or Mailers:--If the currency or other monetary instrument does not accompany the person entering or departing the United States, Form 4790 may be filed by mail on or before the date of entry, departure, mailing, or shipping with the Commissioner of Customs, Attention: Currency Transportation Reports, Washington DC 20229.

C. Travelers.--Travelers carrying currency or other monetary instruments with them shall file Form 4790 at the time of entry into the United States or at the time of departure from the United States with the Customs officer in charge at any Customs port of entry or departure.

An additional report of a particular transportation, mailing, or shipping of currency or the monetary instruments, is not required if a complete and truthful report has already been filed. However, no person otherwise required to file a report shall be excused from liability for failure to do so if, in fact, a complete and truthful report has not been filed. Forms may be obtained from any United States Customs Service office.

PENALTIES.--Civil and criminal penalties, including under certain circumstances a fine of not more than $500,000 and imprisonment of not more than five years, are provided for failure to file a report, supply information, and for filing a false or fraudulent report. In addition, the currency or monetary instrument may be subject to seizure and forfeiture. See section 103.47, 103.48 and 103.49 of the regulations.

DEFINITIONS:

Bank.--Each agent, agency, branch or office within the United States of a foreign bank and each agency, branch or office within the United States of any person doing business in one or more of the capacities listed: (1) a commercial bank or trust company organized under the laws of any state or of the United States; (2) a private bank (3) a savings and loan association or a building and loan association organized under the laws of any state or of the United States; (4) an insured institution as defined in section 401 of the National Housing Act; (5) a savings bank, industrial bank or other thrift institution; (6) a credit union organized under the laws of any state or of the United States; and (7) any other organization chartered under the banking laws of any state and subject to the supervision of the bank supervisory authorities of a state.

Foreign Bank.--A bank organized under foreign law, or an agency, branch or office located outside the United States of a bank. The term does not include an agent agency, branch or office within the United States of a bank organized under foreign law.

Broker or Dealer in Securities.--A broker or dealer in securities, registered or required to be registered with the Securities and Exchange Commission under the Securities Exchange Act of 1934.

IDENTIFICATION NUMBER.--Individuals must enter their social security number, if any. However, aliens who do not have a social security number should enter passport or alien registration number. All others should enter their employer identification number.

Investment Security.--An instrument which: (1) is issued in bearer or registered form; (2) is of a type commonly dealt in upon securities exchanges or markets or commonly recognized in any areas in which it is issued or dealt in as a medium for investment; (3) is either one of a class or series or by its terms is divisible into a class or series of instruments; and (4) evidences a share, participation or other interest in property or in an enterprise or evidences an obligation of the issuer.

Monetary Instruments.--Coin or currency of the United States or of any other country, travelers' checks, money orders, investment securities in bearer form or otherwise in such form that title thereto passes upon delivery, and negotiable instruments (except warehouse receipts or bills of lading) in bearer form or other in such form that title thereto passes upon delivery. The term includes bank checks, travelers' checks and money orders which are signed but on which the name of the payee has been omitted, but does not include bank checks, travelers' checks or money orders made payable to the order of a named person which have not been endorsed or which bear restrictive endorsements.

Person.--An individual, a corporation, a partnership, a trust or estate, a joint stock company, and association, a syndicate, joint venture or other unincorporated organization or group, and all entities cognizable as legal personalties.

SPECIAL INSTRUCTIONS:

You should complete each line which applies to you. **Part II.**--Line 22, enter the exact date you shipped or received currency or monetary instrument(s). Line 23, check the applicable box and give the complete name and address of the shipper or recipient. **Part III.**--Line 26, if currency or monetary instruments of more than one country is involved, attach a schedule showing each kind, country, and amount.

PRIVACY ACT AND PAPERWORK REDUCTION ACT NOTICE

Pursuant to the requirements of Public Law 93-579 (Privacy Act of 1974), notice is hereby given that the authority to collect information on Form 4790 in accordance with 5 U.S.C. 552a(e)(3) is Public Law 91-508; 31 U.S.C. 5316; 5 U.S.C. 301; Reorganization Plan No. 1 of 1950; Treasury Department No.165, revised, as amended; 31 CFR 103 and 44 U.S.C. 3501.

The principal purpose for collecting the information is to assure maintenance of reports or records where such reports or records have a high degree of usefulness in criminal, tax, or regulatory investigations or proceedings. The information collected may be provided to those officers and employees of the Customs Service and any other constituent unit of the Department of the Treasury who have a need for the records in the performance of their duties. The records may be referred to any other department or agency of the Federal Government upon the request of the head of such department or agency.

Disclosure of this information is mandatory. Failure to provide all or any part of the requested information may subject the currency or monetary instruments to seizure and forfeiture as well as subject the individual to civil and criminal liabilities.

Disclosure of the social security number is mandatory. The authority to collect this number is 31 CFR 103.25. The social security number will be used as a means to identify the individual who files the record.

The collection of this information is mandatory pursuant to 31 U.S.C. 5316.

Statement Required by 5 CFR 1320.21: The estimated average burden associated with this collection of information is 10 minutes per respondent or recordkeeper depending on individual circumstances. Comments concerning the accuracy of this burden estimate and suggestions for reducing this burden should be directed to U.S. Customs Service, Paperwork Management Branch, Washington DC 20229. *DO NOT send completed form(s) to this office.*

Form **5471**
(Rev. June 1995)
Department of the Treasury
Internal Revenue Service

Information Return of U.S. Persons With Respect To Certain Foreign Corporations
▶ See separate instructions.

Information furnished for the foreign corporation's annual accounting period (tax year required by section 898) (see instructions) beginning _____ ,19____ , and ending _____ ,19____

OMB No. 1545-0704
File In Duplicate
(see **When and Where To File** in the instructions)

Name of person filing this return

A Identifying number

Number, street, and room or suite no. (or P.O. box number if mail is not delivered to street address)

B Category of filer (see **Who Must File** in the instructions and check applicable box(es)):
(1) ☐ (2) ☐ (3) ☐ (4) ☐ (5) ☐

City or town, state, and ZIP code

C Enter the total percentage of voting stock of the foreign corporation you owned at the end of its annual accounting period ....%

Filer's tax year beginning _____ , 19____ , and ending _____ , 19____

D Person(s) on whose behalf this information return is filed:

(1) Name	(2) Address	(3) Identifying number	(4) Check applicable box(es)		
			Shareholder	Officer	Director

Important: *Fill in all applicable lines and schedules. All information must be in the English language. All amounts must be stated in U.S. dollars unless otherwise indicated.*
Enter the foreign corporation's functional currency ▶

1a Name and address of foreign corporation

b Employer identification number, if any

c Country under whose laws incorporated

d Date of incorporation | **e** Principal place of business | **f** Principal business activity code number | **g** Principal business activity

2 Provide the following information for the foreign corporation's accounting period stated above.

a Name, address, and identifying number of branch office or agent (if any) in the United States

b If a U.S. income tax return was filed, please show:

(i) Taxable income or (loss)	(ii) U.S. income tax paid (after all credits)

c Name and address of foreign corporation's statutory or resident agent in country of incorporation

d Name and address (including corporate department, if applicable) of person (or persons) with custody of the books and records of the foreign corporation, and the location of such books and records, if different

Schedule A — Stock of the Foreign Corporation
Part I—ALL Classes of Stock

(a) Description of each class of stock	(b) Number of shares issued and outstanding	
	(i) Beginning of annual accounting period	(ii) End of annual accounting period

Part II—Additional Information for PREFERRED Stock
(To be completed only by Category (1) filers for foreign personal holding companies)

(a) Description of each class of PREFERRED stock (Note: *This description should match the corresponding description entered in Part I, column (a).*)	(b) Par value in functional currency	(c) Rate of dividend	(d) Indicate whether the stock is cumulative or noncumulative

For Paperwork Reduction Act Notice, see page 1 of the instructions. Cat. No. 49958V Form **5471** (Rev. 6-95)

Form 5471 (Rev. 6-95) Page **2**

Schedule B — U.S. Shareholders of Foreign Corporation (see instructions)

(a) Name, address, and identifying number of shareholder	(b) Description of each class of stock held by shareholder (**Note:** This description should match the corresponding description entered in Schedule A, Part I, column (a).)	(c) Number of shares held at beginning of annual accounting period	(d) Number of shares held at end of annual accounting period	(e) Pro rata share of subpart F income (enter as a percentage)

Schedule C — Income Statement (Complete both columns unless the functional currency is the U.S. dollar. In that case, complete only the U.S. Dollars column.)

Important: Schedule C requests financial accounting information prepared in functional currency in accordance with U.S. GAAP. Each line must also be reported in U.S. dollars translated from functional currency in accordance with U.S. GAAP translation rules. See instructions for special rules for DASTM corporations.

			Functional Currency	U.S. Dollars
Income	1a	Gross receipts or sales		
	b	Returns and allowances		
	c	Subtract line 1b from line 1a		
	2	Cost of goods sold		
	3	Gross profit (subtract line 2 from line 1c)		
	4	Dividends		
	5	Interest		
	6	Gross rents, royalties, and license fees		
	7	Net gain or (loss) on sale of capital assets		
	8	Other income (attach schedule)		
	9	Total income (add lines 3 through 8)		
Deductions	10	Compensation not deducted elsewhere		
	11	Rents, royalties, and license fees		
	12	Interest		
	13	Depreciation not deducted elsewhere		
	14	Depletion		
	15	Taxes (exclude provision for income, war profits, and excess profits taxes)		
	16	Other deductions (attach schedule—exclude provision for income, war profits, and excess profits taxes)		
	17	Total deductions (add lines 10 through 16)		
Net Income	18	Net income or (loss) before extraordinary items, prior period adjustments, and the provision for income, war profits, and excess profits taxes (subtract line 17 from line 9)		
	19	Extraordinary items and prior period adjustments (see instructions)		
	20	Provision for income, war profits, and excess profits taxes (see instructions)		
	21	Current year net income or (loss) per books (line 18 plus line 19 minus line 20)		

Form 5471 (Rev. 6-95)   Page **3**

Schedule E — Income, War Profits, and Excess Profits Taxes Paid or Accrued (see instructions)

	(a) Name of country or U.S. possession	Amount of tax		
		(b) In foreign currency	(c) Spot conversion rate	(d) In U.S. dollars
1	U.S.			
2				
3				
4				
5				
6				
7				
8	Total ▶			

Schedule F — Balance Sheet

Important: Schedule F requests financial accounting information prepared and translated into U.S. dollars in accordance with U.S. GAAP. See instructions for exception for DASTM corporations.

	Assets		(a) Beginning of annual accounting period	(b) End of annual accounting period
1	Cash	1		
2a	Trade notes and accounts receivable	2a		
b	Less allowance for bad debts	2b	( )	( )
3	Inventories	3		
4	Other current assets (attach schedule)	4		
5	Loans to stockholders and other related persons	5		
6	Investment in subsidiaries (attach schedule)	6		
7	Other investments (attach schedule)	7		
8a	Buildings and other depreciable assets	8a		
b	Less accumulated depreciation	8b	( )	( )
9a	Depletable assets	9a		
b	Less accumulated depletion	9b	( )	( )
10	Land (net of any amortization)	10		
11	Intangible assets:			
a	Goodwill	11a		
b	Organization costs	11b		
c	Patents, trademarks, and other intangible assets	11c		
d	Less accumulated amortization for lines 11a, b, and c	11d	( )	( )
12	Other assets (attach schedule)	12		
13	Total assets	13		
	Liabilities and Stockholders' Equity			
14	Accounts payable	14		
15	Other current liabilities (attach schedule)	15		
16	Loans from stockholders and other related persons	16		
17	Other liabilities (attach schedule)	17		
18	Capital stock:			
a	Preferred stock	18a		
b	Common stock	18b		
19	Paid-in or capital surplus (attach reconciliation)	19		
20	Retained earnings	20		
21	Less cost of treasury stock	21	( )	( )
22	Total liabilities and stockholders' equity	22		

Does the foreign corporation have an interest in a partnership or trust? ☐ Yes ☐ No

Form 5471 (Rev. 6-95) Page **4**

Schedule H — Current Earnings and Profits (enter the amounts on lines 1 through 5c in functional currency)

1. Current year net income or (loss) per foreign books of account . . . . **1** _____

2. Net adjustments made to line 1 to determine current earnings and profits according to U.S. financial and tax accounting standards (see instructions):

	Net Additions	Net Subtractions
a Capital gains or losses		
b Depreciation and amortization		
c Depletion		
d Investment or incentive allowance		
e Charges to statutory reserves		
f Inventory adjustments		
g Taxes		
h Other (attach schedule)		

3. Total net additions . . . .
4. Total net subtractions . . . .
5a. Current earnings and profits (line 1 plus line 3 minus line 4) . . . . **5a** _____
 b. DASTM gain or (loss) for foreign corporations that use DASTM (see instructions) . . . . **5b** _____
 c. Combine lines 5a and 5b. . . . . **5c** _____
 d. Current earnings and profits in U.S. dollars (line 5c translated at the weighted average exchange rate as defined in Regulations Section 1.989(b)-1) . . . . **5d** _____
 Enter exchange rate used for line 5d ▶

Schedule I — Summary of Shareholder's Income From Foreign Corporation (see instructions)

1. Subpart F income (line 40b, Worksheet A in the instructions) . . . . **1** _____

2. Earnings invested in U.S. property (line 17, Worksheet B in the instructions) . . . . **2** _____

3. Previously excluded subpart F income withdrawn from qualified investments (line 6b, Worksheet C in the instructions) . . . . **3** _____

4. Previously excluded export trade income withdrawn from investment in export trade assets (line 7b, Worksheet D in the instructions) . . . . **4** _____

5. Earnings invested in excess passive assets (line 21, Worksheet E in the instructions) . . . . . . **5** _____

6. Factoring income . . . . **6** _____

7. Total of lines 1 through 6. Enter here and on your income tax return . . . . **7** _____

8. Dividends received (translated at spot rate on payment date under section 989(b)(1)) . . . . . **8** _____

9. Exchange gain or (loss) on a distribution of previously taxed income . . . . **9** _____

Was any income of the foreign corporation blocked **OR** did any become unblocked during the tax year (see section 964(b))? If the answer to either part of the question is "Yes," check the "Yes" box and attach an explanation . . ☐ Yes ☐ No

SCHEDULE J
(Form 5471)
(Rev. June 1995)

Department of the Treasury
Internal Revenue Service

Accumulated Earnings and Profits (E&P) of Controlled Foreign Corporation

▶ Attach to Form 5471.

OMB No. 1545-0704

Name of person filing Form 5471

Name of foreign corporation

Identifying number

Important. Enter amounts in functional currency.

	(a) Post-1986 Undistributed Earnings (post-86 section 959(c)(3) balance)	(b) Pre-1987 E&P Not Previously Taxed (pre-87 section 959(c)(3) balance)	(c) Previously Taxed E&P (sections 959(c)(1) and (2) balances)			(d) Total Section 964(a) E&P (combine columns (a), (b), and (c))
			(i) Earnings Invested in U.S. Property	(ii) Earnings Invested in Excess Passive Assets	(iii) Subpart F Income	
1 Balance at beginning of year						
2a Current year E&P						
b Current year deficit in E&P						
3 Total current and accumulated E&P not previously taxed (line 1 plus line 2a, minus line 2b)						
4 Amounts included under section 951(a) or reclassified under section 959(c) in current year						
5a Actual distributions or reclassifications of previously taxed E&P						
b Actual distributions of non-previously taxed E&P						
6a Balance of previously taxed E&P at end of year (line 1 plus line 4, minus line 5a)						
b Balance of E&P not previously taxed at end of year (line 3 minus line 4, minus line 5b)						
7 Balance at end of year (Enter amount from line 6a or line 6b, whichever is applicable)						

For Paperwork Reduction Act Notice, see page 1 of the Instructions for Form 5471. Printed on recycled paper

Cat. No. 21111K

Schedule J (Form 5471) (Rev. 6-95)

SCHEDULE M
(Form 5471)
(Rev. June 1995)
Department of the Treasury
Internal Revenue Service

Transactions Between Controlled Foreign Corporation and Shareholders or Other Related Persons

▶ Attach to Form 5471.

OMB No. 1545-0704

Name of person filing Form 5471

Identifying number

Name of foreign corporation

Important: Complete the following summary showing the totals of each of the following types of transactions that took place during the annual accounting period between the foreign corporation and the persons listed in columns (b) through (f). Submit a separate Schedule M for each controlled foreign corporation. All information must be in the English language AND all amounts must be stated in U.S. dollars translated from functional currency at the weighted average exchange rate for the year (as defined in Regulations section 1.989(b)-1). Enter the relevant functional currency and the exchange rate used throughout this schedule ▶

(a) Transactions of foreign corporation	(b) U.S. person filing this return	(c) Any domestic corporation controlled by U.S. person filing this return	(d) Any other foreign corporation controlled by U.S. person filing this return	(e) 10% or more U.S. shareholder of controlled foreign corporation (other than the U.S. person filing this return)	(f) 10% or more U.S. shareholder of any corporation controlling the foreign corporation
1 Sales of stock in trade (inventory)					
2 Sales of property rights (patents, trademarks, etc.)					
3 Compensation received for technical, managerial, engineering, construction, or like services					
4 Commissions received					
5 Rents, royalties, and license fees received					
6 Dividends received (exclude deemed distributions under subpart F and distributions of previously taxed income)					
7 Interest received					
8 Premiums received for insurance or reinsurance					
9 Add lines 1 through 8					
10 Purchases of stock in trade (inventory)					
11 Purchases of tangible property other than stock in trade					
12 Purchases of property rights (patents, trademarks, etc.)					
13 Compensation paid for technical, managerial, engineering, construction, or like services					
14 Commissions paid					
15 Rents, royalties, and license fees paid					
16 Dividends paid					
17 Interest paid					
18 Add lines 10 through 17					
19 Amounts borrowed (enter the maximum loan balance during the year) — see instructions					
20 Amounts loaned (enter the maximum loan balance during the year) — see instructions					

For Paperwork Reduction Act Notice, see page 1 of the Instructions for Form 5471.   Cat. No. 49963O   Schedule M (Form 5471) (Rev. 6-95)

SCHEDULE N
(Form 5471)
(Rev. June 1995)
Department of the Treasury
Internal Revenue Service

Return of Officers, Directors, and 10% Or More Shareholders of a Foreign Personal Holding Company

▶ Attach to Form 5471.

OMB No. 1545-0704

Name of person filing Form 5471 | Identifying number

Name of foreign corporation

Important: All information must be in the English language AND all amounts must be stated in U.S. dollars translated from functional currency at the weighted average exchange rate for the year (as defined in Regulations section 1.989(b)-1). Enter the relevant functional currency and the exchange rate used throughout this schedule ▶

Part I — Shareholder Information

Section A—Outstanding Securities Convertible Into Stock of the Corporation or Options Granted by the Corporation

Description of securities (attach a complete, detailed statement of conversion privileges)	Interest rate (%)	Face value	
		Beginning of year	End of year

Section B—List of Holders of Convertible Securities or Options Granted by the Corporation

Name and address of each holder of convertible securities or options (designate nonresident aliens)	Class of securities	Securities held				Explanation and date of any change in holdings of securities during the year
		Beginning of year		End of year		
		Number	Face value	Number	Face value	

Part II — Income Information

Section A—Computation of Undistributed Foreign Personal Holding Company Income

1	Gross income as defined in section 555 (attach schedule)	1	
2	Deductions allowable under section 161 (attach schedule)	2	
3	Taxable income or (loss) (subtract line 2 from line 1)	3	
4	Adjustments to taxable income or (loss) (see instructions):		
a	Taxes (see instructions)	4a	
b	Charitable contributions	4b	
c	Special deductions disallowed	4c	
d	Net operating loss	4d	
e	Expenses and depreciation applicable to property of the taxpayer	4e	
f	Taxes and contributions to pension trusts	4f	
g	Total adjustments (combine lines 4a through 4f)	4g	
5	Combine line 3 and line 4g	5	
6	Deduction for dividends paid during the tax year. Enter the amount from Section B, line 12	6	
7	Subtract line 6 from line 5	7	
8	Deduction allowed under section 563(c) for dividends paid after close of tax year (see instructions). Attach designation required by Rev. Proc. 90-26, 1990-1 C.B. 512	8	
9	Undistributed foreign personal holding company income (subtract line 8 from line 7)	9	

Section B—Deduction for Dividends Paid During Tax Year (see instructions)

		Date paid		Amount
10	Taxable dividends paid during tax year:			
a	Cash		10a	
b	Property other than cash or the corporation's own securities (indicate nature of property)		10b	
c	Obligations of the corporation (bonds, notes, scrip, etc.)		10c	
11	Consent dividends (attach schedule)		11	
12	Deduction for dividends paid during tax year (add lines 10a through 11). Enter here and on line 6 above		12	

For Paperwork Reduction Act Notice, see page 1 of the Instructions for Form 5471. Cat. No. 61925Q Schedule N (Form 5471) (Rev. 6-95)

Printed on recycled paper

SCHEDULE O
(Form 5471)
(Rev. June 1995)
Department of the Treasury
Internal Revenue Service

Organization or Reorganization of Foreign Corporation, and Acquisitions and Dispositions of Its Stock

▶ Attach to Form 5471.

OMB No. 1545-0704

Name of person filing Form 5471 | Identifying number

Name of foreign corporation

Important: All information must be in the English language AND all amounts must be stated in U.S. dollars. Complete a separate Schedule O for each foreign corporation for which information must be reported.

Part I — To Be Completed by U.S. Officers and Directors

(a) Name of shareholder for whom acquisition information is reported	(b) Address of shareholder	(c) Identifying number of shareholder	(d) Date of original 5% acquisition	(e) Date of additional 5% acquisition

Part II — To Be Completed by U.S. Shareholders

Section A—General Shareholder Information

(a) Name, address, and identifying number of shareholder(s) filing this schedule	(b) For shareholder's latest U.S. income tax return filed, indicate:			(c) Date (if any) shareholder last filed information return under section 6046 for the foreign corporation
	(1) Type of return (enter form number)	(2) Date return filed	(3) Internal Revenue Service Center where filed	

If this return is required because one or more shareholders became U.S. persons, attach a list showing the names of such persons and the date each became a U.S. person.

Section B—U.S. Persons Who Are Officers or Directors of the Foreign Corporation

(a) Name of U.S. officer or director	(b) Address	(c) Social security number	(d) Check appropriate box(es)	
			Officer	Director

Section C—Acquisition of Stock

(a) Name of shareholder(s) filing this schedule	(b) Class of stock acquired	(c) Date of acquisition	(d) Method of acquisition	(e) Number of shares acquired		
				(1) Directly	(2) Indirectly	(3) Constructively

For Paperwork Reduction Act Notice, see page 1 of the Instructions for Form 5471. Cat. No. 61200O

Schedule O (Form 5471) (Rev. 6-95) Page **2**

(f) Amount paid or value given	(g) Name and address of person from whom shares were acquired

Section D—Disposition of Stock

(a) Name of shareholder disposing of stock	(b) Class of stock	(c) Date of disposition	(d) Method of disposition	(e) Number of shares disposed of		
				(1) Directly	(2) Indirectly	(3) Constructively

(f) Amount received	(g) Name and address of person to whom disposition of stock was made

Section E—Organization or Reorganization of Foreign Corporation

(a) Name and address of transferor	(b) Identifying number (if any)	(c) Date of transfer

(d) Assets transferred to foreign corporation			(e) Description of assets transferred by, or notes or securities issued by, foreign corporation
(1) Description of assets	(2) Fair market value	(3) Adjusted basis (if transferor was U.S. person)	

Section F—Additional Information

(a) If the foreign corporation or a predecessor U.S. corporation filed (or joined with a consolidated group in filing) a U.S. income tax return for any of the last 3 years, attach a statement indicating the year for which a return was filed (and, if applicable, the name of the corporation filing the consolidated return), the taxable income or loss, and the U.S. income tax paid (after all credits).

(b) List the date of any reorganization of the foreign corporation that occurred during the last 4 years while any U.S. person held 5% or more (directly or indirectly) of the corporation's stock ▶

(c) If the foreign corporation is a member of a group that make up a chain of ownership, attach a chart, for each unit of which a shareholder owns 5% or more in value of the outstanding stock. The chart must indicate the corporation's position in the chain of ownership and the percentages of stock ownership (see instructions).

Printed on recycled paper

Department of the Treasury
Internal Revenue Service

Instructions for Form 5471
(Revised June 1995)

Information Return of U.S. Persons With Respect to Certain Foreign Corporations

Section references are to the Internal Revenue Code unless otherwise noted.

Paperwork Reduction Act Notice.—We ask for the information on this form to carry out the Internal Revenue laws of the United States. You are required to give us the information. We need it to ensure that you are complying with these laws and to allow us to figure and collect the right amount of tax.

The time needed to complete and file this form and related schedules will vary depending on individual circumstances. The estimated average times are:

Form	Recordkeeping	Learning about the law or the form	Preparing and sending the form to the IRS
5471	87 hr., 32 min.	25 hr., 56 min.	32 hr., 6 min.
Sch. J (5471)	3 hr., 50 min.	1 hr.	1 hr., 6 min.
Sch. M (5471)	26 hr., 33 min.	6 min.	32 min.
Sch. N (5471)	8 hr., 22 min.	2 hr., 47 min.	3 hr., 2 min.
Sch. O (5471)	10 hr., 46 min.	12 min.	23 min.

If you have comments concerning the accuracy of these time estimates or suggestions for making this form and related schedules simpler, we would be happy to hear from you. See the instructions for the tax return with which this form is filed.

General Instructions

Changes To Note

When to File 1995 Revision

The 1995 revision of Form 5471 may be used for returns filed on or after July 1, 1995, but must be used for all returns filed after June 30, 1996. The October 1990 revision of Form 5471 may be used for returns filed prior to July 1, 1996.

Electronic Filing of Form 5471

Form 5471 and the related schedules can now be filed by magnetic media (magnetic tapes, floppy diskettes) or electronically. For more information, see **Electronic Filing of Form 5471** on page 4 of the instructions.

Currency Translation Rules

Final regulations have been issued relating to currency translation. Regulations sections 1.6038-2(h) and 1.6046-1(g) now require that certain amounts be reported in U.S. dollars and/or functional currency. These changes are effective for tax years ending after December 31, 1994, but only for returns filed after December 31, 1995.

Special rules apply to corporations that use the U.S. dollar approximate separate transactions method (DASTM) of accounting under Regulations section 1.985-3.

Changes to Form 5471 and the related schedules include the following:

- Schedule C now contains a "functional currency" column. Filers are now required to report the foreign corporation's income statement amounts in both functional currency and U.S. dollars.

- Schedule H, lines 1 through 5c are now completed in functional currency. On new line 5b, foreign corporations using the dollar approximate separate transactions method must report DASTM gain or loss. On new line 5d, filers are now required to report the foreign corporation's current earnings and profits (E&P) in U.S. dollars (translated from functional currency at the weighted average exchange rate for the year) and the exchange rate used in the translation.

- In the instructions for Schedule I, Worksheets A through E are now completed in functional currency. See the instructions for Schedule I, beginning on page 6.

- Schedule J is now a separate schedule (similar to Schedules M, N, and O) and is completed in functional currency.

Earnings Invested in Excess Passive Assets

The Revenue Reconciliation Act of 1993 (the Act) eliminated the deferral of earnings of a controlled foreign corporation (CFC) that are invested in "excess passive assets" (defined in new section 956A). The amount now required to be included in income of the U.S. shareholder is the shareholder's pro rata share of earnings of the CFC invested in excess passive assets that have not been previously taxed. These rules are effective for earnings accumulated after September 30, 1993. The Act also modified the rules for determining the amount includible in a U.S. shareholder's income if the CFC invested in U.S. property. See sections 956(a) and (b), as modified by the Act.

Schedules I and J and the related instructions were revised to reflect the changes as follows:

- Line 5 of Schedule I was added to report inclusions attributable to earnings invested in excess passive assets.

- In the instructions for Schedule I, Worksheet B was revised and new Worksheet E was added.

- On Schedule J, column (c)(ii) was added to report previously taxed E&P invested in excess passive assets.

Dormant Foreign Corporation

A foreign corporation that qualifies as a dormant foreign corporation can now elect to use a summary filing procedure rather than filing a complete Form 5471 (Rev. Proc. 92-70, 1992-2 C.B. 435). See **Dormant Foreign Corporations** on page 4 for details.

Other Changes

- Item D on page 1 of Form 5471 was formerly Schedule K on page 4 of the previous version of the form.

- Schedules D and G of the October 1990 version of Form 5471 have been eliminated.

- On Schedule I, we have added new line 8 (relating to dividends received from foreign corporations) and new line 9 (relating to exchange gain or loss on a distribution of previously taxed income). Accordingly, Category (4) filers who receive these types of income should now file Schedule I, even if they are not also described in Category (5).

- Schedule J has been revised to state separately the amounts of post-1986 undistributed earnings, pre-1987 earnings not previously taxed, and previously taxed earnings and profits.

- On Schedule M, lines 19 and 20 request maximum balances during the year of gross amounts borrowed from, and gross amounts loaned to, the related parties described in columns (b) through (f). Do not enter aggregate cash flows, year-end loan balances, average balances, or net balances.

Purpose of Form

Form 5471 is used by certain U.S. citizens and residents who are officers, directors, or shareholders in certain foreign corporations. The form and schedules are used to satisfy the reporting requirements of sections 6035, 6038, 6046, and the related regulations.

Who Must File

Generally, the U.S. persons described in **Categories of Filers** below must complete the schedules, statements, and/or other information requested in the chart, **Filing Requirements For Categories of Filers,** on page 2. Read the information for each of the categories of filers carefully to determine which schedules, statements,

Cat. No. 49959G

and/or information apply. Do not duplicate information if the filer is described in more than one filing category. However, complete all schedules that apply. For example, if you are the sole owner of a CFC that is also a foreign personal holding company (i.e., you are described in Categories (1), (4), and (5)), you would complete all four pages of Form 5471 and separate Schedules J, M, and N.

Complete a separate Form 5471 and the applicable schedules for each foreign corporation. Be sure to complete Item B (at the top of page 1 of the form) to indicate the category or categories that describe the filer. If more than one category applies, check all boxes that apply.

If you are filing Form 5471 and applicable schedules for another person who has the same filing requirements, be sure to complete Item D at the top of page 1 of the form. Before completing Item D, read the specific instructions on page 4.

Categories of Filers

Category (1) filer.—This includes a U.S. citizen or resident who is an officer, director, or 10% shareholder of a foreign personal holding company.

A 10% shareholder is any individual who owns, directly or indirectly (within the meaning of section 554), 10% or more in value of the outstanding stock of the foreign personal holding company.

See section 552 for the definition of a foreign personal holding company.

Category (2) filer.—This includes a U.S. citizen or resident who is an officer or director of a foreign corporation in which, since the last time Form 5471 was filed, a U.S. person has acquired (in one or more transactions): **(a)** stock of the foreign corporation that gives that person ownership of 5% or more in value of the outstanding stock of the foreign corporation, or **(b)** an additional 5% or more in value of the outstanding stock. See **Schedule O, Examples of Category (2) Filers,** on page 14.

For purposes of Category (2), a U.S. person is:

1. A citizen or resident of the United States,

2. A domestic partnership,

3. A domestic corporation, and

4. An estate or trust that is not a foreign estate or trust defined in section 7701(a)(31).

See Regulations section 1.6046-1(f)(3) for exceptions pertaining to corporations organized under the laws of certain possessions of the United States.

A U.S. person has acquired stock in a foreign corporation when that person has an unqualified right to receive the stock, even though the stock is not actually issued. See Regulations section 1.6046-1(f)(1) for more details.

(Continued on page 3)

Filing Requirements For Categories of Filers

Required Information	Category of Filer				
	1	2	3	4	5
The identifying information on page 1 (the information above Schedule A)—see **Specific Instructions**	✓	✓	✓	✓	✓
Schedule A, Part I	✓		✓	✓	
Schedule A, Part II	✓				
Schedule B	✓		✓	✓	
Schedules C, E, and F				✓	✓
Schedule H				✓	✓
Schedule I				✓	✓
Separate Schedule J				✓	✓
Separate Schedule M				✓	
Separate Schedule N	✓				
Separate Schedule O, Part I		✓			
Separate Schedule O, Part II			✓		

Additional Filing Requirements

Category (3) filers must attach a statement showing the amount and type of any indebtedness of the foreign corporation to the related persons described in Regulations section 1.6046-1(b)(11). These filers must also attach a statement showing the name, address, identifying number, and number of shares subscribed to by each subscriber to the foreign corporation's stock.

Taxpayers are not required to file the information checked above for a foreign corporation that has elected (under section 953(d)) to be treated as a domestic corporation and has filed a U.S. income tax return for its tax year under that provision.

Foreign Sales Corporations (FSCs).—Category (2) and (3) filers who are shareholders, officers, and directors of a FSC (as defined in section 922) do not have to file Form 5471 and separate Schedule O to report the organization of a FSC. However, any subsequent reorganization, transfer, acquisition, or disposition of stock of the FSC must be reported.

Category (5) shareholders of a FSC are not subject to the subpart F rules for:

- Exempt foreign trade income;
- Deductions that are apportioned or allocated to exempt foreign trade income;
- Nonexempt foreign trade income (other than section 923(a)(2) nonexempt income, within the meaning of section 927(d)(6));
- Any deductions that are apportioned or allocated to the nonexempt foreign trade income described above.

Shareholders of a FSC are subject to the subpart F rules for all other types of FSC income (including section 923(a)(2) nonexempt income (within the meaning of section 927(d)(6)), investment income and carrying charges (as defined in sections 927(c) and (d)(1)), and all other FSC income that is not foreign trade income or investment income or carrying charges). However, Category (5) shareholders of a FSC are not required to file a Form 5471 if the FSC has filed a Form 1120-FSC. See Regulations section 1.921-1T(b)(2), Q&A 3.

Category (3) filer.—This includes:

- A U.S. person who has acquired (in one or more transactions) stock in a foreign corporation that gives the U.S. person ownership of 5% or more in value of the outstanding stock of the foreign corporation;
- A U.S. person who, since the last time Form 5471 was filed, has acquired (in one or more transactions) additional stock of the corporation equal to 5% or more of the value of the outstanding stock of the foreign corporation;
- A U.S. person who owns 5% or more in value of the outstanding stock of the foreign corporation when the foreign corporation is reorganized;
- A U.S. person who disposes of sufficient stock in the foreign corporation to reduce his or her interest to less than 5% of the outstanding value of the stock of the foreign corporation; or
- A person who becomes a U.S. person while owning 5% or more in value of the outstanding stock of the foreign corporation.

For purposes of Category (3), a U.S. person is:

1. A citizen or resident of the United States,
2. A domestic partnership,
3. A domestic corporation, and
4. An estate or trust that is not a foreign estate or trust defined in section 7701(a)(31).

See Regulations section 1.6046-1(f)(3) for exceptions for corporations organized under the laws of certain possessions of the United States.

A U.S. person has acquired stock in a foreign corporation when that person has an unqualified right to receive the stock, even though the stock is not actually issued. See Regulations section 1.6046-1(f)(1) for more details.

See **Examples of Category (3) Filers** on page 15.

Category (4) filer.—This includes a U.S. person who had control of a foreign corporation for an uninterrupted period of at least 30 days during the annual accounting period of the foreign corporation.

Exception. A U.S. person is not required to file for a corporation defined in section 1504(d) that files a consolidated return for the tax year.

For purposes of Category (4), a U.S. person is:

1. A citizen or resident of the United States,
2. A nonresident alien for whom an election is in effect under section 6013(g) to be treated as a resident of the United States,
3. An individual for whom an election is in effect under section 6013(h), relating to nonresident aliens who become residents of the United States during the tax year and are married at the close of the tax year to a citizen or resident of the United States,
4. A domestic partnership,
5. A domestic corporation, and
6. An estate or trust that is not a foreign estate or trust defined in section 7701(a)(31).

However, see Regulations section 1.6038-2(d) for exceptions for corporations organized under the laws of certain possessions of the United States.

A U.S. person has control of a foreign corporation if at any time during that person's tax year it owns (1) stock possessing more than 50% of the total combined voting power of all classes of stock entitled to vote, or (2) more than 50% of the total value of shares of all classes of stock of the foreign corporation.

A person in control of a corporation that, in turn, owns more than 50% of the combined voting power, or the value, of all classes of stock of another corporation is also treated as being in control of such other corporation.

Example. Corporation A owns 51% of the voting stock in Corporation B. Corporation B owns 51% of the voting stock in Corporation C. Corporation C owns 51% of the voting stock in Corporation D. Therefore, Corporation D is controlled by Corporation A.

For more details on "control," see section 6038(e)(1) and Regulations sections 1.6038-2(b) and (c).

Category (5) filer.—This includes a U.S. shareholder who owns stock in a foreign corporation that is a CFC for an uninterrupted period of 30 days or more during any tax year of the foreign corporation, and who owned that stock on the last day of that year.

For purposes of Category (5), a U.S. shareholder is a U.S. person who:

- Owns (either directly, indirectly, or constructively, within the meaning of sections 958(a) and (b)) 10% or more of the total combined voting power of all classes of voting stock of a CFC; or
- Owns (either directly or indirectly, within the meaning of section 958(a)) any stock of a CFC that is also a captive insurance company (as defined in sections 953(c)(1)(B) and 957(b)).

For purposes of Category (5), a U.S. person is:

1. A citizen or resident of the United States,
2. A domestic partnership,
3. A domestic corporation, and
4. An estate or trust that is not a foreign estate or trust defined in section 7701(a)(31).

See section 957(c) for exceptions for corporations organized under the laws of certain possessions of the United States.

A **CFC** is a foreign corporation that has U.S. shareholders that own (either directly, indirectly, or constructively, within the meaning of sections 958(a) and (b)) on any day of the tax year of the foreign corporation, more than:

1. 50% of the total combined voting power of all classes of its voting stock, or
2. 50% of the total value of the stock of the corporation.

When and Where To File

Form 5471 is due when your income tax return is due, including extensions. File two copies of the form and required schedules. Attach one copy to your income tax return. Send the other copy to the Internal Revenue Service Center, Philadelphia, PA 19255.

Penalties

Failure to file information required by section 6038 and the related regulations (Form 5471 and Schedule M).—Any person who fails to file or report all of the information requested will lose a portion of the foreign taxes available for credit under sections 901, 902, and 960. The reduction is 10% of the taxes available for credit for failure to submit the information when required. Furthermore, if the failure continues for 90 days or more after notice of the failure by the IRS, an additional 5% reduction is made for each 3-month period, or fraction thereof, during which the failure continues after the 90-day period has expired. See section 6038(c)(2) for limits on the amount of this penalty.

Also, a $1,000 penalty is imposed for each annual accounting period of each foreign corporation for failure to furnish any information described in Regulations sections 1.6038-2(f) and (g) (within the time prescribed by Regulations section 1.6038-2(i)). Furthermore, if the required information is not filed within 90 days after the IRS has mailed a notice of the failure to the U.S. person, an additional $1,000 penalty (per foreign corporation) is charged for each 30-day period, or fraction thereof, during which the failure continues after the 90-day period has expired. The additional penalty is limited to a maximum of $24,000 for each failure. See section 6038(c)(3) and Regulations section 1.6038-2(k)(2)(vi) for rules coordinating these penalties.

Criminal penalties under sections 7203, 7206, and 7207 may apply for failure to file or for filing false or fraudulent information.

Failure to file information required by sections 6035 and 6046 and the related regulations (Form 5471 and Schedules N and O).—Any person who fails to file or report all of the information requested may be subject to a $1,000 penalty for each such failure for each reportable transaction (section 6679(a)). Furthermore, criminal penalties under sections 7203, 7206, and 7207 may apply for failure to file or for filing false or fraudulent information.

Note: *Any person required to file Form 5471 and Schedule J, M, N, or O who agrees to have another person file the form and schedule for him or her may be subject to the above penalties if the other person does not file a correct and proper form and schedule.*

Electronic Filing of Form 5471

Form 5471 and the related Schedules J, M, N, and O can be filed by magnetic media (magnetic tapes, floppy diskettes) or electronically (via modem to modem). Approval must be received from the IRS prior to filing. The reporting agent can request approval by submitting an application, **Form 9041,** Application for Electronic/Magnetic Media Filing of Business and Employee Benefit Plan Returns (this form can be obtained by calling 1-800-829-6945). The application should be mailed to: **Internal Revenue Service,** Philadelphia Service Center, Magnetic Media Office, D.P. 115, 11601 Roosevelt Blvd., Philadelphia, PA 19154. The application can be submitted year round.

If unable to obtain Form 9041, a letter of application requesting approval can be submitted. The request should include the following:

- Organization name, address, and identification number;
- Name and title of person to contact;
- Telephone number and best time to call;
- Expected return volume; and
- Method of magnetic media, and whether the software will be developed or modified for commercial use.

Computer-Generated Form 5471 and Schedules

Computer-generated printouts of Form 5471 and its schedules may be filed. Generally, all computer-generated forms must receive prior approval each year from the IRS. Be sure to attach the approval letter to Form 5471. Please submit all requests for approval to: Internal Revenue Service, Attention: Substitute Forms Program, PC:FP:FS, 1111 Constitution Avenue, NW, Room 2712, Washington, DC 20224.

Every year, the IRS issues a Revenue Procedure to provide guidance for filers of computer-generated forms. In addition, every year the IRS issues **Pub. 1167,** Substitute Printed, Computer-Prepared, and Computer-Generated Tax Forms and Schedules, which reprints the most recent applicable Revenue Procedure. At the time these instructions went to print, Pub. 1167 could be ordered by calling 1-800-829-3676.

Dormant Foreign Corporations

Rev. Proc. 92-70, 1992-2 C.B. 435, provides a summary filing procedure for filing Form 5471 for a dormant foreign corporation (defined in Sec. 3 of the Rev. Proc.). If the filer elects the summary procedure, only page 1 of Form 5471 is completed for each dormant foreign corporation as follows:

1. Write "Filed Pursuant To Rev. Proc. 92-70 for Dormant Foreign Corporations" across the top margin.

2. Complete filer items such as:
- Name and address;
- Identifying number (Item A);
- Filing category (Item B);
- Stock ownership percentage (Item C); and
- Tax year.

3. Complete the following corporate items:
- The dormant foreign corporation's annual accounting period (within the meaning of section 6038(e)(2)) (below the title of the form);
- Name and address (Item 1a);
- Employer identification number (EIN), if any (Item 1b);
- Country of incorporation (Item 1c); and
- Date of incorporation (Item 1e).

File page 1 in duplicate with each filer's regularly filed income tax return. See **When and Where To File.** Also, see Rev. Proc. 92-70 for more details.

Treaty-Based Return Positions

U.S. persons that adopt a return position that any treaty of the United States (including, but not limited to, an income tax treaty, an estate and gift tax treaty, or a friendship, commerce, and navigation treaty) overrides or modifies any provision of the Internal Revenue Code and causes (or potentially causes) a reduction of any tax incurred at any time, generally must disclose that return position on **Form 8833,** Treaty-Based Return Position Disclosure Under Section 6114 or 7701(b).

Failure to make such a report may result in a $1,000 penalty ($10,000 in the case of a C corporation) (see section 6712).

Specific Instructions

Important. Fill in all applicable lines and sections. All information reported must be in the English language. If the information required in a given section exceeds the space provided within that section, **do not** write "see attached" in the section and **do not** attach all of the information on additional sheets. Instead, complete all entry spaces in the section and attach the remaining information on additional sheets. The additional sheets must conform with the IRS version of that section.

Annual Accounting Period

Enter, in the space provided below the title of Form 5471, the annual accounting period of the foreign corporation for which you are furnishing information. Except for information contained on Schedule O, report information for the tax year of the foreign corporation that ends with or within your tax year. When filing Schedule O, report acquisitions, dispositions, and organizations or reorganizations that occurred during your tax year.

Specified Foreign Corporations.—For a specified foreign corporation, the annual accounting period is generally required to be the tax year of the corporation's majority U.S. shareholder. See section 898(c) for details.

A specified foreign corporation is any foreign corporation: **(1)** that is treated as a CFC under subpart F **or** that is a foreign personal holding company; and **(2)** that meets the more than 50% U.S. ownership requirements of section 898(b)(2).

If you are preparing Form 5471 for a specified foreign corporation, see Rev. Proc. 90-26, 1990-1 C.B. 512, for wording that must be entered in the upper left corner on page 1 of Form 5471. This wording pertains to whether the corporation made an election under section 898(c)(1)(B) and whether the corporation changed its tax year to conform to the tax year required by section 898.

Note: *A specified foreign corporation may elect to change its required annual accounting period back to the taxable year it used immediately before conforming to the tax year required by section 898. This is applicable for returns due (including extensions) and timely filed after March 14, 1995, but no later than March 14, 1997. For more details, see Notice 95-13, 1995-15 I.R.B. 21.*

Name Change

If either the name of the person filing this return or the corporation whose activities are being reported has changed since the last time information was reported, attach a statement that explains the change and shows the prior name.

Item A

The identifying number of an individual is his or her social security number. The identifying number of all others is their EIN. If a U.S. corporation that owns stock in a foreign corporation is a member of a consolidated group, list the common parent as the person filing the return and enter its EIN in Item A. Identify the direct owner in Item D.

Item C

Enter the total percentage of the voting stock of the foreign corporation you owned directly, indirectly, or constructively at the end of the corporation's annual accounting period.

Item D—Person(s) On Whose Behalf This Information Return Is Filed

One person may file Form 5471 and the applicable schedules for other persons who have the same filing requirements. For example, if you and one or more other persons are required to furnish information for the same foreign corporation for the same period, a joint information return that contains the required information may be filed with your income tax return or with the income tax return of any one of the other persons. However, for Category (3) filers, the required information may only be filed by another person having an equal or greater interest (measured in terms of value of stock of the foreign corporation).

The person that files the required information for other persons must complete Item D. In addition, a separate Schedule I must be filed for each person described in Category 5.

Other persons for whom required information is filed.—

1. A U.S. citizen or resident described in Category (1) that is a 10% shareholder that does not own 10% or more in value of the outstanding stock directly but is required to file Form 5471 solely by attribution of another U.S. person's stock ownership does not have to file if the direct owner is an individual who furnishes all the information required.

2. A U.S. officer or director described in Category (2) does not have to file Form 5471 if:

   a. Immediately after a reportable stock acquisition, three or fewer U.S. persons own 95% or more in value of the outstanding stock of the foreign corporation and the U.S. person making such acquisition files a return for such acquisition under Category (3), **or**

   b. The U.S. person(s) for which such U.S. officer or director is required to file Form 5471 does not directly own an interest in the foreign corporation and is required to furnish the information solely because of attribution of stock ownership from a U.S. person under Regulations section 1.6046-1(i) and the person from whom the stock ownership is attributed furnishes all of the information required.

3. A U.S. person described in Category (3) does not have to file Form 5471 if that person does not directly own an interest in the foreign corporation and is required to furnish the information solely because of attribution of stock ownership from another U.S. person under Regulations section 1.6046-1(i) and the person from whom the stock ownership is attributed furnishes all of the information required.

4. A U.S. person described in Category (4) that does not directly own an interest in the foreign corporation and must file Form 5471 solely because of the attribution of stock ownership rules of Regulations section 1.6038-2(c) does not have to file if the person from whom the stock ownership is attributed files all the information required.

5. A U.S. person described in Category (5) may file a joint Form 5471 with another U.S. person described in either Category (4) or Category (5) according to Regulations sections 1.6038-2(j)(1) and (3).

Filing requirements.— Except for members of the filer's consolidated return group, all persons identified in Item D must attach a statement to their income tax returns that: **(a)** indicates that their filing requirements have been or will be satisfied, **(b)** lists the name, address, and identifying number of the return with which the information was or will be filed, and **(c)** identifies the IRS Service Center where the return was or will be filed.

Currency Translation

Enter the foreign corporation's functional currency in the space indicated above items 1a and 1b on page 1 of the form. Regulations sections 1.6038-2(h) and 1.6046-1(g) require that certain amounts be reported in U.S. dollars and/or in the foreign corporation's functional currency. The specific instructions for the affected schedules state these requirements, including special rules for a foreign corporation that uses the U.S. dollar approximate separate transactions method of accounting under Regulations section 1.985-3.

Items 1f and 1g

See the last page of these instructions for a list of business code numbers and descriptions of principal business activities.

Schedule B

Category (1), (3), and (4) filers must complete Schedule B for U.S. persons that owned (at any time during the annual accounting period), directly or indirectly through foreign entities, 5% or more in value of any class of the corporation's outstanding stock.

Column (e).—Use column (e) to report the shareholder's allocable percentage of the foreign corporation's subpart F income or, for a foreign personal holding company, foreign personal holding company income.

Schedule C

Schedule C requires an income statement prepared in functional currency in accordance with U.S. Generally Accepted Accounting Principles (GAAP). Each line item on Schedule C must also be reported in U.S. dollars translated from functional currency in accordance with U.S. GAAP translation rules. If the foreign corporation uses the U.S. dollar approximate separate transactions method of accounting (DASTM) under Regulations section 1.985-3, the functional currency column should reflect local hyperinflationary currency amounts computed in accordance with U.S. GAAP, and the U.S. dollar column should reflect such amounts translated into dollars under U.S. GAAP translation rules. Differences between this U.S. dollar GAAP column and the U.S. dollar income or loss figured for tax purposes under Regulations section 1.985-3(c) should be accounted for on Schedule H. See the instructions for Schedule H.

Line 19.—The terms "extraordinary items" and "prior period adjustments" have the same meaning given to them by U.S. GAAP (see Opinion No. 30 of the Accounting Principles Board and Statement No. 16 of the Financial Accounting Standards Board).

Line 20.—Enter the income, war profits, and excess profits taxes deducted in accordance with U.S. GAAP.

Note: *Differences between this functional currency amount and the amount of taxes that reduce U.S. E&P should be accounted for on line 2g of Schedule H.*

Schedule E

List income, war profits, and excess profits taxes paid or accrued to the United States and to any foreign country or U.S. possession for the annual accounting period. Report these amounts in column (b) in the local currency in which the taxes are payable. Translate these amounts into U.S. dollars at the exchange rate as of the time the taxes were paid (or, if unpaid, at the year-end rate). Identify the exchange rate used in column (c) and report the translated dollar amount in column (d).

Schedule F

Schedule F generally requires a balance sheet prepared and translated into U.S. dollars in accordance with U.S. GAAP.

Exception. If the foreign corporation uses DASTM, Schedule F should reflect the tax balance sheet prepared and translated into U.S. dollars according to Regulations section 1.985-3(d), and not a U.S. GAAP balance sheet.

Schedule H

Use Schedule H to report the foreign corporation's current E&P figured in functional currency for U.S. tax purposes.

Special rules for DASTM.—If the foreign corporation uses DASTM, enter on line 1 the dollar GAAP income or (loss) from line 21 of Schedule C, and use Schedule H to reflect adjustments made in figuring income or loss in dollars for tax purposes. DASTM gain or loss figured under Regulations section 1.985-3(d) should be reported on line 5b. Enter the sum of lines 5a and 5b on both lines 5c and 5d.

Lines 2a through 2h.—Certain adjustments (required by Regulations sections 1.964-1(b) and (c)) must be made to the foreign corporation's line 1 net book income or (loss) to determine its E&P. These adjustments may include both positive and negative adjustments to conform the foreign book income to U.S. GAAP and to U.S. tax accounting principles. If the foreign corporation's books are maintained in functional currency in accordance with U.S. GAAP, enter on line 1 the functional currency GAAP income or (loss) from line 21 of Schedule C, rather than starting with foreign book income, and show GAAP-to-tax adjustments on lines 2a through 2h.

Lines 2b and 2c.—Generally, depreciation, depletion, and amortization allowances must be based on the historical cost of the underlying asset, and depreciation must be figured according to section 167 (or, if 20% or more of the foreign corporation's gross income is from U.S. sources, on a straight line basis according to Regulations section 1.312-15).

Line 2f.—Inventories must be taken into account according to the rules of sections 471 (incorporating the provisions of section 263A) and 472 and the related regulations.

Line 2g.—See the instructions for Schedule C, line 20.

Line 2h.—Enter the net amount of any additional adjustments not included on lines 2a through 2g. List these additional adjustments on a separate schedule. Attach this separate schedule to Form 5471.

Line 5b.—DASTM gain or (loss), reflecting unrealized exchange gain or loss, should be reported on line 5b only for foreign corporations that use DASTM.

Line 5d.—Enter the line 5c functional currency number translated into U.S. dollars at the weighted average exchange rate as defined in Regulations section 1.989(b)-1. Specify the exchange rate used. If the foreign corporation uses DASTM, enter on line 5d the same amount entered on line 5c.

Blocked income.—The E&P of the foreign corporation, as reflected on Schedule H, must not be reduced by all or any part of such E&P that could not have been distributed by the foreign corporation due to currency or other restrictions or limitations imposed under the laws of any foreign country.

Schedule I

Use Schedule I to report in U.S. dollars the U.S. shareholder's pro rata share of income from the foreign corporation reportable under subpart F and other income realized from a corporate distribution.

Lines 1 through 4

Subpart F income.—Generally, the income of a foreign corporation with U.S. shareholders is not taxed to those U.S. shareholders until the income is repatriated to the United States (e.g., through the payment of dividends to the U.S. shareholders or in the form of gain on the disposition of the U.S. shareholders' stock in the foreign corporation). However, this deferral of U.S. tax is not available to U.S. shareholders of CFCs with certain types of income, including subpart F income. See sections 951 and 952.

Generally, the subpart F income of a CFC includes:

- Adjusted net foreign base company income (lines 1 through 21 of Worksheet A);
- Adjusted net insurance income and adjusted net related person insurance income (lines 22 and 23 of Worksheet A);
- International boycott income (line 24 of Worksheet A);
- Illegal bribes, kickbacks, and other payments (line 25 of Worksheet A); and

- Income from a country described in section 952(a)(5) (line 26 of Worksheet A).

Certain CFC investments that may make earnings ineligible for deferral include:

- Earnings invested in U.S. property (Worksheet B);
- Amounts withdrawn from qualified investments in less developed countries and amounts withdrawn from qualified investments in foreign base company shipping operations (Worksheet C);
- Amounts withdrawn from investment in export trade assets (Worksheet D); and
- Earnings invested in excess passive assets (Worksheet E).

In addition, if the subpart F income of any CFC for any tax year was reduced because of the current E&P limitation (see the instructions for line 31 of Worksheet A), any excess of the E&P of the CFC for any subsequent tax year over the subpart F income of the CFC for the tax year must be recharacterized as subpart F income.

Line 5

Complete Worksheet E. Enter on line 5 of Schedule I the amount from line 21 of Worksheet E. This amount is the shareholder's pro rata share of the CFC's earnings invested in excess passive assets, computed according to section 956A and translated into U.S. dollars at the year-end spot rate (as provided in section 989(b)).

Line 6

Enter the factoring income (as defined in section 864(d)(1)) if no subpart F income is reported on line 1a, Worksheet A, because of the operation of the de minimis rule (see lines 1a, 10, and 12 of Worksheet A and the related instructions).

Line 7

Add lines 1 through 6. Enter the result here and on your income tax return. If you are preparing Form 5471 for a corporate U.S. shareholder, enter the result on Schedule C, Form 1120, or on the comparable line of other corporate income tax returns. If you are preparing Form 5471 for a noncorporate U.S. shareholder, enter the result on Schedule B, Form 1040, or on the comparable line of other noncorporate income tax returns.

Line 8

Enter the dividends you received from the foreign corporation that have not been previously taxed under subpart F in the current year or in any prior year.

Line 9

If previously taxed E&P described in section 959(a) or (b) was distributed, enter the amount of foreign currency gain or (loss) on the distribution, computed under section 986(c). See Notice 88-71, 1988-2 C.B. 374, for rules for computing section 986(c) gain or (loss). If you are preparing Form 5471 for a corporate U.S. shareholder, include the gain or (loss) as "other income" on Form 1120, or on the comparable line of other corporate income

tax returns. If you are preparing Form 5471 for a noncorporate U.S. shareholder, include the result as "other income" on Form 1040, or on the comparable line of other noncorporate income tax returns.

Worksheet A

Line 1a.—Enter on this line: **(a)** dividend income; **(b)** interest income (except any interest from conducting a banking business and that is "export financing interest" (as defined in section 904(d)(2)(G))); **(c)** income from rents and royalties (except rents and royalties from actively conducting a trade or business and that are received from a person other than a "related person" (as defined in section 954(d)(3))); and **(d)** income from annuities. Do not include certain income received from related persons (described in section 954(c)(3)). Interest income includes factoring income arising when a person acquires a trade or service receivable (directly or indirectly) from a related person. The income is treated as interest on a loan to the obligor under section 864(d)(1) and is generally not eligible for the de minimis, export financing, and related party exceptions to the inclusion of subpart F income. Furthermore, a trade or service receivable acquired or treated as acquired by a CFC from a related U.S. person is considered an investment in U.S. property for purposes of section 956 (Worksheet B) if the obligor is a U.S. person.

Line 1b.—Enter the excess of gains over losses from the sale or exchange of: **(a)** property that produces the type of income reportable on line 1a; **(b)** an interest in a trust, partnership, or REMIC; or **(c)** property that does not produce any income.

Do **not** include on this line the following: **(a)** for any regular dealer in property, gains and losses from the sale or exchange of any such "dealer property" or gains and losses from bona fide hedging transactions reasonably necessary to be a dealer in such property, and **(b)** gains and losses from the sale or exchange of any property that, in the hands of the CFC, is property described in section 1221(1).

Line 1c.—Enter the excess of gains over losses from transactions (including futures, forward, and similar transactions) in any commodities. See section 954(c)(1)(C) for exceptions.

Line 1d.—Enter the excess of foreign currency gains over foreign currency losses (see section 988(b) for definitions), except for transactions directly related to the business needs of a CFC.

Line 1e.—Enter any income equivalent to interest, including income from commitment fees (or similar amounts) for loans actually made.

Lines 10 and 12. De minimis rule.—If the sum of foreign base company income (determined without regard to the deductions of section 954(b)(5)) and the gross insurance income (as defined in section 954(b)(3)(C)) (line 9) for the tax year is less than the smaller of 5% of gross income for income tax purposes (line 10) or $1 million, no portion of the gross income for the tax year is treated as foreign base company income or insurance income. In this case, enter zero on line 12 and skip lines 13 through 23. Otherwise, go on to line 13.

Lines 11, 13, and 14. Full inclusion rule.—If the sum of the foreign base company income (determined without regard to the deductions of section 954(b)(5)) and the gross insurance income (line 9) for the tax year exceeds 70% of gross income (for income tax purposes) (line 11), the entire gross income for the tax year must (subject to the exception for certain income subject to high foreign taxes (described below), the section 952(b) exclusion, and the deductions to be taken into account under section 954(b)(5)) be treated as foreign base company income or insurance income (whichever is appropriate). In this case, enter total gross income (for income tax purposes) on line 13. Otherwise, enter zero.

Lines 15g, 16d, 17d, 18d, 20d, 22d, and 23d. Exception for certain income subject to high foreign taxes.—Foreign base company income and insurance income does not include any item of income received by a CFC if the taxpayer establishes that such income was subject to an effective rate of income tax imposed by a foreign country that is greater than 90% of the maximum rate of tax specified in section 11. This rule does not apply to foreign base company oil-related income as described in section 954(a)(5). See Regulations section 1.954-1T(d) for more information.

Line 22. Adjusted net insurance income.—In determining a shareholder's pro rata share of the subpart F income of a CFC, insurance income is any income that:

• Is attributable to the issuing (or reinsuring) of any insurance or annuity contract: **(1)** for property in, liability from an activity in, or for the lives or health of residents of a country other than the country under the laws of which the CFC is created or organized, or **(2)** for risks not described in **(1)** above, resulting from any arrangement in which another corporation receives a substantially equal amount of premiums or other consideration for issuing (or reinsuring) a contract described in **(1)** above; and

• Would (subject to the modifications provided in sections 953(b)(1) and 953(b)(2)) be taxed under subchapter L (insurance company tax) if such income were income of a domestic insurance company.

Line 23. Adjusted net related person insurance income.—In determining a shareholder's pro rata share of the subpart F income of a CFC, related person insurance income is any insurance income (within the meaning of section 953(a)) attributable to a policy of insurance or reinsurance for which the person insured (directly or indirectly) is a U.S. shareholder (as defined in section 953(c)(1)(A)) in a CFC, or a related person (as defined in section 953(c)(6)) to such a shareholder. In such case, the pro rata share referred to above is to be determined under the rules of section 953(c)(5).

Exceptions. The above definition does not apply to any foreign corporation if:

• At all times during the foreign corporation's tax year, less than 20% of the total combined voting power of all classes of stock of the corporation entitled to vote, and less than 20% of the total value of the corporation, is owned (directly or indirectly under the principles of section 883(c)(4)) by persons who are (directly or indirectly) insured under any policy of insurance or reinsurance issued by the corporation or who are related persons to any such person;

• The related person insurance income (determined on a gross basis) of the corporation for the tax year is less than 20% of its insurance income for the tax year determined regardless of the provisions of section 953(a)(1) that limit insurance income to income from countries other than the country in which the corporation was created or organized; or

• The corporation: **(1)** elects to treat its related person insurance income for the tax year as income effectively connected with the conduct of a trade or business in the United States; **(2)** elects to waive all treaty benefits (other than from section 884) for related person insurance income; and **(3)** meets any requirement the IRS may prescribe to ensure that any tax on such income is paid. This election will not be effective if the corporation was a disqualified corporation (as defined in section 953(c)(3)(E)) for the tax year for which the election was made or for any prior tax year beginning after 1986. See section 953(c)(3)(D) for special rules for this election.

Mutual life insurance companies.—The related person insurance income rules also apply to mutual life insurance companies under regulations prescribed by the Secretary. For these purposes, policyholders must be treated as shareholders.

Line 24. International boycott income.—If a CFC or a member of a controlled group (within the meaning of section 993(a)(3)) that includes the CFC has operations in, or related to, a country (or with the government, a company, or a national of a country) that requires participation in or cooperation with an international boycott as a condition of doing business within such country or with the government, company, or national of that country, a portion of the income of the CFC is included in subpart F income. The amount included is determined by multiplying the income of the CFC (other than income included under section 951 and U.S. source effectively connected business income described in section 952(b)) by the international boycott factor. The international boycott factor is a fraction determined on Schedule A (Form 5713).

Special rule.—If the shareholder of a CFC can clearly demonstrate that the income earned for the tax year is from specific operations, then, instead of applying the international boycott factor, the addition to subpart F income is the amount specifically from the operations in which there was participation in or cooperation with an international boycott. See Schedule B (Form 5713).

Line 25. Illegal bribes, kickbacks, and other payments.—Under section 952(a)(4), the sum of the amounts of any illegal bribes, kickbacks, or other payments (within the meaning of section 162(c)) paid by or on behalf of the corporation, directly or indirectly, to an official, employee, or agent of a government is considered subpart F income.

Line 26. Income from a country described in section 952(a)(5).—The income of a CFC from any country described in section 901(j) will be deemed to be income to the U.S. shareholders of such CFC. As of the date these instructions were revised, the countries described in section 901(j) included: Cuba, Iran, Iraq, Libya, North Korea, Sudan, Syria, and Vietnam.

Line 28. Exclusion of U.S. income.—Subpart F income does not include any U.S. source income (which, for these purposes, includes all carrying charges and all interest, dividends, royalties, and other investment income received or accrued by a FSC) that is effectively connected with a CFC's conduct of a trade or business in the United States unless that item is exempt from taxation (or is subject to a reduced rate of tax) pursuant to a treaty obligation of the United States.

Line 31. E&P limitation.—The subpart F income of a CFC is limited to its current year E&P, computed under the special rule of section 952(c)(3).

The amount included in the gross income of a U.S. shareholder of a CFC under section 951(a)(1)(A)(i) for any tax year and attributable to a qualified activity must be reduced by the shareholder's pro rata share of any qualified deficit (see section 952(c)(1)(B)).

Also, see section 952(c)(1)(C) for certain current year deficits of a member of the same chain of corporations that may be considered in determining subpart F income.

Worksheet A—Foreign Base Company Income and Insurance Income and Summary of U.S. Shareholder's Pro Rata Share of Subpart F Income of a CFC (see instructions)

Enter the amounts on lines 1a through 40a in functional currency.

1 **Gross foreign personal holding company income:**
   a Dividends, interest, royalties, rents, and annuities (section 954(c)(1)(A)) (excluding amounts described in sections 954(c)(2) and (3))) . . . | 1a
   b Excess of gains over losses from certain property transactions (section 954(c)(1)(B)) . . . . | 1b
   c Excess of gains over losses from commodity transactions (section 954(c)(1)(C)) . . . . | 1c
   d Excess of foreign currency gains over foreign currency losses (section 954(c)(1)(D)) . . . . | 1d
   e Income equivalent to interest (section 954(c)(1)(E)) . . . . . . | 1e

2 Gross foreign personal holding company income. Add lines 1a through 1e . . . . | 2
3 Gross foreign base company sales income (see section 954(d)) . . . . | 3
4 Gross foreign base company services income (see section 954(e)) . . . . | 4
5 Gross foreign base company shipping income (see section 954(f)) after application of sections 954(b)(6) and (7) . . . . | 5
6 Gross foreign base company oil-related income (see section 954(g)) after application of section 954(b)(8) | 6
7 Gross foreign base company income. Add lines 2 through 6 . . . . | 7
8 Gross insurance income (see sections 953 and 954(b)(3)(C) and the instructions for lines 22 and 23) | 8
9 Gross foreign base company income and gross insurance income. Add lines 7 and 8 . . . | 9
10 Enter 5% of total gross income (as computed for income tax purposes) . . . . | 10
11 Enter 70% of total gross income (as computed for income tax purposes) . . . . . . | 11
12 If line 9 is less than line 10 and less than $1 million, enter -0- on this line and skip lines 13 through 23 | 12
13 If line 9 is more than line 11, enter total gross income (as computed for income tax purposes) | 13
14 **Total adjusted gross foreign base company income and insurance income** (enter the greater of line 9 or line 13) . . . . | 14

15 **Adjusted net foreign personal holding company income:**
   a Enter amount from line 2 . . . . | 15a
   b Expenses directly related to amount on line 2 . . . . . . | 15b
   c Subtract line 15b from line 15a . . . . | 15c
   d Related person interest expense (see section 954(b)(5)) . . . . | 15d
   e Other expenses allocated and apportioned to the amount on line 2 under section 954(b)(5) . . . . | 15e
   f Net foreign personal holding company income. Subtract the sum of lines 15d and 15e from line 15c . . . . | 15f
   g Net foreign personal holding company income excluded under high-tax exception . . . . | 15g
   h Subtract line 15g from line 15f . . . . | 15h

16 **Adjusted net foreign base company sales income:**
   a Enter amount from line 3 . . . . | 16a
   b Expenses allocated and apportioned to the amount on line 3 under section 954(b)(5) . . . . | 16b
   c Net foreign base company sales income. Subtract line 16b from line 16a | 16c
   d Net foreign base company sales income excluded under high-tax exception | 16d
   e Subtract line 16d from line 16c . . . . | 16e

17 **Adjusted net foreign base company services income:**
   a Enter amount from line 4 . . . . | 17a
   b Expenses allocated and apportioned to line 4 under section 954(b)(5) | 17b
   c Net foreign base company services income. Subtract line 17b from line 17a | 17c
   d Net foreign base company services income excluded under high-tax exception | 17d
   e Subtract line 17d from line 17c . . . . | 17e

18 **Adjusted net foreign base company shipping income:**
   a Enter amount from line 5 . . . . | 18a
   b Expenses allocated and apportioned to line 5 under section 954(b)(5) | 18b
   c Net foreign base company shipping income. Subtract line 18b from line 18a | 18c
   d Net foreign base company shipping income excluded under high-tax exception | 18d
   e Subtract line 18d from line 18c . . . . | 18e

Worksheet A (continued) (See instructions.)

19	**Adjusted net foreign base company oil-related income:**		
a	Enter amount from line 6	19a	
b	Expenses allocated and apportioned to line 6 under section 954(b)(5)	19b	
c	Subtract line 19b from line 19a		19c
20	**Adjusted net full inclusion foreign base company income:**		
a	Enter the excess, if any, of line 13 over line 9	20a	
b	Expenses allocated and apportioned under section 954(b)(5)	20b	
c	Net full inclusion foreign base company income. Subtract line 20b from line 20a	20c	
d	Net full inclusion foreign base company income excluded under high-tax exception	20d	
e	Subtract line 20d from line 20c		20e
21	**Adjusted net foreign base company income.** Add lines 15h, 16e, 17e, 18e, 19c, and 20e		21
22	**Adjusted net insurance income** (other than related person insurance income):		
a	Enter amount from line 8 (other than related person insurance income)	22a	
b	Expenses allocated and apportioned to the amount from line 8 under section 953	22b	
c	Net insurance income. Subtract line 22b from line 22a	22c	
d	Net insurance income excluded under high-tax exception	22d	
e	Subtract line 22d from line 22c		22e
23	**Adjusted net related person insurance income:**		
a	Enter amount from line 8 that is related person insurance income	23a	
b	Expenses allocated and apportioned to related person insurance income under section 953	23b	
c	Net related person insurance income. Subtract line 23b from line 23a	23c	
d	Net related person insurance income excluded under high-tax exception	23d	
e	Subtract line 23d from line 23c		23e
24	International boycott income (section 952(a)(3))		24
25	Illegal bribes, kickbacks, and other payments (section 952(a)(4))		25
26	Income from a country described in section 952(a)(5)		26
27	Subpart F income before application of sections 952(b) and (c) and section 959(b). Add lines 21, 22e, 23e, and 24 through 26		27
28	Enter portion of line 27 that is U.S. source income effectively connected with a U.S. trade or business (section 952(b))	28	
29	Exclusions under section 959(b)	29	
30	Total subpart F income. Subtract the sum of lines 28 and 29 from line 27		30
31	Current E&P		31
32	Enter the smaller of line 30 or line 31		32
33	Shareholder's pro rata share of line 32	33	
34	Shareholder's pro rata share of export trade income	34	
35	Subtract line 34 from line 33	35	
36	Divide the number of days in the tax year that the corporation was a CFC by the number of days in the tax year and multiply the result by line 35	36	
37	Dividends paid to any other person with respect to your stock during the tax year	37	
38	Divide the number of days in the tax year you did not own such stock by the number of days in the tax year and multiply the result by line 35	38	
39	Enter the smaller of line 37 or line 38	39	
40a	**Shareholder's pro rata share of subpart F income.** Subtract line 39 from line 36		40a
b	Translate the amount on line 40a from functional currency to U.S. dollars at the weighted average exchange rate (as defined in Regulations section 1.989(b)-1). Enter the result here and on line 1, Schedule I		40b

Worksheet B

Under sections 951(a)(1)(B) and 956, U.S. shareholders are generally taxed on the amount of earnings that a CFC invests in U.S. property. Worksheet B is used by a U.S. shareholder to determine his or her share of the amount subject to tax.

Only earnings of a CFC that have not been distributed or otherwise previously taxed are subject to these rules. Thus, the amount of previously **untaxed** earnings limits the section 956 inclusion. A CFC's investment in U.S. property in excess of this limit will not be included in the taxable income of the CFC's U.S. shareholders.

Further, U.S. shareholders are only taxed on earnings invested in U.S. property to the extent the investments exceed the CFC's previously **taxed** earnings. The balances in the previously taxed accounts of prior section 956 inclusions (see section 959(c)(1)(A) and current or prior subpart F inclusions (see section 959(c)(2)) reduce what would otherwise be the current section 956 inclusion.

Note: *The previously taxed accounts should be adjusted to reflect any reclassification of subpart F inclusions that reduced prior section 956 or 956A inclusions (see section 959(a)(2) and (3), Worksheet E, and Schedule J).*

Distributions are also taken into account before the section 956 inclusion is determined. Distributions generally are treated as coming first from (and thus reducing the balances of) the previously taxed accounts. Thus, the U.S. shareholders must **(1)** compute the current subpart F inclusion (potentially increasing that previously taxed account); **(2)** take into account current distributions (potentially reducing the previously taxed and untaxed accounts); and **(3)** compute the current section 956 inclusion (potentially increasing or reclassifying the previously taxed accounts).

Worksheet B applies for tax years of a CFC beginning after September 30, 1993, and to tax years of the U.S. shareholder in which or with which the tax year of the CFC ends. U.S. property is measured on a quarterly average basis. For purposes of this worksheet, the amount taken into account with respect to U.S. property is its adjusted basis for earnings and profits purposes, reduced by any liability the property is subject to. See sections 956(c) and (d) for the definition of U.S. property.

The amount of U.S. property held (directly or indirectly) by the CFC does not include any item that was acquired by the foreign corporation before it became a CFC, except for the property acquired before the foreign corporation became a CFC that exceeds the applicable earnings (as defined in sections 956(b) and 956A(b)) accumulated during periods before it became a CFC.

If the foreign corporation ceases to be a CFC during the tax year: **(1)** the determination of the U.S. shareholder's pro rata share will be made based upon the stock owned (within the meaning of section 958(a)) by the U.S. shareholder on the last day on which the foreign corporation is a CFC; **(2)** the CFC's U.S. property for the taxable year will be determined only by taking into account quarters ending on or before such last day (and investments in U.S. property as of the close of subsequent quarters should be recorded as zero on line 1); and **(3)** in determining applicable earnings, current earnings and profits will include only earnings and profits that are allocable (on a pro rata basis) to the part of the year during which the foreign corporation is a CFC.

Worksheet B—U.S. Shareholder's Pro Rata Share of Earnings of a CFC Invested in U.S. Property
Enter the amounts on lines 1 through 16 in functional currency.

1	Amount of U.S. property (as defined in sections 956(c) and (d)) held (directly or indirectly) by the CFC as of the close of:		
a	The first quarter of the tax year.	1a	
b	The second quarter of the tax year	1b	
c	The third quarter of the tax year	1c	
d	The fourth quarter of the tax year.	1d	
2	Number of quarter-ends the foreign corporation was a CFC during the tax year ▶	2	
3	Average amount of U.S. property held (directly or indirectly) by the CFC as of the close of each quarter of the tax year. (Add lines 1a through 1d. Divide this amount by the number on line 2.)	3	
4	U.S. shareholder's pro rata share of the amount on line 3.	4	
5	U.S. shareholder's earnings and profits described in section 959(c)(1)(A) after reductions (if any) for current year distributions	5	
6	Subtract line 5 from line 4	6	
7	Applicable earnings:		
a	Current earnings and profits	7a	
b	Line 7a plus accumulated earnings and profits	7b	
8	Enter the greater of line 7a or line 7b	8	
9	Distributions made by the CFC during the tax year	9	
10	Subtract line 9 from line 8	10	
11	Earnings and profits described in section 959(c)(1)	11	
12	Subtract line 11 from line 10	12	
13	U.S. shareholder's pro rata share of the amount on line 12	13	
14	U.S. shareholder's earnings invested in U.S. property. (Enter the smaller of line 6 or line 13)	14	
15	Amount on line 14 that is excluded from the U.S. shareholder's gross income under section 959(a)(2)	15	
16	Subtract line 15 from line 14	16	
17	Translate the amount on line 16 from functional currency to U.S. dollars at the year-end spot rate (as provided in section 989(b)). Enter the result here and on line 2 of Schedule I	17	

Worksheet C—U.S. Shareholder's Pro Rata Share of Previously Excluded Subpart F Income of a CFC Withdrawn From Qualified Investments in Less Developed Countries and From Qualified Investments in Foreign Base Company Shipping Operations

Enter the amounts on lines 1 through 6a in functional currency.

1. Decrease in qualified investments in less developed countries (see Regulations section 1.955-1(b)(1)) and foreign base company shipping operations (see Regulations section 1.955A-1(b)(1)) **1**
2. Limitation (see Regulations section 1.955-1(b)(2)):
   a. Enter the sum of E&P for the tax year and E&P accumulated for prior tax years beginning after 1962 . . . . **2a**
   b. Enter the sum of amounts invested in less developed countries or foreign base company shipping operations and excluded from foreign base company income for all prior tax years, minus the sum of such amounts withdrawn for such years (see Regulations section 1.955-1(b)(2)(i)) . . **2b**
3. Enter the smaller of line 2a or line 2b **3**
4. Previously excluded subpart F income withdrawn for the tax year (enter the smaller of line 1 or line 3) **4**
5. U.S. shareholder's pro rata share of line 4 (see Regulations section 1.955-1(c)) **5**
6a. Divide the number of days in the tax year that the foreign corporation was a CFC by the number of days in the tax year and multiply the result by line 5 . . . . **6a**
  b. Translate the amount on line 6a from functional currency to U.S. dollars at the weighted average exchange rate (as defined in Regulations section 1.989(b)-1). Enter the result here and on line 3, Schedule I . . **6b**

Worksheet D—U.S. Shareholder's Pro Rata Share of Previously Excluded Export Trade Income of a CFC Withdrawn From Investment in Export Trade Assets

Enter the amounts on lines 1 through 7a in functional currency.

1. Decrease in investments of the CFC in export trade assets (see Regulations section 1.970-1(d)(3)) **1**
2. U.S. shareholder's pro rata share of line 1 . . . . **2**
3. U.S. shareholder's pro rata share of the sum of E&P of the CFC for the tax year and E&P accumulated for prior tax years beginning after 1962 (see Regulations section 1.970-1(c)(2)(ii)) **3**
4. Limitation under section 970(b) (see Regulations section 1.970-1(c)(2)(i)):
   a. U.S. shareholder's pro rata share of the sum of the amounts by which the CFC's subpart F income for prior tax years was reduced under section 970(a) **4a**
   b. U.S. shareholder's pro rata share of the sum of the amounts that were not included in subpart F income of the CFC for prior tax years because of Regulations section 1.972-1 . . . . **4b**
   c. Add lines 4a and 4b **4c**
   d. U.S. shareholder's pro rata share of the sum of the amounts that were previously included in his or her gross income for prior tax years under section 951(a)(1)(A)(ii) because of section 970(b) **4d**
5. Subtract line 4d from line 4c **5**
6. Enter the smallest of line 2, 3, or 5 . . . . **6**
7a. Divide the number of days in the tax year that the foreign corporation was a CFC by the number of days in the tax year and multiply the result by line 6 . . . . **7a**
  b. Translate the amount on line 7a from functional currency to U.S. dollars at the weighted average exchange rate (as defined in Regulations section 1.989(b)-1). Enter the result here and on line 4, Schedule I **7b**

Worksheet E

Under sections 951(a)(1)(C) and 956A, U.S. shareholders are generally taxed on the amount of earnings that a CFC invests in excess passive assets. Worksheet E is used by a U.S. shareholder to determine his or her share of the amount subject to tax.

Only earnings accumulated in tax years of a CFC beginning after September 30, 1993 that have not been distributed or otherwise previously taxed are subject to these rules. Thus, the amount of previously **untaxed** earnings accumulated in post-September 30, 1993, years limits the section 956A inclusion. A CFC's investment in excess passive assets in excess of this limit will not be included in the taxable income of the CFC's U.S. shareholders.

Further, U.S. shareholders are only taxed on earnings invested in excess passive assets to the extent the investments exceed the CFC's previously **taxed** earnings. The balances in the previously taxed accounts of prior section 956A inclusions (see section 959(c)(1)(B) and current or prior subpart F inclusions arising in post-September 30, 1993, years (see section 959(c)(2))) reduce what would otherwise be the current section 956A inclusion.

Note: *The previously taxed accounts should be adjusted to reflect any reclassification of subpart F inclusions that* reduced current or prior section 956, or prior 956A, inclusions (see section 959(a)(2) and (3), Worksheet B, and Schedule J).

The previously taxed and untaxed accounts must be adjusted for the application of section 956 before the application of section 956A (see section 956A(a)(2)). Distributions are also taken into account before the section 956A inclusion is determined. Distributions generally are treated as coming first from (and thus reducing the balances of) the previously taxed accounts. Thus, U.S. shareholders must: **(1)** compute the current subpart F inclusion (potentially increasing that previously taxed account); **(2)** take into account current distributions (potentially reducing the previously taxed and untaxed

Worksheet E—U.S. Shareholder's Pro Rata Share of the CFC's Earnings Invested in Excess Passive Assets

Enter the amounts on lines 1 through 20 in functional currency.

1	Amount of passive assets (defined in section 956A(c)(2)) held by the CFC as of the close of:	
a	The first quarter of the tax year	1a
b	The second quarter of the tax year	1b
c	The third quarter of the tax year	1c
d	The fourth quarter of the tax year	1d
2	Number of quarter-ends the foreign corporation was a CFC during the tax year ▶	2
3	Average amount of passive assets held by the CFC as of the close of each quarter of the tax year. (Add lines 1a through 1d. Divide this sum by the number on line 2.)	3
4	Total assets held by the CFC as of the close of:	
a	The first quarter of the tax year.	4a
b	The second quarter of the tax year	4b
c	The third quarter of the tax year	4c
d	The fourth quarter of the tax year.	4d
5	Average total assets held by the CFC as of the close of each quarter of the tax year. (Add lines 4a through 4d. Divide this sum by the number on line 2.)	5
6	Multiply line 5 by 25%	6
7	Excess passive assets (subtract line 6 from line 3)	7
8	U.S. shareholder's pro rata share of the amount on line 7	8
9	U.S. shareholder's earnings and profits described in section 959(c)(1)(B) after reductions (if any) for current year distributions.	9
10	Subtract line 9 from line 8	10
11	Applicable earnings:	
a	Current earnings and profits.	11a
b	Line 11a plus accumulated earnings and profits	11b
12	Enter the greater of line 11a or line 11b.	12
13	Distributions made by the CFC during the tax year	13
14	Subtract line 13 from line 12	14
15	Earnings and profits described in section 959(c)(1) accumulated in tax years beginning after September 30, 1993 (determined after application of section 951(a)(1)(B))	15
16	Subtract line 15 from line 14	16
17	U.S. shareholder's pro rata share of the amount on line 16	17
18	U.S. shareholder's share of earnings invested in excess passive assets (smaller of line 10 or line 17).	18
19	Amount of line 18 excluded from gross income under section 959(a)(3)	19
20	Subtract line 19 from line 18	20
21	Translate the amount on line 20 from functional currency to U.S. dollars at the year-end spot rate (as provided in section 989(b)). Enter the result here and on line 5 of Schedule I	21

accounts); **(3)** compute the current section 956 inclusion (potentially reclassifying the subpart F previously taxed account); and **(4)** compute the current 956A inclusion (potentially increasing or reclassifying the previously taxed accounts).

Worksheet E applies for tax years of a CFC beginning after September 30, 1993, and to tax years of the U.S. shareholder in which or with which the tax year of the CFC ends. Excess passive assets are measured on a quarterly average basis.

In determining excess passive assets, the amount taken into account for an asset is its adjusted basis as determined for purposes of computing earnings and profits. A passive asset generally is an asset that produces passive income, as defined for passive foreign investment company purposes (sections 1296 and 1297), but excludes assets that are U.S. property under section 956. The term "excess passive assets" means the excess (if any) of the quarterly average amount of passive assets of the CFC, over 25 percent of the quarterly average amount of total assets of the CFC.

In determining the amount of excess passive assets of a CFC, all CFCs that are members of the same CFC group (defined in section 956A(d)(2)) are treated as one CFC. The amount of excess passive assets determined for that one CFC is allocated among the members of the CFC group in proportion to their respective amounts of applicable earnings.

If the foreign corporation ceases to be a CFC during the tax year: **(1)** the determination of the U.S. shareholder's pro rata share will be made based on the stock owned (within the meaning of section 958(a)) by the U.S. shareholder on the last day on which the foreign corporation is a CFC; **(2)** the amount of the CFC's excess passive assets for the tax year will be determined only by taking into account quarters ending on or before such last day (and passive and total assets as of the close of subsequent quarters should be recorded as zero on lines 1 and 4); and **(3)** in determining applicable earnings, current earnings and profits will include only earnings and profits that are allocable (on a pro rata basis) to the part of the year during which the foreign corporation is a CFC.

Schedule J

Use Schedule J to report accumulated E&P in functional currency, computed under sections 964(a) and 986(b).

Column (a)

Use column (a) to report the opening balance, current year additions and subtractions, and the closing balance in the foreign corporation's post-1986 undistributed earnings pool. Line 3 (E&P as of the close of the tax year, before actual or deemed distributions during the year s the denominator of the deemed-paid credit fraction under section 902(c)(1).

Column (b)

Use column (b) to report the aggregate amount of the foreign corporation's pre-1987 section 964(a) E&P accumulated since 1962 and not previously distributed or deemed distributed. These amounts are figured in U.S. dollars using the rules of section 1.964-1(a) through (e), translated into the foreign corporation's functional currency according to Notice 88-70, 1988-2 C.B. 369.

Column (c)

Use column (c) to report the running balance of the foreign corporation's previously taxed earnings and profits (PTI), or section 964(a) E&P accumulated since 1962 that have resulted in deemed inclusions under subpart F. Pre-1987 U.S. dollar PTI should be translated into the foreign corporation's functional currency using the rules of Notice 88-70 and added to post-1986 amounts in the appropriate PTI category. Include in column (c)(i) PTI attributable to, or reclassified as, investments in U.S. property (section 959(c)(1)(A) amounts). Include in column (c)(ii) PTI attributable to, or reclassified as, earnings invested in excess passive assets (section 959(c)(1)(B) amounts). Include in column (c)(iii) PTI attributable to subpart F income net of any reclassifications (section 959(c)(2) amounts).

Column (d)

Use column (d) to report the opening and closing balance of the foreign corporation's accumulated E&P. This amount is the sum of post-1986 undistributed earnings, pre-1987 section 964(a) E&P not previously taxed, and PTI.

Schedule M

Every U.S. person described in Category (4) must file Schedule M to report the transactions of the foreign corporation's annual accounting period ending with or within the U.S. person's tax year.

If a U.S. corporation that owns stock in a foreign corporation is a member of a consolidated group, list the common parent as the U.S. person filing the Schedule M.

Column b.—Use column (b) to report transactions between the CFC and the Category (4) person filing the return.

Lines 6 and 16.—Report on these lines dividends received and paid by the foreign corporation that have not been previously taxed under subpart F in the current year or in any prior year.

Lines 19 and 20.—Lines 19 and 20 request the largest outstanding balances during the year of gross amounts borrowed from, and gross amounts loaned to, the related parties described in columns (b) through (f). Do not enter aggregate cash flows, year-end loan balances, average balances, or net balances. Do not include open account balances resulting from sales and purchases reported under other items listed on Schedule M that arise and are collected in full in the ordinary course of business.

Schedule N

Note: *In computing a shareholder's taxable income (on the shareholder's income tax return), actual dividends are translated into U.S. dollars at the spot rate on the date the dividend is included in income. Deemed inclusions of undistributed foreign personal holding company income are translated into U.S. dollars at the weighted average exchange rate for the foreign corporation's tax year (as defined in Regulations section 1.989(b)-1).*

Who Must File

Every U.S. citizen or resident described in Category (1) must file Schedule N to report the activities of a foreign personal holding company. The information is submitted for the company's annual accounting period that ends with or within the officer's, director's, or shareholder's tax year.

Whether an individual is a Category (1) filer is determined on the date Form 5471 is required to be filed. If no individual qualifies as of that date, the determination is made on the last day of the foreign corporation's tax year in which there was such a person who was a U.S. citizen or resident.

If the corporation ceased to be a foreign personal holding company during the tax year or after the tax year ended, you must still file Schedule N if it was a foreign personal holding company at any time during the tax year.

First-time Filer.—If this is the first time you are submitting information required under section 6035, attach the following:

- A statement of stock ownership showing that during the corporation's tax year more than 50% in value of its outstanding stock was owned, directly or indirectly, by or for not more than five individual citizens or residents of the United States.

- A detailed statement of the conversion privileges of any outstanding securities that are convertible to the corporation's stock.

- A detailed statement of the respective rights of the various classes of shareholders if more than one class of stock is outstanding.

Exception. This information does not need to be submitted if it was previously furnished by another person.

Foreign Personal Holding Company

A foreign corporation qualifies as a foreign personal holding company if:
(a) at any time during the tax year more than 50% of the combined voting power of all classes of stock entitled to vote or the total value of the stock of the corporation is owned (directly or indirectly) by or for a group of five or fewer U.S. citizens or residents; and **(b)** the foreign corporation meets the "gross income test" (described below).

The following entities do not qualify as foreign personal holding companies:

- A corporation exempt from income tax under subchapter F (sections 501 through 528);

- A corporation organized and doing business under the banking and credit laws of a foreign country if it is established to the satisfaction of the Secretary that the corporation is not being used to avoid or evade taxes that would normally be imposed upon its shareholders. If the corporation meets this test, the Secretary will issue a certificate that the corporation is not a foreign personal holding company. Shareholders that meet this exception must attach a copy of the Secretary's certificate to their income tax return for each tax year that they are shareholders in the corporation.

Gross income test.—This test is met if at least 60% of the foreign corporation's gross income (as defined in section 555(a)) is foreign personal holding company income (defined below).

Once a foreign personal holding company meets the gross income test, the minimum percentage is lowered to 50% for any subsequent tax year. The foreign corporation will, however, continue to be considered a foreign personal holding company until either: **(a)** the stock requirement test is not met, or **(b)** the end of 3 consecutive tax years in each of which less than 50% of the gross income is foreign personal holding company income.

Foreign personal holding company income.—This type of income includes dividend income, interest income, rental income (unless such income constitutes 50% or more of the gross income of the foreign corporation), income from royalties, and income from annuities. It also includes gains from the sale or exchange of stock or securities (except for regular dealers of stock or securities), certain gains from commodities transactions, and certain income from estates and trusts, personal service contracts, and the use of the foreign corporation's property by a shareholder. See section 553 for more information.

Part I—Shareholder Information

Section A

List the outstanding securities of the foreign personal holding company that are convertible into the stock of the foreign personal holding company. List the interest rate and the face value of the securities at the beginning and end of the corporation's annual accounting period. Also list any options granted by the corporation during its tax year.

Section B

Identify each person who is the holder of convertible securities in the foreign personal holding company. Also, enter the class of securities held, the number and face value at the beginning and end of the corporation's tax year, and an explanation of any change in the holdings for each person holding the convertible securities.

Enter the name and address of each person granted an option for the stock of the foreign personal holding company.

Part II—Income Information

Section A

Line 4a. Taxes.—Enter the difference between the taxes deducted in computing taxable income and the taxes allowable under section 556(b)(1) in computing undistributed foreign personal holding company income.

Attach a schedule showing **(1)** the nature of income on which Federal income tax was paid or withheld at the source; **(2)** when and where the tax was paid or withheld; **(3)** the amount of tax paid or accrued; and **(4)** the tax year to which the tax relates.

Also, attach a schedule of income, war profits, and excess profits taxes of foreign countries and U.S. possessions accrued during the tax year not allowable as a deduction because a foreign tax credit was claimed.

Line 4b. Charitable contributions.— Enter the difference between the charitable contributions deducted in computing taxable income and the charitable contributions allowable under section 556(b)(2) in computing undistributed foreign personal holding company income. See section 556(b)(2) and the related regulations.

The carryover of charitable contributions made in a prior year is not allowed as a deduction in computing undistributed foreign personal holding company income for any tax year.

Line 4c. Special deductions disallowed.—The special deductions described in section 556(b)(3) are not allowed in computing undistributed foreign personal holding company income. Therefore, they must be added back to taxable income in computing undistributed foreign personal holding company income. Enter these amounts on line 4c as a positive number.

Line 4d. Net operating loss.—In computing undistributed foreign personal holding company income, only the amount of the net operating loss (as defined in section 172(c)) for the preceding tax year computed without the deductions provided in sections 241 through 247, 249, and 250 is allowed. Enter on line 4d the difference between this amount and the net operating loss deduction allowed in computing taxable income.

Line 4e. Expenses and depreciation applicable to property of the taxpayer.— Enter the total expenses limited by section 556(b)(5) as a positive number. In computing undistributed foreign personal holding company income, section 556(b)(5) limits the allowance of deductions for trade or business expenses and depreciation that are allocable to the operation and maintenance of the property owned or operated by a foreign personal holding company. These deductions will not be allowed in excess of the aggregate amount of the rent or other compensation received for the use of, or the right to use, the property unless it is established to the satisfaction of the Commissioner that:

1. The rent or other compensation received was the highest obtained, or, if none was received, that none was obtainable;

2. The property was held in the course of a business carried on for profit; and

3. Either there was reasonable expectation that the operation of the property would result in a profit or the property was necessary to the conduct of the business.

If excess deductions are claimed, attach a statement for each property showing the following:

1. A description of the property;

2. The cost or other basis to the corporation and the nature and value of the consideration paid for the property;

3. The name and address of the person from whom the property was acquired and the date the property was acquired;

4. The name and address of the person to whom the property was leased or rented, or the person permitted to use the property, and the number of shares of stock, if any, held by the person and the members of his or her family;

5. The nature (cash, securities, services, etc.) and the gross amount of rent or other compensation received or accrued for the use of, or the right to use, the property during the tax year and for each of the 5 preceding years and the amount of expense incurred for, and the depreciation sustained on, the property for such years;

6. Evidence that the rent or other compensation was the highest obtainable or, if none was received or accrued, a statement of the reason that none was received or accrued;

7. A copy of the contract, lease, or rental agreement;

8. The purpose for which the property was used;

9. The business carried on by the corporation for which the property was held and the gross income, expenses, and taxable income from the conduct of that business for the tax year and for each of the 5 preceding years;

10. The reasons for acquiring the property, for expecting that it would be profitable, and for using the property in the business of the corporation; and

11. Any other information in support of the deductions.

Line 4f. Taxes and contributions to pension trusts not allowable under section 556(b)(6).—Enter the total amount of any deductions taken in computing taxable income under the provisions of section 164(e), relating to taxes of a shareholder paid by the corporation, and section 404, relating to pension, etc., trusts.

Line 8. Deduction allowed under section 563(c) for dividends paid after close of tax year.—Enter all dividends paid after the close of the tax year and on or before the 15th day of the 3rd month following the close of the year if the foreign personal holding company designated such dividends as taken into account under section 563(c).

Note: *This amount may not exceed the amount entered on line 7. See section 563(c) for additional information.*

Section B

The deduction for dividends paid is the sum of the dividends paid during the tax year and the consent dividends for the tax year (determined under section 565). See sections 561 and 562.

Attach a copy of each dividend resolution. Also attach a concise statement of the pertinent facts relating to the payment of each dividend, clearly specifying **(a)** the medium of payment; **(b)** if not paid in money, the fair market value and adjusted basis (or face value, if paid in the corporation's own obligations) on the date of distribution of the property; and **(c)** the manner in which the fair market value and adjusted basis were determined.

Schedule O

Schedule O is used to report the organization or reorganization of a foreign corporation and the acquisition or disposition of its stock. Every U.S. citizen or resident described in Category (2) (examples are listed below) must complete Schedule O, Part I. Every U.S. person described in Category (3) (examples are listed below) must complete Schedule O, Part II. See Regulations section 1.6046-1(i) for rules on determining when U.S. persons constructively own stock of a foreign corporation and therefore are subject to the section 6046 filing requirements.

Examples of Category (2) Filers

1. Mr. Harris is a U.S. citizen who is a director of a foreign corporation. Mr. Johnson, also a U.S. citizen, acquired stock of that foreign corporation in the following transactions:

a. On March 1, 1994, Mr. Johnson acquires 2% in value of the foreign corporation's outstanding stock;

b. On October 1, 1994, Mr. Johnson acquires an additional 2% in value of the foreign corporation's outstanding stock; and

c. On December 1, 1994, Mr. Johnson acquires an additional 2% in value of the foreign corporation's outstanding stock.

Mr. Harris is required to report Mr. Johnson's December 1, 1994, transaction because Mr. Johnson at that point owned 5% or more in value of the outstanding stock of the foreign corporation.

2. The facts are the same as above. Also, Mr. Johnson acquires an additional 4% in value of the foreign corporation's outstanding stock on March 1, 1995; and on April 1, 1995, Mr. Johnson acquires an additional 2% in value of the foreign corporation's outstanding stock.

Mr. Harris does not have to complete Schedule O for the March 1, 1995, transaction because Mr. Johnson had not acquired an additional 5% or more in value of the outstanding stock of the foreign corporation since Mr. Harris last filed Form 5471 and Schedule O. Mr. Harris is, however, required to complete Schedule O for the April 1, 1995, transaction because Mr. Johnson had, at that time, acquired an additional 5% or more in value of the foreign corporation's outstanding stock.

Examples of Category (3) Filers

1. On June 10, 1993, a calendar year domestic corporation, Z, acquires 6% in value of the outstanding stock of a foreign corporation. Z completes Form 5471 and Schedule O to report this transaction. On July 7, 1994, Z acquires an additional 4% in value of the outstanding stock of the foreign corporation and on September 2, 1994, Z acquires an additional 2% in value of the foreign corporation's outstanding stock. Z is not required to complete Schedule O for the July 7, 1994, transaction, but Z must complete Schedule O to report the September 2, 1994, transaction because that transaction gives Z an additional 5% or more in value of the outstanding stock of the foreign corporation from the last time Z became liable for completing Schedule O (June 10, 1993).

2. On May 1, 1994, D, a domestic corporation, owns 15% in value of the outstanding stock of a foreign corporation. On August 7, 1994, the foreign corporation was reorganized. As a result, D then owned 7% in value of the foreign corporation's outstanding stock. D must complete Schedule O to report this transaction.

3. The facts are the same as in Example 2 above. Additionally, on October 1, 1994, D donates 3% in value of the outstanding stock of the foreign corporation to a charitable organization. D must complete Schedule O to report this transaction because the transaction reduces D's interest in the foreign corporation to less than 5% in value of its outstanding stock.

Part I

Column (d).—Enter the date on which the shareholder first owned 5% or more in value of the outstanding stock of the foreign corporation (i.e., the date on which the shareholder became a person described in Regulations section 1.6046-1(a)(2)(i)(a)).

Column (e).—Enter the date on which the shareholder acquired (whether in one or more transactions) an additional 5% or more in value of the outstanding stock of the foreign corporation (i.e., the date on which the shareholder became a person described in Regulations section 1.6046-1(a)(2)(i)(b)).

Part II

Section C—Acquisition of Stock

Section C is completed by shareholders who are completing Schedule O because they have acquired sufficient stock in a foreign corporation. If the shareholder acquired the stock in more than one transaction, use a separate line to report each transaction.

Column (d).—Enter the method of acquisition (e.g., purchase, gift, bequest, trade, etc.).

Column (e)(2).—Enter the number of shares acquired indirectly (within the meaning of section 958(a)(2)) by the shareholder listed in column (a).

Column (e)(3).—Enter the number of shares constructively owned (within the meaning of section 958(b)) by the shareholder listed in column (a).

Section D—Disposition of Stock

Shareholders who dispose of their interest (or part) in a foreign corporation must complete Section D.

Column (d).—Enter the method of disposition (e.g., sale, bequest, gift, trade, etc.).

Example for Section D

In 1992, Mr. Jackson, a U.S. citizen, purchased 10,000 shares of common stock of foreign corporation X. The purchase represented 10% ownership of the foreign corporation.

On July 1, 1994, Mr. Jackson made a gift of 5,000 shares of foreign corporation X to his son, John. Because Mr. Jackson has reduced his holding in the foreign corporation by 5%, he is required to complete Form 5471 and Schedule O. To show the required information about the disposition, Mr. Jackson completes Section D as follows:

- Enters his name in column (a).
- Enters "common" in column (b).
- Enters "July 1, 1994," in column (c).
- Enters "gift" in column (d).
- Enters "5,000" in column (e)(1).
- Enters "-0-" in column (f) because the disposition was by gift.
- Enters the name and address of his son, John, in column (g).

Section F

Example for Item (c)

Mr. Lyons acquires a 10% ownership in foreign corporation F. F is the 100% owner of two foreign corporations, FI and FJ. F is also a 50% owner of foreign corporation FK. In addition, F is 90% owned by foreign corporation W.

Mr. Lyons completes and files Form 5471 and Schedule O for the corporations in which he is a 5% or more shareholder.

In addition, Mr. Lyons is required to submit a schedule if the foreign corporation is a member of a chain of corporations, and to indicate if he is a 5% or more shareholder in any of those corporations.

Mr. Lyons would prepare a list showing the corporations in the following order:

- Corporation W
- Corporation F
- Corporation FI
- Corporation FJ
- Corporation FK

Then Mr. Lyons is required to indicate that he is a 5% or more shareholder in corporations F, FI, FJ, and FK.

Codes for Principal Business Activity

These codes for the Principal Business Activity are designed to classify enterprises by the type of activity in which they are engaged to facilitate the administration of the Internal Revenue Code. Though similar in format and structure to the Standard Industrial Classification (SIC) codes, they should not be used as SIC codes.

Using the list below, enter on page 1, item 1f, the code number for the specific industry group from which the largest percentage of "total receipts" is derived.

If, as its principal business activity, the corporation (1) purchases raw materials, (2) subcontracts out for labor to make a finished product from the raw materials, and (3) retains title to the goods, the corporation is considered to be a manufacturer and must enter one of the codes (2010 through 3998) under "Manufacturing."

Agriculture, Forestry, and Fishing
Code
- 0400 Agricultural production
- 0600 Agricultural services (except veterinarians), forestry, fishing, hunting, and trapping

Mining
Metal mining
- 1010 Iron ores
- 1070 Copper, lead and zinc, gold and silver ores
- 1098 Other metal mining
- 1150 Coal mining

Oil and gas extraction
- 1330 Crude petroleum, natural gas, and natural gas liquids
- 1380 Oil and gas field services

Nonmetalic minerals, except fuels
- 1430 Dimension, crushed and broken stone; sand and gravel
- 1498 Other nonmetallic minerals, except fuels

Construction
General building contractors and operative builders
- 1510 General building contractors
- 1531 Operative builders
- 1600 Heavy construction contractors

Special trade contractors
- 1711 Plumbing, heating, and air conditioning
- 1731 Electrical work
- 1798 Other special trade contractors

Manufacturing
Food and kindred products
- 2010 Meat products
- 2020 Dairy products
- 2030 Preserved fruits and vegetables
- 2040 Grain mill products
- 2050 Bakery products
- 2060 Sugar and confectionery products
- 2081 Malt liquors and malt
- 2088 Alcoholic beverages, except malt liquors and malt
- 2089 Bottled soft drinks, and flavorings
- 2096 Other food and kindred products
- 2100 Tobacco manufacturers

Textile mill products
- 2228 Weaving mills and textile finishing
- 2250 Knitting mills
- 2298 Other textile mill products

Apparel and other textile products
- 2315 Men's and boys' clothing
- 2345 Women's and children's clothing
- 2388 Other apparel and accessories
- 2390 Miscellaneous fabricated textile products

Lumber and wood products
- 2415 Logging, sawmills, and planing mills
- 2430 Millwork, plywood, and related products
- 2498 Other wood products, including wood buildings and mobile homes
- 2500 Furniture and fixtures

Code
Paper and allied products
- 2625 Pulp, paper, and board mills
- 2699 Other paper products

Printing and publishing
- 2710 Newspapers
- 2720 Periodicals
- 2735 Books, greeting cards, and miscellaneous publishing
- 2799 Commercial and other printing, and printing trade services

Chemicals and allied products
- 2815 Industrial chemicals, plastics materials and synthetics
- 2830 Drugs
- 2840 Soap, cleaners, and toilet goods
- 2850 Paints and allied products
- 2898 Agricultural and other chemical products

Petroleum refining and related industries (including those integrated with extraction)
- 2910 Petroleum refining (including integrated)
- 2998 Other petroleum and coal products

Rubber and misc. plastics products
- 3050 Rubber products, plastics footwear, hose and belting
- 3070 Misc. plastics products

Leather and leather products
- 3140 Footwear, except rubber
- 3198 Other leather and leather products

Stone, clay, and glass products
- 3225 Glass products
- 3240 Cement, hydraulic
- 3270 Concrete, gypsum, and plaster products
- 3298 Other nonmetallic mineral products

Primary metal industries
- 3370 Ferrous metal industries; misc. primary metal industries
- 3380 Nonferrous metal industries

Fabricated metal products
- 3410 Metal cans and shipping containers
- 3428 Cutlery, hand tools, and hardware; screw machine products, bolts, and similar products
- 3430 Plumbing and heating, except electric and warm air
- 3440 Fabricated structural metal products
- 3460 Metal forgings and stampings
- 3470 Coating, engraving, and allied services
- 3480 Ordnance and accessories, except vehicles and guided missiles
- 3490 Misc. fabricated metal products

Machinery, except electrical
- 3520 Farm machinery
- 3530 Construction and related machinery
- 3540 Metalworking machinery
- 3550 Special industry machinery
- 3560 General industrial machinery
- 3570 Office, computing, and accounting machines
- 3598 Other machinery except electrical

Code
Electrical and electronic equipment
- 3630 Household appliances
- 3665 Radio, television, and communication equipment
- 3670 Electronic components and accessories
- 3698 Other electrical equipment
- 3710 Motor vehicles and equipment

Transportation equipment, except motor vehicles
- 3725 Aircraft, guided missiles and parts
- 3730 Ship and boat building and repairing
- 3798 Other transportation equipment, except motor vehicles

Instruments and related products
- 3815 Scientific instruments and measuring devices; watches and clocks
- 3845 Optical, medical, and ophthalmic goods
- 3860 Photographic equipment and supplies
- 3998 Other manufacturing products

Transportation and Public Utilities
Transportation
- 4000 Railroad transportation
- 4100 Local and interurban passenger transit
- 4200 Trucking and warehousing
- 4400 Water transportation
- 4500 Transportation by air
- 4600 Pipe lines, except natural gas
- 4700 Miscellaneous transportation services

Communication
- 4825 Telephone, telegraph, and other communication services
- 4830 Radio and television broadcasting

Electric, gas, and sanitary services
- 4910 Electric services
- 4920 Gas production and distribution
- 4930 Combination utility services
- 4990 Water supply and other sanitary services

Wholesale Trade
Durable
- 5008 Machinery, equipment, and supplies
- 5010 Motor vehicles and automotive equipment
- 5020 Furniture and home furnishings
- 5030 Lumber and construction materials
- 5040 Sporting, recreational, photographic, and hobby goods, toys and supplies
- 5050 Metals and minerals, except petroleum and scrap
- 5060 Electrical goods
- 5070 Hardware, plumbing and heating equipment and supplies
- 5098 Other durable goods

Nondurable
- 5110 Paper and paper products
- 5129 Drugs, drug proprietaries, and druggists' sundries
- 5130 Apparel, piece goods, and notions
- 5140 Groceries and related products
- 5150 Farm-product raw materials
- 5160 Chemicals and allied products
- 5170 Petroleum and petroleum products
- 5180 Alcoholic beverages
- 5190 Misc. nondurable goods

Retail Trade
Building materials, garden supplies, and mobile home dealers
- 5220 Building materials dealers
- 5251 Hardware stores
- 5265 Garden supplies and mobile home dealers
- 5300 General merchandise stores

Food stores
- 5410 Grocery stores
- 5490 Other food stores

Automotive dealers and service stations
- 5515 Motor vehicle dealers
- 5541 Gasoline service stations
- 5598 Other automotive dealers
- 5600 Apparel and accessory stores
- 5700 Furniture and home furnishings stores
- 5800 Eating and drinking places

Code
Misc. retail stores
- 5912 Drug stores and proprietary stores
- 5921 Liquor stores
- 5995 Other retail stores

Finance, Insurance, and Real Estate
Banking
- 6030 Mutual savings banks
- 6060 Bank holding companies
- 6090 Banks, except mutual savings banks and bank holding companies

Credit agencies other than banks
- 6120 Savings and loan associations
- 6140 Personal credit institutions
- 6150 Business credit institutions
- 6199 Other credit agencies

Security, commodity brokers and services
- 6210 Security brokers, dealers, and flotation companies
- 6299 Commodity contracts brokers and dealers; security and commodity exchanges; and allied services

Insurance
- 6355 Life insurance
- 6356 Mutual insurance, except life or marine and certain fire or flood insurance companies
- 6359 Other insurance companies
- 6411 Insurance agents, brokers, and service

Real estate
- 6511 Real estate operators and lessors of buildings
- 6516 Lessors of mining, oil, and similar property
- 6518 Lessors of railroad property and other real property
- 6530 Condominium management and cooperative housing associations
- 6550 Subdividers and developers
- 6599 Other real estate

Holding and other investment companies, except bank holding companies
- 6744 Small business investment companies
- 6749 Other holding and investment companies except bank holding companies

Services
- 7000 Hotels and other lodging places
- 7200 Personal services

Business services
- 7310 Advertising
- 7389 Business services, except advertising

Auto repair; misc. repair services
- 7500 Auto repair and services
- 7600 Misc. repair services

Amusement and recreation services
- 7812 Motion picture production, distribution, and services
- 7830 Motion picture theaters
- 7900 Amusement and recreation services, except motion pictures

Other services
- 8015 Offices of physicians, including osteopathic physicians
- 8021 Offices of dentists
- 8040 Offices of other health practitioners
- 8050 Nursing and personal care facilities
- 8060 Hospitals
- 8071 Medical laboratories
- 8099 Other medical services
- 8111 Legal services
- 8200 Educational services
- 8300 Social services
- 8600 Membership organizations
- 8911 Architectural and engineering services
- 8930 Accounting, auditing, and bookkeeping
- 8980 Miscellaneous services (including veterinarians)

Form **8300**
(Rev. August 1997)
Department of the Treasury
Internal Revenue Service

Report of Cash Payments Over $10,000 Received in a Trade or Business
▶ See instructions for definition of cash.
▶ Use this form for transactions occurring after July 31, 1997.
Please type or print.

OMB No. 1545-0892

1 Check appropriate box(es) if: **a** ☐ Amends prior report;   **b** ☐ Suspicious transaction.

Part I — Identity of Individual From Whom the Cash Was Received

2 If more than one individual is involved, check here and see instructions . . . . ▶ ☐

3 Last name	4 First name	5 M.I.	6 Taxpayer identification number

7 Address (number, street, and apt. or suite no.)   **8** Date of birth ▶ M M D D Y Y Y Y (see instructions)

9 City	10 State	11 ZIP code	12 Country (if not U.S.)	13 Occupation, profession, or business

14 Document used to verify identity: **a** Describe identification ▶
   b Issued by   **c** Number

Part II — Person on Whose Behalf This Transaction Was Conducted

15 If this transaction was conducted on behalf of more than one person, check here and see instructions . . . . . ▶ ☐

16 Individual's last name or Organization's name	17 First name	18 M.I.	19 Taxpayer identification number

20 Doing business as (DBA) name (see instructions)   Employer identification number

21 Address (number, street, and apt. or suite no.)   **22** Occupation, profession, or business

23 City	24 State	25 ZIP code	26 Country (if not U.S.)

27 Alien identification: **a** Describe identification ▶
   b Issued by   **c** Number

Part III — Description of Transaction and Method of Payment

28 Date cash received M M D D Y Y Y Y	29 Total cash received $ .00	30 If cash was received in more than one payment, check here . . . ▶ ☐	31 Total price if different from item 29 $ .00

32 Amount of cash received (in U.S. dollar equivalent) (must equal item 29) (see instructions):

   a U.S. currency $ _____ .00 (Amount in $100 bills or higher $ _____ .00)
   b Foreign currency $ _____ .00 (Country ▶ _____)
   c Cashier's check(s) $ _____ .00 ⎫
   d Money order(s) $ _____ .00 ⎬ Issuer's name(s) and serial number(s) of the monetary instrument(s) ▶
   e Bank draft(s) $ _____ .00 ⎪
   f Traveler's check(s) $ _____ .00 ⎭

33 Type of transaction
   a ☐ Personal property purchased   **f** ☐ Debt obligations paid
   b ☐ Real property purchased   **g** ☐ Exchange of cash
   c ☐ Personal services provided   **h** ☐ Escrow or trust funds
   d ☐ Business services provided   **i** ☐ Bail bond
   e ☐ Intangible property purchased   **j** ☐ Other (specify) ▶

34 Specific description of property or service shown in 33. (Give serial or registration number, address, docket number, etc.) ▶

Part IV — Business That Received Cash

35 Name of business that received cash   **36** Employer identification number

37 Address (number, street, and apt. or suite no.)   Social security number

38 City	39 State	40 ZIP code	41 Nature of your business

42 Under penalties of perjury, I declare that to the best of my knowledge the information I have furnished above is true, correct, and complete.

Signature of authorized official   Title of authorized official

43 Date of signature M M D D Y Y Y Y   **44** Type or print name of contact person   **45** Contact telephone number ( )

For Paperwork Reduction Act Notice, see page 4.   Cat. No. 62133S   Form **8300** (Rev. 8-97)

Form 8300 (Rev. 8-97) Page **2**

Multiple Parties
(Complete applicable parts below if box 2 or 15 on page 1 is checked)

Part I — Continued—Complete if box 2 on page 1 is checked

3 Last name	4 First name	5 M.I.	6 Taxpayer identification number

7 Address (number, street, and apt. or suite no.)	8 Date of birth ▶ (see instructions) M M D D Y Y Y Y

9 City	10 State	11 ZIP code	12 Country (if not U.S.)	13 Occupation, profession, or business

14 Document used to verify identity: **a** Describe identification ▶
b Issued by **c** Number

---

3 Last name	4 First name	5 M.I.	6 Taxpayer identification number

7 Address (number, street, and apt. or suite no.)	8 Date of birth ▶ (see instructions) M M D D Y Y Y Y

9 City	10 State	11 ZIP code	12 Country (if not U.S.)	13 Occupation, profession, or business

14 Document used to verify identity: **a** Describe identification ▶
b Issued by **c** Number

Part II — Continued—Complete if box 15 on page 1 is checked

16 Individual's last name or Organization's name	17 First name	18 M.I.	19 Taxpayer identification number

20 Doing business as (DBA) name (see instructions)	Employer identification number

21 Address (number, street, and apt. or suite no.)	22 Occupation, profession, or business

23 City	24 State	25 ZIP code	26 Country (if not U.S.)

27 Alien identification: **a** Describe identification ▶
b Issued by **c** Number

---

16 Individual's last name or Organization's name	17 First name	18 M.I.	19 Taxpayer identification number

20 Doing business as (DBA) name (see instructions)	Employer identification number

21 Address (number, street, and apt. or suite no.)	22 Occupation, profession, or business

23 City	24 State	25 ZIP code	26 Country (if not U.S.)

27 Alien identification: **a** Describe identification ▶
b Issued by **c** Number

Item You Should Note

Clerks of Federal or State courts must now file Form 8300 if more than $10,000 in cash is received as bail for an individual(s) charged with certain criminal offenses. For these purposes, a clerk includes the clerk's office or any other office, department, division, branch, or unit of the court that is authorized to receive bail. If a person receives bail on behalf of a clerk, the clerk is treated as receiving the bail.

If multiple payments are made in cash to satisfy bail and the initial payment does not exceed $10,000, the initial payment and subsequent payments must be aggregated and the information return must be filed by the 15th day after receipt of the payment that causes the aggregate amount to exceed $10,000 in cash. In such cases, the reporting requirement can be satisfied either by sending a single written statement with an aggregate amount listed or by furnishing a copy of each Form 8300 relating to that payer. Payments made to satisfy separate bail requirements are not required to be aggregated. See Treasury Regulations section 1.6050I-2.

Casinos must file Form 8300 for nongaming activities (restaurants, shops, etc.).

General Instructions

Who must file.—Each person engaged in a trade or business who, in the course of that trade or business, receives more than $10,000 in cash in one transaction or in two or more related transactions, must file Form 8300. Any transactions conducted between a payer (or its agent) and the recipient in a 24-hour period are related transactions. Transactions are considered related even if they occur over a period of more than 24 hours if the recipient knows, or has reason to know, that each transaction is one of a series of connected transactions.

Keep a copy of each Form 8300 for 5 years from the date you file it.

Voluntary use of Form 8300.—Form 8300 may be filed voluntarily for any suspicious transaction (see **Definitions**), even if the total amount does not exceed $10,000.

Exceptions.—Cash is not required to be reported if it is received:

- By a financial institution required to file **Form 4789,** Currency Transaction Report.
- By a casino required to file (or exempt from filing) **Form 8362,** Currency Transaction Report by Casinos, if the cash is received as part of its gaming business.
- By an agent who receives the cash from a principal, if the agent uses all of the cash within 15 days in a second transaction that is reportable on Form 8300 or on Form 4789, and discloses all the information necessary to complete Part II of Form 8300 or Form 4789 to the recipient of the cash in the second transaction.
- In a transaction occurring entirely outside the United States. See **Pub. 1544,** Reporting Cash Payments Over $10,000 (Received in a Trade or Business), regarding transactions occurring in Puerto Rico, the Virgin Islands, and territories and possessions of the United States.
- In a transaction that is not in the course of a person's trade or business.

When to file.—File Form 8300 by the 15th day after the date the cash was received. If that date falls on a Saturday, Sunday, or legal holiday, file the form on the next business day.

Where to file.—File the form with the Internal Revenue Service, Detroit Computing Center, P.O. Box 32621, Detroit, MI 48232, or hand carry it to your local IRS office.

Statement to be provided.—You must give a written statement to each person named on a required Form 8300 on or before January 31 of the year following the calendar year in which the cash is received. The statement must show the name, telephone number, and address of the information contact for the business, the aggregate amount of reportable cash received, and that the information was furnished to the IRS. Keep a copy of the statement for your records.

Multiple payments.—If you receive more than one cash payment for a single transaction or for related transactions, you must report the multiple payments any time you receive a total amount that exceeds $10,000 within any 12-month period. Submit the report within 15 days of the date you receive the payment that causes the total amount to exceed $10,000. If more than one report is required within 15 days, you may file a combined report. File the combined report no later than the date the earliest report, if filed separately, would have to be filed.

Taxpayer identification number (TIN).—You must furnish the correct TIN of the person or persons from whom you receive the cash and, if applicable, the person or persons on whose behalf the transaction is being conducted. **You may be subject to penalties for an incorrect or missing TIN.**

The TIN for an individual (including a sole proprietorship) is the individual's social security number (SSN). For certain resident aliens who are not eligible to get an SSN and nonresident aliens who are required to file tax returns, it is an IRS Individual Taxpayer Identification Number (ITIN). For other persons, including corporations, partnerships, and estates, it is the employer identification number.

If you have requested but are not able to get a TIN for one or more of the parties to a transaction within 15 days following the transaction, file the report and attach a statement explaining why the TIN is not included.

Exception: *You are not required to provide the TIN of a person who is a nonresident alien individual or a foreign organization **if** that person does not have income effectively connected with the conduct of a U.S. trade or business **and** does not have an office or place of business, or fiscal or paying agent, in the United States. See Pub. 1544 for more information.*

Penalties.—You may be subject to penalties if you fail to file a correct and complete Form 8300 on time and you cannot show that the failure was due to reasonable cause. You may also be subject to penalties if you fail to furnish timely a correct and complete statement to each person named in a required report. A minimum penalty of $25,000 may be imposed if the failure is due to an intentional disregard of the cash reporting requirements.

Penalties may also be imposed for causing, or attempting to cause, a trade or business to fail to file a required report; for causing, or attempting to cause, a trade or business to file a required report containing a material omission or misstatement of fact; or for structuring, or attempting to structure, transactions to avoid the reporting requirements. These violations may also be subject to criminal prosecution which, upon conviction, may result in imprisonment of up to 5 years or fines of up to $250,000 for individuals and $500,000 for corporations or both.

Definitions

Cash.—The term "cash" means the following:

- U.S. and foreign coin and currency received in any transaction.
- A cashier's check, money order, bank draft, or traveler's check having a face amount of $10,000 or less that is received in a **designated reporting transaction** (defined below), or that is received in any transaction in which the recipient knows that the instrument is being used in an attempt to avoid the reporting of the transaction under section 6050I.

Note: *Cash does not include a check drawn on the payer's own account, such as a personal check, regardless of the amount.*

Designated reporting transaction.—A retail sale (or the receipt of funds by a broker or other intermediary in connection with a retail sale) of a consumer durable, a collectible, or a travel or entertainment activity.

Retail sale.—Any sale (whether or not the sale is for resale or for any other purpose) made in the course of a trade or business if that trade or business principally consists of making sales to ultimate consumers.

Consumer durable.—An item of tangible personal property of a type that, under ordinary usage, can reasonably be expected to remain useful for at least 1 year, and that has a sales price of more than $10,000.

Collectible.—Any work of art, rug, antique, metal, gem, stamp, coin, etc.

Travel or entertainment activity.—An item of travel or entertainment that pertains to a single trip or event if the combined sales price of the item and all other items relating to the same trip or event that are sold in the same transaction (or related transactions) exceeds $10,000.

Exceptions.—A cashier's check, money order, bank draft, or traveler's check is not considered received in a designated reporting transaction if it constitutes the proceeds of a bank loan or if it is received as a payment on certain promissory notes, installment sales contracts, or down payment plans. See Pub. 1544 for more information.

Person.—An individual, corporation, partnership, trust, estate, association, or company.

Recipient.—The person receiving the cash. Each branch or other unit of a person's trade or business is considered a separate recipient unless the branch receiving the cash (or a central office linking the branches), knows or has reason to know the identity of payers making cash payments to other branches.

Transaction.—Includes the purchase of property or services, the payment of debt, the exchange of a negotiable instrument for cash, and the receipt of cash to be held in escrow or trust. A single transaction may not be broken into multiple transactions to avoid reporting.

Suspicious transaction.—A transaction in which it appears that a person is attempting to cause Form 8300 not to be filed, or to file a false or incomplete form. The term also includes any transaction in which there is an indication of possible illegal activity.

Specific Instructions

You must complete all parts. However, you may skip Part II if the individual named in Part I is conducting the transaction on his or her behalf only.

Item 1.—If you are amending a prior report, check box 1a. Complete the appropriate items with the correct or amended information only. Complete all of Part IV. Staple a copy of the original report to the amended report.

To voluntarily report a suspicious transaction (see **Definitions**), check box 1b. You may also telephone your local IRS Criminal Investigation Division or call 1-800-800-2877.

Part I

Item 2.—If two or more individuals conducted the transaction you are reporting, check the box and complete Part I for any one of the individuals. Provide the same information for the other individual(s) on the back of the form. If more than three individuals are involved, provide the same information on additional sheets of paper and attach them to this form.

Item 6.—Enter the taxpayer identification number (TIN) of the individual named. See **Taxpayer identification number (TIN)** under **General Instructions** for more information.

Item 8.—Enter eight numerals for the date of birth of the individual named. For example, if the individual's birth date is July 6, 1960, enter 07 06 1960.

Item 13.—Fully describe the nature of the occupation, profession, or business (for example, "plumber," "attorney," or "automobile dealer"). Do not use general or nondescriptive terms such as "businessman" or "self-employed."

Item 14.—You must verify the name and address of the named individual(s). Verification must be made by examination of a document normally accepted as a means of identification when cashing checks (for example, a driver's license, passport, alien registration card, or other official document). In item 14a, enter the type of document examined. In item 14b, identify the issuer of the document. In item 14c, enter the document's number. For example, if the individual has a Utah driver's license, enter "driver's license" in item 14a, "Utah" in item 14b, and the number appearing on the license in item 14c.

Part II

Item 15.—If the transaction is being conducted on behalf of more than one person (including husband and wife or parent and child), check the box and complete Part II for any one of the persons. Provide the same information for the other person(s) on the back of the form. If more than three persons are involved, provide the same information on additional sheets of paper and attach them to this form.

Items 16 through 19.—If the person on whose behalf the transaction is being conducted is an individual, complete items 16, 17, and 18. Enter his or her TIN in item 19. If the individual is a sole proprietor and has an employer identification number (EIN), you must enter both the SSN and EIN in item 19. If the person is an organization, put its name as shown on required tax filings in item 16 and its EIN in item 19.

Item 20.—If a sole proprietor or organization named in items 16 through 18 is doing business under a name other than that entered in item 16 (e.g., a "trade" or "doing business as (DBA)" name), enter it here.

Item 27.—If the person is **NOT** required to furnish a TIN (see **Taxpayer identification number (TIN)** under **General Instructions**), complete this item. Enter a description of the type of official document issued to that person in item 27a (for example, "passport"), the country that issued the document in item 27b, and the document's number in item 27c.

Part III

Item 28.—Enter the date you received the cash. If you received the cash in more than one payment, enter the date you received the payment that caused the combined amount to exceed $10,000. See **Multiple payments** under **General Instructions** for more information.

Item 30.—Check this box if the amount shown in item 29 was received in more than one payment (for example, as installment payments or payments on related transactions).

Item 31.—Enter the total price of the property, services, amount of cash exchanged, etc. (for example, the total cost of a vehicle purchased, cost of catering service, exchange of currency) if different from the amount shown in item 29.

Item 32.—Enter the dollar amount of each form of cash received. Show foreign currency amounts in U.S. dollar equivalent at a fair market rate of exchange available to the public. **The sum of the amounts must equal item 29.** For cashier's check, money order, bank draft, or traveler's check, provide the name of the issuer and the serial number of each instrument. Names of all issuers and all serial numbers involved must be provided. If necessary, provide this information on additional sheets of paper and attach them to this form.

Item 33.—Check the appropriate box(es) that describe the transaction. If the transaction is not specified in boxes a–i, check box j and briefly describe the transaction (for example, car lease, boat lease, house lease, aircraft rental).

Part IV

Item 36.—If you are a sole proprietorship, you must enter your SSN. If your business also has an EIN, you must provide the EIN as well. All other business entities must enter an EIN.

Item 41.—Fully describe the nature of your business, for example, "attorney," "jewelry dealer." Do not use general or nondescriptive terms such as "business" or "store."

Item 42.—This form must be signed by an individual who has been authorized to do so for the business that received the cash.

Paperwork Reduction Act Notice

The requested information is useful in criminal, tax, and regulatory investigations, for instance, by directing the Federal Government's attention to unusual or questionable transactions. Trades or businesses are required to provide the information under 26 U.S.C. 6050I.

You are not required to provide the information requested on a form that is subject to the Paperwork Reduction Act unless the form displays a valid OMB control number. Books or records relating to a form or its instructions must be retained as long as their contents may become material in the administration of any Internal Revenue law. Generally, tax returns and return information are confidential, as required by Code section 6103.

The time needed to complete this form will vary depending on individual circumstances. The estimated average time is 21 minutes. If you have comments concerning the accuracy of this time estimate or suggestions for making this form simpler, you can write to the Tax Forms Committee, Western Area Distribution Center, Rancho Cordova, CA 95743-0001. DO NOT send this form to this office. Instead, see **Where To File** on page 3.

Department of the Treasury

Internal Revenue Service

Publication 1544
(Rev. Aug. 97)
Cat. No. 12696A

Reporting Cash Payments of Over $10,000
(Received in a Trade or Business)

Get forms and other information faster and easier by:
COMPUTER
• World Wide Web • http://www.irs.ustreas.gov
• FTP • ftp.irs.ustreas.gov
• IRIS at FedWorld • (703) 321-8020
FAX
• From your FAX machine, dial • (703) 487-4160
See *How To Get More Information* in this publication.

Introduction

If, in a 12-month period, you receive more than $10,000 in cash from one buyer as a result of a transaction in your trade or business, you must report it to the Internal Revenue Service (IRS) on Form 8300, *Report of Cash Payments Over $10,000 Received in a Trade or Business*.

This publication explains why, when, and where to report these cash payments. It also discusses the substantial penalties for not reporting them.

Some organizations do not have to file Form 8300, including financial institutions who must file Form 4789, *Currency Transaction Report*, and casinos who must file Form 8362, *Currency Transaction Report by Casinos*. They are not discussed in this publication.

This publication explains key issues and terms related to Form 8300. You should also read the instructions attached to the form. They explain what to enter on each line.

Why Report These Payments?

Congress passed the Tax Reform Act of 1984 and the Anti-Drug Abuse Act of 1988. These Acts require you to report certain cash payments of over $10,000.

Often smugglers and drug dealers use large cash payments to "launder" money from illegal activities. Laundering means converting "dirty" or illegally-gained money to "clean" money.

The government can often trace this laundered money through the payments you report. Your compliance with the law provides valuable information that can stop those who evade taxes and those who profit from the drug trade and other criminal activities.

Who Must File Form 8300?

Generally, any person in a trade or business who receives more than $10,000 in cash in a single transaction or in related transactions must file Form 8300.

For example, you may have to file Form 8300 if you are a dealer in jewelry, furniture, boats, aircraft, or automobiles; a pawnbroker; an attorney; a real estate broker; an insurance company; or a travel agency. Special rules for clerks of federal or state courts are discussed later under *Bail for certain criminal offenses*.

However, you do not have to file Form 8300 if the transaction is not related to your trade or business. For example, if you own a jewelry store and sell your personal automobile for more than $10,000 in cash, you would not submit a Form 8300 for that transaction.

Transaction defined. A "transaction" occurs when:

- Goods, services, or property are sold.
- Property is rented.
- Cash is exchanged for other cash.
- A contribution is made to a trust or escrow account.

- A loan is made or repaid.
- Cash is converted to a negotiable instrument, such as a check or a bond.

Person defined. A "person" includes an individual, a company, a corporation, a partnership, an association, a trust, or an estate.

Exempt organizations, including employee plans, are also "persons." But, exempt organizations do not have to file Form 8300 for a more-than-$10,000 charitable cash contribution they receive since it is not received in the course of a trade or business.

Foreign transactions. You do not have to file Form 8300 if the entire transaction (including the receipt of cash) takes place outside of:

- The 50 states,
- The District of Columbia,
- Puerto Rico, or
- A possession or territory of the United States.

However, you must file Form 8300 if any part of the transaction (including the receipt of cash) occurs in Puerto Rico or a possession or territory of the United States and you are subject to the Internal Revenue Code.

Bail for certain criminal offenses. Any clerk of a Federal or state court who receives more than $10,000 in cash as bail for an individual charged with any of the following criminal offenses must file Form 8300:

1) Any Federal offense involving a controlled substance,
2) Racketeering,
3) Money laundering, and
4) Any state offense substantially similar to (1), (2), or (3) above.

For more information about the rules that apply to court clerks, see Section 1.6050I–2 of the Income Tax Regulations.

What Payments Must Be Reported?

You must file Form 8300 to report cash paid to you if it is:

1) Over $10,000,
2) Received as:
   a) One lump sum of over $10,000,
   b) Installment payments that cause the total cash received within one year of the initial payment to total more than $10,000, or
   c) Other previously unreportable payments that cause the total cash received within a 12-month period to total more than $10,000,
3) Received in the course of your trade or business,
4) Received from the same buyer (or agent), and
5) Received in a single transaction or in related transactions (defined later).

What Is Cash?

Cash is:

1) The coins and currency of the United States (and any other country), and
2) Cashier's checks, bank drafts, traveler's checks, and money orders you receive, if they have a face amount of *$10,000 or less* and you receive them in:
   a) A designated reporting transaction (defined later), or
   b) Any transaction in which you know the payer is trying to avoid the reporting of the transaction on Form 8300.

Note. Cash may include a cashier's check even if it is called a "treasurer's check" or "bank check."

Cash does not include a check drawn on an individual's personal account.

A cashier's check, bank draft, traveler's check, or money order with a face amount of *more than $10,000* is not treated as cash. (These items are not defined as cash and you do not have to file Form 8300 when you receive them because, if they were bought with currency, the bank or other financial institution that issued them must file a report on Form 4789.)

Example 1. You are a coin dealer. Bob Green buys gold coins from you for $13,200. He pays for them with $6,200 in U.S. currency and a cashier's check having a face amount of $7,000. The cashier's check is treated as cash. You have received more than $10,000 cash and must file Form 8300 for this transaction.

Example 2. You are a retail jeweler. Mary North buys an item of jewelry from you for $12,000. She pays for it with a personal check payable to you in the amount of $9,600 and traveler's checks totaling $2,400. Because the personal check is not treated as cash, you have not received more than $10,000 cash in the transaction. You do not have to file Form 8300.

Example 3. You are a boat dealer. Emily Jones buys a boat from you for $16,500. She pays for it with a cashier's check payable to you in the amount of $16,500. The cashier's check is not treated as cash because its face amount is more than $10,000. You do not have to file Form 8300 for this transaction.

Designated Reporting Transaction

A designated reporting transaction is the retail sale of any of the following:

1) A consumer durable, such as an automobile or boat. A consumer durable is property, other than land or buildings, that:
   a) Is suitable for personal use,
   b) Can reasonably be expected to last at least one year under ordinary use,
   c) Has a sales price of more than $10,000, and
   d) Can be seen or touched (tangible property).

   For example, a $20,000 car is a consumer durable, but a $20,000 dump truck or factory machine is not. The car is a consumer durable even if you sell it to a buyer who will use it in a business.

2) A collectible (a work of art, rug, antique, metal, gem, stamp, or coin).
3) Travel or entertainment, if the total sales price of all items sold for the same trip or entertainment event in one transaction (or related transactions) is more than $10,000.

To figure the total sales price of all items sold for a trip or entertainment event, you include the sales price of items such as airfare, hotel rooms, and admission tickets.

Example. You are a travel agent. Ed Johnson asks you to charter a passenger airplane to take a group to a sports event in another city. He also asks you to book hotel rooms and admission tickets for the group. In payment, he gives you two money orders, each for $6,000. You have received more than $10,000 cash in this designated reporting transaction. You must file Form 8300.

Retail sale. The term "retail sale" means any sale made in the course of a trade or business that consists mainly of making sales to ultimate consumers.

Thus, if your business consists mainly of making sales to ultimate consumers, all sales you make in the course of that business are retail sales. This includes any sales of items that will be resold.

Broker or intermediary. A designated reporting transaction includes the retail sale of items (1), (2), or (3) of the preceding list, even if the funds are received by a broker or other intermediary, rather than directly by the seller.

Exceptions to Definition of Cash

A cashier's check, bank draft, traveler's check, or money order you received in a designated reporting transaction is not treated as cash if one of the following exceptions applies.

Exception for certain bank loans. A cashier's check, bank draft, traveler's check, or money order is not treated as cash if it is the proceeds from a bank loan. As proof that it is from a bank loan, you may rely on a copy of the loan document, a written statement or lien instruction from the bank, or similar proof.

Example. You are a car dealer. Mandy White buys a new car from you for $11,500. She pays you with $2,000 of U.S. currency and a cashier's check for $9,500 payable to you and her. You can tell that the cashier's check is the proceeds of a bank loan because it includes instructions to you to have a lien put on the car as security for the loan. For this reason, the cashier's check is not treated as cash. You do not have to file Form 8300 for the transaction.

Exception for certain installment sales. A cashier's check, bank draft, traveler's check, or money order is not treated as cash if it is received in payment on a promissory note or an installment sales contract (including a lease that is considered a sale for federal tax purposes). However, this exception applies only if:

1) You use similar notes or contracts in other sales to ultimate consumers in the ordinary course of your trade or business, and

2) The total payments for the sale that you receive on or before the 60th day after the sale are 50 % or less of the purchase price.

Exception for certain down payment plans. A cashier's check, bank draft, traveler's check, or money order is not treated as cash if you received it in payment for a consumer durable or collectible, and all three of the following statements are true.

1) You receive it under a payment plan requiring:
   a) One or more down payments, and
   b) Payment of the rest of the purchase price by the date of sale.
2) You receive it more than 60 days before the date of sale.
3) You use payment plans with the same or substantially similar terms when selling to ultimate consumers in the ordinary course of your trade or business.

Exception for travel and entertainment. A cashier's check, bank draft, traveler's check, or money order received for travel or entertainment is not treated as cash if all three of the following statements are true.

1) You receive it under a payment plan requiring:
   a) One or more down payments, and
   b) Payment of the rest of the purchase price by the earliest date that any travel or entertainment item (such as airfare) is furnished for the trip or entertainment event.
2) You receive it more than 60 days before the date on which the final payment is due.
3) You use payment plans with the same or substantially similar terms when selling to ultimate consumers in the ordinary course of your trade or business.

Taxpayer Identification Number (TIN)

You must furnish the correct TIN of the person or persons from whom you receive the cash. If the transaction is conducted on the behalf of another person or persons, you must furnish the TIN of that person or persons. If you do not know a person's TIN, you have to ask for it. You may be subject to penalties for an incorrect or missing TIN.

There are three types of TINs.

1) The TIN for an individual, including a sole proprietor, is the individual's social security number (SSN).
2) The TIN for a nonresident alien individual who needs a TIN but is not eligible to get an SSN is an IRS individual taxpayer identification number (ITIN). An ITIN has nine digits, similar to an SSN.
3) The TIN for other persons, including corporations, partnerships, and estates, is the employer identification number.

Exception. A nonresident alien individual or a foreign organization does not have to have a TIN, and so you do not have to furnish a TIN for them, if all the following are true.

1) The individual or organization does not have income effectively connected with the conduct of a trade or business in the United States, or an office or place of business or fiscal or paying agent in the United States, at any time during the year.
2) The individual or organization does not file a Federal tax return.
3) In the case of a nonresident alien individual, the individual has not chosen to file a joint federal income tax return with a spouse who is a U.S. citizen or resident.

What Is A Related Transaction?

Any transactions between a buyer (or an agent of the buyer) and a seller that occur within a 24-hour period are related transactions. If you receive over $10,000 in cash during two or more transactions with one buyer in a 24-hour period, you must treat the transactions as one transaction and report the payments on Form 8300.

For example, if you sell two products for $6,000 each to the same customer in one day and the customer pays you in cash, these are related transactions. Because they total $12,000 (more than $10,000), you must file Form 8300.

More than 24 hours between transactions. Transactions are related even if they are more than 24 hours apart if you know, or have reason to know, that each is one of a series of connected transactions.

For example, you are a travel agent. A client pays you $8,000 in cash for a trip. Two days later, the same client pays you $3,000 more in cash to include another person on the trip. These are related transactions, and you must file Form 8300 to report them.

What About Suspicious Transactions?

If you receive $10,000 or less in cash, you may voluntarily file Form 8300 if the transaction appears to be suspicious.

A transaction is suspicious if it appears that a person is trying to cause you not to file Form 8300 or is trying to cause you to file a false or incomplete Form 8300, or if there is a sign of possible illegal activity.

If you are suspicious, you are encouraged to call the local IRS Criminal Investigation Division as soon as possible. Or, you can call toll free 1–800–800–2877.

When, Where, and What To File

The amount you receive and when you receive it determine when you must file. Generally, you must file Form 8300 within 15 days after receiving a payment. If the Form 8300 due date (the 15th or last day you can timely file the form) falls on a Saturday, Sunday, or holiday, it is delayed until the next day that is not a Saturday, Sunday, or holiday.

More than one payment. In some transactions, the buyer may arrange to pay you in cash installment payments. If the first payment is more than $10,000, you must file Form 8300 within 15 days. If the first payment is not more than $10,000, you must add the first payment and any later payments made within one year of the first payment. When the total cash payments are more than $10,000, you must file Form 8300 within 15 days.

After you file Form 8300, you must start a new count of cash payments received from that buyer. If you receive more than $10,000 in additional cash payments from that buyer within a 12-month period, you must file another Form 8300. You must file the form within 15 days of the payment that causes the additional payments to total more than $10,000.

If you are already required to file Form 8300 and you receive additional payments within the 15 days before you must file, you can report all the payments on one form.

Example. On January 10, you receive a cash payment of $11,000. You receive additional cash payments on the same transaction of $4,000 on February 15, $5,000 on March 20, and $6,000 on May 12. By January 25, you must file a Form 8300 for the $11,000 payment. By May 27, you must file an additional Form 8300 for the additional payments that total $15,000.

Where to file. You can mail the form to the address given in the Form 8300 instructions, or you can hand carry it to your local IRS office.

Required statement to buyer. You must give a written statement to each person named on any Form 8300 you must file. The statement must show the name and address of your business, the name and phone number of a contact person, and the total amount of reportable cash you received from the person during the year. It must state that you are also reporting this information to the IRS.

You must send this statement to the buyer by January 31 of the year after the year in which you received the cash that caused you to file the form.

 You must keep a copy of every Form 8300 you file for 5 years.

Examples

Example 1. Pat Brown is the sales manager for Small Town Cars. On July 1, 1997, Jane Smith buys a new car from Pat and pays $18,000 in cash. Pat asks for identification from Jane to get the necessary information to complete Form 8300. A filled-in form is shown in this publication.

Pat must mail the form to the address shown in the form's instructions by July 16, 1997. He must also send a statement to Jane by January 31, 1998.

Example 2. Using the same facts given in Example 1, suppose Jane had arranged to make cash payments of $6,000 each on July 1, August 1, and September 1. Pat would have to file a Form 8300 by August 16 because he would have received two cash payments within one year (July and August) that total over $10,000. Pat would not have to report the remaining $6,000 cash payment because it is not more than $10,000. However, he could report it if he felt it was a suspicious transaction.

Penalties

There are *civil penalties* for failure to:

- File a correct Form 8300 by the date it is due, and
- Provide the required statement to those named in the Form 8300.

If you intentionally disregard the requirement to file a correct Form 8300 by the date it is due, the penalty is the larger of:

1) $25,000, or
2) The amount of cash you received and were required to report (up to $100,000).

There are *criminal penalties* for:

- Willful failure to file Form 8300,
- Willfully filing a false or fraudulent Form 8300,
- Stopping or trying to stop Form 8300 from being filed, and
- Setting up, helping to set up, or trying to set up a transaction in a way that would make it seem unnecessary to file Form 8300.

If you willfully fail to file Form 8300, you can be fined up to $250,000 ($500,000 for corporations) or sentenced to up to 5 years in prison, or both. These dollar amounts are based on Section 3571 of Title 18 of the U.S. Code.

The penalties for failure to file may also apply to any person (including a payer) who attempts to interfere with or prevent the seller (or business) from filing a correct Form 8300. This includes any attempt to structure the transaction in a way that would make it seem unnecessary to file Form 8300. Structuring means breaking up a large cash transaction into small cash transactions.

How To Get More Information

You can get help from the IRS in several ways.

Free publications and forms. To order free publications and forms, call 1–800–TAX–FORM (1–800–829–3676). You can also write to the IRS Forms Distribution Center nearest you. Check your income tax package for the address. Your local library or post office also may have the items you need.

For a list of free tax publications, order Publication 910, *Guide to Free Tax Services.* It also contains an index of tax topics and related publications and describes other free tax information services available from IRS, including tax education and assistance programs.

If you have access to a personal computer and modem, you also can get many forms and publications electronically. See *Quick and Easy Access To Tax Help and Forms* in your income tax package for details.

Tax questions. You can call the IRS with your tax questions. Check your income tax package or telephone book for the local number, or you can call 1–800–829–1040.

TTY/TDD equipment. If you have access to TTY/TDD equipment, you can call 1–800–829–4059 to ask tax questions or to order forms and publications. See your income tax package for the hours of operation.

Form 8362
(Rev. July 1997)
Department of the Treasury
Internal Revenue Service

Currency Transaction Report by Casinos
▶ Use this revision for reportable transactions occuring after June 30, 1997.
▶ Please type or print.
(Complete all applicable parts—see instructions.)

OMB No. 1506-0005

1 If this Form 8362 (CTRC) is submitted to **amend a prior report** check here: ☐ and attach a copy of the original CTRC to this form.

Part I — Person(s) Involved in Transaction(s)

Section A—Person(s) on Whose Behalf Transaction(s) Is Conducted (Customer)

2 ☐ Multiple persons

3 Individual's last name or Organization's name

4 First name

5 M.I.

6 Permanent address (number, street, and apt. or suite no.)

7 SSN or EIN

8 City **9** State **10** ZIP code **11** Country (if not U.S.) **12** Date of birth M M D D Y Y Y Y

13 Method used to verify identity: **a** ☐ Examined identification credential/document **b** ☐ Known customer - information on file **c** ☐ Organization

14 Describe identification credential: **a** ☐ Driver's license/State I.D. **b** ☐ Passport **c** ☐ Alien registration **d** ☐ Other _____
e Issued by: _____ **f** Number:

15 Customer's Account Number

Section B—Individual(s) Conducting Transaction(s) – If other than above (Agent)

16 ☐ Multiple agents

17 Individual's last name

18 First name

19 M.I.

20 Permanent address (number, street, and apt. or suite no.)

21 SSN

22 City **23** State **24** ZIP code **25** Country (if not U.S.) **26** Date of birth M M D D Y Y Y Y

27 Method used to verify identity: **a** ☐ Examined identification credential/document **b** ☐ Known customer - information on file

28 Describe identification credential: **a** ☐ Driver's license/State I.D. **b** ☐ Passport **c** ☐ Alien registration **d** ☐ Other _____
e Issued by: _____ **f** Number:

Part II — Amount and Type of Transaction(s) (Complete all items that apply.)

29 ☐ Multiple transactions

30 CASH IN: (in U.S. dollar equivalent)

- **a** Purchase(s) of casino chips, tokens, and other gaming instruments $ _____
- **b** Deposit(s) (front money or safekeeping) _____
- **c** Payment(s) on credit (including markers) _____
- **d** Bet(s) of currency _____
- **e** Currency received from wire transfer(s) out _____
- **f** Purchase(s) of casino check(s) _____
- **g** Currency exchange(s) _____
- **h** Other (specify) _____
- **i** Enter total amount of CASH IN transaction(s) ▶ $ _____

31 CASH OUT: (in U.S. dollar equivalent)

- **a** Redemption(s) of casino chips, tokens, and other gaming instruments $ _____
- **b** Withdrawal(s) of deposit (front money or safekeeping) _____
- **c** Advance(s) on credit (including markers) _____
- **d** Payment(s) on bet(s) (including slot jackpot(s)) _____
- **e** Currency paid from wire transfer(s) in _____
- **f** Negotiable instrument(s) cashed (including checks) _____
- **g** Currency exchange(s) _____
- **h** Travel and complimentary expenses and gaming incentives _____
- **i** Payment for tournament, contest or other promotions _____
- **j** Other (specify) _____
- **k** Enter total amount of CASH OUT transaction(s) ▶ $ _____

32 Date of transaction (see instructions) M M D D Y Y Y Y

33 Foreign currency used _____ (Country)

Part III — Casino Reporting Transaction(s)

34 Casino's trade name

35 Casino's legal name

36 Employer identification number (EIN)

37 Address (number, street, and apt. or suite no.) where transaction occurred

38 City **39** State **40** ZIP code

Sign Here ▶

41 Title of approving official

42 Signature of approving official

43 Date of signature M M D D Y Y Y Y

44 Type or print preparer's name

45 Type or print name of person to contact

46 Contact telephone number ( )

For Paperwork Reduction Act Notice, see page 2.   Cat. No. 62291Z   Form **8362** (Rev. 7-97)

Form 8362 (Rev. 7-97) Page **2**

Multiple Persons or Multiple Agents
(Complete applicable parts below if box 2 or box 16 on page 1 is checked.)

Part I Continued

Section A—Person(s) on Whose Behalf Transaction(s) Is Conducted (Customer)

| 3 Individual's last name or Organization's name | 4 First name | 5 M.I. |

| 6 Permanent address (number, street, and apt. or suite no.) | 7 SSN or EIN |

| 8 City | 9 State | 10 ZIP code | 11 Country (if not U.S.) | 12 Date of birth M M D D Y Y Y Y |

13 Method used to verify identity: **a** ☐ Examined identification credential/document   **b** ☐ Known customer - information on file   **c** ☐ Organization

14 Describe identification credential: **a** ☐ Driver's license/State I.D.   **b** ☐ Passport   **c** ☐ Alien registration   **d** ☐ Other _____
 e Issued by: **f** Number:

15 Customer's Account Number

Section B—Individual(s) Conducting Transaction(s) – If other than above (Agent)

| 17 Individual's last name | 18 First name | 19 M.I. |

| 20 Permanent address (number, street, and apt. or suite no.) | 21 SSN |

| 22 City | 23 State | 24 ZIP code | 25 Country (if not U.S.) | 26 Date of birth M M D D Y Y Y Y |

27 Method used to verify identity: **a** ☐ Examined identification credential/document   **b** ☐ Known customer - information on file

28 Describe identification credential: **a** ☐ Driver's license/State I.D.   **b** ☐ Passport   **c** ☐ Alien registration   **d** ☐ Other _____
 e Issued by: **f** Number:

Paperwork Reduction Act Notice.—The requested information is useful in criminal, tax, and regulatory investigations and proceedings. Financial institutions are required to provide the information under 31 U.S.C. 5313 and 31 CFR Part 103, commonly referred to as the Bank Secrecy Act (BSA). The BSA is administered by the U.S. Department of the Treasury's Financial Crimes Enforcement Network (FinCEN). You are not required to provide the requested information unless a form displays a valid OMB control number.

The time needed to complete this form will vary depending on individual circumstances. The estimated average time is 19 minutes. If you have comments concerning the accuracy of this time estimate or suggestions for improving this form, you may write to the **Tax Forms Committee,** Western Area Distribution Center, Rancho Cordova, CA 95743-0001. **DO NOT** send this form to this address. Instead, see **When and Where To File** below.

General Instructions

Form 8362.—Use the July 1997 revision of Form 8362 for reportable transactions occurring after June 30, 1997. Use the May 1992 revision of Form 8362 for reportable transactions occurring before July 1, 1997.

Suspicious Transactions.—If a transaction is greater than $10,000 in currency as well as suspicious, casinos must file a Form 8362 and are encouraged to report suspicious transactions and activities on **Form TDF 90-22.47,** Suspicious Activity Report (SAR). Banks and other depository institutions currently are required to use the SAR to report suspicious activities. A SAR for casinos is under development and, once issued, a casino will use this SAR for reporting a suspicious transaction or activity, rather than reporting such activity on Form TDF 90-22.47.

DO NOT use Form 8362 to **(1)** report suspicious transactions involving $10,000 or less in currency OR **(2)** indicate that a transaction of more than $10,000 is suspicious.

When a suspicious activity requires immediate attention, casinos should telephone 1-800-800-CTRS, Monday through Friday, from 9:00 a.m. to 6:00 p.m. Eastern Standard Time (EST). An Internal Revenue Service (IRS) employee will direct the call to the local office of the IRS Criminal Investigation Division (CID). In an emergency, consult directory assistance for the local IRS CID office.

Who Must File.—Any organization duly licensed or authorized to do business as a casino or gambling casino in the United States (except casinos located in Nevada) and having gross annual gaming revenues in excess of $1 million must file Form 8362. This includes the principal headquarters and every domestic branch or place of business of the casino.

Note: *Nevada casinos must file Form 8852, Currency Transaction Report by Casinos - Nevada (CTRC-N), to report transactions as required under Nevada Regulation 6A.*

What To File.—A casino must file Form 8362 for each transaction involving either currency received (Cash In) or currency disbursed (Cash Out) of more than $10,000 in a gaming day. A gaming day is the normal business day of the casino by which it keeps its books and records for business, accounting, and tax purposes. Multiple transactions must be treated as a single transaction if the casino has knowledge that: **(1)** they are made by or on behalf of the same person, and **(2)** they result in either Cash In or Cash Out by the casino totalling more than $10,000 during any one gaming day. Reportable transactions may occur at a casino cage, gaming table, and/or slot machine. The casino should report both Cash In and Cash Out transactions by or on behalf of the same customer on a single Form 8362. **DO NOT** use Form 8362 to report receipts of currency in excess of $10,000 by nongaming businesses of a casino (e.g., a hotel); instead, use **Form 8300,** Report of Cash Payments Over $10,000 Received in a Trade or Business.

Exceptions.—A casino does not have to report transactions with domestic banks, currency dealers or exchangers, or commercial check cashers.

Identification Requirements.—All individuals (except employees conducting transactions on behalf of armored car services) conducting a reportable transaction(s) for themselves or for another person must be identified by means of an official or otherwise reliable record.

Acceptable forms of identification include a driver's license, military or military dependent identification cards, passport, alien registration card, state issued identification card, cedular card (foreign), or a combination of other documents that contain an individual's name and address and preferably a photograph and are normally acceptable by financial institutions as a means of identification when cashing checks for persons other than established customers.

For casino customers granted accounts for credit, deposit, or check cashing, or on whom a CTRC containing verified identity has been filed, acceptable identification information obtained previously and maintained in the casino's internal records may be used as long as the following conditions are met. The customer's identity is reverified periodically, any out-of-date identifying information is updated in the internal records, and the date of each reverification is noted on the internal record. For example, if documents verifying an individual's identity were examined and recorded on a signature card when a deposit or credit account was opened, the casino may rely on that information as long as it is reverified periodically.

When and Where To File.—File each Form 8362 by the 15th calendar day after the day of the transaction with the:

IRS Detroit Computing Center
ATTN: CTRC
P.O. Box 32621
Detroit, MI 48232-5604

A casino must retain a copy of each Form 8362 filed for 5 years from the date of filing.

Penalties.—Civil and/or criminal penalties may be assessed for failure to file a CTRC or supply information, or for filing a false or fraudulent CTRC. See 31 U.S.C. 5321, 5322, and 5324.

Definitions.—For purposes of Form 8362, the terms below have the following meanings:

Agent. Any individual who conducts a currency transaction on behalf of another individual or organization.

Currency. The coin and paper money of the United States or of any other country that is circulated and customarily used and accepted as money.

Customer. Any person involved in a currency transaction whether or not that person participates in the casino's gaming activities.

Person. An individual, corporation, partnership, trust or estate, joint stock company, association, syndicate, joint venture, or any other unincorporated organization or group.

Organization. Person other than an individual.

Transaction In Currency (Currency Transaction). The **physical** transfer of currency from one person to another.

Negotiable Instruments. All checks and drafts (including business, personal, bank, cashier's, and third-party), traveler's checks, money orders, and promissory notes, whether or not they are in bearer form.

Specific Instructions

Note: *Additional information that cannot fit on the front and back of Form 8362 must be submitted on plain paper attached to Form 8362. Type or print the individual's or organization's name and identifying number, date of transaction, and casino's name and employer identification number (i.e., Items 3, 4, 5, 7, 32, 34, 35, and 36) as well as identify the specific item number on all additional sheets. This will ensure that if a sheet becomes separated, it will be associated with the appropriate Form 8362.*

Item 1. Amends prior report.—Check Item 1 if this Form 8362 amends a previously filed report. Staple a copy of the original report behind the amended one. Complete Part III in its entirety, but complete only those other entries that are being amended.

Part I. Person(s) Involved in Transaction(s)

Note: *Section A must be completed in all cases. If an individual conducts a transaction on his/her own behalf, complete only section A; leave Section B BLANK. If a transaction is conducted by an individual on behalf of another person(s), complete Section A for each person on whose behalf the transaction is conducted; complete Section B for the individual conducting the transaction.*

Section A. Person(s) on Whose Behalf Transaction(s) Is Conducted (Customer)

Item 2. Multiple persons.—Check Item 2 if this transaction is being conducted on behalf of more than one person. For example, if John and Jane Doe cash a check made out to them jointly at the casino, more than one individual has conducted the transaction. Enter information in Section A for one of the individuals; provide information for the other individual on page 2, Section A. Attach additional sheets as necessary.

Items 3, 4, and 5. Individual/Organization name.—If the person on whose behalf the transaction(s) is conducted is an individual, put his/her last name in Item 3, first name in Item 4 and middle initial in Item 5. If there is no middle initial, leave Item 5 BLANK. If the transaction is conducted on behalf of an organization, enter the name in Item 3 and leave Items 4 and 5 BLANK, but identify the individual conducting the transaction in Section B. If an organization has a separate "doing business as (DBA)" name, enter in Item 3 the organization's legal name (e.g., Smith Enterprises, Inc.) followed by the name of the business (e.g., DBA Smith Casino Tours). In this case, use Items 4 and 5 if more space is needed.

Items 6, 8, 9, 10, and 11. Address.—Enter the permanent street address, city, two-letter state abbreviation used by the U.S. Postal Service, and ZIP code of the person identified in Item 3. Also, enter in Item 6 the apartment or suite number and road or route number. Do not enter a P.O. box number unless the person has no street address. If the person is from a foreign country, enter any province name as well as the appropriate two-letter country code (e.g., "CA" for Canada, "JA" for Japan, etc.). If the country is the United States, leave Item 11 BLANK.

Item 7. Social security number (SSN) or Employer identification number (EIN).—Enter the SSN (if an individual) or EIN (if other than an individual) of the person identified in Items 3 through 5. If that individual is a nonresident alien individual who does not have an SSN, enter "NONE" in this space.

Item 12. Date of birth.—Enter the customer's date of birth (DOB) if it is known to the casino through an existing internal record or reflected on an appropriate identification document or credential presented to the casino to verify the customer's identity (see **Identification Requirements** above). Internal casino records can include those for casino customers granted accounts for credit, deposit, or check cashing, or on whom a CTRC containing verified identity has been filed. If such records do not indicate the DOB, a casino should ask the customer for the DOB. If the DOB is not available from any of these sources, the casino should enter NOT AVAILABLE in the space. Eight numerals must be inserted for each date. Enter the date in the format "mmddyyyy", where "mm" is the month, "dd" is the day, and "yyyy" is the year. Zero (0) should precede any single-digit number. For example, if the individual's birth date is June 1, 1948, enter "06 01 1948" in Item 12.

Item 13. Method used to verify identity.—If an individual conducts the transaction(s) on his/her own behalf, his/her name and address **must** be verified by examination of an official credential/document or internal record containing identification information on a known customer (see **Identification Requirements** above). Check box **a** if you examined an official identification credential/document. Check box **b** if you examined an acceptable internal casino record (i.e., credit, deposit, or check cashing account record, or a CTRC worksheet) containing previously verified identification information on a "known customer." Check box **c** if the transaction is conducted on behalf of an organization. If box **a** or **b** is checked, you **must** complete Item 14. If box **c** is checked, do not complete Item 14.

Item 14. Describe identification credential.—If a driver's license, passport, or alien registration card was used to verify the individual's identity, check as appropriate box **a, b,** or **c**. If you check box **d,** you must specifically identify the type of document used (e.g., enter "military ID" for a military or military/dependent identification card). A statement such as "known customer" in box **d** is **not** sufficient for completion of Form 8362. Enter in Item 14e the two-letter state postal code, two-letter country code, or the name of the issuer for that document, and enter in Item 14f the number shown on that official document.

Item 15. Customer account number.—Enter the account number which corresponds to the transaction being reported and which the casino has assigned to the person whose name is entered in Item 3. If the person has more than one account number affected by the transaction, enter the account number that corresponds to the majority of currency being reported. If the transaction does not involve an account number, enter "NOT APPLICABLE" in the space.

Section B. Individual(s) Conducting Transaction(s) – If Other Than Above (Agent)

Complete Section B if an individual conducts a transaction on behalf of another person(s) listed in Section A. If an individual conducts a transaction on his/her own behalf, leave Section B BLANK.

Item 16. Multiple agents.—If, during a gaming day, more than one individual conducts transactions on behalf of an individual or organization listed in Section A, check this box and complete Section B. List one of the individuals on the front of the form and the other individual(s) on page 2, Section B. Attach additional sheets as necessary.

Items 17, 18, and 19. Name of individual.—Enter the individual's last name in Item 17, first name in Item 18, and middle initial in Item 19. If there is no middle initial, leave Item 19 BLANK. For example, if John Doe, an employee of the Error Free Rock Band, cashes an $11,000 check for the band, Error Free Rock Band is identified in Section A, and John Doe is identified in Section B.

Items 20, 22, 23, 24, and 25. Address.—Enter the permanent street address, including ZIP code, of the individual conducting the transaction. If the individual is from a foreign country, enter any province name and the appropriate two-letter country code.

Item 21. Social security number (SSN).—Enter the SSN of the individual identified in Items 17 through 19. If that individual is a nonresident alien who does not have an SSN, enter "NONE" in the space.

Item 26. Date of birth.—Enter the individual's date of birth. For proper format, see the instructions under **Item 12** above.

Item 27. Method used to verify identity.—Any individual listed in Items 17 through 19 must present an official document to verify his/her name and address. See the instructions under **Item 13** above for more information. After completing Item 27, you must also complete Item 28.

Item 28. Describe identification credential.—Describe the identification credential used to verify the individual's name and address. See the instructions under **Item 14** above for more information.

Part II. Amount and Type of Transaction(s)

Part II identifies the type of transaction(s) reported and the amount(s) involved. You must complete all items that apply.

Item 29. Multiple transactions.—Check this box if multiple currency transactions, none of which individually exceeds $10,000, comprise this report.

Items 30 and 31. Cash in and cash out.—Enter in the appropriate spaces provided in Items 30 and/or 31, the specific currency amount for each "type of transaction" for a reportable Cash In or Cash Out. If the casino engages in a Cash In or a Cash Out transaction that is not listed in Items 30a through 30g or Items 31a through 31i, specify the type of transaction and the amount of currency in Item 30h or 31j, respectively. Enter the total amount of the reportable Cash In transaction(s) in Item 30i. Enter the total amount of the reportable Cash Out transaction(s) in Item 31k.

If less than a full dollar amount is involved, increase the figure to the next higher dollar. For example, if the currency total is $20,500.25, show it as $20,501.00.

If there is a currency exchange, list it separately with both the Cash In and Cash Out totals. If foreign currency is exchanged, use the U.S. dollar equivalent on the day of the transaction.

Payment(s) on credit, Item 30c, includes all forms of cash payments made by a customer on a credit account or line of credit, or in redemption of markers or counter checks. Currency received from wire transfer(s) out, Item 30e, applies to cash received from a customer when the casino sends a wire transfer on behalf of a customer.

Currency paid from wire transfer(s) in, Item 31e, applies to cash paid to a customer when the casino receives a wire transfer on behalf of a customer. Travel and complimentary expenses and gaming incentives, Item 31h, includes reimbursements for a customer's travel and entertainment expenses and cash complementaries ("comps").

Determining Whether Transactions Meet The Reporting Threshold

Only cash transactions that, alone or when aggregated, exceed $10,000 should be reported on Form 8362. A casino must report multiple currency transactions when it has knowledge that such transactions have occurred. This includes knowledge gathered through examination of books, records, logs, information retained on magnetic disk, tape or other machine-readable media, or in any manual system, and similar documents and information that the casino maintains pursuant to any law or regulation or within the ordinary course of its business.

Cash In and Cash Out transactions for the same customer are to be aggregated separately and must not be offset against one another. If there are both Cash In and Cash Out transactions which **each** exceed $10,000, enter the amounts in Items 30 and 31 and report on a single Form 8362.

Example 1. Person A purchases $11,000 in chips with currency (one Cash In entry); and later receives currency from a $6,000 redemption of chips and a $2,000 slot jackpot win (two Cash Out entries). Complete Form 8362 as follows:

Cash In of "$11,000" is entered in Item 30a (purchase of chips) and Cash In Total of "$11,000" is entered in Item 30i. No entry is made for Cash Out. The two Cash Out transactions equal only $8,000, which does not meet the BSA reporting threshold.

Example 2. Person B deposits $5,000 in currency to his front money account and pays $10,000 in currency to pay off an outstanding credit balance (two Cash In entries); receives $7,000 in currency from a wire transfer (one Cash Out entry); and presents $2,000 in small denomination U.S. currency to be exchanged for an equal amount in U.S. $100 bills. Complete Form 8362 as follows:

Cash In of "$5,000" is entered in Item 30b (deposit), "$10,000" is entered in Item 30c (payment on credit), "$2,000" is entered in Item 30g (currency exchange), and Cash In Total of "$17,000" is entered in Item 30i. In determining whether the transactions are reportable, the currency exchange is aggregated with both the Cash In and the Cash Out amounts. The result is a reportable $17,000 Cash In transaction. No entry is made for Cash Out. The total Cash Out amount only equals $9,000, which does not meet the BSA reporting threshold.

Example 3. Person C deposits $7,000 in currency to his front money account and pays $9,000 in currency to pay off an outstanding credit balance (two Cash In entries); receives $2,500 in currency from a withdrawal from a safekeeping account, $2,500 in currency from a wire transfer and cashes a personal check of $7,500 (three Cash Out entries); and presents Canadian dollars which are exchanged for $1,500 in U.S. dollar equivalent. Complete Form 8362 as follows:

Cash In of "$7,000" is entered in Item 30b (deposit), "$9,000" is entered in Item 30c (payment on credit), "$1,500" is entered in Item 30g (currency exchange), and a Cash In total of "$17,500" is entered in Item 30i. Cash Out of "$2,500" is entered in Item 31b (withdrawal of deposit), "$2,500" is entered in Item 31e (wire transfer), "$7,500" is entered in Item 31f (negotiable instrument cashed), "$1,500" is entered in Item 31g (currency exchange) and a Cash Out Total of "$14,000" is entered in Item 31k. In this example, both the Cash In and Cash Out totals exceed $10,000, and each must be reflected on Form 8362.

Example 4. Person D purchases $10,000 in chips with currency and places a $10,000 cash bet (two Cash In entries); and later receives currency for an $18,000 redemption of chips and $20,000 from a payment on a cash bet (two Cash Out entries). Complete Form 8362 as follows:

Cash In of "$10,000" is entered in Items 30a and 30d and a Cash In total of "$20,000" is entered in Item 30i. Cash Out of "$18,000" is entered in Item 31a (redemption of chips), "$20,000" is entered in Item 31d (payment on bets) and a Cash Out Total of "$38,000" is entered in Item 31k. In this example, both the Cash In and Cash Out totals exceed $10,000, and each must be reflected on Form 8362.

Item 32. Date of transaction.—Enter the gaming day on which the transaction occurred (see **What To File** above). For proper format, see the instructions for **Item 12** above.

Item 33. Foreign currency.—If foreign currency is involved, identify the country of issuance by entering the appropriate two-letter country code. If multiple foreign currencies are involved, identify the country for which the largest amount in U.S. dollars is exchanged.

Part III. Casino Reporting Transaction(s)

Item 34. Casino's trade name.—Enter the name by which the casino does business and is commonly known. Do not enter a corporate, partnership, or other entity name, unless such name is the one by which the casino is commonly known.

Item 35. Casino's legal name.—Enter the legal name as shown on required tax filings, only if different from the trade name shown in Item 34. This name will be defined as the name indicated on a charter or other document creating the entity, and which is identified with the casino's established EIN.

Item 36. Employer identification number (EIN).—Enter the casino's EIN.

Items 37, 38, 39, and 40. Address.—Enter the street address, city, state, and ZIP code of the casino (or branch) where the transaction occurred. **Do not** use a P.O. box number.

Items 41 and 42. Title and signature of approving official.—The official who is authorized to review and approve Form 8362 must indicate his/her title and sign the form.

Item 43. Date the form is signed.—The approving official must enter the date the Form 8362 is signed. For proper format, see the instructions for **Item 12** above.

Item 44. Preparer's name.—Type or print the full name of the individual preparing Form 8362. The preparer and the approving official may be different individuals.

Items 45 and 46. Contact person/telephone number.—Type or print the name and commercial telephone number of a responsible individual to contact concerning any questions about this Form 8362.

Form **8621**
(Rev. April 1997)
Department of the Treasury
Internal Revenue Service

Return by a Shareholder of a Passive Foreign Investment Company or Qualified Electing Fund

▶ See separate instructions.

OMB No. 1545-1002

Attachment Sequence No. **69**

Name of shareholder

Identifying number (see page 2 of instructions)

Number, street, and room or suite no. (If a P.O. box, see page 2 of instructions.)

Your tax year: calendar year 19 ..... or other tax year
beginning   19   and ending   19   .

City or town, state, and ZIP code or country

Check type of shareholder filing the return: ☐ Individual ☐ Corporation ☐ Partnership ☐ S Corporation ☐ Nongrantor Trust ☐ Estate

Name of passive foreign investment company (PFIC) or qualified electing fund (QEF)

Employer identification number (if any)

Address (Enter number, street, city or town, and country.)

Tax year of company or fund: calendar year 19 ..... or other tax year beginning .... 19 ..... and ending   19   .

Part I — Elections

1 ☐ I, a shareholder of a PFIC, elect to treat the PFIC as a QEF. (Section 1295.) (See page 2 of the instructions for information to attach when making this election.) *Complete lines 6a through 7c of Part II.*

2 ☐ I, a shareholder on the first day of a PFIC's first tax year as a QEF, elect to recognize gain on the deemed sale of my interest in the PFIC. (Section 1291(d)(2)(A).)
Enter gain or loss on line 10f of Part III.

3 ☐ I, a shareholder on the first day of a PFIC's first tax year as a QEF that is a controlled foreign corporation (CFC), elect to treat an amount equal to my share of the post-1986 earnings and profits of the CFC as an excess distribution. (Section 1291(d)(2)(B).)
Enter this amount on line 10e. (See page 3 of the instructions for tax years over which the excess distribution is allocated.)

4 ☐ I, a shareholder of a QEF, elect to extend the time for payment of tax on the undistributed earnings and profits of the QEF until this line 4 election is terminated. (Section 1294.) *Complete lines 8a through 9c of Part II to calculate the tax that may be deferred.*
Note: *If any portion of line 6a or line 7a is includible under section 551 or 951, you may **not** make this election. Also, see sections 1294(c) and 1294(f) and the related regulations for events that terminate this election.*

5 ☐ I, a shareholder of a former PFIC, elect to recognize gain on the deemed sale of my interest in the PFIC on the last day of the foreign corporation's last tax year as a PFIC as defined in section 1296(a). (Section 1297(b)(1).)
Enter gain or loss on line 10f.

Part II — Income From a Qualified Electing Fund (QEF). All QEF shareholders complete lines 6a through 7c. If you are making the line 4 election, also complete lines 8a through 9c.

6a Enter your pro rata share of the ordinary earnings of the QEF	**6a**
b Enter the portion of line 6a that is included in income under section 551 or 951 or that may be excluded under section 1293(g)	**6b**
c Subtract line 6b from line 6a. Enter this amount on your tax return as dividend income	**6c**
7a Enter your pro rata share of the net capital gain of the QEF	**7a**
b Enter the portion of line 7a that is included in income under section 551 or 951 or that may be excluded under section 1293(g)	**7b**
c Subtract line 7b from line 7a. This amount is long-term capital gain. Enter this amount in Part II of the Schedule D used for your income tax return	**7c**
8a Add lines 6c and 7c	**8a**
b Enter the total amount of cash and the fair market value of other property distributed or deemed distributed to you during the tax year of the QEF (See page 3 of instructions.)	**8b**
c Enter the portion of line 8a to the extent not already included in line 8b that is attributable to shares in the QEF that you disposed of, pledged, or otherwise transferred during the tax year	**8c**
d Add lines 8b and 8c	**8d**
e Subtract line 8d from line 8a, and enter the difference (if zero or less, enter amount in brackets)	**8e**

If no portion of line 6a or line 7a is includible in income under section 551 or 951 and line 8e is greater than zero, you may make the line 4 election with respect to the amount on line 8e.

Computation of Tax for Which the Time for Payment Is Extended

9a Enter the total tax for total taxable income for the tax year	**9a**
b Enter the total tax for the tax year determined without regard to the amount entered on line 8e	**9b**
c Subtract line 9b from line 9a. This is the deferred tax, the time for payment of which is extended by making the line 4 election. See instructions	**9c**

For Paperwork Reduction Act Notice, see page 1 of separate instructions. Cat. No. 64174H Form **8621** (Rev. 4-97)

Form 8621 (Rev. 4-97) Page **2**

Part III — Distributions and Disposition of Stock in a Section 1291 Fund (See instructions on page 3.)
Complete a separate Part III for each excess distribution.

10a Enter your total distributions from the PFIC during the current tax year. If the holding period of the PFIC stock began in the current tax year, this amount is dividend income to the extent there are accumulated earnings and profits **10a**

b Enter the total distributions, reduced by the portions of such distributions that were excess distributions but not included in income under section 1291(a)(1)(B), made by the company for each of the 3 years preceding the current tax year (or if shorter, the portion of the shareholder's holding period before the current tax year) **10b**

c Divide line 10b by 3. (See instructions if the number of preceding tax years is less than 3.) . **10c**

d Multiply line 10c by 125%. Enter the lesser of line 10a or line 10d as a dividend on your income tax return **10d**

e Subtract line 10d from line 10a. This amount, if more than zero, is the total excess distribution. If zero or less and you did not dispose of stock during the tax year, **do not** complete the rest of Part III. See instructions if you received more than one distribution during the current tax year . . . **10e**

f Enter gain or loss from the disposition of stock of a section 1291 fund or former section 1291 fund. If a gain, complete lines 11a through 11f. If a loss, show it in brackets and do not complete the rest of Part III **10f**

11 On an attached statement for each distribution and disposition, show your holding period for each share of stock or block of shares held and:

a Allocate the excess distribution to each day in your holding period. Add all amounts that are allocated to days in each tax year.

b Enter the total of the amounts determined in line 11a that are allocable to the current tax year and tax years before the foreign corporation became a PFIC (pre-PFIC tax years). Enter these amounts on your income tax return as other income. (See instructions.) **11b**

c To determine the increase in tax for each tax year in your holding period (other than the current tax year and pre-PFIC years), multiply the amount allocated to each tax year by the highest rate of tax under section 1 or section 11, whichever applies, in effect for that tax year. Add the increases in tax computed for all years and enter the aggregate increases in taxes (before credits) here **11c**

d Foreign tax credit. (See instructions.) **11d**

e Subtract line 11d from line 11c. Enter this amount on your income tax return as "additional tax". (See instructions.) **11e**

f Determine interest on each net increase in tax (increase in tax less any foreign tax credit) determined in line 11e by using the rates and method under section 6621. Enter the aggregate amount of interest here. (See instructions.) **11f**

Part IV — Status of Prior Year Section 1294 Elections and Termination of Section 1294 Elections
Complete a separate column for each outstanding election. Complete lines 9 and 10 only if there is a partial termination of the section 1294 election.

	(i)	(ii)	(iii)	(iv)	(v)	(vi)
1 Tax year of outstanding election	,19	,19	,19	,19	,19	,19
2 Undistributed earnings to which the election relates						
3 Deferred tax						
4 Interest accrued on deferred tax (line 3) as of the filing date						
5 Event terminating election						
6 Earnings distributed or deemed distributed during the tax year						
7 Deferred tax due with this return						
8 Accrued interest due with this return						
9 Portion of deferred tax outstanding after partial termination of section 1294 election						
10 Portion of interest accrued after partial termination of section 1294 election						

![IRS Logo] **Department of the Treasury**
Internal Revenue Service

Instructions for Form 8621
(Revised April 1997)
Return by a Shareholder of a Passive Foreign Investment Company or Qualified Electing Fund

Section references are to the Internal Revenue Code unless otherwise noted.

Paperwork Reduction Act Notice.— We ask for the information on this form to carry out the Internal Revenue laws of the United States. You are required to give us the information. We need it to ensure that you are complying with these laws and to allow us to figure and collect the right amount of tax.

You are not required to provide the information requested on a form that is subject to the Paperwork Reduction Act unless the form displays a valid OMB control number. Books or records relating to a form or its instructions must be retained as long as their contents may become material in the administration of any Internal Revenue law. Generally, tax returns and return information are confidential as required by Code section 6103.

The time needed to complete and file this form will vary depending on individual circumstances. The estimated average time is:

Recordkeeping .... 12 hr., 12 min.

Learning about the law or the form .... 3 hr., 41 min.

Preparing and sending the form to the IRS .... 4 hr., 2 min.

If you have comments concerning the accuracy of these time estimates or suggestions for making this form simpler, we would be happy to hear from you. You can write to the Tax Forms Committee, Western Area Distribution Center, Rancho Cordova, CA 95743-0001. **DO NOT** send the tax form to this office. Instead, see **When and Where To File** below.

Changes To Note

- The Small Business Job Protection Act of 1996 clarified that foreign trade income of foreign sales corporations (FSCs) and export trade income of export trade corporations (ETCs) is not passive income for purposes of the definition of a passive foreign investment company (PFIC) (section 1296(b)(2)(D)). This provision is effective for tax years of foreign corporations beginning after 1986.
- Final regulations have been issued that provide rules for making the deemed sale and deemed dividend elections under section 1291(d)(2). These regulations apply to a shareholder of a PFIC that elects under section 1295 to treat the PFIC as a qualified electing fund (QEF) for a tax year after the first tax year during the shareholder's holding period that the foreign corporation was a PFIC. These regulations, effective December 27, 1996, are applicable as of April 1, 1995. For more information, see Regulations sections 1.1291-9 and 1.1291-10.

General Instructions

Who Must File

Generally, a U.S. person must file Form 8621 for each tax year in which that U.S. person is a shareholder in a PFIC. A separate Form 8621 must be filed for each PFIC in which stock is held.

The PFIC provisions apply to U.S. persons who are direct or indirect shareholders of a PFIC. Generally, a U.S. person is an indirect shareholder of a PFIC if it is:

1. A direct or indirect owner of a pass-through entity that is a direct or indirect shareholder of a PFIC;

2. A shareholder of a PFIC that is a shareholder of another PFIC; or

3. A 50% or more shareholder in a non-PFIC foreign corporation that is a shareholder of a PFIC.

Interest holder of pass-through entities.— The following interest holders must file Form 8621:

1. A U.S. person that is an interest holder of a foreign pass-through entity that is a direct or indirect shareholder of a PFIC;

2. A U.S. person that is considered (under sections 671 through 679) the owner of PFIC stock held in trust; and

3. A U.S. partnership, S corporation, trust (other than a trust that is subject to sections 671 through 679 for the PFIC stock), or estate that is a direct or indirect owner of a PFIC.

However, U.S. persons that are interest holders of pass-through entities described in **3** above must file Form 8621 if the pass-through entity fails to file or the U.S. person is required to recognize any income under either section 1291 or section 1293.

Chain of ownership.— If the shareholder owns one PFIC and through that PFIC owns one or more other PFICs, the shareholder must either file a Form 8621 for each PFIC in the chain, or complete Form 8621 for the first PFIC and, in an attachment, provide the information required on Form 8621 for each of the other PFICs in the chain.

Shareholder of a section 1291 fund.— A direct or indirect shareholder of a PFIC that is a section 1291 fund uses Form 8621 to report a PFIC distribution or disposition. An indirect shareholder may be taxed on the distribution paid to the direct owner of the section 1291 fund and on a disposition of the stock indirectly owned.

Shareholder of a QEF.— A direct or indirect shareholder that elects to be treated as a shareholder of a QEF must file Form 8621 as part of its election, and with its return for each succeeding tax year. The shareholder of the QEF uses Form 8621 to report its share of the current earnings of the QEF and to make the election to extend the time for payment of tax on its share of the undistributed earnings of the QEF. Certain shareholders of a QEF also use Form 8621 to make a deemed dividend or deemed sale election to purge the section 1291 fund years from their holding period.

When and Where To File

Form 8621 must be filed by the due date, including extensions, of the shareholder's income tax return. File two copies of the form. Attach one copy to the shareholder's income tax return. Send the other copy to the Internal Revenue Service Center, P.O. Box 21086, Philadelphia, PA 19114.

If you are not required to file an income tax return or other return for the tax year, file one copy of Form 8621 with the Internal Revenue Service Center, P.O. Box 21086, Philadelphia, PA 19114.

When To Make Elections

Generally, the Line 1 election must be made by the due date, including extensions, of the shareholder's income tax return for the first year the PFIC is treated as a QEF. However, see section 1295(b)(2) for an exception.

The Line 2 or Line 3 election must be made by the due date, including extensions, of the shareholder's original income tax return (or by filing an amended return within 3 years of the due date, as extended) for the tax year that includes the date of the deemed sale or deemed dividend.

Generally, the Line 4 election must be made by the due date, including extensions, of the shareholder's income tax return for the tax year for which the election is being made. See Regulations section 1.1294-1T(c)(2) for an exception.

The Line 5 election is made with the original return or by filing an amended return (within 3 years of the due date (as extended) of the shareholder's original return) for the tax year that includes the date of the deemed sale.

Definitions

Passive Foreign Investment Company (PFIC)

A foreign corporation is a PFIC if:

1. 75% or more of the corporation's gross income for its tax year is passive income (as defined in section 1296(b)); or

2. At least 50% of the average value of the corporation's assets for its tax year is attributable to assets used in the production of passive income or held for the production of passive income.

A controlled foreign corporation (CFC) must use the adjusted basis of its assets when determining PFIC status. Other foreign corporations use fair market value unless they elect to use the adjusted basis of their assets when determining if they are PFICs.

Cat. No. 10784P

When determining if a foreign corporation that owns at least 25% (by value) of another corporation is a PFIC, the foreign corporation is treated as holding a proportionate share of the assets and as receiving a proportionate share of the income of the 25%-or-more owned corporation.

Qualified Electing Fund (QEF)

A PFIC is a QEF if the U.S. person who is a direct or indirect shareholder of the PFIC elected under section 1295 to treat the foreign corporation as a QEF for the PFIC's tax year that ends during the tax year of the shareholder for which the shareholder made the election. Once the election is made, it applies to all subsequent years that the foreign corporation is a PFIC. The election may be revoked only with the consent of the IRS. A separate QEF election must be made for each PFIC the shareholder wants to treat as a QEF.

Tax Consequences for Shareholders of a QEF

A shareholder of a QEF must include in gross income its share of the annual earnings of the QEF, but may elect to extend the time for payment of tax on undistributed earnings. Income from a QEF is computed in Part II of Form 8621.

A shareholder of a pedigreed QEF (defined in Regulations section 1.1291-9(j)(2)(ii)) only reports section 1293 amounts for tax years of the QEF in which it qualifies as a PFIC under section 1296(a). In contrast, a shareholder of an unpedigreed QEF (defined in Regulations section 1.1291-9(j)(2)(iii)) reports section 1293 amounts for each tax year of the foreign corporation because it is a PFIC under section 1297(b)(1), even if it does not qualify as a PFIC under section 1296(a).

Basis adjustments.— A shareholder's basis in the stock of a QEF is increased by the amount of earnings that is included in gross income and decreased by a distribution of previously taxed income.

Section 1291 Fund

A PFIC is a section 1291 fund if the shareholder did not elect to treat the PFIC as a QEF. A QEF may also be a section 1291 fund if the shareholder made the QEF election for a tax year after the foreign corporation's first tax year as a PFIC during the shareholder's holding period but did not make the Line 2 or Line 3 election.

Tax Consequences for Shareholders of a Section 1291 Fund

Shareholders of a section 1291 fund are subject to special rules when they receive a distribution from, or dispose of the stock of, a section 1291 fund. A distribution may be partly or wholly an excess distribution. Gain from the disposition of a section 1291 fund is treated as an excess distribution.

Excess distributions.— An excess distribution is the part of the distribution received in the current tax year that is greater than 125% of the average of the distributions made during the 3 preceding tax years. No part of a distribution received or deemed received during the first tax year of the shareholder's holding period of the stock will be treated as an excess distribution.

The excess distribution is determined on a per share basis. See section 1291(b)(3) for adjustments that are made when determining if a distribution is an excess distribution.

The excess distribution is allocated to each day in the shareholder's holding period of the stock of the section 1291 fund.

Portions of an excess distribution are treated differently. The portions allocated to the days in the current tax year and the shareholder's tax years in its holding period before the foreign corporation qualified as a PFIC (pre-PFIC years) are taxed as ordinary income. The portions allocated to the days in the shareholder's tax years (other than the current tax year) in its holding period when the foreign corporation was a PFIC are not included in income, but are subject to the deferred tax amount, as defined in section 1291(c). Excess distributions are computed in Part III of Form 8621.

Additional Information Required

A shareholder of a PFIC must attach certain information to Form 8621. This information includes:

1. The number of shares in each class of stock owned by the shareholder at the beginning of its tax year;

2. Any changes in the number of shares in each class of stock during its tax year and the dates of such changes; and

3. The number of shares in each class of stock at the end of its tax year.

Specific Instructions

Address and Identifying Number

Address.— Include the suite, room, or other unit number after the street address. If the Post Office does not deliver mail to the street address and the shareholder has a P.O. box, enter the box number instead of the street address.

Identifying number.— Individuals, enter a social security number or an IRS taxpayer identification number. All other entities, enter employer identification number.

Part I—Elections

Line 1–Election To Treat the PFIC as a QEF (Section 1295)

Who makes the election.— A U.S. person that owns stock of a PFIC, including a shareholder that owns stock of the PFIC in bearer form, may make this election.

In a chain of ownership, only the first U.S. person that owns stock in a PFIC may make the QEF election. For example, if a U.S. person is a partner in a U.S. partnership and the partnership is a shareholder in a PFIC, the election is made by the partnership. All U.S. persons that are partners in that partnership are bound by the QEF election. If a U.S. person is a partner in a foreign partnership, the QEF election is made by the U.S. person and binds only the electing person.

The common parent of an affiliated group of corporations that joins in the filing of a consolidated income tax return makes the QEF election for all members of the affiliated group that are shareholders in a PFIC. An election by a common parent is effective for all members of the group that own stock in the PFIC at the time the election is made and at any time thereafter.

Making the election.— To make the election

1. Check the box on line 1;

2. Attach the "Shareholder Section 1295 Election Statement," the "PFIC Annual Information Statement" (see below), and Form 8621 to a timely filed income tax return for the tax year the election is effective.

3. Attach a copy of the election statement to the duplicate Form 8621 sent to the Philadelphia Service Center at the time the election is made. See **When and Where To File** on page 1.

For more information on making the election, see Notice 88-125, 1988-2 C.B. 535.

Termination of the election.— The IRS may revoke the QEF election if the shareholder does not produce the following when requested:

1. Copies of the books and records of the PFIC substantiating that the PFIC's ordinary earnings and net capital gain are figured according to U.S. income tax principles; and

2. Copies of books and records to verify the shareholder's pro rata share of the QEF's ordinary earnings and net capital gain.

Shareholder Section 1295 Election Statement

Attach a statement to your income tax return with the words "Shareholder Section 1295 Election Statement" written at the top of the statement. Include the following:

1. A statement that you are making the section 1295 election.

2. The first tax year to which the election applies.

3. The first tax year of the PFIC to which the election applies.

4. The number of shares in each class of stock of the PFIC that you hold.

5. The country and date of incorporation of the PFIC.

PFIC Annual Information Statement

Generally, the PFIC Annual Information Statement must be filed with your income tax return for the first year for which the QEF election is made. It must also be filed with your return for the tax year for which the election is in effect (see **Exception,** below). The statement must include the following:

1. The first and last day of the PFIC's tax year that ends with or within your tax year.

2. Your pro rata share of the ordinary earnings and the net capital gain of the PFIC or sufficient information so that you can determine your share of ordinary earnings and net capital gain.

3. The amount of money and the fair market value of other property distributed or deemed distributed to you during the year.

4. A statement that the PFIC will permit you to inspect and copy its permanent books of accounts, records, and other documents so that it can be determined that the QEF's ordinary earnings and net capital gain are calculated according to U.S. income tax principles.

Exception. If you hold stock in a PFIC through a nominee or a shareholder of record, you may submit a statement issued by the nominee or shareholder of record instead of the PFIC Annual Information Statement. The statement must show your pro rata share of the PFIC's ordinary earnings and net capital gain. This statement is acceptable if the PFIC issues an annual information statement to the nominee or shareholder of record and the annual statement is the basis for the information contained in the statement issued by the nominee or shareholder of record.

Alternative Documentation

Occasionally, the IRS will consider requests for alternative documentation to verify the ordinary earnings and net capital gain of the PFIC. For more information, see Notice 88-125.

Line 2–Deemed Sale Election

A U.S. person that elected to treat a PFIC as a QEF for a foreign corporation's tax year following its first tax year as a PFIC included in the shareholder's holding period may make this election. A shareholder making this election is deemed to have sold the PFIC's stock as of the first day of the PFIC's first tax year as a QEF (the qualification date) for its fair market value. The gain from the deemed sale is taxed as an excess distribution. The election may be made for stock on which the shareholder will realize a loss, but that loss cannot be recognized. The basis of the stock is increased by the gain recognized, if any, and the holding period of the stock begins on the qualification date.

For more information on making this election, see Regulations section 1.1291-10.

Making the election.— To make the election, check the box on line 2. Enter the gain or loss on line 10f of Part III. If a gain is entered, complete the rest of Part III.

Line 3–Deemed Dividend Election

A U.S. person that elected to treat a PFIC that is also a CFC as a QEF for the foreign corporation's tax year following its first tax year as a PFIC included in the shareholder's holding period may make this election. A shareholder making this election is treated as receiving a dividend of its pro rata share of the post-1986 earnings and profits of the PFIC on the qualification date. The deemed dividend is taxed as an excess distribution, and is allocated only to the days in the shareholder's holding period that are both after 1986 and when the foreign corporation was a PFIC.

For purposes of this election, the term "post-1986 earnings and profits" means earnings and profits of the PFIC accumulated in tax years beginning after 1986 during which the CFC was a PFIC and while the shareholder held the stock, and ending on the day before the qualification date.

For purposes of the deemed dividend election, the shareholder's holding period is treated as ending on the day before the deemed dividend. The basis of the shareholder's stock is increased by the deemed dividend amount. The shareholder's holding period after the deemed dividend begins on the qualification date.

The post-1986 earnings and profits may be reduced (but not below zero) by the part thereof that the shareholder satisfactorily demonstrates was previously included in the income of a U.S. person. The shareholder demonstrates this by attaching to Form 8621 a statement listing:

1. The name, address, and identifying number of the U.S. person and the amount that was included in income;
2. The tax year in which the amount was included in income; and
3. The law under which the amount was previously included in income.

For more information on making this election, see Regulations section 1.1291-9.

Making the election.— To make the election, check the box on line 3. Enter the dividend on line 10e and complete the rest of Part III.

Line 4–Election To Extend Time for Payment of Tax on Undistributed Earnings

A shareholder of a QEF may elect to extend the time for payment of the tax on its share of the undistributed earnings of the fund for the current tax year. If a U.S. partnership is a shareholder of a QEF, the election is made at the partner level. If this election is made, interest will be imposed on the amount of the deferred tax.

The election cannot be made for any earnings on shares disposed of during the tax year or for a tax year that any portion of the shareholder's pro rata share of the fund's earnings is included in income under section 551 or section 951.

For more information, see Temporary Regulations section 1.1294-1T(d)(2)

Making the election.— To make the election, check the box on line 4 and complete Part II.

Line 5–Election To Recognize Gain on Deemed Sale of PFIC

This election may be made by a U.S. person that is a shareholder of a section 1291 fund that no longer qualifies as a PFIC under either the income or asset test of section 1296(a). A shareholder making this election is treated as selling the stock of the foreign corporation on the last day of the last tax year of the foreign corporation in which it qualified as a PFIC (termination date) for its fair market value on that date. The election is made for the tax year that includes the termination date. The gain from the deemed sale is taxed as an excess distribution. You may make the election for the stock on which you will realize a loss, but you may not recognize the loss. Your basis in the stock is increased by the gain recognized, if any, and the holding period of the stock begins on the day after the deemed sale.

For more information, see Temporary Regulations section 1.1297-3T(b)(2).

Making the election.— To make the election, check the box on line 5. Enter the gain or loss on line 10f. If a gain, complete the rest of Part III. Also, see Part IV for annual reporting requirements for outstanding section 1294 elections.

Part II—Income From a QEF

Note: *All line references in Parts II and III to Form 1120 and Form 1040 are to the 1996 forms.*

Lines 6 and 7

Lines 6a and 7a.— Enter on lines 6a and 7a your pro rata share of the ordinary earnings and net capital gain of the QEF. The QEF should provide these amounts or information that will help you determine your pro rata share.

Lines 6b and 7b.— Your share of the ordinary earnings and the net capital gain of the QEF is reduced by the amounts you include in income under section 551 or 951 for the tax year with respect to the QEF. Your share of these amounts may also be reduced as provided in section 1293(g).

Line 6c.— This amount is treated as an ordinary dividend on your tax return.

Individuals, include this amount in the total on Form 1040, line 9.

Corporations, include this amount in the total on Form 1120, Schedule C, line 13.

Line 8

If you receive a distribution from the QEF during the current tax year, the distribution is first treated as a distribution out of the earnings and profits of the QEF accumulated during the year. If the total amount distributed (line 8b) exceeds the amount included in income (line 8a), the excess is treated as distributed out of the most recently accumulated earnings and profits and is taxable to you unless you satisfactorily demonstrate that the excess was previously included in the income of a U.S. person. To satisfactorily demonstrate this, the QEF shareholder must attach a statement to Form 8621 that includes:

1. The name, address, and identifying number of the U.S. person that included the amount in income;
2. The tax year in which the amount was included in income; and
3. The law under which the amount was previously included in income.

Line 9

Line 9a.— Enter the total tax (from Form 1120, Schedule J, line 10, or Form 1040, line 51) on your total taxable income (including your share of undistributed earnings of the QEF) for the tax year.

The term "undistributed earnings" means the excess, if any, of the amount included in gross income under section 1293(a) over the sum of the amount of any distribution and the portion of the amount attributable to stock in the QEF that you transferred or otherwise disposed of before the end of the QEF's tax year.

Line 9b.— Calculate your total tax as if your total taxable income did not include your share of the undistributed earnings of the QEF (line 8e). Enter this amount on line 9b.

Line 9c.— Corporations, enter this tax on Form 1120, Schedule J, in brackets to the left of the line entry space for line 10. Subtract that amount from the total of lines 6 through 9 and enter the difference on line 10.

Individuals, enter this tax on Form 1040 in brackets to the left of the line entry space for line 51. Subtract that amount from the total of lines 45 through 50, and enter the difference on line 51.

Part III—Distributions and Disposition of Stock in a Section 1291 Fund

Note: *A distribution to a corporation claiming the foreign tax credit for deemed paid foreign taxes includes foreign taxes deemed paid. See Form 1118, Foreign Tax Credits—Corporations (Rev. July 1994), Schedule C, Part I, column 9 and Part II, column 10 for the gross-up amount.*

Line 10

Line 10c.— Divide the amount on line 10b by 3. If the number of tax years in your holding period preceding the current tax year is less than 3, divide the amount on line 10b by that number.

Line 10d.— Report the dividend as follows:

Corporations, include this amount on Form 1120, Schedule C. line 13.

Individuals, include this amount as part of the total on Form 1040, line 9.

Line 10e.— If there was more than one distribution during the year, the excess distribution is apportioned among all actual distributions. Each apportioned amount is treated as a separate excess distribution.

Line 10f.— Gain recognized on the disposition of stock of a section 1291 fund is treated as an excess distribution. Losses are not recognized. Stock of a section 1291 fund is considered disposed of if it is sold, transferred, or pledged.

Line 11

Lines 11a and 11b.— Determine the taxation of the excess distribution on a separate sheet and attach it to Form 8621.

1. Divide the amount on line 10e or 10f, whichever applies, by the number of days in your holding period. The holding period of the

stock is treated as ending on the date of distribution or disposition. If the Line 3 election is made, special rules apply to the holding period. See the instructions for line 3.

  2. Determine the amount allocated to each tax year in your holding period by adding the amounts allocated to the days in each such tax year.

  3. Add the amounts allocated to the pre-PFIC and current tax years. Enter the sum on line 11b.

This amount is treated as ordinary income on your tax return. Individuals, enter this amount on Form 1040, line 21. Corporations, enter this amount on Form 1120, page 1, line 10.

Line 11c.— An increase in tax is determined for each PFIC year in your holding period (other than the current tax year) by multiplying the part of the excess distribution allocated to each year (as determined on line 11a) by the highest rate of tax in effect for that tax year that would have been applicable to you.

Line 11d.— To figure the foreign tax credit, the shareholder of a section 1291 fund figures the total creditable foreign taxes attributable to the distribution. This amount includes the direct foreign taxes paid by the shareholder on the distribution (for example, withholding taxes) and for 10% or greater corporate shareholders, any taxes deemed paid under section 902. Both the direct and indirect foreign taxes must be creditable under general foreign tax credit principles and the shareholder must choose to claim the foreign tax credit for the current tax year.

The excess distribution taxes (the creditable foreign taxes attributable to an excess distribution) are determined by apportioning the total creditable foreign taxes between the part of the distribution that is an excess distribution and the part that is not.

The excess distribution taxes are allocated in the same manner as the excess distribution is allocated. See **Excess distributions** on page 2. Those taxes allocated to pre-PFIC and the current tax years are taken into account for the current tax year under the general rules of the foreign tax credit.

The excess distribution taxes allocated to a PFIC year only reduce the increase in tax figured for that tax year (but not below zero). No carryover of any unused excess distribution taxes is allowed.

When you dispose of stock, the above foreign tax credit rules apply only to the part of the gain that, without regard to section 1291, would be treated under section 1248 as a dividend.

Line 11e.— This amount is the aggregate increase in tax and is included on your tax return as additional taxes.

Individuals, enter this amount on Form 1040 to the left of the line 38 entry space. Write "Sec. 1291" next to the amount and include the amount as part of the total for line 38.

Corporations, enter this amount on Form 1120, Schedule J, to the left of the entry space for line 3. Write "Sec. 1291" next to the amount and include it as part of the total for line 3. Other entities should use the comparable line on their income tax returns.

Line 11f.— Interest is charged on each net increase in tax for the period beginning on the due date (without regard to extensions) of your income tax return for the tax year to which an increase in tax is attributable and ending with the due date (without regard to extensions) of your income tax return for the tax year of the excess distribution.

Individuals, enter the interest at the bottom right margin of Form 1040, page 1 and label it as "Sec. 1291 interest." Include this amount in your check or money order payable to the Internal Revenue Service. If you would otherwise receive a refund, reduce the refund by the interest due.

Corporations, enter this interest at the bottom right margin of Form 1120, page 1, and label it as "Sec. 1291 interest." Include this amount in your check or money order payable to the Internal Revenue Service. If you would otherwise receive a refund, reduce the refund by the interest due.

Part IV

Status of Prior Year Section 1294 Elections and Termination of Section 1294 Elections

Temporary Regulations section 1.1294-1T(h) requires each person who has made a section 1294 election to **(a)** annually report the status of that election and **(b)** report the termination of any section 1294 election that occurred during the tax year.

Line 1.— Enter the last day of each tax year for which you made a section 1294 election that is outstanding. Do not include an election made in the current tax year.

Line 2.— Enter the undistributed earnings of the QEF on which the payment of tax was extended by the section 1294 election entered on line 1. If the election was partially terminated in a prior year, enter the remaining undistributed earnings.

Line 3.— Enter the tax for which payment was extended by the section 1294 election entered on line 1. If the election was partially terminated in a previous tax year, enter the balance of the deferred tax.

Line 4.— Enter the accrued interest (determined under section 6621) on the deferred tax. This is the interest accrued from the due date (not including extensions) of the return for the year for which the section 1294 election was made until the date the current year's return is filed.

Line 5.— Enter the event(s) that occurred during the tax year that terminated one or more of the section 1294 elections reported on line 1. A section 1294 election may be terminated voluntarily. However, an election will terminate when any of the following events occur:

• An actual or deemed distribution of earnings to which the election is attributable (a loan, pledge, or guarantee by the QEF to or for the benefit of the taxpayer may cause a deemed distribution of the earnings);

• A disposition of stock in the fund, including a pledge by the taxpayer of stock as security for a loan; or

• A change of status of the QEF (i.e., a foreign corporation that is no longer a QEF or PFIC).

Line 6.— Enter the earnings distributed or deemed distributed as a result of the events described on line 5. Earnings are treated as distributed out of the most recently accumulated earnings. Accordingly, an event will first terminate the most recently made election. An election may be terminated in whole or in part depending on the event causing the termination. A distribution of earnings will terminate an election only to the extent the election is attributable to the earnings distributed. A loan, pledge, or guarantee by the QEF will terminate an election to the extent of the lower of the undistributed earnings or the amount loaned, secured, or guaranteed. A disposition of stock will terminate all elections with respect to the undistributed earnings attributable to that stock. A change in status of the QEF will terminate all elections.

Line 7.— Enter the deferred tax due from the termination of the section 1294 election. The deferred tax entered on line 3 is due if the election was completely terminated. If the election was only partially terminated, a proportionate amount of the deferred tax is due. That amount is determined by multiplying the amount entered on line 3 by a fraction, in which the numerator is the amount entered on line 6 and the denominator is the amount entered on line 2. The deferred tax is due by the due date of the shareholder's income tax return (without regard to extensions) for the year of termination.

When the election is terminated, corporations include the deferred tax as part of the total for Form 1120, Schedule J, line 10. Also enter the deferred tax to the left of line 10 and label it as "Sec. 1294 deferred tax."

Individuals must enter the deferred tax as part of the total for Form 1040, line 51. Also enter the deferred tax to the left of line 51, and label it as "Sec. 1294 deferred tax."

Line 8.— Enter the interest accrued on the deferred tax. Interest accrues beginning on the due date (without regard to extensions) of your tax return for the tax year in which the section 1294 election is made, and ending with the due date (without regard to extensions) of your tax return for the tax year of the termination. Interest is computed using the rates and methods under section 6621.

Corporations, enter the amount of section 1294 interest at the bottom right margin of Form 1120, page 1 and label it as "Sec. 1294 interest." Corporations, also include this amount in your check or money order payable to the Internal Revenue Service. If you would otherwise receive a refund, reduce the refund by the interest due.

Individuals must enter the interest from line 8 at the bottom right margin of Form 1040, page 1, and label it as "Sec. 1294 interest." Also include this amount in your check or money order payable to the Internal Revenue Service. If you would otherwise receive a refund, reduce the amount of the refund by the amount of interest due.

Lines 9 and 10.— Complete lines 9 and 10 only if you have partially terminated your section 1294 election. Enter on line 9 the part of the deferred tax outstanding after the partial termination of the section 1294 election. This amount should equal line 3 minus line 7.

Enter on line 10 the accrued interest remaining after the partial termination of the section 1294 election. This amount should equal line 4 minus line 8.

Department of the Treasury

TD F 90-22.1 (10/92)

SUPERSEDES ALL PREVIOUS EDITIONS

Report of Foreign Bank and Financial Accounts

For the calendar year 19 ......

Do not file this form with your Federal Tax Return.

Form Approved: OMB No. 1505-0063

This form should be used to report financial interest in or signature authority or other authority over one or more bank accounts, securities accounts, or other financial accounts in foreign countries as required by Department of the Treasury Regulations (31 CFR 103). You are not required to file a report if the aggregate value of the accounts did not exceed $10,000. Check all appropriate boxes. **See instructions on back for definitions.** File this form with Dept. of the Treasury, P.O. Box 32621, Detroit, MI 48232.

1 Name (Last, First, Middle)

2 Social security number or employer identification number if other than individual

3 Name in item 1 refers to
- [ ] Individual
- [ ] Partnership
- [ ] Corporation
- [ ] Fiduciary

4 Address (Street, City, State, Country, ZIP)

5 [ ] I had signature authority over one or more foreign accounts, but had no "financial interest" in such accounts (see Instruction J). Indicate for these accounts:

a Name and social security number or taxpayer identification number of each owner _____

b Address of each owner _____

(Do not complete item 9 for these accounts)

6 [ ] I had a "financial interest" in one or more foreign accounts owned by a domestic corporation, partnership or trust which is required to file TD F 90-22.1 (See instruction L). Indicate for these accounts:

a Name and taxpayer identification number of each such corporation, partnership or trust _____

b Address of each such corporation, partnership or trust _____

(Do not complete item 9 for these accounts)

7 [ ] I had a "financial interest" in one or more foreign accounts, but the total maximum value of these accounts (see instruction I) did not exceed $10,000 at any time during the year. (If you checked this box, do not complete item 9.)

8 [ ] I had a "financial interest" in 25 or more foreign accounts. (If you checked this box, do not complete item 9.)

9 If you had a "financial interest" in one or more but fewer than 25 foreign accounts which are required to be reported, and the total maximum value of the accounts exceeded $10,000 during the year (see instruction I), write the total number of those accounts in the box below:

Complete items **a** through **f** below for one of the accounts and attach a separate TD F 90-22.1 for each of the others. Items 1, 2, 3, 9, and 10 must be completed for each account.

Check here if this is an attachment: [ ]

a Name in which account is maintained

b Name of bank or other person with whom account is maintained

c Number and other account designation, if any

d Address of office or branch where account is maintained

e Type of account. (If not certain of English name for the type of account, give the foreign language name and describe the nature of the account. Attach additional sheets if necessary.)
- [ ] Bank Account
- [ ] Securities Account
- [ ] Other (specify)

f Maximum value of account (see instructions I)
- [ ] Under $10,000
- [ ] $10,000 to $50,000
- [ ] $50,000 to $100,000
- [ ] Over $100,000

10 Signature

11 Title (Not necessary if reporting a personal account)

12 Date

Privacy Act Notification

Pursuant to the requirements of Public Law 93-579 (Privacy Act of 1974), notice is hereby given that the authority to collect information on TD F 90-22.1 in accordance with 5 U.S.C. 552(e)(3) is Public Law 91-508; 31 U.S.C. 1121; 5 U.S.C. 301, 31 CFR Part 103.

The principal purpose of collecting the information is to assure maintenance of reports or records where such reports or records have a high degree of usefulness in criminal, tax, or regulatory investigations or proceedings. The information collected may be provided to those officers and employees of any constituent unit of the Department of the Treasury who have a need for the records in the performance of their duties. The records may be referred to any other department or agency of the Federal Government upon the request of the head of such department or agency for use in a criminal, tax, or regulatory investigation or proceeding.

Disclosure of this information is mandatory. Civil and criminal penalties, including under certain circumstances a fine of not more than $500,000 and imprisonment of not more than five years, are provided for failure to file a report, supply information, and for filing a false or fraudulent report.

Disclosure of the social security number is mandatory. The authority to collect this number is 31 CFR 103. The social security number will be used as a means to identify the individual who files the report.

Cat. No. 12996D

Instructions

A. Who Must File a Report.—Each United States person who has a financial interest in or signature authority or other authority over bank, securities, or other financial accounts in a foreign country, which exceeds $10,000 in aggregate value at any time during the calendar year, must report that relationship each calendar year by filing TD F 90-22.1 with the Department of the Treasury on or before June 30, of the succeeding year.

An officer or employee of a commercial bank which is subject to the supervision of the Comptroller of the Currency, the Board of Governors of the Federal Reserve System, or the Federal Deposit Insurance Corporation need not report that he has signature or other authority over a foreign bank, securities, or other financial account maintained by the bank unless he has a personal financial interest in the account.

In addition, an officer or employee of a domestic corporation whose securities are listed upon national securities exchanges or which has assets exceeding $1 million and 500 or more shareholders of record need not file such a report concerning his signature authority over a foreign financial account of the corporation, if he has no personal financial interest in the account and has been advised in writing by the chief financial officer of the corporation that the corporation has filed a current report which includes that account.

B. United States Person.—The term "United States person" means (1) a citizen or resident of the United States, (2) a domestic partnership, (3) a domestic corporation, or (4) a domestic estate or trust.

C. When and Where to File.—This report shall be filed on or before June 30 each calendar year with the Department of the Treasury, Post Office Box 32621, Detroit, MI 48232, or it may be hand carried to any local office of the Internal Revenue Service for forwarding to the Department of the Treasury, Detroit, MI.

D. Account in a Foreign Country.—A "foreign country" includes all geographical areas located outside the United States, Guam, Puerto Rico, and the Virgin Islands.

Report any account maintained with a bank (except a military banking facility as defined in Instruction E) or broker or dealer in securities that is located in a foreign country, even if it is a part of a United States bank or other institution. Do not report any account maintained with a branch, agency, or other office of a foreign bank or other institution that is located in the United States, Guam, Puerto Rico, and the Virgin Islands.

E. Military Banking Facility.—Do not consider as an account in a foreign country, an account in an institution known as a "United States military banking facility" (or "United States military finance facility") operated by a United States financial institution designated by the United States Government to serve U.S. Government installations abroad, even if the United States military banking facility is located in a foreign country.

F. Bank, Financial Account.—The term "bank account" means a savings, demand, checking, deposit, loan or any other account maintained with a financial institution or other person engaged in the business of banking. It includes certificates of deposit.

The term "securities account" means an account maintained with a financial institution or other person who buys, sells, holds, or trades stock or other securities for the benefit of another.

The term "other financial account" means any other account maintained with a financial institution or other person who accepts deposits, exchanges or transmits funds, or acts as a broker or dealer for future transactions in any commodity on (or subject to the rules of) a commodity exchange or association.

G. Financial Interest.—A financial interest in a bank, securities, or other financial account in a foreign country means an interest described in either of the following two paragraphs:

1. A United States person has a financial interest in each account for which such person is the owner of records or has legal title, whether the account is maintained for his or her own benefit or for the benefit of others including non-United States persons. If an account is maintained in the name of two persons jointly, or if several persons each own a partial interest in an account, each of those United States persons has a financial interest in that account.

2. A United States person has a financial interest in each bank, securities, or other financial account in a foreign country for which the owner of record or holder of legal title is: (a) a person acting as an agent, nominee, attorney, or in some other capacity on behalf of the U.S. person; (b) a corporation in which the United States person owns directly or indirectly more than 50 percent of the total value of shares of stock; (c) a partnership in which the United States person owns an interest in more than 50 percent of the profits (distributive share of income); or (d) a trust in which the United States person either has a present beneficial interest in more than 50 percent of the assets or from which such person receives more than 50 percent of the current income.

H. Signature or Other Authority Over an Account.—

Signature Authority.—A person has signature authority over an account if such person can control the disposition of money or other property in it by delivery of a document containing his or her signature (or his or her signature and that of one or more other persons) to the bank or other person with whom the account is maintained.

Other authority exists in a person who can exercise comparable power over an account by direct communication to the bank or other person with whom the account is maintained, either orally or by some other means.

I. Account Valuation.—For items 7, 9, and Instruction A, the maximum value of an account is the largest amount of currency and non-monetary assets that appear on any quarterly or more frequent account statement issued for the applicable year. If periodic account statements are not so issued, the maximum account asset value is the largest amount of currency and non-monetary assets in the account at any time during the year. Convert foreign currency by using the official exchange rate at the end of the year. In valuing currency of a country that uses multiple exchanges rates, use the rate which would apply if the currency in the account were converted into United States dollars at the close of the calendar year.

The value of stock, other securities or other non-monetary assets in an account reported on TD F 90-22.1 is the fair market value at the end of the calendar year, or if withdrawn from the account, at the time of the withdrawal.

For purposes of items 7, 9, and Instruction A, if you had a financial interest in more than one account, each account is to be valued separately in accordance with the foregoing two paragraphs.

If you had a financial interest in one or more but fewer than 25 accounts, and you are unable to determine whether the maximum value of these accounts exceeded $10,000 at any time during the year, check item 9 (do not check item 7) and complete item 9 for each of these accounts.

J. United States Persons with Authority Over but No Interest in an Account.—Except as provided in Instruction A and the following paragraph, you must state the name, address, and identifying number of each owner of an account over which you had authority, but if you check item 5 for more than one account of the same owner, you need identify the owner only once.

If you check item 5 for one or more accounts in which no United States person had a financial interest, you may state on the first line of this item, in lieu of supplying information about the owner, "No U.S. person had any financial interest in the foreign accounts." This statement must be based upon the actual belief of the person filing this form after he or she has taken reasonable measures to endure its correctness.

If you check item 5 for accounts owned by a domestic corporation and its domestic and/or foreign subsidiaries, you may treat them as one owner and write in the space provided, the name of the parent corporation, followed by "and related entities," and the identifying number and address of the parent corporation.

K. Consolidated Reporting.—A corporation which owns directly or indirectly more than 50 percent interest in one or more other entities will be permitted to file a consolidated report on TD F 90-22.1, on behalf of itself and such other entities provided that a listing of them is made part of the consolidated report. Such reports should be signed by an authorized official of the parent corporation.

If the group of entities covered by a consolidated report has a financial interest in 25 or more foreign financial accounts, the reporting corporation need only note that fact on the form, it will, however, be required to provide detailed information concerning each account when so requested by the Secretary or his delegate.

L. Avoiding Duplicate Reporting.—If you had financial interest (as defined in instruction G2(b), (c), or (d)) in one or more accounts which are owned by a domestic corporation, partnership or trust which is required to file TD F 90-22.1 with respect to these accounts in lieu of completing item 9 for each account you may check item 6 and provide the required information.

M. Providing Additional Information.—Any person who does not complete item 9, shall when requested by the Department of the Treasury provide the information called for in item 9.

N. Signature (Item 10).—*This report must be signed* by the person named in item 1. If the report is being filed on behalf of a partnership, corporation, or fiduciary, it must be signed by an authorized individual.

O. Penalties.—For criminal penalties for failure to file a report, supply information, and for filing a false or fraudulent report, see 31 U.S.C. 5322(a), 31 U.S.C. 5322(b), and 18 U.S.C. 1001.

The estimated average burden associated with this collection of information is 10 minutes per respondent or recordkeeper depending on individual circumstances. Comments concerning the accuracy of this burden estimate and suggestions for reducing the burden should be directed to the Department of the Treasury, Office of Financial Enforcement, Room 5000 Treasury Annex Building, Washington, DC 20220, and to the Office of Management and Budget, Paperwork Reduction Project (1505-0063), Washington, DC 20503.

Suspicious Activity Report

FRB: FR 2230	OMB No. 7100-0212
FDIC: 6710/06	OMB No. 3064-0077
OCC: 8010-9,8010-1	OMB No. 1557-0180
OTS: 1601	OMB No. 1550-0003
NCUA: 2362	OMB No. 3133-0094
TREASURY: TD F 90-22.47	OMB No. 1506-0001

ALWAYS COMPLETE ENTIRE REPORT

Expires September 30, 1998

1 Check appropriate box:
 a ☐ Initial Report b ☐ Corrected Report c ☐ Supplemental Report

Part I Reporting Financial Institution Information

2 Name of Financial Institution

3 Primary Federal Regulator
 a ☐ Federal Reserve d ☐ OCC
 b ☐ FDIC e ☐ OTS
 c ☐ NCUA

4 Address of Financial Institution

5 City 6 State 7 Zip Code 8 EIN or TIN

9 Address of Branch Office(s) where activity occurred

10 Asset size of financial institution $ .00

11 City 12 State 13 Zip Code

14 If institution closed, date closed (MMDDYY) ___/___/___

15 Account number(s) affected, if any
 a _____
 b _____

16 Have any of the institution's accounts related to this matter been closed?
 a ☐ Yes b ☐ No If yes, identify _____

Part II Suspect Information

17 Last Name or Name of Entity 18 First Name 19 Middle Initial

20 Address 21 SSN, EIN or TIN (as applicable)

22 City 23 State 24 Zip Code 25 Country 26 Date of Birth (MMDDYY) ___/___/___

27 Phone Number - Residence (include area code) ( )

28 Phone Number - Work (include area code) ( )

29 Occupation

30 Forms of Identification for Suspect:
 a ☐ Driver's License b ☐ Passport c ☐ Alien Registration d ☐ Other _____
 e Number _____ f Issuing Authority _____

31 Relationship to Financial Institution:
 a ☐ Accountant d ☐ Attorney g ☐ Customer j ☐ Officer
 b ☐ Agent e ☐ Borrower h ☐ Director k ☐ Shareholder
 c ☐ Appraiser f ☐ Broker i ☐ Employee l ☐ Other _____

32 Is insider suspect still affiliated with the financial institution?
 a ☐ Yes
 b ☐ No   If no, specify { c ☐ Suspended e ☐ Resigned
                           d ☐ Terminated }

33 Date of Suspension, Termination, Resignation (MMDDYY) ___/___/___

34 Admission/Confession
 a ☐ Yes b ☐ No

Part III — Suspicious Activity Information

35 Date of suspicious activity (MMDDYY) ___ / ___ / ___

36 Dollar amount involved in known or suspicious activity $ .00

37 Summary characterization of suspicious activity:
- a ☐ Bank Secrecy Act/Structuring/Money Laundering
- b ☐ Bribery/Gratuity
- c ☐ Check Fraud
- d ☐ Check Kiting
- e ☐ Commercial Loan Fraud
- f ☐ Consumer Loan Fraud
- g ☐ Counterfeit Check
- h ☐ Counterfeit Credit/Debit Card
- i ☐ Counterfeit Instrument (other)
- j ☐ Credit Card Fraud
- k ☐ Debit Card Fraud
- l ☐ Defalcation/Embezzlement
- m ☐ False Statement
- n ☐ Misuse of Position or Self-Dealing
- o ☐ Mortgage Loan Fraud
- p ☐ Mysterious Disappearance
- q ☐ Wire Transfer Fraud

r ☐ Other _____

38 Amount of loss prior to recovery (if applicable) $ .00

39 Dollar amount of recovery (if applicable) $ .00

40 Has the suspicious activity had a material impact on or otherwise affected the financial soundness of the institution?
a ☐ Yes   b ☐ No

41 Has the institution's bonding company been notified?
a ☐ Yes   b ☐ No

42 Has any law enforcement agency already been advised by telephone, written communication, or otherwise? If so, list the agency and local address.
Agency _____

43 Address

44 City   45 State   46 Zip Code

Part IV — Witness Information

47 Last Name   48 First Name   49 Middle Initial

50 Address   51 SSN

52 City   53 State   54 Zip Code   55 Date of Birth (MMDDYY) ___ / ___ / ___

56 Title   57 Phone Number (include area code) ( )   58 Interviewed a ☐ Yes b ☐ No

Part V — Preparer Information

59 Last Name   60 First Name   61 Middle Initial

62 Title   63 Phone Number (include area code) ( )   64 Date (MMDDYY) ___ / ___ / ___

Part VI — Contact for Assistance (If different than Preparer Information in Part V)

65 Last Name   66 First Name   67 Middle Initial

68 Title   69 Phone Number (include area code) ( )

70 Agency (If applicable)

Part VII Suspicious Activity Information Explanation/Description

Explanation/description of known or suspected violation of law or suspicious activity. This section of the report is **critical**. The care with which it is written may make the difference in whether or not the described conduct and its possible criminal nature are clearly understood. Provide below a chronological and **complete** account of the possible violation of law, including what is unusual, irregular or suspicious about the transaction, using the following checklist as you prepare your account. If necessary, continue the narrative on a duplicate of this page.

a **Describe** supporting documentation and retain for 5 years.
b **Explain** who benefited, financially or otherwise, from the transaction, how much, and how.
c **Retain** any confession, admission, or explanation of the transaction provided by the suspect and indicate to whom and when it was given.
d **Retain** any confession, admission, or explanation of the transaction provided by any other person and indicate to whom and when it was given.
e **Retain** any evidence of cover-up or evidence of an attempt to deceive federal or state examiners or others.
f **Indicate** where the possible violation took place (e.g., main office, branch, other).
g **Indicate** whether the possible violation is an isolated incident or relates to other transactions.
h **Indicate** whether there is any related litigation; if so, specify.
i **Recommend** any further investigation that might assist law enforcement authorities.
j **Indicate** whether any information has been excluded from this report; if so, why?

For Bank Secrecy Act/Structuring/Money Laundering reports, include the following additional information:

k **Indicate** whether currency and/or monetary instruments were involved. If so, provide the amount and/or description.
l **Indicate** any account number that may be involved or affected.

Paperwork Reduction Act Notice: The purpose of this form is to provide an effective and consistent means for financial institutions to notify appropriate law enforcement agencies of known or suspected criminal conduct or suspicious activities that take place at or were perpetrated against financial institutions. This report is required by law, pursuant to authority contained in the following statutes. Board of Governors of the Federal Reserve System: 12 U.S.C. 324, 334, 611a, 1844(b) and (c), 3105(c) (2) and 3106(a). Federal Deposit Insurance Corporation: 12 U.S.C. 93a, 1818, 1881-84, 3401-22. Office of the Comptroller of the Currency: 12 U.S.C. 93a, 1818, 1881-84, 3401-22. Office of Thrift Supervision: 12 U.S.C. 1463 and 1464. National Credit Union Administration: 12 U.S.C. 1766(a), 1786(q). Financial Crimes Enforcement Network: 31 U.S.C. 5318(g). Information collected on this report is confidential (5 U.S.C. 552(b)(7) and 552a(k)(2), and 31 U.S.C. 5318(g)). The Federal financial institutions regulatory agencies and the U.S. Departments of Justice and Treasury may use and share the information. Public reporting and recordkeeping burden for this information collection is estimated to average 36 minutes per response, and includes time to gather and maintain data in the required report, review the instructions, and complete the information collection. Send comments regarding this burden estimate, including suggestions for reducing the burden, to the Office of Management and Budget, Paperwork Reduction Project, Washington, DC 20503 and, depending on your primary Federal regulatory agency, to Secretary, Board of Governors of the Federal Reserve System, Washington, DC 20551; or Assistant Executive Secretary, Federal Deposit Insurance Corporation, Washington, DC 20429; or Legislative and Regulatory Analysis Division, Office of the Comptroller of the Currency, Washington, DC 20219; or Office of Thrift Supervision, Enforcement Office, Washington, DC 20552; or National Credit Union Administration, 1775 Duke Street, Alexandria, VA 22314; or Office of the Director, Financial Crimes Enforcement Network, Department of the Treasury, 2070 Chain Bridge Road, Vienna, VA 22182.

sale of any stock, bond, certificate of deposit, or other monetary instrument or investment security, or any other payment, transfer, or delivery by, through, or to a financial institution, by whatever means effected) conducted or attempted by, at or through the financial institution and involving or aggregating $5,000 or more in funds or other assets, if the financial institution knows, suspects, or has reason to suspect that:

i. The transaction involves funds derived from illegal activities or is intended or conducted in order to hide or disguise funds or assets derived from illegal activities (including, without limitation, the ownership, nature, source, location, or control of such funds or assets) as part of a plan to violate or evade any law or regulation or to avoid any transaction reporting requirement under Federal law;

ii. The transaction is designed to evade any regulations promulgated under the Bank Secrecy Act; or

iii. The transaction has no business or apparent lawful purpose or is not the sort in which the particular customer would normally be expected to engage, and the financial institution knows of no reasonable explanation for the transaction after examining the available facts, including the background and possible purpose of the transaction.

The Bank Secrecy Act requires all financial institutions to file currency transaction reports (CTRs) in accordance with the Department of the Treasury's implementing regulations (31 CFR Part 103). These regulations require a financial institution to file a CTR whenever a currency transaction exceeds $10,000. If a currency transaction exceeds $10,000 and is suspicious, the institution must file both a CTR (reporting the currency transaction) and a suspicious activity report (reporting the suspicious or criminal aspects of the transaction). If a currency transaction equals or is below $10,000 and is suspicious, the institution should only file a suspicious activity report.

2. A financial institution is required to file a suspicious activity report no later than 30 calendar days after the date of initial detection of facts that may constitute a basis for filing a suspicious activity report. If no suspect was identified on the date of detection of the incident requiring the filing, a financial institution may delay filing a suspicious activity report for an additional 30 calendar days to identify a suspect. In no case shall reporting be delayed more than 60 calendar days after the date of initial detection of a reportable transaction.

3. This suspicious activity report does not need to be filed for those robberies and burglaries that are reported to local authorities, or (except for savings associations and service corporations) for lost, missing, counterfeit or stolen securities that are reported pursuant to the requirements of 17 CFR 240.17f-1.

HOW TO MAKE A REPORT:

1. Send each completed suspicious activity report to:

    FinCEN, Detroit Computing Center, P.O. Box 33980, Detroit, MI 48232

2. For items that do not apply or for which information is not available, leave blank.

3. Complete each suspicious activity report in its entirety, even when the suspicious activity report is a corrected or supplemental report.

4. Do not include supporting documentation with the suspicious activity report. Identify and retain a copy of the suspicious activity report and all original supporting documentation or business record equivalent for 5 years from the date of the suspicious activity report. All supporting documentation must be made available to appropriate authorities upon request.

5. If more space is needed to complete an item (for example, to report an additional suspect or witness), a copy of the page containing the item should be used to provide the information.

6. Financial institutions are encouraged to provide copies of suspicious activity reports to state and local authorities, where appropriate.

Suspicious Activity Report
Instructions

Safe Harbor Federal law (31 U.S.C. 5318(g)(3)) provides complete protection from civil liability for all reports of suspected or known criminal violations and suspicious activities to appropriate authorities, including supporting documentation, regardless of whether such reports are filed pursuant to this report's instructions or are filed on a voluntary basis. Specifically, the law provides that a financial institution, and its directors, officers, employees and agents, that make a disclosure of any possible violation of law or regulation, including in connection with the preparation of suspicious activity reports, "shall not be liable to any person under any law or regulation of the United States or any constitution, law, or regulation of any State or political subdivision thereof, for such disclosure or for any failure to notify the person involved in the transaction or any other person of such disclosure."

Notification Prohibited Federal law (31 U.S.C. 5318(g)(2)) requires that a financial institution, and its directors, officers, employees and agents who, voluntarily or by means of a suspicious activity report, report suspected or known criminal violations or suspicious activities may not notify any person involved in the transaction that the transaction has been reported.

In situations involving violations requiring immediate attention, such as when a reportable violation is ongoing, the financial institution shall immediately notify, by telephone, appropriate law enforcement and financial institution supervisory authorities in addition to filing a timely suspicious activity report.

WHEN TO MAKE A REPORT:

1. All financial institutions operating in the United States, including insured banks, savings associations, savings association service corporations, credit unions, bank holding companies, nonbank subsidiaries of bank holding companies, Edge and Agreement corporations, and U.S. branches and agencies of foreign banks, are required to make this report following the discovery of:

    a. **Insider abuse involving any amount.** Whenever the financial institution detects any known or suspected Federal criminal violation, or pattern of criminal violations, committed or attempted against the financial institution or involving a transaction or transactions conducted through the financial institution, where the financial institution believes that it was either an actual or potential victim of a criminal violation, or series of criminal violations, or that the financial institution was used to facilitate a criminal transaction, and the financial institution has a substantial basis for identifying one of its directors, officers, employees, agents or other institution-affiliated parties as having committed or aided in the commission of a criminal act regardless of the amount involved in the violation.

    b. **Violations aggregating $5,000 or more where a suspect can be identified.** Whenever the financial institution detects any known or suspected Federal criminal violation, or pattern of criminal violations, committed or attempted against the financial institution or involving a transaction or transactions conducted through the financial institution and involving or aggregating $5,000 or more in funds or other assets, where the financial institution believes that it was either an actual or potential victim of a criminal violation, or series of criminal violations, or that the financial institution was used to facilitate a criminal transaction, and the financial institution has a substantial basis for identifying a possible suspect or group of suspects. If it is determined prior to filing this report that the identified suspect or group of suspects has used an "alias," then information regarding the true identity of the suspect or group of suspects, as well as alias identifiers, such as drivers' licenses or social security numbers, addresses and telephone numbers, must be reported.

    c. **Violations aggregating $25,000 or more regardless of a potential suspect.** Whenever the financial institution detects any known or suspected Federal criminal violation, or pattern of criminal violations, committed or attempted against the financial institution or involving a transaction or transactions conducted through the financial institution and involving or aggregating $25,000 or more in funds or other assets, where the financial institution believes that it was either an actual or potential victim of a criminal violation, or series of criminal violations, or that the financial institution was used to facilitate a criminal transaction, even though there is no substantial basis for identifying a possible suspect or group of suspects.

    d. **Transactions aggregating $5,000 or more that involve potential money laundering or violations of the Bank Secrecy Act.** Any transaction (which for purposes of this subsection means a deposit, withdrawal, transfer between accounts, exchange of currency, loan, extension of credit, purchase or

INDEX

A Society of Suspects 111, 136
ABA Banking Journal 68, 135, 136
Above the Law 111, 133
Akron Tax Journal 134
Alderman & Kennedy 104, 105, 106, 107, 133
Alexander v. United States 54
American Bankers Association 81
American Bar Association 87
American Express 9, 45
Ameritrust v. Derakhshan 112
Ames, Aldrich 41
asset protection   90, 98, 99, 101, 103, 109, 110, 112, 113, 114, 115, 116, 118, 119, 120, 125, 127, 128, 131
    asset protection trust 110, 113, 126
    conflict of law 84, 86, 88, 90, 99
        comity 86
        dual criminality 55, 86, 91, 100
        revenue rule 90
    limited partnership 59, 109, 113, 115, 116, 117, 118
        charging order 116
        Revised Uniform Limited Partnership Act 115
        Uniform Limited Partnership Act 115, 116
    corporations .... v, 25, 54, 59, 88, 109, 113, 114, 126, 138, 198
    excise tax 124, 127
    flight capital 110, 112
    fraudulent conveyance 96, 97
        Statute of Elizabeth 96, 97, 98, 126, 128
    pension and retirement plans 112, 125
    tenancy by the entireties 119
    ultra vires actions (effect on) 114
Axelrod 110, 133

Bamford 107, 133
bankruptcy 43, 49, 109, 110, 111, 112, 114, 117, 119, 129
Bank Secrecy Act   17, 20, 50, 55, 56, 59, 60, 61, 62, 63, 64, 65, 73, 74, 79, 80, 120, 121, 122
    cash transactions 6, 8, 9, 17, 56, 62, 66, 108, 109, 121
        Currency Transaction Report   v, 10, 55, 60, 61, 62, 65, 66, 68, 79, 93, 121, 138, 192, 226
        Form 4790 (Report of International Transportation of Currency or Monetary Instruments) .... v, 55, 61, 65, 81, 121, 122, 138, 196
        Form 8300 .... v, 63, 64, 81, 121, 138, 218
            designated reporting transaction 55, 63

Foreign Bank Account Reporting Form (Form TD F 90-22.1)   v,   64,   123,   124, 138, 234
    monetary instruments 55, 60, 61, 62, 64, 67, 80, 81, 84, 120, 121, 122
        money orders 55, 56, 60, 62, 63, 68, 84, 122
    structuring 9, 60, 61, 62, 79, 109, 121
    suspicious transactions 9, 63, 65, 66, 67, 68, 79, 83, 84, 90, 92, 93, 95
bearer shares 26, 114, 122, 125, 126
Bennis v. Michigan 72, 119
Bertoli v. Malone 104
black market 8, 17
Bureau of Alcohol, Tobacco, and Firearms 108
Bureau of Justice Assistance 4
Bush, George 31, 82

Califano, Joseph 69
California Bankers Association v. Shultz 20, 57, 108
Campbell 103, 130, 133
capital flight 89, 103, 104, 109
Caplin & Drysdale, Chartered v. United States 3, 48, 54
Citicorp 45
Civil Law 115, 127, 128, 129
    forced heirship 127, 128
    per stirpes 127
    Power of Attorney 124, 128
Clinton, Bill 33
Common Law (decisional law)   19, 45, 46, 94, 95, 96, 97, 99, 103, 104, 108, 111, 112, 115, 120, 126, 127, 128, 129, 137
Commonwealth 95, 96, 98, 99, 126, 127, 134
    dependent territories 84, 90, 92, 95, 96, 126
    Statute of Westminster 95
Comprehensive Forfeiture Act 70, 71, 73, 76
Comptroller of the Currency 108
Computer Matching and Privacy Protection Act 70
Constitutional Criminal Procedure 133
Copeland, Cary 6
Council of Europe .... iv, 82, 90, 93, 100, 134, 135
Criminal Referral Report 65
Crown   iv 71, 84, 90, 94, 95, 96, 97, 98, 99, 103, 107, 108, 109, 111, 112, 116, 118, 125, 126, 127, 128
    Letters Patent 95
    Parliament 95, 96, 97, 127
    prerogative 95, 125, 127
    Prime Minister 96
    Privy Council 95, 96, 97, 134
    Customs Service 19, 108

Drug Enforcement Administration (DEA) 5, 7, 11, 14, 37, 70, 81, 108

debit card 8, 123
Deficit Reduction Act 59, 70
Dennis 3
Department of Defense 35
Department of Justice 3, 4, 6, 37, 53, 54, 66, 72, 111
Department of Transportation 70
Doe v. United States 86, 105
Dominican Republic 88
Douglas, William 2
Dun and Bradstreet 108
Eggar, Roscoe 27

Emergency Banking Act 31, 32
Employee Retirement Income Security Act (ERISA) 112
Endangered Species Act 6
English Common Law 45, 70, 94, 95, 96, 97, 99, 103, 111, 116, 126, 128, 129
Etim v. United States 109
European Convention on Human Rights 94, 135
Evans v. Dale 52
Evans v. Galardi 116
Ex Parte Casperson 115
Executive Order 31, 32, 33, 35, 37, 69, 82, 96
expatriation 131
expectation of privacy 19, 103, 104, 105, 106, 107, 108, 109
   aerial surveillance 106
   attorney-client privilege 39, 95, 109, 110, 111
   correspondence
      mail cover 21, 22, 41, 87, 108
      mail drops 22
      Pretty Good Privacy (PGP) 130
   electronic surveillance 37, 38, 39, 40, 41
      bugs 38, 40
      cellular telephone 107
   cluster modeling 44
   compelled consent 86, 127
   curtilage 105, 106
   divorce 15, 16, 39, 46, 52, 119
   financial privacy 2, 3, 19, 59, 61, 103, 120
   paper trail 106, 121
   public records 43, 44, 45, 114
   telephone privacy
      caller ID 42, 129
      dialed number recorder 129, 130
      reverse directory 42
      wiretaps 37, 38, 39, 40
   Tournier v. National Provincial and Union Bank of England 103
   trash 106

factoring 122
Fair Credit Reporting Act 42, 43, 46
Family Support Act 34
Federal Bureau of Investigation (FBI)   10, 12, 13, 16, 17, 21, 36, 37, 41, 44, 45, 57, 81, 90, 96, 107, 108, 134
    National Crime Information Center 16, 44, 57, 70
    Federal Communications Commission 38
Federal Deposit Insurance Act 5
Federal Deposit Insurance Corporation 108
Federal Register 30, 62, 131
Federal Reserve 7, 32, 60, 80, 99, 108, 123
Financial Action Task Force (FATF) 92, 93, 94, 98
Financial Times 123
Fischer 134
Fisher v. United States 58
Fleming v. Nestor 112
forfeiture
    civil forfeiture 4, 5, 6, 62, 71, 72, 73, 76, 77, 84, 89, 119
        Admiralty (procedures in) 95
        bona fide purchaser (rights of) 53, 93
        burden of proof 4, 72, 91, 93, 117, 131
        guilt   (effect of on) 4, 9
        hearsay (evidence to support) 72, 90
        informants 3, 8, 10, 11, 12, 72, 90, 110, 111
            immunity (of to prosecution) 91, 111
        legal fictions (of) 53
            personality (of property) 71
            non-punitive 96, 115, 128
            relation-back doctrine 53, 112
            taint doctrine 7, 71
            plea bargains (in) 91
    criminal forfeiture 53, 54
    deodand 71, 76
    ex parte (procedures in) 26, 72, 118
    ink drop theory (of) 71
    innocent owners (rights of) 4, 72, 119
    outlawry 71, 76, 110, 111, 127
    predicate offenses (for) 48, 50, 52, 53, 55, 76, 92, 110
    proceeds (liable to)   4, 6, 7, 11, 24, 26, 48, 50, 52, 65, 67, 74, 76, 77, 78, 89, 90, 91, 92, 123
    real estate (vulnerability to) 29, 30, 35, 43, 56, 82, 108, 124
    retroactive (application of) 5, 24, 25
    third party (rights in) .... ii, 24, 58, 67, 86, 112, 129
Freedom of Information Act 69, 80

Gary Allen Report   14
General Accounting Office (GAO) 28

Germany	88, 90, 92, 93, 128
Gilmore	134
Grenada	88, 92, 94

H.J., Inc. v. Northwestern Bell Co.	52
Hardy	14
Helman v. Anderson	116

Immigration and Naturalization Service 70, 108
In re Air Crash in Bali, Indonesia 105
In re Marc Rich & Co. 105
In re Priestly 117
In re Tucker 90
Internal Revenue Service (IRS)   6, 8, 10, 13, 14, 16, 17, 21, 22, 23, 24, 25, 26, 27, 28, 29, 30, 34, 35, 45, 55, 57, 58, 60, 61, 62, 63, 64, 66, 68, 70, 78, 80, 81, 82, 83, 108, 112, 113, 114, 117, 119, 120, 121, 124, 131, 133, 134
    administrative subpoena 24, 42, 43, 59
    Compliance 2000 30
    Criminal Investigation Division 8, 14, 61
    estate tax 23, 25, 117, 131
    income tax 13, 21, 23, 29, 64, 81, 123, 126
    independent contractor 27
    Market Segment Specialization Program 29
    Strategic Plan 26, 27, 28, 29
    tax avoidance 53, 131
    tax evasion 25, 57, 58, 80
    tax fraud 25, 53, 64, 74, 78, 117
    tax lien 43, 109, 112, 119
intelligence agencies
    AUSTRAC 109
    Central Intelligence Agency (CIA) ....
        DESIST database 21
    Financial Crimes Enforcement Network (FinCEN)   iii, 30, 45, 56, 57, 64, 69, 78, 80, 81, 94, 99, 108, 109, 111, 120, 123, 134, 135
        Deposit Tracking System 81, 82, 94, 109
        Operation Gateway 82
    MI-5 .... 38, 107, 108
    National Security Agency (NSA) 35, 99, 108
        Foreign Intelligence Surveillance Court 37, 38
        Project Minaret 36
        Project Shamrock 36

    National Criminal Information Network (NCIN) 109, 111
    TRACFIN 109
International Emergency Economic Powers Act (IEEPA) 33, 75, 82
International Herald Tribune 123
international judicial assistance

Memoranda of Understanding..88, 90
treaties 4, 25, 55, 82, 86, 88, 89, 90, 93, 95, 96, 100, 105, 125
Convention on Laundering, Search, Seizure, and Confiscation of the Proceeds from Crime 93, 134
Convention on Mutual Administrative Assistance in Tax Matters 82, 90
Mutual Legal Assistance Treaties (MLATs) .... iv, 55, 84, 88, 89, 100
tax treaties...88
United Nations Convention Against Illicit Traffic in Narcotic Drugs and Psychotropic Substances...91
International Taxation 131
Introduction to Comparative Law, An 103, 136
Irish Republican Army..108
Isenbergh 131

Jacobson v. United States 14
joint tenancy 119
jurisdiction 20, 22, 23, 25, 31, 32, 46, 77, 84, 86, 87, 88, 89, 91, 93, 94, 95, 97, 98, 99, 103, 105, 106, 111, 113, 114, 116, 117, 118, 120, 122, 123, 124, 125, 126, 127, 128
in rem 71, 123
in personam 71, 103, 105, 106, 111, 127, 128

Kerry 8, 79, 80, 84, 89
Klein v. Klein 116
Kronenberg v. Commissioner 131

Lessard & Williamson 103, 134
LEXIS-NEXIS 108
life insurance 112, 124
London Daily Telegraph.. 108

mail fraud 49, 50, 51, 110
McClean 134
McCollum 77
Medco Containment Services 47
Medicaid 6, 8, 70
Medical Information Bureau 46, 70
Medicare 6, 45, 70
Merryman & Clark 134
Metromail 47, 48, 108
Mexico 88, 89, 90, 131
money laundering 9, 10, 14, 25, 54, 57, 73, 77, 78, 79, 80, 83, 86, 91, 92, 100, 110, 120
Money Laundering Control Act 72, 73, 77, 78, 79
mutual funds 29, 111, 126
Qualified Electing Fund... v, 138, 228
National Emergencies Act...32

National Security Council	108
Netherlands	88, 89, 90, 92, 93
Nilsson	135
Nixon, Richard	32, 39, 57
North American Free Trade Agreement	28
numismatic coins	122
Office of Thrift Supervision	5
offshore financial centers	86, 94, 103, 109, 111, 113, 120, 128
Austria	88, 89, 91, 92, 94
Bahamas	89, 91, 94, 103, 131
Barbados	88, 91, 94
Belize	94, 131
Bermuda	84, 88, 94
British Virgin Islands	89, 90, 94, 103
Cayman Islands	84, 89, 90, 94, 99, 103, 131, 137
Channel Islands	90, 94
Cook Islands	94, 97, 98, 113, 126, 127
International Companies Act	98
International Trusts Act	97, 98, 126
Costa Rica	88
Cyprus	88, 93, 94
Gibraltar	84, 94, 103
Guernsey	94
Hong Kong	94, 103
Isle of Man	94, 103, 112
Jersey	94
Liechtenstein	94, 98, 128
Luxembourg	88, 89, 90, 92, 93
Malaysia	92, 94
Malta	88, 94
Mauritius	92, 94
Montserrat	84, 89, 90, 94
Panama	79, 89
Seychelles	92, 94
Singapore	94, 103
Sri Lanka	92, 94
St. Christopher and Nevis	94
Switzerland	iv, 21, 55, 88, 89, 90, 92, 93, 94, 99, 100, 101, 109, 111, 129
Turks & Caicos Islands	84, 89, 94, 96
Vanuatu	94
Western Samoa	94
Olmstead v. United States	38
Omnibus Crime Control Act	38
Palmyra, The	71
passports	34, 63, 79, 130, 131

Paul v. Davis 20
Physician Computer Network 47
Pittsburgh Press, The 4, 135
Postal Service 20, 21, 31, 56, 108
      Postal Inspection Service 22
Pratt 109
precious metals 31, 56, 64
Prentice-Hall Online 108
Privacy Act 20, 30, 68, 69, 70, 80, 113
probate 128
Project Match 69
Protect Yourself and Your Fees 109, 135
Puzzle Palace, The   107, 133

Quigley 99, 135

Racketeering in Corrupt Organizations Act (RICO)   iii, 48, 50, 51, 52, 53, 54, 55, 56,
    71, 73, 74, 76, 77, 110, 135
RAGS Couture, Inc. v. Hyatt 51
Raikos v. Bloomfield State Bank 60
Reagan, Ronald 37, 39
Regan, Don 8
Religious Technology Center v. Wollersheim 52
Right to Financial Privacy Act 20, 59, 80, 84, 113
Ristau & Abbell 135
Rosen 110, 135
Rudnick 4
Safe Streets Act 38
safety deposit box 24, 124, 125
Sark 94
Scheckloth v. Bustamonte 19
SEC v. Jerry T. O'Brien 112
Secret Service 36, 108
securities fraud 49, 89
single-premium variable benefit life assurance policy 112
Smith, D. 110, 135

Social Security Act 33
Social Security Number 13, 15, 26, 29, 33, 43, 44, 47, 63, 66, 79, 114
Spencer 107
States of Injustice 107
Statewatch 107, 134
Supreme Court   2, 3, 14, 19, 20, 25, 46, 48, 52, 53, 54, 57, 58, 71, 72, 104, 105,
    106, 112, 119, 137

Tax Reform Act (1976) 34
Tax Reform Act (1986) 28

Terry v. Ohio 19
Thornburgh 3
Trading With the Enemy Act 31, 76
Tupper v. Kroc 116
Turning Up the Heat: MI-5 After the Cold War 108

U.S. Constitution
    Bill of Rights 104
        Eighth Amendment 54
        Fifth Amendment 58, 59, 104
            property rights 24, 94
            right to silence 104
        Fourth Amendment 19, 58, 104, 105, 106
            probable cause   3, 7, 19, 20, 21, 22, 26, 37, 38, 54, 72, 89, 104, 106, 129
            searches and seizures 19, 104
            warrants 19, 20, 26, 84, 104, 106, 107
        Sixth Amendment 54, 77, 133

United States v. $11,580 122
United States v. $145,139 109
United States v. $173,081.04 122
United States v. 2525 Leroy Lane 119
United States v. Accounts No. 3034504504 and 144-07143 72
United States v. All Funds 84
United States v. All Monies ($477,048.62) 76
United States v. All the Inventories of the Businesses Known as Khalife Bros. Jewelry 76
United States v. Alvarez-Machain 105
United States v. Aversa 9
United States v. Bank of Nova Scotia 105
United States v. Beecroft 51
United States v. Bryan 127
United States v. Caceres 53
United States v. Carlton 25
United States v. Chadwick 19
United States v. Clines 124
United States v. Daccaret 123
United States v. Doe 20, 58, 105
United States v. Dunn 106
United States v. Giraldi and Reategui 10
United States v. Hennsel 137
United States v. Hooper 57
United States v. Hyppolite 106
United States v. James Daniel Good Real Property 72
United States v. Kellogg 79
United States v. Lot 111 B 72
United States v. MacKay 60

United States v. Meza 84
United States v. Miller 20, 58, 112
United States v. Montague 76
United States v. Morales-Vasquez 122
United States v. Noriega 54, 58
United States v. Porcelli 54
United States v. Raniere 114
United States v. Rylander 127
United States v. Real Property in Mecklenberg County 77
United States v. Regan 117
United States v. Rodgers 119
United States v. Sandini 119
United States v. Scanio 109
United States v. Sellers 105
Universal Declaration of Human Rights 112, 131

Vale v. Louisiana 19, 106
Vander Zee 10, 136
Wallace v. United States 110
Whalen v. Roe 46
wire fraud 9, 50
wire transfers 63, 66, 68, 93

Zeldin 6
Zweigert & Kotz 103, 136

Other Special Reports Available from Scope International

The Passport Report
by Dr WG Hill

Why entrust your life and freedom to any one government?

With only one passport you are accountable to politicians who can regard you as an expendable resource. But this need not be the case. With two or more passports, you will not belong to any one country. Your mobility is ensured and your personal and financial independence can be preserved.

A second passport could save your life, your money and your freedom. This valuable document can open up opportunities you never thought possible.

It is a fact that many countries have well-established but little-known procedures for issuing passports. Knowledge of these 'exceptions' allows intrepid individuals to obtain multiple foreign passports, and thus choose the countries most suitable for their purposes.

Having researched 147 different countries throughout the world, Dr Hill has selected 120+ that he feels you should know about. More than half of these are major countries covered in considerable detail.

Absolutely everything you require to legally obtain dual nationality is now inside this comprehensive and unmatched Report. So, save yourself thousands in legal fees, cut out bureaucratic bunglers and avoid hours of haggling. Learn all there is to know from this single exhaustive publication. It will open your eyes to options you've never thought of before.

The Passport Report contains almost 500 pages packed with unique information. It is the most detailed and useful book of its kind. Should you manage to find another Report on the subject which you feel is more comprehensive, we guarantee that we will not only refund the cost of our publication, but also pay for the other Report as well.

The Tax Exile Report
by Marshall J Langer

The Blueprint on how to Legally Avoid Taxes

Your taxes are higher than you think they are!
Did you know that in many countries you pay tax at three levels? Federal, state and local. Are you aware that **overall tax rates of 50 per cent or more are common now in most major industrial nations?** This is because of crafty schemes ingeniously called 'tax reform' employed by the US government and adopted by many other high-tax countries. They have cleverly lowered tax rates, while at the same time they have increased the amount of taxes that they collect from you.

More than just a book on tax havens
The Tax Exile Report is not your average tax manual. Unlike most other books on the subject Langer sets out legally and thoroughly the entire process of becoming a tax exile. He takes a look at the special problems involved in leaving certain high-tax countries, including Britain, the US and many European countries. He also explains how to plan around US anti-expatriation rules and departure taxes imposed by other countries. And, exclusive to Scope International, he reveals **The Tax Octopus** - the eight different criteria the US government and other high-tax countries use to tax you on your income and your capital.

Marshall Langer's book covers the whole process from leaving your old country to arriving at your new home. He gives you the facts so you will be able to make your own decision without having to rely solely on advice from expensive lawyers. It is the only book on the subject that sets out thoroughly the legal process of becoming a tax exile. You could save thousands, even millions from the information contained in this easy-to-read Report. Beat the bureaucrats. Save your fortune from unfair taxes. Become a tax exile TODAY.

Think Like a Tycoon
By Dr WG Hill

How to make a million in three years or less!

*D*iscover the amazing formula that every single super-rich person has used to gain wealth.

Yes, it is possible to become a millionaire in three years or less, plus at the same time have three times more fun out of life. Most people can only dream about becoming wealthy. They have all the wrong ideas. "Why are some people rich? Why am I not successful?" The author, Dr Hill, reveals in the first chapter how to avoid mistakes that keep 94 per cent of the population just plodding along in a miserable rut, dissatisfied with everything.

You'll learn step by step how Dr Hill became a multi-millionaire. It really is easy once you know how. No need to crawl up a corporate ladder for 30 years. Hill shows you how to do it simply and quickly.

You cannot go wrong with this ingenious volume. If you apply its practical concepts *you will surely be a millionaire within a few years*. Take the first step on your path to riches.

PT - The Perpetual Traveller
by Dr WG Hill

*D*o you want to escape the control over your life and property now held by modern Big Brother government? With *PT the book*, you can discover true personal and financial freedom by breaking free and becoming a PT.

In a nutshell, a PT merely arranges his or her paperwork in such a way that all governments consider him a tourist - a person who is just **P**assing **T**hrough. The advantage is that by being thought of by government officials as a person who is merely **P**arked **T**emporarily, a PT is not subjected to taxes, military service, lawsuits, or persecution for partaking in innocent but forbidden pursuits or pleasures.

"Becoming a PT is not a static thing that you can do once, and then, like obtaining a diploma, just hang it on the wall. PT is a way of thinking, something far more than a mere occupation or even a lifestyle. It is a state of being... The variations and possibilities are infinite - PT's have real freedom in an unfree world."

WG Hill

Unlimited, untaxed wealth and the power to dispose of it as you please is one of the major benefits of becoming a PT. *PT the book*, will raise your consciousness as to the nature of freedom and ways to rid yourself of limitations.

Can you afford to have only one flag? Not if your net worth is, or may soon be, over $250,000! *PT the book*, explains the **Five Flag Theory** on how to defend your wealth.

Flag 1: *Passport & Citizenship*. Finding a country unconcerned about offshore citizens or what they do outside its borders.
Flag 2: *Business Base*. Places where you make your money.
Flag 3: *Domicile*. A tax haven with good communications.
Flag 4: *Asset Repository*. An anonymous base for your assets.

Other Special Reports Available from Scope International

Flag 5: *Playgrounds*. Places where you would actually spend your time physically.

PT the book, fully explains all Five Flags. It is a complete guide to getting the most from life. It covers:

- Dual and multiple nationality.
- Tax avoidance (NOT evasion!).
- The ideal offshore investment.
- Where (and where not) to keep your money.
- Personal and financial privacy.
- Divorce and child custody.
- Crossing borders without hassle.
- Avoiding trouble from bureaucrats.

PT's 300+ pages are also packed with many case histories, details of real-life consultations along with plenty of serious and very useful advice. It includes a comprehensive and valuable **Resource List** giving numerous names, contacts and addresses which will allow you to commence your personal plan for complete financial and personal freedom immediately.

The Tax Haven Report
by Adam Starchild

Tax havens need not be the exclusive preserve of the ultra-rich. People of average means need no longer be captive to the State in today's modern jet-set era. In *The Tax Haven Report*, Adam Starchild reveals these secrets of the ultra-rich so that we lesser mortals can take advantage of the many benefits tax havens have to offer.

As modern governments continue to expand and swallow human rights, deficits and taxes grow. All free-minded individuals must seek a means to protect their assets from this out of control monster. As Starchild explains, it is legally possible to pay absolutely no taxes. Your government may want you to think otherwise, but a very important point remains unnoticed. **While tax evasion is illegal, tax avoidance is not.** This distinction is crucial, and thus Starchild explains it at great length.

For entrepreneurs and businessmen, he explains the ins and outs of tax haven corporations and trusts, including how they are formed, how they are controlled, where they can be located and most importantly, how they can seriously reduce, if not eliminate, the tax burden of your business.

This Report is essential reading for anyone interested in reducing their tax burden. With over 240 pages of vital information we are certain that you can develop a successful plan to reduce your tax burden as a direct result of reading this Report.

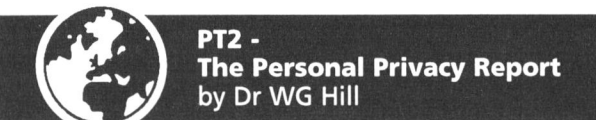

PT2 -
The Personal Privacy Report
by Dr WG Hill

PT2 - The Personal Privacy Report is the sequel to Hill's classic *PT*. It is the essential counterpart and shows you how best you can put into practice the ideas contained in PT. In more than 200 fact-filled pages you will learn about the little-known tactics and techniques of living tax free including:

- How you can triple your interest earnings.
- How you can gain when currencies move.
- The six best ways to transfer cash across borders.
- How to keep your communications confidential.
- The ten best low-profile mail tips.

and much, much more...

Banking in Silence
by Dr WG Hill

The complete manual on how to protect your money

Banking in Silence is the only book of its kind. The subject of secret banking has only ever been skimmed by other writers. Hill investigates it from beginning to end.

You will learn about:

- Over 40 banking havens.
- Offshore corporations and trusts.
- Borrowing money privately.
- Secret accounts.
- Why reporting requirements don't work.
- Obtaining alternate ID.

Find out where the smart money goes. This comprehensive Report reveals unbelievable secrets about France, Greece, Ireland, The Netherlands, and the Dutch Antilles.

Obtain a copy of *Banking in Silence* today and find out:

- How to earn tax-free profits legally.
- How to move money silently into your offshore account.
- How to avoid reporting requirements.
- How to benefit from a new financial privacy program.
- How to obtain an anonymous corporate credit card.

With *Banking in Silence* you and your money can achieve total anonymity and safety.

The Computer Privacy Report
by Dr WG Hill

Roam the globe electronically, raking in TAX-FREE income 24 hours a day

Technology is advancing at a dizzying rate. Do not be afraid. In his most controversial Report yet, Dr WG Hill shows you how to keep your private electronic affairs private.

With computers, your office need have no address, no staff, not even so much as a single desk. But you can make millions! You can be open 24 hours a day, 365 days a year. And you don't have to pay any taxes. This explosive new Report will give you all the tools you need. Say goodbye to bureaucracy and Big Brother forever!

Dr Hill helps you set up and operate the secure paperless office. You will learn how to use the most advanced privacy-protection tricks to keep this office safe from outsiders, con-men, competitors, ex-wives and governments.

You will find out:

- How to fax the world at next to no cost.
- How to encrypt messages.
- Which keys are most effective for keeping information private.
- How to stay anonymous on the information network.
- The best ways to secure your passwords and passphrases.

Computers are the future. But you must protect yourself now. Prepare yourself for the 21st Century!

Other Special Reports Available from Scope International

The Russia Report
by Michael Kavanagh

A gold-mine of opportunity

*R*ussia is a country of enormous opportunity. This Report shows you what's on offer and how to turn it to your advantage. Avoid some of the pitfalls foreign entrepreneurs often walk into. The author not only describes the mechanics of doing business in Russia but makes valid suggestions on how to do it.

If you are considering doing serious business in Russia, you need to establish a 100 per cent Foreign Owned Company there. The author outlines the procedures, detailing all the appropriate documents that are required. Once you have set up your 100 per cent Foreign Owned Company, the author guides you through what to do next, and how to avoid tax complications.

The good news is that moving money in and out of Russia is a lot simpler than it used to be. Whether or not you set up a company there, at some point you'll need to come to terms with the Russian banking system. Revealed in this unique Report is the possibility for a foreign company to lend a Russian company money secured against shares in a bank. As the Russian economy begins to settle, ownership of a functioning bank will be greatly sought after.

Business Opportunities

This in-depth chapter reviews some of the most attractive business opportunities in Russia, along with some to avoid. Potentially very lucrative the author's suggestions concern exporting goods and services to Russia.

The Russia Report **also deals with the practicalities for the foreign visitor including:**

- Visas and how to obtain them.
- How to get there and what to expect in Customs.
- Getting around the cities.
- Recommendations of where and where not to eat.
- Affordable private and office accommodation.

This Report is the essential guide for anyone concerned about seizing opportunities. Over 175 fact-filled pages of priceless information.

The Austria & Liechtenstein Report
by Dr Reinhard Stern

*F*ew people are aware that banks in Austria offer all the same advantages of their Swiss counterparts - plus the only true bank secrecy laws remaining in Europe.

The author Dr Stern outlines:

- The dos and don'ts of investing in Austria.
- The accounts available to foreigners.
- Where the best banks are.
- How to live and do business in Austria without paying taxes.
- How to establish residency.
- How the policy of banking super-secrecy can enable you to open accounts or purchase securities, future options and bullion coins anonymously.

Dr Stern also introduces Liechtenstein, answering vital questions on this Principality, including:

- Setting up accounts.
- Attractive fund management plans and bank secrecy.
- Advice on taxes, and how to avoid them by setting up private trusts and anonymous commercial *Anstalts*.

Dr Stern is a banking and privacy expert. Learn from his experience and discover true financial independence.

The Isle Of Man Report
by Scope International

The perfect base for your offshore company?

The Isle of Man is an emerging offshore centre which is attracting the attention of investors and business owners. There are no capital gains taxes, no inheritance taxes, no wealth taxes and no gift taxes. In fact most international financial transactions and business are carried out TAX FREE. There are only two forms of direct taxation and MANY exemptions.

In this new and expanded Report you will find all you will need to know to establish yourself in one of the world's most prestigious tax havens. You will discover the logistics of setting up your own private offshore company. The legal requirements from incorporating a company right through to winding it up are set out step by step.

You will also discover:
- How to obtain residence and work permits.
- How to obtain citizenship and passport.
- The financial services available.
- The laws surrounding partnerships.
- Isle of Man trusts.
- Business and individual tax systems.

and much, much more.

All the secrets are revealed in this up-and-coming haven for those who want to keep what's rightfully theirs. The only jurisdiction in the EU where you can run a full trading operation, fully registered for VAT, but totally exempt from all income and capital taxes. Profit from the amazing advantages of this island.

The Monaco Report
by Scope International

How to become a legal resident of tax-free Monte Carlo, Monaco

*S*ay goodbye to income, wealth and capital gains taxes! Monaco is ideal for your personal and company needs. Take advantage of the strict levels of confidentiality in Monégasque banks.

There are many places where you could live and be free of income taxes, inheritance and estate taxes and real estate taxes. But most are too isolated, too cold, too hot, too Third World, or simply too dull. Monaco is the only tax haven offering non-stop action. This masterfully written Report goes into the question of how to earn a living, manage a business, handle investments, and forming corporations or trusts. The moves to win the game are all in *The Monaco Report*.

Other Special Reports Available from Scope International

Two Reports in one volume. Double value for money!

Discover a hidden haven for those few that are in the know.

- Property is still affordable.
- Lowest prices in Europe on a huge selection of goods.

Without any big fuss or fanfare Andorra now has a thriving 100 per cent privately owned, local service-based economy. Their unregulated banking system is among the safest in the world. It is sound, prosperous, computerized, streamlined, discreet and very customer orientated. Some of the wealthiest people in the world prefer Andorra's banks to those famed institutions of Switzerland.

Dr Hill uncovers secret enclaves which could be your key to tax freedom. Along with its natural breathtaking beauty, Andorra, the mini-Switzerland, is now seen as one of the most favourable tax havens in Europe.

Plus... The Gibraltar Report

The Rock of Gibraltar is one of the best places in the world to register your tax haven company, your trust, your car, yacht or airplane. Dr Hill examines in great detail the financial advantages of Gibraltar. He also considers quality of living, the real estate market, where to get one of the best car deals in the Europe and how to get the most out of Gibraltar.

Chapters include:

Confidential Banking in Gibraltar, How to Set Up Your Own Tax Haven Corporation, Owning a Home in Next-Door Spain. With the vital information supplied, including a Resource List of important contacts, your feet will hit the Rock running.

Switzerland's secret semi-tropical tax haven

Dr WG Hill, the world's leading expert on personal tax havens, predicts that Campione, a strange accident of history, anomaly of geography and climatic freak, will be one of the most fashionable tax havens of the next decade. This Report shows anyone how to become a legal resident of this soon-to-be discovered enclave of the super rich.

Campione is a unique semi-autonomous community located entirely within Switzerland. As a separate country from Switzerland, it is *not* subject to *any* Swiss laws, Swiss taxes or Swiss tax treaties.

Campione is a part of the EU with all the benefits of passport-free, visa-free travel, and the right of its citizens to travel, work, engage in commerce or perform services anywhere in the EU.

"Property values could continue to escalate like nowhere else in the world," says Hill. This Special Report gives the who, what, where, why, when and how. Hill feels that Campione is a great place to escape to, while still relatively uncongested.

The Swiss Report takes you inside this remarkable country and the institutions that make it tick. The Report describes Switzerland's banks and it's world renowned bank secrecy. Author Marshall Langer believes that by using Switzerland correctly it can be a base for you to earn money at a nil rate of tax.

This Report answers the questions:

- Is Switzerland more free than the US or the UK?
- Should you move there at all?
- How do you avoid or reduce Swiss taxes?
- How can you use Swiss bank accounts and the Swiss secrecy laws to your advantage?

If you want to be anonymous with your assets, Switzerland is the place to go!

*P*erhaps the greatest benefit of any tax haven is that you do not have to live there! *The Channel Island Report* gives all the details of a tax haven which meets this criterion. It is inexpensive and the initial arrangements can all be completed by mail. This particular tax haven is 100 per cent English speaking, and has tougher bank secrecy laws than Switzerland.

How to do it...

Basically, one rents or buys suitable accommodation, arranges for appropriate identity documents, and establishes a means whereby telephone messages and mail may be held or forwarded. A checking account is opened, credit cards are obtained, and presto, the move is complete.

A mere change of legal address could typically double the income of many people. Learn how to establish and maintain a tax haven domicile on a Channel Island (UK) for £50 per month.

Capital Preservation Through Global Investing

Investing globally is one of the most successful ways to accomplish capital preservation and growth. In *The Wealth Report*, Adam Starchild reveals how you can create an ultimate global portfolio of investments to hedge against inflation, taxes, confiscations, market fluctuations, currency devaluations, economic and political turmoil...

Starchild reveals the little-known investment secrets that he has been giving to his clients for the past few decades. He concentrates not only on preserving your wealth effectively, but also on building it safely and securely. His recommendations are not high-flying investment tips, but rather solid, conservative recommendations that over time will help build a healthy nestegg for you.

You will learn how to build a secret stash of cash that

- You can use at any time.
- Is tax-free and seizure-proof.
- Pays competitive dividends and interest.
- Has no government reporting requirements *(even for Americans!).*

In fact if you had put $10,000 each year into this investment for the last twenty years you would have $590,697 today!

Everything you need to get yourself started on a global path to a secure fortune is in *The Wealth Report.*

Other Special Reports Available from Scope International

The Tax-Free Car Report
by Dr WG Hill

Discover how to own a luxury car tax free, use it for a year or so and then sell it for a profit. And not just once but again and again! This is your chance to own the car of your dreams tax free. People are doing it everyday. However, these amazing deals are not publicized.

You will discover:

- where to obtain the lowest factory-list prices in the world.
- the longest lasting tax-free license plates.
- the nine golden rules of international car ownership.
- little-known secrets about tax-free plates.
- the premier source for right-hand drive vehicles.
- everything you need to know about permanent registration.

The potential buyer has the global market at his feet. The United States in particular offers amazing deals on quality luxury cars. There are also excellent deals to be made in the Middle East and the South Pacific. The author, Dr Hill, discusses 14 countries in detail.

Over 110 dealers names, addresses and telephone numbers are listed to help you on your way. Dr Hill discusses the entire process of buying tax free.

During the past twenty years the author, Dr WG Hill, has personally owned a Rolls, Ferrari, and several Mercedes all tax-free. Let him show you how to save up to 50 per cent off the retail price. Learn everything you need to know to enjoy trouble-free, permanently tax-free international motoring. Those who take Dr Hill's advice are guaranteed to succeed.

The Malta Report
by Ross Shaw

Explore the emerging Investors' Paradise.

Recent developments have seen Malta develop into a promising financial centre and tax haven. Get your foot in the door early.

The Malta Report gives you the necessary head start.

The areas covered in depth include:

- Residency incentives.
- Real Estate opportunities.
- Offshore companies & Trusts.
- Expatriate Perks.
- Relocation tips.

The Maltese government's desire to attract foreign business provides many opportunities for the potential investor. There are no restrictions on 100 per cent foreign ownership and control of companies. You are also guaranteed repatriation of capital and profits.

In this new Report just published you will learn about the many perks and incentives used to encourage people to take up residency in Malta:

- no VAT or Customs Duty on the import of your personal effects.
- no death duty, gift duty or wealth tax on real estate transfers.

Take advantage of Malta as an offshore banking centre.
A qualified accountant, the author reveals:

- that there are no restrictions on transfer (in or out) of large sums of foreign currency.
- how nonresidents can receive gross interest on savings.
- how you can acquire major credit cards, including Visa and Eurocard, with no security pledge.

Discover the advantages of living and investing in this beautiful island.

The Business Havens Report
by Adam Starchild

Make The Right Choice For Your Business

Business havens are countries and regions where the investor is given significant incentives to establish an active business. Some are well-known, many are not and most remain well-kept secrets. Adam Starchild covers them all ensuring you have access to tomorrow's profit opportunities today.

During the preparation of this ground-breaking Report, Starchild traveled extensively. His investigations reveal an international goldmine of profit potential.

The *Business Havens Report* shows you exactly where to find:
- Tax-free business jurisdictions.
- Tax holidays.
- Long-term, low-interest loans.
- Reduced rents for office/factory space.
- Low cost, educated and motivated labor.

and many other vital benefits for your business.

The Report covers over 20 first-rate havens with the most advantageous, pro-business policies in the world today. In comprehensive detail Starchild uncovers countries and regions to suit all variety of business and personal requirements. Spanning the West Indies, South America, North America, Europe, the Middle East, South East Asia and the Western Pacific, the Report constitutes a truly global compendium of profit opportunity.

Every aspect of each individual haven is expertly assessed and analysed. Starchild is highly experienced in this field and covers all the factors you need to consider before establishing your operation in a business haven. In each haven Starchild covers:

- History, geography and people.
- Government and policy.
- Incentives available.
- The Economic and financial system.
- Tax laws and the tax system.
- Communication systems and infrastructure.
- Emerging markets and future opportunities.
- Lifestyle.
- Contact information.

...and much, much more.

This Report is an indispensable guide to international business relocation and the amazing profit opportunities it can generate.

For full details and prices on all these Special Reports contact Richard or Stewart at Scope International on:
Tel: (01705) 631751. **Fax:** (01705) 631322
(Overseas: +44 1705)